THE BOOK OF LISTS #3

THE PEOPLE'S ALMANAC®
PRESENTS
THE BOOK OF LISTS #3

BY

AMY WALLACE
DAVID WALLECHINSKY
IRVING WALLACE

WILLIAM MORROW AND COMPANY, INC.

NEW YORK   1983

Library of Congress Cataloging in Publication Data

Main entry under title:

The Book of lists #3.

Includes index.
1. Encyclopedias and dictionaries.   I. Wallace, Amy.
II. Wallechinsky, David, 1948-   .   III. Wallace,
Irving, 1916-   .   IV. Title: Book of lists number
three.
AG106.B65   1983   031′.02   82-20373
ISBN 0-688-01647-2

Printed in the United States of America

First Edition

1 2 3 4 5 6 7 8 9 10

Page design by Gene Siegel

This book is dedicated
to the memory of

Michael Toohey

THEY WROTE THE ORIGINAL MATERIAL

When "THE EDS." is used, it means the material has been contributed by the editors of *The Book of Lists 3.*

A.E.	Ann Elwood	J.M.P.	Jill M. Phillips
A.S.	Aleen Stein	J.N.	Jim Natal
A.T.	Anita Taylor	J.R.L.	James R. Longacre
A.Ti.	Alan Tigay	J.S.A.	Jeffrey S. Alexander
A.W.	Amy Wallace	K.A.	Kayti Adkins
C.D.	Carol Dunlap	K.A.M.	Kenneth A. Michaelis
C.O.M.	Carol Orsag-Madigan	K.C.	Kathleen Campbell
C.R.M.	Claude R. Mowry	K.P.	Karen Pedersen
C.S.	Carl Sifakis	L.B.C.	Lowell B. Chase
D.B.	Danny Biederman	L.C.	Loren Coleman
D.F.	David Fluke	L.K.S.	Laurie K. Strand
D.H.	Doug Huff	L.O.	Laurel Overman
D.L.	Don Lessem	L.R.	Lawrence Roberts
D.O.	David Owen	M.B.T.	Marguerite B. Thompson
D.R.	Dan Riley	M.E.P.	Marc E. Paavola
D.W.	David Wallechinsky	M.H.	Moss Hall
E.F.	Ed Fishbein	M.J.H.	Michael J. Hayes
E.H.C.	Ernest H. Corfine	M.J.T.	Michael J. Toohey
E.N.	Edward Nizalowski	M.MC.	Mary McLaughlin
F.B.	Fern Bryant	M.S.	Michael Sheeter
F.H.	Frank Henry	N.C.S.	Nancy C. Sorel
H.G.	Helen Ginsburg	N.F.	Neva Fluke
I.W.	Irving Wallace	N.W.	Nigel Watson
J.A.	John Ascenzi	R.B.	Ron Birnbach
J.E.	John Eastman	R.J.F.	Rodger J. Fadness
J.E.W.	John E. Williams	R.J.R.	R. John Rapsys
J.L.	Jack Luzzatto	R.K.R.	R. Kent Rasmussen
J.M.B.E.	John M. B. Edwards	R.S.	Ray Spangenburg

CONTENTS

ON LISTING

If imitation is truly the sincerest form of flattery, then we have been flattered constantly since we created and wrote *The Book of Lists* in 1977 and its successor, *The Book of Lists 2*, in 1980. Ever since we started this unusual approach to providing entertainment and information, America and the world have been happily listing. We have had, at last count, over 25 imitators, who have been bringing out volumes of lists on such specialized subjects as sports, crime, movies, television, rock music, money, children, food, literature, Texas, the Bible, and Jewish life. Imitators began to spring up everywhere—Canada, Great Britain, and Germany have published their own versions of lists.

Fortunately, most countries in the world preferred to translate our own original *Book of Lists*. *Lists 1* and 2 have been published in Great Britain and translated in France, Germany, Sweden, Norway, Denmark, Finland, Holland, Spain, Greece, Turkey, Japan, Argentina, Brazil, and Mexico. We've received letters from readers in 50 countries outside the U.S., including Bahrain, the Channel Islands, Cuba, Fiji, Ghana, India, Kuwait, Malawi, Thailand, and Tonga.

Highly encouraged, we plunged into the task of creating, researching, and writing *The Book of Lists 3*.

All during its preparation, we were asked by the press and other media and by readers if we would ever run out of lists. We always had one answer. Run out of lists? Never! As long as human beings continue to populate this rotund planet, as long as they make things happen, as long as each day becomes part of civilization's long history, as long as history goes on discussing its wonders, material for lists will continue to flourish and will be nonending.

That's what made it possible for us to make *The Book of Lists 3* all new once more—new ideas for lists, new factual material, new fun and information.

One standard that we set from the outset has remained unchanged. This is our absolute insistence on truth and accuracy in each item in every list. This standard has driven us to go to great lengths in our researches and in verifying our findings. For example, we had gathered together, over a period of years, material for two lists, one called "19 Stupid Thieves," the other called "9 Ordinary Men Who Played King." Much of this material was based on old newspaper clippings. Since the clippings might have been exaggerated, or untrue, we spent months hunting down the subjects of these articles, contacting a myriad of people. When we were satisfied that the stories were accurate, we included them in this volume. (Unfortunately, a lot of seemingly great stories fall by the wayside.)

Also, we have tried to uncover as much material as we could on various subjects or items. Here are some more examples of our efforts to obtain information firsthand. When we heard someone had written a novel without once using the letter "e," we were fascinated but could hardly believe it. So we searched for that rare novel and actually found and purchased a copy. That led to an authentic item for a list of books written without the use of that single letter of the alphabet. When we became interested in knowing what are the most-hated household tasks, we took matters into our own hands. We hired the Gallup Poll people to make a private survey for us, and that became a list for this book. When we wondered which great scientists might have won the Nobel Prize, but didn't, we questioned Nobel Prize laureates in physics, chemistry, and medicine, asking which of their famous colleagues had been ignored. We soon had another unique list.

Like our previous books, *The Book of Lists 3* tries to provide a balance between the lighthearted and the serious. It is fun to read a list of what people would do to get a million dollars (76% of the men and 58% of the women would be unfaithful to their mates) or a list of the most popular names people give cats, or commas that have changed moments in history, or murder victims who were the hardest to kill. On the other side of the coin are lists on the jobs with the least unemployment, on nuclear accidents, on drunken politicians, on famous draft dodgers, and on nations that are the cruelest to animals.

We have tried to fill this book with fresh features. For a list entitled "10 Famous Cartoonists Select Their Own Favorite Cartoons" such greats as Charles Addams, Jules Feiffer, and Charles Schulz have generously allowed us to reproduce their choices.

Also, numerous celebrities have written exclusive lists for us on the subjects in which they specialize. We are including lists written by Stephen King, Dizzy Gillespie, Walter Matthau, Yehudi Menuhin, Lucille Ball, Bjorn Borg, Nathan Pritikin, Doris Lessing, Edwin Newman, Ansel Adams, Erma Bombeck, Thor Heyerdahl, and dozens of others.

Important and fascinating as these contributions are, the most important and fascinating ideas for lists and entries for lists have come from our readers. Their variety and originality have been astounding, and a source of enormous pleasure to us. Much of the grass-roots reader material has been incorporated in these pages.

Once more we want to thank our brilliant and lively readers, and once more we want to invite them to continue sending us ideas for future lists. We want the next all-new edition of this book to be even more comprehensive and entertaining than the first three. Tell us what you like most about this book, what we have overlooked, and what we can do to improve it. Send us any unusual information you've read or heard about. Those clippings you've so long saved. Everything and anything that might fit. Don't be listless. Let's have fun together. Of course, we'll pay you for your ideas if we use them. Our address is:

The Book of Lists
P.O. Box 49699
Los Angeles, Calif. 90049

AMY WALLACE
DAVID WALLECHINSKY
IRVING WALLACE

THE BOOK OF LISTS #3

1
WE, THE PEOPLE

NAME DROPPERS: 38 PEOPLE BETTER KNOWN BY THEIR MIDDLE NAMES

1. Henry Beaty, U.S. actor and director (Warren Beatty)
2. Eleanor Carter, U.S. first lady (Rosalynn)
3. Arthur Chamberlain, British statesman (Neville)
4. Leroy Cleaver, U.S. civil rights leader (Eldridge)
5. Stephen Cleveland, U.S. president (Grover)
6. Alfred Cooke, British journalist (Alistair)
7. John Coolidge, U.S. president (Calvin)
8. Harold Crane, U.S. poet (Hart)
9. William Crawford, U.S. actor (Broderick)
10. Achille Debussy, French composer (Claude)
11. Mary Fawcett, U.S. actress (Farrah)
12. William Gable, U.S. actor (Clark)
13. Francis Harte, U.S. writer (Brett "Bret")
14. Herbert McLuhan, Canadian educator and writer (Marshall)
15. Terence McQueen, U.S. actor (Stephen "Steve")

Terence McQueen.

Charles Redford.   Ernestine Russell.

16. George Newhart, U.S. comedian (Robert "Bob")
17. James Niven, British actor (David)
18. Patrick O'Neal, U.S. actor (Ryan)
19. Olive Osmond, U.S. singer (Marie)
20. Margaret Pauley, U.S. newscaster (Jane)
21. Eldred Peck, U.S. actor (Gregory)
22. David Peckinpah, U.S. director (Samuel "Sam")
23. William Rains, British actor (Claude)
24. Charles Redford, U.S. actor (Robert)
25. Anna Roosevelt, U.S. first lady (Eleanor)
26. David Rusk, U.S. statesman (Dean)
27. Ernestine Russell, U.S. actress (Jane)
28. Alfred Runyon, U.S. journalist and writer (Damon)
29. Lynn Ryan, U.S. baseball pitcher (Nolan)
30. Arnold Sevareid, U.S. newscaster (Eric)
31. Edith Shearer, U.S. actress (Norma)
32. Robert Shriver, U.S. attorney (Sargent)
33. Marvin Simon, U.S. playwright (Neil)
34. Michael Stallone, U.S. actor and director (Sylvester)
35. Newton Tarkington, U.S. novelist (Booth)
36. Aaron Ward, U.S. merchant (Montgomery)
37. George Welles, U.S. actor and director (Orson)
38. Thomas Wilson, U.S. president (Woodrow)

—A.T.

8 THINGS PEOPLE WOULD BE WILLING TO DO FOR A MILLION DOLLARS

In December, 1980, *Psychology Today* magazine ran a questionnaire to discover its readers' feelings and fantasies about money. In general, the more than 20,000 people who responded to the survey were young, married, and middle class. The average age was 35, 45% were married. About 90% had spent at least some time in college, and 42% had gone on to graduate school. Almost half the respondents earned more than $25,000 per year.

	Men	Women
1. Have sexual relations with a stranger (once)	76%	58%
2. Move to a foreign country	65%	59%
3. Take a job I didn't like	55%	54%
4. Marry someone I didn't love	23%	21%
5. Tell a lie about a business associate	22%	10%
6. Steal something	21%	10%
7. Bribe someone or take a bribe	18%	10%
8. Divorce my spouse	12%	10%

Note: Since respondents were asked to circle all statements to which they would answer "yes," percentages add up to more than 100%.
SOURCE: Reprinted from *Psychology Today* magazine, copyright 1981, Ziff-Davis Publishing Company.

10 NON-NAZIS WHO ADMIRED HITLER

1. GEORGE BERNARD SHAW (1856–1950)

This British playwright was a lifelong political radical and an admirer of what he called "Supermen," into which category fell certain extremist dictators. Disgusted with the ineptitude of parliamentary democracy during the interwar period, he supported Oswald Mosley and the British Union of Fascists and professed admiration for both Hitler and Mussolini. In Shaw's 1938 play *Geneva,* he condoned the anti-Semitic excesses of a dictator named "Battler" (Hitler). The 82-year-old Shaw's friends considered this, regrettably, as evidence of the onset of senility.

2. KNUT HAMSUN (1859–1952)

Hamsun, who won a Nobel Prize for his novels celebrating the Norwegian soul, was a longtime Anglophobe who applauded Prussian militarism during W.W. I and Nazism during W.W. II. He urged his countrymen not to resist the Nazi invasion in 1940 (the real enemy was Britain, he explained) and visited Hitler in 1943. Arrested in 1945 for collaboration with the enemy, Hamsun was released as a mental incompetent, a convenient verdict in view of his age and the veneration in which his work was held.

3. HENRY FORD (1863–1947)

Automotive pioneer "Heinrich" Ford was known in Germany as "a great individualist and a great anti-Semite," chiefly for his publication of defamatory newspaper articles and books about the Jews. Hitler praised him in *Mein Kampf*, hung his picture prominently at Nazi headquarters in Munich, and sought financial support from him. Ford built a plant to manufacture military vehicles in Germany, although he had refused a comparable British venture. "At least Germany keeps its people at work," said Ford, who did not know Hitler personally. In 1938, on Ford's 75th birthday, he became the first American to receive Hitler's Supreme Order of the German Eagle.

4. WILLIAM RANDOLPH HEARST (1863–1951)

During W.W. I, the megalomaniac publisher and leading U.S. proponent of yellow journalism was accused of having pro-German sympathies because he favored U.S. neutrality. In 1934, while visiting Germany's spas, he interviewed Hitler, whom he described as "certainly an extraordinary man." Allegedly he also negotiated the expansion of his news service into Germany, in return for which the Hearst newspapers ran articles written by Göring and other Nazis espousing their cause. Hitler was a tyrant, Hearst admitted privately, but no one else could stem the tide of Communism, which the publisher considered a greater threat than Nazism.

5. DAVID LLOYD GEORGE (1863–1945)

Having lost a bid for reelection in 1935, Britain's W.W. I prime minister was peevish and at loose ends. When he visited Germany the following year, he was received with flattering deference by Hitler. Lloyd George in turn expressed approval of the new German motorways, high employment, and other Nazi accomplishments. He returned home to write newspaper articles lauding Hitler as "a born leader" who was "indeed a great man." He also replaced a wall in his country home, imitating the Führer's example at Berchtesgaden, with a massive sheet of plate glass.

6. CHARLES COUGHLIN (1891–1979)

Father Coughlin, the Depression-era Catholic "radio priest" from the Shrine of the Little Flower in Michigan, was a major spokesman for the radical right in the U.S. His Christian Front organization espoused Nazi ideals and methods, including paramilitary platoons formed to promote "sanity and right thinking." Coughlin maintained contacts with high-ranking Nazis and disseminated their propaganda in his magazine, *Social Justice*. He also reached 30–40 million listeners with his weekly radio program. He was silenced by the U.S. government in 1942.

7. EDWARD VIII (1894–1972)

While Prince of Wales and during his brief reign as king of England, the Duke of Windsor was thought to be partial to the Germans, from whom he descended on his mother's side. He was also considered somewhat deficient in judgment if not totally irresponsible, as evidenced by his abdication in order to marry American divorcée Wallis Simpson in 1936. The following year, flouting the official British position in regard to Nazism, the couple visited Germany as not-quite-private citizens. The duke was reported in the press as even offering a "modified Nazi salute." The Windsors went to Germany seeking the status denied them in Britain, it was said—and left feeling they had been badly used.

8. JUAN PERÓN (1895–1974)

As the Argentine military attaché in Chile during the 1930s, Perón was accused of being a Nazi spymaster. His next assignment was to Italy, where he was deeply impressed by the fascist "politics of spectacle." He toured Nazi Germany before returning home to create a state-controlled labor movement designed on the fascist model, possibly with fascist financial assistance. After the war in Europe ended, amid rumors of a Fourth Reich in Argentina, Perón was elected his country's president, a position he held until overthrown in 1955.

9. IDI AMIN (1925–   )

Ugandan dictator Amin praised the memory of Hitler, to whom he planned to erect a memorial, and did his worst to emulate the Führer's example. In 1972 he implemented his own "final solution" to the problem of the numerous East Indians and Pakistanis in Uganda. (They were known as the Jews of East Africa because they controlled both trade and the professions there.) Amin gave them 90 days to leave the country, taking with them only $100 apiece. The dictator, who liquidated some 300,000 Ugandans as well, was also said to resemble his idol for sheer brutality and for his long and demented harangues. Deposed in 1979, he reportedly took refuge in Libya and Saudi Arabia.

10. NGUYEN CAO KY (1930–   )

This flamboyant ace pilot who became the U.S.-backed premier of South Vietnam between 1965 and 1967 was called "the Cowboy" because he wore a pearl-handled revolver with his tailored flying suits. In politics, however, he favored the Nazi model. "I admire Hitler because he pulled his country together when it was in a terrible state in the early thirties," he once told a journalist. "We need four or five Hitlers in Vietnam."

—C.D.

21 SETS OF EXACT CONTEMPORARIES: PEOPLE WHOSE YEARS OF BIRTH AND OF DEATH WERE THE SAME

1. 1874–1965 Winston Churchill (British statesman) and W. Somerset Maugham (British writer)
2. 1875–1965 Syngman Rhee (Korean statesman) and Albert Schweitzer (French medical missionary)
3. 1878–1967 John Masefield (British poet) and Carl Sandburg (U.S. poet)
4. 1882–1941 James Joyce (Irish writer) and Virginia Woolf (British writer)
5. 1885–1957 Louis B. Mayer (U.S. film producer) and Erich von Stroheim (U.S. actor and director)
6. 1888–1953 Eugene O'Neill (U.S. playwright) and Jim Thorpe (U.S. athlete)
7. 1888–1959 Raymond Chandler (U.S. writer) and John Foster Dulles (U.S. statesman)
8. 1889–1945 Adolf Hitler (German dictator) and Robert Benchley (U.S. humorist)
9. 1889–1967 Charles Bickford (U.S. actor) and Claude Rains (British actor)
10. 1890–1969 Dwight D. Eisenhower (U.S. statesman) and Ho Chi Minh (Vietnamese statesman)

Dwight D. Eisenhower.

Ho Chi Minh.

11. 1892–1973 Joe E. Brown (U.S. actor), Pearl Buck (U.S. writer), and J. R. R. Tolkien (British writer)
12. 1893–1964 Cedric Hardwicke (British actor), Harpo Marx (U.S. actor), and Cole Porter (U.S. composer)
13. 1894–1961 Dashiell Hammett (U.S. writer) and James Thurber (U.S. humorist)
14. 1895–1967 Bert Lahr (U.S. actor) and Paul Muni (U.S. actor)
15. 1895–1972 J. Edgar Hoover (U.S. FBI director) and Edmund Wilson (U.S. writer)
16. 1898–1976 Chou En-lai (Chinese statesman) and Paul Robeson (U.S. singer and actor)
17. 1902–1974 Vittorio De Sica (Italian director and actor) and Ed Sullivan (U.S. TV personality)
18. 1905–1965 Constance Bennett (U.S. actress), Clara Bow (U.S. actress), and Red Nichols (U.S. musician)
19. 1906–1964 Gracie Allen (U.S. comedienne) and William Bendix (U.S. actor)
20. 1909–1959 Max Baer (U.S. boxer) and Errol Flynn (U.S. actor)
21. 1925–1968 Robert F. Kennedy (U.S. politician) and Wes Montgomery (U.S. musician)

—R.K.R.

11 PEOPLE WHO BECAME FOODS

1. SAMUEL BENEDICT

After a long, hard night of partying in 1894, New York socialite Samuel Benedict confronted the Waldorf-Astoria maître d'hôtel and asked for the following hangover remedy: a piece of buttered toast topped with a poached egg, bacon, and hollandaise sauce. The maître d' complied but substituted an English muffin for the toast, and ham for the bacon. Since then, Eggs Benedict has become a popular dish more for its flavor than for its medicinal properties.

2. FRANÇOIS RENÉ DE CHATEAUBRIAND

As a young man, Chateaubriand (1768–1848) witnessed the storming of the Bastille and fought on the side of the Royalists in the French revolution. He journeyed to America, where he explored the Mississippi and Ohio rivers. On his return to Europe, he earned fame as a novelist, playwright, and social critic. Ironically, in spite of all his adventures and accomplishments, Chateaubriand is best remembered today because of a cut of meat prepared for him by his chef, Montmireil. Beefsteak Chateaubriand is a thick cut of tenderloin from the center of the filet mignon, usually served with a béarnaise sauce.

3. SYLVESTER GRAHAM

Graham (1794–1851) was America's premier health-food fanatic. During the 1840s, he traveled far and wide denouncing both white bread and meat, and extolling the benefits of fruits, vegetables, whole grains, and their inevitable consequence—bowel regularity. He was frequently harassed by bakers and butchers, whose livelihoods were threatened by such rhetoric as, "Meat is a powerful constipator which stimulates sexual excess." The nutritional guru and his true believers—among them Horace Greeley, Thomas Edison, and Mormon prophet Joseph Smith—would no doubt feel vindicated today, since many of Graham's theories have since been proved. However, the whole wheat crackers that he developed and named after himself have evolved into sugary treats containing bleached flour and preservatives.

4.–5. JAMES LOGAN and RUDOLF BOYSEN

During the late 1850s, Indiana-born schoolteacher James Logan (1841–1921) drove an ox team west to California, where the young man found fortune in a law practice and fame in horticulture. He developed the loganberry by planting California blackberries between Texas Early blackberries and Red Antwerp raspberries. In the early 1900s, a Californian named Rudolf Boysen (1895?–1950) combined the hybrid loganberry with the blackberry and raspberry to produce a new variety of trailing blackberry, which he called the boysenberry.

6. NELLIE MELBA

Australian-born Helen Porter Mitchell (1861–1931) didn't study opera until age 21, yet she quickly earned worldwide fame under the stage name Nellie Melba. While staying at the Savoy in London, Dame Nellie was accidentally served burnt toast. To the chef's surprise, the diva found the crisp slices of bread delicious. With this endorsement, Melba toast was put on the menu in her honor. A peach, raspberry, and ice-cream dessert was also named after the singer.

7. JOHN MONTAGU, 4TH EARL OF SANDWICH

According to legend, Montagu (1718–1792) was in the middle of a card game when he asked a servant to place some cold roast beef between two pieces of toast, so he could eat with one hand while he played cards with the other. Revisionists have argued that the earl was actually writing or hunting when he ordered the first sandwich, but from what is known of him, the card-game story is the most plausible. Forty-eight-hour card games were among the earl's more wholesome pursuits. As a member of the notorious Hellfire Club, he was an enthusiastic participant in drunken orgies and black masses. It is not known whether Montagu found the sandwich a convenient snack to accompany his other vices as well.

EARL OF SANDWICH

8. PIERRE PÉRIGNON

Dom Pérignon (1638–1715) entered the religious life at age 15. A blind man, his acute senses of taste and smell aided him in making and improving the wines of the Benedictine monastery near Épernay, where he was a cellarmaster. It was Dom Pérignon who perfected the process of fermenting champagne in the bottle—he literally put in the all-important bubbles. Moët et Chandon vineyards later honored Pérignon's accomplishment by naming its finest vintage after him. Ironically, the blind man who renounced the world and its pleasures also made New Year's Eve what it is today.

9. CHARLES WILLIAM POST

It was C. W. Post (1854–1914) who made Battle Creek, Mich., the breakfast-food capital of America. There, in 1891, he established La Vita Inn, a retreat devoted to healing through mental suggestion. In 1894, he began experimenting with foods and developed Postum, a coffee substitute made from grain. Over the years, Post was to lend his name to assorted breakfast foods and become, quite literally, a household word.

10. JOHN D. ROCKEFELLER

By 1899, oil tycoon John D. Rockefeller (1839–1937) was well on his way to his first billion. So when a diner at Antoine's restaurant in New Orleans proclaimed that a new oyster dish was "as rich as Rockefeller," it was no faint praise. Thereafter, the recipe for oysters broiled with vegetables and seasonings on a bed of rock salt was called Oysters Rockefeller.

11. JAMES H. SALISBURY

In 1886, this British physician prescribed a cure-all for pulmonary tuberculosis, hardening of the arteries, gout, colitis, asthma, bronchitis, rheumatism, and pernicious anemia. He stipulated that well-done ground beef be eaten three times a day and that a glass of hot water be drunk before and after each meal. The so-called "Salisbury steak"—basically a hamburger without a bun—is hardly the gourmet dish it sounds. During both W.W. I and W.W. II, patriotic extremists fought a stateside campaign to substitute "Salisbury steak" for the German word "hamburger," but their efforts failed for the most part. However, the term "Salisbury steak" still endures, since it looks better on a menu than "hamburger, plain."

—M.J.T.

13 FAMOUS FATHERS-IN-LAW OF FAMOUS SONS-IN-LAW

Father-in-Law	Son-in-Law
1. Lou Boudreau (1917–) U.S. baseball player	Denny McLain (1944–) U.S. baseball player

2. Cecil B. De Mille (1881–1959)
   U.S. director, producer
   Anthony Quinn (1915–   )
   U.S. actor
3. Henry Fonda (1905–1982)
   U.S. actor
   Tom Hayden (1940–   )
   U.S. politician
4. William Godwin (1756–1836)
   British philosopher, writer
   Percy Bysshe Shelley (1792–1822)
   British poet
5. Clark Griffith (1869–1955)
   U.S. baseball player, manager,
   and club owner
   Joe Cronin (1906–   )
   U.S. baseball player, manager,
   and executive
6. Tom Harmon (1919–   )
   U.S. sportscaster
   Rick Nelson (1940–   )
   U.S. singer
7. Franz Liszt (1811–1886)
   Hungarian pianist, composer
   Richard Wagner (1813–1883)
   German composer
8. Thomas Mann (1875–1955)
   German novelist
   W. H. Auden (1907–1973)
   British poet
9. Eugene O'Neill (1888–1953)
   U.S. playwright
   Charlie Chaplin (1889–1977)
   British actor, director,
   producer
10. Richard Simon (1899–1960)
    U.S. publisher
    James Taylor (1948–   )
    U.S. singer
11. Arturo Toscanini (1867–1957)
    Italian conductor
    Vladimir Horowitz (1904–   )
    U.S. pianist
12. Kurt Vonnegut, Jr. (1922–   )
    U.S. author
    Geraldo Rivera (1943–   )
    U.S. television journalist
13. Richard Widmark (1914–   )
    U.S. actor
    Sandy Koufax (1935–   )
    U.S. baseball player

—T.S.

9 ORDINARY MEN WHO PLAYED KING

1. GIUSEPPE BARTOLEONI (1780?–1848?), king of Tavolara

One day in 1833, Carlo Alberto (1798–1849), king of Sardinia, instructed the captain of his ship to leave him on the island of Tavolara—located off the coast of Sardinia—for a few hours of solitary hunting. After a short time, the king was approached by a huge man over 7 ft. tall. The man was the sole inhabitant of the island, and the king was so impressed with his harmonious life-style that he declared him king of Tavolara. The hermit identified himself as Giuseppe Bartoleoni, a shepherd from Maddalena—an island north of Sardinia. Carlo Alberto found this hard to believe. Most people of the time—especially peasants—were illiterate, but Giuseppe was fluent in several languages and extremely well-educated. He was also the head of two families; one wife and children lived on another island while a second wife and children lived on yet a third island. He sent for both to live with him in his new kingdom, and because he was a sovereign, the Italian government failed in its attempt to prosecute him for bigamy. Paolo, his eldest son, was named his successor upon his father's death in the late 1840s.

11

2. PATRICK WATKINS (fl. c. 1810), king of the Galapagos

Watkins, a redheaded Irish seaman, left his British whaling ship for the isolation of the Galapagos Islands off the coast of Ecuador. Crowning himself king, Patrick grew potatoes and pumpkins, which he sold to ships that stopped at the islands. He considered all of the Galapagos his domain and even pressed some unsuspecting sailors into slavery. To share his throne, he picked up a "queen" in Payta, Peru. Unfortunately, local police there found Patrick hiding on board a ship and put him in prison, where he eventually died.

3. ANTOINE-ORÉLIE de TOUNENS (?–1880), king of Araucanía

Tounens, an adventuresome French lawyer, succeeded in winning the favor of the Araucanían Indians, a belligerent agrarian people of southern Chile. He was crowned Antoine-Orélie I. After a time, the natives grew restless and chased the hapless monarch back to France, lock, stock, and crown. Upon his death, Antoine left the throne to his secretary, Gustave Achille Laviarde, who took the name Achille I and "ruled in exile" from Paris.

4. DAVID O'KEEFE (?–1901?), king of Yap

In 1871, O'Keefe, an Irish immigrant who had settled in Savannah, Ga., said good-bye to his wife and daughter and left for China. En route he was shipwrecked on Yap, a group of islands in the West Pacific Ocean southwest of Guam. Adjusting well to island life, he acquired real estate from local chiefs and, in a few short years, became king. He even designed a royal emblem (an American flag waving over the letters "O'K") and erected a castle on one of the islands. Not forgetting Mrs. O'Keefe, he sent money home to Savannah twice a year. His tranquil reign was upset one day when the tribal chiefs presented him with a suitable queen. Ever mindful of Mrs. O'Keefe, he tried to sidestep this bigamous marriage. But the chiefs were insistent. Reluctantly, King David accepted Queen Dollyboy—reluctantly at first, that is, since the royal couple eventually produced seven children. In 1901, O'Keefe sent word to wife no. 1 that he was coming home. With two of his Yapese sons, he boarded the ship *Santa Cruz*. It was lost at sea.

5. BARON JAMES A. HARDEN-HICKEY (1854–1898), king of Trinidad

"I propose to take possession of the Island of Trinidad under a maxim of international law which declares that anybody may seize and hold waste land that is not claimed by anybody else." So declared Baron Harden-Hickey—the Francophile American novelist, Catholic-turned-Buddhist/Theosophist, and author of a how-to-do-it book on suicide—in 1893 as he prepared to assume the throne as King James I. Although his kingdom was not *the* Trinidad in the West Indies, but rather a small uninhabited island 700 mi. off the coast of Brazil, Harden-Hickey fully expected to be welcomed into the family of nations. But it was not to be. While Harden-Hickey recruited suitable subjects and issued fancy postage stamps and 1,000-franc bonds from a Manhattan office, Great Britain and Brazil haggled over possession of the South Atlantic rock. In 1896, Great Britain abandoned its claim. Brazil, assured of no further British occupation, left the island to the turtles. And lost in the shuffle was the would-be king, his crown gathering dust in a trunk. Two years later,

Baron Harden-Hickey, taking a page from his own book, committed suicide in El Paso, Tex.

6. JOHN DAVIS MURRAY (1870?–?), king of Christmas Island

In 1891 Murray, a mechanical engineer who graduated from Purdue University, went to work for the British-owned Phosphate Mining and Shipping Company. The firm dispatched him to Christmas Island, southwest of Java, to oversee its phosphate mines there. Since most of the miners were native islanders, it was decided that the surest way to get things done was to make Murray king, complete with full executive and judicial powers. In 1910, while in London, he met a young woman and decided to get married. The prospect of royal life on a remote island held little appeal for the bride, so King John dutifully relinquished his throne.

7. CARL HAFFKE (fl. 1900), king of the Ilocanos

A German immigrant, Haffke first found work as a Western Union messenger in Omaha, Neb. He later joined the navy and, serving under Admiral Dewey during the Spanish-American War, ended up in the Philippines, where he was a court stenographer. In due time, he became acquainted with various Ilocano chieftains. When a cholera epidemic wiped out the royal family, Haffke was offered the crown. He accepted but not before making sure that the venture would turn a profit: He demanded up front a onetime six-figure tribute from the tribe, a 5% cut of all tribal profits, and the customary royal perks, including servants. In exchange for this, he agreed to serve as sovereign, purchase farm machinery, and teach the natives modern agricultural techniques. After a year on the throne, King Carlos I, longing for the Cornhusker State, visited his home. He looked up an old girl friend while there and, failing to convince her of the charms of the Philippines, abdicated to practice law in Nebraska.

8. EDWARD THOMPSON (?–1910?), king of Naikeva

Dumped by his girl friend in his hometown of Albion, Ill., Thompson sought solace at sea and wound up in the Fijis. On Naikeva Island, he rebounded into the arms of Princess Lakanita, the king's daughter. Still, Thompson pressed on to other adventures on other islands. Then one day, a messenger from Naikeva brought him word that insurgents on the island were threatening to topple the monarchy. Thompson hastily returned to Naikeva and joined the battle. Although the king died in action and Thompson was wounded, loyalists managed to put down the rebellion. While convalescing, Thompson rekindled his romance with Princess Lakanita and decided, after all, to settle down. Assuming the throne, he ruled Naikeva until his death 25 years later.

9. FAUSTIN E. WIRKUS (1894–1948), king of La Gonave

In 1925, Wirkus, a 31-year-old U.S. Marine Corps sergeant stationed in Haiti, volunteered for the post of district commander on the island of La Gonave, just 40 mi. from the mainland. The position entailed supervising the collection of taxes to be paid to the capital of Port-au-Prince. He was warned his job would be complicated by the islanders' occult customs—including voodoo—but Wirkus was intent on his mission. When he landed, by an incredible coincidence, the people opened

Faustin E. Wirkus, King of La Gonave, with Queen Ti Memenne.

their hearts to him and proclaimed him King Faustin II. (It appeared that in 1848 a Negro man named Soulouque had become emperor of Haiti and its surrounding islands. He had declared himself King Faustin I. Why he chose the name Faustin, no one knows.) When Wirkus was born in Pittston, Pa., in 1894, his parents could not decide on a name and left the choice to their Catholic priest, who—again, for some unknown reason—christened the boy Faustin. When Wirkus arrived on La Gonave, he learned from Queen Ti Memenne the legend that Faustin I would return. Even though Wirkus was white, the natives believed him to be the fulfillment of the prophecy and crowned him King Faustin II a few weeks later. Wirkus retained his post of district commander and his title of king for 4 years, until his duty was officially terminated in 1929. He returned to a hero's welcome in the U.S. in the early 1930s, lived in New York for a brief time lecturing and writing on voodoo, and then rejoined the marines when W.W. II began. He died from cancer in a New York military hospital.

—W.A.D. & L.O.

11 DAYS ON WHICH ONE CELEBRITY DIED AND ANOTHER WAS BORN

1. May 21, 1471
    Died: Henry VI of England
    Born: Albrecht Dürer, German artist

2. Dec. 2, 1859
    Died: John Brown, U.S. abolitionist
    Born: Georges Seurat, French painter

3. July 14, 1904
    Died: Paul Kruger, South African statesman
    Born: Isaac Bashevis Singer, Polish-born U.S. writer

4. Sept. 27, 1917
    Died: Edgar Degas, French artist
    Born: Louis Auchincloss, U.S. lawyer and writer

5. Aug. 3, 1924
    Died: Joseph Conrad, Polish-born British writer
    Born: Leon Uris, U.S. writer

6. May 12, 1925
    Died: Amy Lowell, U.S. poet
    Born: Yogi Berra, U.S. baseball player

7. Nov. 20, 1925
    Died: Alexandra, Queen Consort of Edward VII of the United
        Kingdom
    Born: Robert Kennedy, U.S. politician

8. May 19, 1935
    Died: T. E. Lawrence, British soldier and writer
    Born: David Hartman, U.S. actor

9. June 2, 1941
    Died: Lou Gehrig, U.S. baseball player
    Born: Stacy Keach, U.S. actor

10. Nov. 21, 1945
    Died: Robert Benchley, U.S. writer and actor
    Born: Goldie Hawn, U.S. actress

Robert Benchley.

Goldie Hawn.

11. Dec. 25, 1946
    Died: W. C. Fields, U.S. actor
    Born: Larry Csonka, U.S. football player

—R.K.R.

20 PHILOSOPHERS WHO NEVER MARRIED

1. Plato (427?–347 B.C.), Greek
2. St. Augustine (354–430), Numidian (Roman subject)
3. St. Thomas Aquinas (1225–1274), Italian
4. Thomas Hobbes (1588–1679), British
5. René Descartes (1596–1650), French
6. Blaise Pascal (1623–1662), French
7. John Locke (1632–1704), British
8. Benedict Spinoza (1632–1677), Dutch
9. Gottfried Wilhelm von Leibnitz (1646–1716), German
10. Voltaire (1694–1778), French
11. David Hume (1711–1776), Scottish
12. Immanuel Kant (1724–1804), German
13. Arthur Schopenhauer (1788–1860), German
14. Sorën Aabye Kierkegaard (1813–1855), Danish
15. Herbert Spencer (1820–1903), British
16. Friedrich Nietzsche (1844–1900), German
17. George Santayana (1863–1952), Spanish-American
18. Ludwig Josef Johann Wittgenstein (1889–1951), Austrian
19. Jean-Paul Sartre (1905–1980), French
20. Simone Weil (1909–1943), French

—L.B.C.

6 MEN ASKED TO LEAD BOTH SIDES

1. HENRY IV (1553–1610)

The ruler of a small kingdom in the Pyrenees, Henry of Navarre was asked to lead both the Protestant and Catholic political movements in France in the 16th century. At first, since he was a Protestant, Henry headed the Protestant faction. However, he inherited the throne of France in 1589 and became King Henry IV. In 1593, he converted to Catholicism, commenting, "Paris is well worth a mass." In 1594, he entered that city and was crowned.

2. ALBERT SIDNEY JOHNSTON (1803–1862)

In 1860, Gen. Albert Sidney Johnston, the commander of the U.S. Army Department of the Pacific, was asked to take the position of second-in-command of the Union Army by President Abraham Lincoln. About a year later, President Jefferson Davis offered him the post of second-ranking general in the Confederate Army. A native of Texas, Johnston resigned his commission in the U.S. Army and accepted the Confederate offer.

3. ROBERT E. LEE (1807–1870)

In April, 1861, President Abraham Lincoln offered Robert E. Lee the field command of all Union forces. A few days later, the new Confederate government of his native state of Virginia asked Lee to take command of that state's military forces. Even though he opposed slavery and the secession of states from the Union, and believed that the South could not win the war, he accepted the Confederate offer because of his loyalty to Virginia.

Robert E. Lee.

4. VICTORIANO HUERTA (1854–1916)

Mexican president Francisco Madero gave command of government troops in Mexico City to General Victoriano Huerta in order to suppress a coup which had broken out on Feb. 9, 1913. During the next 10 days, Huerta, who felt no real loyalty to Madero, met with the rebel leader, Félix Díaz. Díaz, with his eye on the presidency, was looking for an able military commander. However, Huerta had no intention of playing second fiddle even to Díaz. The general joined the rebels, successfully overthrew President Madero, and made himself president of Mexico.

5. HERBERT HOOVER (1874–1964)

After administering relief programs in Europe following W.W. I, Herbert Hoover returned to the U.S. as a popular political figure. However, his political affiliations were unknown, with the result that both Democrats and Republicans courted him and offered him leadership positions. In 1920, Hoover announced he would accept the Republican nomination for president. When the Republicans knew Hoover was no longer thinking of joining the Democratic party, they decided to run party regular Warren Harding for president that year instead of Hoover, to whom they gave the job of secretary of commerce.

6. DWIGHT D. EISENHOWER (1890–1969)

In 1952, after serving as the commander of NATO, Gen. Eisenhower returned to the U.S., where both the Democratic and Republican parties asked him to be their presidential candidate in that year's election. After several months of indecisiveness about whether he wanted to enter politics and, if so, which party he should join, Eisenhower accepted the Republican offer and was nominated as the GOP presidential candidate. He won the election in 1952 and was reelected four years later.

—R.J.F.

18 AMERICANS YOU DIDN'T KNOW WERE PART INDIAN

1. JOHNNY CASH (1932–   )

Country singer; one fourth Cherokee.

2. CHER (1946–   )
Singer; part Cherokee.

3. CHARLES CURTIS (1860–1936)
Vice-president under Herbert Hoover; one fourth Kansa.

4. REDD FOXX (1922–   )
   Comedian; grandson of a full-blooded Seminole.

5. JAMES GARNER (1928–   )
   Actor; part Cherokee.

6. JIMI HENDRIX (1942–1970)
   Musician; part Cherokee.

7. LENA HORNE (1917–   )
   Singer; great-granddaughter of a full-blooded Blackfoot.

Lena Horne.

8. CORDELL HULL (1871–1955)
   Statesman and Nobel Peace Prize laureate; his mother was part Cherokee.

9. WAYLON JENNINGS (1937–   )
   Country and Western singer; part Comanche and Cherokee.

10. ROBERT RAUSCHENBERG (1925–   )
    Artist; one fourth Cherokee.

11. JOHNNIE RAY (1927–   )
    Rock 'n' roll singer; part Blackfoot.

12. BURT REYNOLDS (1936–   )
    Actor; one fourth Cherokee.

13. LYNN RIGGS (1899–1954)
    Screenwriter and playwright who wrote the original work upon which *Oklahoma!* was based; one half Cherokee.

14. ORAL ROBERTS (1918–   )
    Evangelist; inherited Cherokee blood from his mother's side.

15. ROY ROGERS (1912–   )
    Actor and singer; great-great grandson of a Choctaw woman.

16. WILL ROGERS (1879–1935)
    Humorist; about one fourth Cherokee.

17. CHARLES STEVENS (1893–1964)
    Actor whose film career spanned from 1915 *(The Birth of a Nation)* to 1962 *(The Outsider*—the story of Ira Hayes); grandson of Apache chief Geronimo.

18. MAJ. GEN. CLARENCE TINKER (1887–1942)
    First American general killed after Pearl Harbor in W.W. II; one eighth Osage.

—W.A.D. & THE EDS.

2
AMERICA, AMERICA

RANKING THE PRESIDENTS

On Jan. 10, 1982, the *Chicago Tribune* published the results of a survey in which leading historians, authors, and political scholars were asked to rate the U.S. presidents. Setting his or her own criteria, this is how the 49 respondents ranked the 10 best and the 10 worst presidents:

THE TOP 10 PRESIDENTS (WITH BEST NO. 1)

1. Abraham Lincoln
2. George Washington
3. Franklin Roosevelt
4. Theodore Roosevelt
5. Thomas Jefferson
6. Woodrow Wilson
7. Andrew Jackson
8. Harry Truman
9. Dwight Eisenhower
10. James Polk

THE 10 WORST PRESIDENTS (WITH WORST NO. 1)

1. Warren Harding
2. Richard Nixon
3. James Buchanan
4. Franklin Pierce
5. Ulysses Grant
6. Millard Fillmore
7. Andrew Johnson
8. Calvin Coolidge
9. John Tyler
10. Jimmy Carter

Source: Copyright, 1982, *Chicago Tribune*. Used with permission.

9 CLOSE ENCOUNTERS WITH RICHARD NIXON

1. CAB CALLOWAY

On Apr. 29, 1969, President Nixon held a black-tie dinner in honor of pianist-composer Duke Ellington's 70th birthday. Among the show-business personalities who were invited to attend the affair was entertainer Cab Calloway. As Calloway passed down the reception line, shaking hands with such dignitaries as the Shah of Iran, he finally reached Nixon, who gave him a big smile as he approached. Nixon grasped Calloway's hand in both of his and said, "Ah, Mr. Ellington, it's so good you're here. Happy, happy birthday. Pat and I just love your music." Not wanting to embarrass the president of the United States, Calloway smiled, thanked him, and moved on.

2. A SMALL GIRL

President Nixon was shaking hands and talking with members of a crowd at an airport when a little girl shouted to him, "How is Smokey the Bear?" referring to the famous fire-fighting symbol who was then residing at the Washington Zoo. Nixon smiled at the girl and turned away, but she kept waving and asking her question. Unable to make out her words, Nixon sought help from his aide-de-camp, Steve Bull. Bull whispered, "Smokey the Bear, Washington National Zoo." Nixon walked over to the little girl, shook her hand, and said, "How do you do, Miss Bear?"

3. ANTIWAR PROTESTORS

Following the invasion of Cambodia and the death of four students at Kent State University in 1970, thousands of people poured into Washington, D.C., in preparation for a major antiwar demonstration. Unable to sleep the morning of May 9, Nixon called his valet, Manolo Sanchez, and asked him if he had ever seen the Lincoln Memorial after dark. Sanchez had not, so Nixon said, "Let's go." Accompanied by several Secret Service agents, they toured the memorial and emerged at about 5:00 A.M. On the steps outside, they encountered a small group of students from Alfred State College, who had been talking politics with a park policeman. Nixon chatted amiably with the young people and soon a crowd of 40 or 50 sleepy protestors had gathered. When the protestors began asking political questions, the president became vague and somewhat evasive, preferring to launch into a long monologue about his world travels instead. When one student said he was from California, Nixon talked about surfing; when three others said they were from Syracuse, he remarked, "Oh, the Orangemen, that's a good football team." Some protestors became so discouraged that they walked away. One Syracuse student, Lynn Shatzkin, commented, "He didn't look anyone in the eyes; he was mumbling; when people asked him to speak up he would boom one word and no more. . . . I always thought Nixon was just a man who disagreed with me, but that's not what he is. He's obviously a very sick person who's had too much pressure and cracked. I'm just wondering who's running the country."

After the conversation, Nixon had breakfast at the Mayflower Hotel and ate corned beef hash with a poached egg for the first time in five years.

4.–5. DON LEADBETER AND FRENCH GENDARME

On Oct. 28, 1970, motorcycle policeman Don Leadbeter was leading a presidential motorcade in St. Petersburg, Fla., when he was hit by a truck and severely injured. Nixon rushed over to express his sympathies. Leadbeter replied by apologizing for delaying the motorcade. Then, after an awkward silence, the president blurted out, "Do you like the work?"

In 1974, in Paris to attend the funeral of Georges Pompidou, Nixon asked the same question of a French policeman who was struggling to hold back an enthusiastic crowd. Unfortunately, the beleaguered gendarme did not understand English.

6. RICH LITTLE

The comedian, famed for his realistic impersonation of Richard Nixon, attended a reception for the president at his estate in San Clemente, Calif. After actress Debbie Reynolds was introduced to Nixon, she turned to Little and said, "Go ahead, Rich, do your impersonation of the president." After a pause, Little did a brief impression of Nixon, who watched politely, shook his hand, and continued down the receiving line. Later Nixon asked an aide, "Who was that fellow with the strange voice imitating?"

7. ELVIS PRESLEY

When Elvis learned that a certain Hollywood celebrity was an undercover agent for the Federal Narcotics Bureau, he decided that he, too, wanted to be an agent. If that couldn't be arranged, then he at least wanted a Federal Narcotics Bureau badge. Uninterested in the honorary shield offered him by Deputy Narcotics Director John Finlator, Elvis took his case straight to the president, who invited him to the Oval Office. When Nixon saw Elvis's costume, he said, "Boy, you sure do dress kind of wild, don't you?" to which Elvis replied, "Mr. President, you've got your show to run and I've got mine." After offering to help Nixon with his antidrug campaign, Elvis got his badge, but it failed to curb his own fatal drug addiction.

8. ANTHONY CALOMARIS

Calomaris was a teenager who lived next door to J. Edgar Hoover on Thirtieth Place in Washington, D.C. One night, during a newspaper strike in April, 1974, Hoover held a secret dinner party for Nixon. However, word of the president's visit to the home of the FBI director leaked out, and when Nixon prepared to leave, he was shocked to discover TV cameramen waiting for him outside. Calomaris was also there, and when the president emerged, the young man asked for his autograph. It was Calomaris's lucky night; he ended up with four autographs of Richard Nixon. "He didn't seem to want to talk to the television people," said Calomaris, "and when I gave him my writing pad, he just kept turning the pages and signing his name."

9. STANLEY ROCKWELL

Mr. Rockwell, an insurance salesman from West Hartford, Conn., was standing at a pay phone in Nantucket in mid-September, 1980, talking to his wife, Betty, when he noticed Richard Nixon step off a nearby yacht. Calling out to the ex-president, Rockwell asked Nixon if he wouldn't say a few words to his wife. Glad to oblige, Nixon picked up the phone and said, "Betty, who's this woman your husband's with?" Then he smiled at Rockwell and walked away.

—D.W.

3 ROCKS THAT LOOK LIKE U.S. PRESIDENTS

John F. Kennedy in Maui, Hawaii.

Abraham Lincoln in Washington state.

Richard Nixon in Krista, Crete.

SOURCE: John Mitchell, *Simulacra*. London: Thames & Hudson, 1979.

EDWARD ASNER'S FIRST 5 INTERNATIONAL ACTS HE WOULD PERFORM OR DOMESTIC LAWS HE WOULD PROPOSE IF HE WERE PRESIDENT OF THE UNITED STATES

The outspoken president of the Screen Actors Guild first gained a large following in his role as Lou Grant on the *Mary Tyler Moore Show*. From 1977 to 1982 he starred in the *Lou Grant Show*, which won six Emmys and four Golden Globes. A longtime liberal, Asner is a member of the American Civil Liberties Union, Americans for Democratic Action, and Common Cause.

1. Declaration of the illegality of war, combined with total disarmament.

2. All 18-year-olds must have 18 months to two years of national service, with an option of other than military, such as VISTA-Peace Corps-type (e.g., forestry, highways, innercity ghettos, Indian reservations, etc.), with automatic crediting for GI Bill. No exemptions, including disabled.

3. Declaration making it illegal to starve. Every citizen to receive monies sufficient to live on (this to include food, clothing, shelter). Jobs must be regarded as nonessential, those desiring them strictly in terms of joy-of-job, not necessity. Cost of living to be geared and controlled through wage-price controls so that guaranteed living allowances remain sufficient.

4. Worldwide research, investigation, and eventual land reapportionment. Worldwide protection and safeguard of all animal and plant species, as well as primitive peoples. Worldwide policing and prosecution against all forms of pollution.

5. Total funding and restructuring of the penal system.

—Exclusive for *The Book of Lists 3*

ELDRIDGE CLEAVER'S FIRST 5 INTERNATIONAL ACTS HE WOULD PERFORM OR DOMESTIC LAWS HE WOULD PROPOSE IF HE WERE PRESIDENT OF THE UNITED STATES

Onetime minister of information for the militant Black Panthers and author of two books, Eldridge Cleaver fled criminal charges and remained in exile abroad for seven years. Cleared of any major crimes, he returned to the U.S. After a period as an evangelist, he is now studying Mormonism and works for a tree service firm. He is married and has two children.

1. Establish a National Identification Card, based on a "great census," in which maximum effort is made to count everybody. We then could put America on the computer; ferret out illegals, spies, terrorists, fugitives; streamline procedures; and trim down bureaucracy.

2. Conduct a Comprehensive Monetary and Banking Reform, implementing Section 31 of the Federal Reserve Act. Cancel the national debt. Restore to Congress the constitutional duty of issuing and controlling our money supply. Outlaw fractional banking. Abolish open-market committees.

3. Establish a National Health and Retirement Plan, based on the vision that human beings deserve the very best that knowledge and technology can provide, and that, after a lifetime of productive contribution to society, citizens should retire rich instead of poor and dependent.

4. Promote a Goods and Services Access Security Plan, with the goal of breaking the ancient domination of our lives by fear of privation, by guar-

anteeing and aggressively delivering food, clothing, shelter, telephonic communication, and transportation to all citizens.

5. Realign world forces and issues: (1) Reaffirm goal of the American Revolution of establishing a world democratic order. (2) Reject the U.N. as a mixed bag of feudalistic, totalitarian, and undemocratic values and practices. (3) Establish a world council of democratic nations.

—Exclusive for *The Book of Lists 3*

10 U.S. POLITICIANS WHO APPEARED DRUNK IN PUBLIC

1. DANIEL WEBSTER (1851)

Webster spent nearly three decades in one federal office or another. As he approached the end of his distinguished career he grew increasingly dependent on alcohol, regularly drinking brandy and water while speaking. In 1851 this practice caused him trouble at a ceremony marking the completion of the Boston–Montreal Railroad. Then secretary of state, Webster ignored the point of the ceremony and delivered a rambling speech on American history. The governor general of Canada, one of the honored guests, was so enraged by the performance that he almost stormed off the platform.

2. ANDREW JOHNSON (1865)

Johnson was drunk when he took the oath of office as vice-president. Because of that, he delivered a bizarre speech focusing on his humble origins, which prompted the New York *World* to editorialize: "And think that one frail life stands between this insolent, clownish creature and the presidency! May God bless and spare Abraham Lincoln." Johnson, however, was not to blame. He was not an alcoholic, and he had been drinking only to ease the pain of a bout with typhoid fever.

3. B. GRATZ BROWN (1872)

Brown, the governor of Missouri, was Horace Greeley's running mate on the Democrats' national ticket in 1872. His drinking habits during the campaign earned him the nickname "Boozy Gratz" and played a role in the ticket's defeat. His most memorable performance occurred at Yale University, where he drunkenly disparaged the school, its students, and the entire eastern part of the country, calling them effete and backward.

4. MARION ZIONCHECK (1936)

Zioncheck was one of the zaniest characters ever to sit in the House of Representatives. He came from Seattle and was initially elected in Roosevelt's 1932 landslide. In 1936 he went on a spree that involved a

Andrew Johnson was so drunk during his vice-presidential inauguration that he could barely repeat the Oath of Office.

good deal of drinking. The most notable incident in the binge occurred when Zioncheck took his battered car on a wild ride through Washington's streets and over its sidewalks before arriving at the White House, where he left some gifts for the president—a box of Ping-Pong balls, an empty moth ball container, and a bag of empty beer bottles.

5. JIM FOLSOM (1962)

Folsom had been elected governor of Alabama twice before and had a good chance at a third term until he appeared drunk on a TV program on the eve of the Democratic primary in 1962. Folsom forgot the names of his children, then gave an extended imitation of a cuckoo clock. The performance cost him the election and ended his career as an important politician in Alabama.

6. THOMAS DODD (1965)

Two years before his fellow senators censured Dodd for using campaign contributions for personal purposes, the Connecticut Democrat put on a memorable performance on the steps of the Senate Office Building. After an afternoon of drinking, Dodd was so inebriated that, according to witnesses, he required two secretaries to aid him in reaching his car.

7. CARL ALBERT (1972)

Albert, the speaker of the House of Representatives, was driving home from work when he had the misfortune of colliding with two parked cars. Newspaper reports quoted witnesses as saying that Albert was "obviously drunk." According to these observers, he told the police who came to investigate: "Leave me alone. I'm Carl Albert, speaker of the House. You can't touch me . . . I just got you raises."

8. WILBUR MILLS (1974)

As chairman of the House Ways and Means Committee, Mills was one of the most powerful men in Washington. But that power was taken away shortly after an intoxicated Mills and his companion, stripper Fanne Foxe, were stopped by police for speeding. The hysterical Fanne fell or jumped into the nearby Tidal Basin. Two months later, Mills appeared with her on the stage of a Boston burlesque house. He then sought medical treatment.

9. FRANK HORTON (1976)

A Republican representative from New York, Horton carved out a special niche for himself in the history of congressional car chases when he reached speeds exceeding 78 mph one summer night on the New York State Thruway. He ultimately pleaded guilty to charges of drunk driving and speeding, was fined, and served a short term in jail.

10. HERMAN TALMADGE (1979)

Talmadge, senator from Georgia for more than two decades, faced up to the fact that he had a drinking problem after tottering onto the Senate floor as controversy over his financial dealings was raging. Soon afterward, he entered an alcohol abuse program.

—E.F.

THE TOP 7 U.S. POLITICAL ACTION COMMITTEES (PACs)

In 1946, when Richard Nixon first ran for Congress, he lashed out at opponent Jerry Voorhis as the candidate of the CIO-PAC. In those early days of the cold war, the CIO-PAC was considered by right-wingers to be a Communist-front organization, if not openly controlled by "Moscow."

(Voorhis did not in fact have the endorsement of the CIO-PAC, but the charge nonetheless helped send Nixon to Washington.) Since then, however, the right has come to appreciate the utility of the PAC as an organizational form. Under the 1971 Federal Election Campaign Act (as amended in 1974 to help prevent Watergate-style dirty tricks), with its limit on individual donations of $1,000 per candidate, the PAC has emerged as a major conduit for conservative campaign funding. Of the following 7 PACs—as ranked by the Federal Election Commission in order of funds raised in 1979–1980—four are militantly conservative in orientation and two more were formed by professional associations with pronounced conservative leanings.

1. NATIONAL CONGRESSIONAL CLUB (NCC)

NCC was founded in 1972 as the private political party of conservative Republican Senator-elect Jesse Helms of North Carolina, for the purpose of raising funds to pay his campaign expenses. Having amassed the ample sum of $7.5 million for Helms's reelection in 1978, NCC extended its aid to other conservative candidates, fellow believers in such right-wing causes as restoration of prayer in the schools and termination of legal aid to the poor. (To avoid the legal ceiling of $10,000 donated by a PAC to any one candidate, NCC created its own ad agency, Jefferson Marketing, providing in-kind services on which there are no limits.) In 1980 NCC broke PAC fund-raising records by collecting $7,874,000, of which $4.5 million went to elect Ronald Reagan. In 1981 alone, NCC reported a war chest of $5.3 million for use against pro-abortion, probusing, spendthrift liberals.

2. NATIONAL CONSERVATIVE POLITICAL ACTION COMMITTEE (NCPAC)

In 1980 a little-known group founded by John ("Terry") Dolan, only a year out of Georgetown Law School, claimed credit for helping defeat such key Senate liberals as Birch Bayh, George McGovern, and Frank Church. "A rooster who takes credit for the dawn," skeptics said of NCPAC, while others deplored Dolan's kamikaze political tactics. (To help defeat a pro-abortion liberal, NCPAC did not hesitate to televise the specter of dead fetuses.) In 1979–1980 NCPAC raised $7.7 million. By bankrolling saturation media campaigns in 1980—up to 200 TV ads weekly and 72 radio spots daily in target electoral districts—NCPAC maximized impact while avoiding federal limits on contributions per candidate. In 1982, with $3.1 million at its disposal, NCPAC announced a "hit list" headed by House Majority leader Jim Wright (D-Tex.); Daniel Patrick Moynihan, liberal Democratic senator from New York; and Democratic presidential hopeful Ted Kennedy.

3. FUND FOR A CONSERVATIVE MAJORITY (FCM)

Established in 1969, FCM was an early supporter of Ronald Reagan's presidential ambitions. Unlike the Republican party, which supports liberal party members, FCM specifically seeks conservative candidates dedicated to "the rebirth of America on all fronts." Under the leadership of Robert C. Heckman, FCM's Citizens for Reagan (not to be confused with Reagan's own Citizens for the Republic) spent $2.5 million on the 1980 presidential election. With Reagan in the White House, FCM conducted direct-mail and telephone campaigns in favor of his tax-cut programs. In 1982 FCM announced its intention to back candidates loyal to Reagan, hoping to elect six new conservative senators, three pro-Reagan governors, and 300 state legislators. In addition, FCM sponsored a "Repeal O'Neill" drive, hoping to unseat the speaker of the House of Representatives by electing a Republican majority in the House.

4. REALTORS POLITICAL ACTION COMMITTEE (RPAC)

The largest of the trade association political action committees, RPAC (formed by the National Association of Realtors) was established in 1969 to identify and help elect candidates sympathetic to real-estate interests. Of funds raised—$2.74 million in 1979–1980—less was disbursed on national elections than on elections at the local level. Although claiming to be bipartisan, RPAC showed a definite bias to the right: in the 1979–1980 federal elections, it gave $1.1 million to Republicans, only $504,365 to Democrats. It was also very supportive of President Reagan's efforts to curtail federal spending. In 1981 Reagan appointed a past president of the National Association of Realtors, Donald Hovde, undersecretary of the Department of Housing and Urban Development.

5. CITIZENS FOR THE REPUBLIC (CFTR)

CFTR was established in California in 1977 as Ronald Reagan's personal power vehicle, using leftover funds from his 1976 candidacy as seed money to finance other conservative Republican candidates. In the 1980 elections 131 winners were backed by the CFTR. Of those, 98 were nonincumbents. After Reagan's election in 1980, CFTR (under the chairmanship of his aide Lyn Nofziger) began funding a nationwide advertising campaign in favor of his tax-cut program. Reagan's incumbency, however, took some of the urgency out of the movement: CFTR was the only one of six major conservative PACs to report a decline in funds raised in 1981 as compared to 1979.

6. UAW VOLUNTARY COMMUNITY ACTION PROGRAM (UAW-V-CAP)

Under federal law, union dues may not be spent on federal elections. The United Auto Workers therefore established its own PAC, under the authority of elected union officials, to solicit funds from members for the express purpose of seeking economic and social justice through the electoral process. Of $1,792,406 raised in 1979–1980, most went to support moderate and liberal Democratic candidates in the Northeast and Midwest, including 18 of 19 Democratic congressional candidates in Michigan. UAW-V-CAP also conducts voter registration drives, leadership training institutes, and propaganda of the anti-Reagan strain, taking particularly strong exception to Reaganomics with its trickle-down theory and tax breaks for the wealthy.

7. AMERICAN MEDICAL POLITICAL ACTION COMMITTEE (AMPAC)

Tax-exempt organizations are also prohibited from making political contributions, a restriction the American Medical Association circumvents through its own PAC. Established in 1961, AMPAC collects money from AMA members to further its specific and general legislative interests. More than simply opposing government interference in the profession, AMPAC also seeks to further a business climate favorable to its affluent constituents, many of them medical corporations in their own right. (In selecting candidates to support, an AMPAC spokesman explained, "We don't keep voting records. Our candidates do not view government as the answer to our problems.") AMPAC is generally secretive about the recipients of its funds, but it is known that it gave $100,000 in 1978 to members of the House committee with jurisdiction over hospital cost containment legislation.

—C.D.

THE 6 BEST SECRETARIES OF STATE

David L. Porter, associate professor of history at William Penn College in Oskaloosa, Ia., polled 50 diplomatic historians in the U.S., asking each to nominate candidates for the best—and the worst—secretaries of state. Among the suggested criteria: the secretary's success in defining and achieving his diplomatic goals; the political and moral leadership he exerted on foreign affairs; the impact of his actions on the course of American history.

1. JOHN QUINCY ADAMS, who served (1817–1825) under President James Monroe, was the first choice of over 80% of the respondents. Stern, cerebral, conscientious, and articulate, he negotiated the acquisition of Florida from Spain in 1819 and collaborated with the president in formulating the Monroe Doctrine.

2. WILLIAM H. SEWARD served (1861–1869) Presidents Abraham Lincoln and Andrew Johnson. Seward helped keep France and Britain from recognizing the Confederacy during the Civil War, persuaded France to withdraw its troops from Mexico after that war ended, and successfully engineered the purchase of Alaska from Russia in 1867.

3. HAMILTON FISH served (1869–1877) President Ulysses S. Grant. Calm, judicious, and untainted by the corruption that permeated the Grant administration, Fish helped settle the thorny Alabama claims controversy with Britain in 1871, directed negotiations that settled American claims against Spain, and signed a commercial reciprocity treaty with Hawaii in 1875, helping to pave the way for later annexation.

4. CHARLES EVANS HUGHES served (1921–1925) Presidents Harding and Coolidge. Hughes presided over the Washington Conference for Limitation of Armament (1921–1922), which froze for a decade naval armament among the U.S., Britain, and France, and he brought about the 1922 Nine Power Treaty, which called upon its signatories to maintain an Open Door policy toward China and respect China's independence.

5. GEORGE C. MARSHALL served (1947–1949) President Harry Truman. The first professional soldier ever to become secretary—and the man who held the post for the shortest time among the top secretaries of state—Marshall helped establish the postwar policy of containment. He promulgated the Truman Doctrine, which provided military aid for Greece and Turkey, developed the Marshall Plan for rebuilding postwar Europe, and helped foster the Organization of American States and the North Atlantic Treaty Organization.

6. DEAN ACHESON, Marshall's successor, also served (1949–1953) President Truman. Acheson helped create NATO, brought West Germany into the European defense system, and implemented a policy of armed intervention in Korea.

Source: *American Heritage,* December, 1981.

THE 5 WORST SECRETARIES OF STATE

1. JOHN SHERMAN served (1897–1898) President McKinley. An Ohio senator (and the younger brother of General William Tecumseh Sherman), John Sherman was 74 at the time of his appointment—made

John Sherman, voted the worst Secretary of State.

purely in order to create a vacancy in the Senate for McKinley's mentor, Mark Hanna, to fill. In failing health and absentminded—he once forgot entirely that his department was engaged in annexing Hawaii—Sherman resigned when an assistant secretary was invited to attend Cabinet meetings in his stead.

2. ROBERT SMITH, a Pennsylvanian who had served as secretary of the Navy under Jefferson, was appointed in 1809 by James Madison when a Senate cabal barred the president from appointing the man he really wanted, Albert Gallatin. Madison, who had himself been secretary of state, planned to direct foreign policy in any case. Smith was inept and unschooled in diplomacy—Madison complained that he personally had to rewrite all the secretary's papers—and was replaced in 1811 by James Monroe.

3. ELIHU WASHBURNE, President Grant's first secretary of state, served the shortest of all terms—just five days (Mar. 5 to Mar. 10, 1869). An Illinois congressman and longtime political ally of the new president, Washburne was made secretary out of gratitude for past favors—and perhaps to add luster to his next appointment: minister to France. His successor, Hamilton Fish, would prove one of the ablest secretaries.

4. JOHN FOSTER DULLES served (1953–1959) under President Eisenhower. A stern, pious lawyer and diplomat, Dulles was ranked among the worst because of his dangerous tendency toward overstatement—he was the champion of "brinkmanship" and "massive retaliation"—that caused distrust among America's allies and bewilderment among its potential adversaries.

5. WILLIAM JENNINGS BRYAN, three times Democratic candidate for president, was made secretary of state in 1913 because he had thrown his support to Woodrow Wilson at the 1912 Democratic convention. Bryan knew little of foreign affairs: His chief concern when asked to take the job was whether he would be expected to serve intoxicants. Assured that he would not, he accepted, only to find his unbending pacifism increasingly out of favor with the growing interventionist spirit of the president and public. Bryan resigned in 1915, charging that Wilson's notes to the Germans following the sinking of the *Lusitania* were too belligerent.

SOURCE: *American Heritage,* December, 1981.

DENIS HAYES'S FIRST 5 ACTS HE WOULD PERFORM IF HE WERE IN CHARGE OF THE DEPARTMENT OF ENERGY

An enthusiastic supporter of solar energy, Hayes became a leader in environmental causes while still a student. In 1970 he coordinated the celebration of Earth Day, and eight years later he organized Sun Day.

Soon afterward he founded the Solar Lobby in Washington, D.C. In 1979, the 34-year-old Hayes was appointed director of the Dept. of Energy's Solar Energy Research Institute in Golden, Colo.

1. Introduce legislation establishing a $20 per barrel tariff on imported oil, to be phased in over five years. Early revenues would be earmarked to fill the Strategic Petroleum Reserve and to upgrade the energy efficiencies of poor people's homes.

2. Introduce legislation to phase in a 50¢ per gallon tax on gasoline, diesel, and aviation fuel. Half the revenues would support a Transportation Trust Fund. Half would finance a Renewable Energy Development Authority, governed by an independent board of directors.

3. Update and widely disseminate all the consumer information now being suppressed by the Reagan Administration. People need objective, trustworthy information about which appliances—furnaces, etc.—are most efficient and cost-effective.

4. Cancel the Clinch River Breeder Reactor; halt completion of the Barnwell Nuclear Reprocessing Facility; and enlist our allies in a major campaign to provide assistance to third-world countries pursuing nonnuclear alternatives.

5. Discourage dull gray suits, dull gray buildings, dull gray furniture, dull gray reports, and dull gray thinking.

—Exclusive for *The Book of Lists 3*

FRANCES MOORE LAPPE'S FIRST 5 ACTS SHE WOULD PERFORM IF SHE WERE HEAD OF THE DEPARTMENT OF AGRICULTURE

In 1975 Lappé founded the Institute for Food and Development Policy as an outgrowth of her passionate concern about the world's food shortage. She believes that food scarcity is directly linked to political, cultural, and economic factors. Lappé's widely read books include *Diet for a Small Planet* and *Food First,* in which she stresses the importance of "choosing a diet that is good both for our bodies and for the earth."

1. Reform the Dept. of Agriculture as the Dept. of Agriculture and Nutrition, explicitly linking the production of food and the meeting of human nutritional needs.

2. Establish local and regional "Sustainable Agriculture Boards" (elected and comprised of farmers, consumers, and agricultural scientists) to arrive at regional plans for the protection of farmland and topsoil and a return to significant regional food self-sufficiency.

3. Declare a national goal of reducing dependency on petrochemical fertilizers and pesticides through a national research and educational campaign in which a network of farmers serve as teachers and organizers.

4. Reverse the trend toward monopoly control of farmland by prohibiting nonfarm corporations or foreign interests from owning farmland, directing government help only to family-sized farms or cooperatives (that is, no support for farms larger than can be justified on the grounds of efficiency), and setting a ceiling on the acres of farmland any one family can own or control.

5. Establish an elected National Food Export Board responsible for overseeing and controlling food exports in light of domestic food needs and the impact of our food exports abroad.

—Exclusive for *The Book of Lists 3*

ANSEL ADAMS'S 10 MOST PHOTOGENIC SITES IN THE U.S.

One of the greatest photographers of the 20th century, Adams is best known for his scenes of the American West. He has been a member of the Sierra Club since 1919. Always an innovator, in the 1940s Adams organized the first academic department of photography. He is still an active lecturer, writer, and teacher.

1. Yosemite Valley (Yosemite National Park, California)
2. The High Sierra (California)
3. Big Sur Region (California)
4. Northern New Mexico
5. Most of Arizona
6. Teton National Park (Wyoming)
7. Olympic National Park (Washington)
8. Some of Utah
9. Some of New England
10. Golden Gate National Recreation Area (California)

—Exclusive for *The Book of Lists 3*

The Yosemite Valley, photographed by Ansel Adams.

THE 10 BEST STATES TO RETIRE TO

Chase Econometrics, a subsidiary of Chase Manhattan Bank, ranked 48 states, using a point system, within the conterminous U.S. according to their desirability for the average retiree; Hawaii and Alaska were not included due to a lack of sufficient data. Among the factors which analysts examined were weather conditions, housing, property taxes, living costs, unemployment, medical facilities, public transportation, and cultural and leisure activities. In case you're wondering, sunny California ranked no. 17.

		Points
1.	Utah	305
2.	Louisiana	295
3.	South Carolina	280
4.	Nevada	260
5.	Texas	230
6.	New Mexico	200
7.	Alabama	185
8.	Arizona	175
9.	Florida	160
10.	Georgia	155

SOURCE: "The Best States to Retire To" by Raymond Schuessler, in *Modern Maturity*, October/November, 1981.

THE 10 WORST STATES TO RETIRE TO

		Points
1.	Massachusetts	−498
2.	Maine	−428
3.	New Jersey	−390
4.	Vermont	−385
5.	Rhode Island	−373
6.	New York	−355
7.	New Hampshire	−300
8.	Connecticut	−285
9.	North Dakota	−280
10.	Minnesota	−265

SOURCE: "The Best States to Retire To" by Raymond Schuessler, in *Modern Maturity*, October/November, 1981.

10 PLACES THAT CONSUME THE MOST ALCOHOL

To understand fully the implications of this list, certain things must be kept in mind: The high consumption rate of intoxicants in such locations as Nevada and the District of Columbia are explained at least partly by tourism. Because the price of alcohol is lower in some states, such as New Hampshire and Vermont, many people come from nearby states to purchase their liquor. The first three columns of figures indicate beverage volume consumed in the form of distilled spirits, wine, and beer; the fourth column shows total alcohol consumption. The numbers represent U.S. gallons. All data are based on a drinking-age population 14 years and over.

	Distilled Spirits	Wine	Beer	Total Alcohol Volume
1. Nevada	8.97	6.62	49.68	7.05
2. District of Columbia	7.51	7.32	31.74	5.72
3. New Hampshire	7.14	4.19	44.06	5.66
4. Alaska	4.16	3.53	31.63	3.73
5. Vermont	3.86	3.63	33.62	3.70
6. California	3.22	5.29	31.49	3.57
7. Colorado	3.51	3.66	33.41	3.54
8. Wyoming	3.32	1.73	40.59	3.51
9. Wisconsin	3.06	2.15	39.96	3.42
10. Arizona	2.78	3.00	39.52	3.41

SOURCE: Merton M. Hyman, Marilyn M. Zimmerman, Carol Gurioli, and Alice Helrich, *Drinking, Drinkers and Alcohol-Related Mortality and Hospitalizations*. New Brunswick, N.J.: Rutgers University Center of Alcohol Studies, 1980.

10 STATES THAT CONSUME THE LEAST ALCOHOL

	Distilled Spirits	Wine	Beer	Total Alcohol Volume
1. Utah	1.50	1.07	21.59	1.77
2. Arkansas	1.76	.87	21.48	1.85
3. West Virginia	1.91	.69	21.42	1.89
4. Kentucky	1.90	.71	22.15	1.92
5. Kansas	1.60	.89	25.33	1.96
6. Tennessee	1.75	.83	25.61	2.02
7. Alabama	2.12	.91	21.87	2.03

8. Oklahoma	2.02	1.07	24.00	2.10
9. Indiana	1.88	1.21	26.70	2.18
10. North Carolina	2.09	1.63	24.21	2.22

SOURCE: Merton M. Hyman, Marilyn M. Zimmerman, Carol Gurioli, and Alice Helrich, *Drinking, Drinkers and Alcohol-Related Mortality and Hospitalizations*. New Brunswick, N.J.: Rutgers University Center of Alcohol Studies, 1980.

10 CELEBRITIES WHO RENOUNCED THEIR U.S. CITIZENSHIP

1. JOSEPHINE BAKER, dancer and singer

Born in St. Louis, Mo., in 1906. She joined a traveling dance troupe at age 16, and by 1925, she was a Parisian star. She decided to remain in France, and she became a naturalized French citizen in 1937. During her visit to the U.S. in 1963, she took part in the civil-rights march on Washington, D.C., and in 1973 she performed onstage in New York City. She died in Paris in 1975.

2. JEFFERSON DAVIS, president of the Confederate States of America

Born in present-day Fairview, Ky., in 1808. The well-respected senator from Mississippi withdrew from the U.S. Senate in January, 1861, and was named provisional president of the Confederate States of America a few weeks later. These acts caused him to lose his U.S. citizenship. After the Confederacy's defeat, Davis was imprisoned until May, 1867. Although he was urged to request a presidential pardon, he refused to do so, contending that he had committed no crime. As a result, he died in New Orleans in 1889 without having regained his citizenship. In October, 1978, President Jimmy Carter signed an amnesty bill which restored Davis's citizenship, retroactive to Dec. 25, 1868.

3. W. E. B. DU BOIS, sociologist and civil-rights activist

Born in Great Barrington, Mass., in 1868. A prominent advocate of Pan-Africanism and black nationalism, Du Bois played an important role in the development of the NAACP. In later life he became increasingly radical in his beliefs and joined the Communist party in 1961. The following year he moved to Ghana and renounced his U.S. citizenship. He died in Accra, Ghana, in 1963.

4. T. S. ELIOT, poet and playwright

Born in St. Louis, Mo., in 1888. After graduating from Harvard, he continued his studies at the University of Paris. He returned to the U.S. and taught briefly at Harvard but returned to Europe in 1914 and made his home in London. In 1927 he sparked controversy when he renounced his U.S. citizenship and became a British subject—the first major literary figure to do so since Henry James. Eliot died in London in 1965.

40

5. ERIC ERICKSON, W.W. II spy for the Allies

Born in Brooklyn, N.Y., in 1889. After many years of experience as an oil salesman in the Orient, he decided to begin his own oil importing business in Sweden and became a Swedish citizen in 1936. In December, 1939, he was approached by Laurence Steinhardt, U.S. ambassador in Moscow, to work for U.S. intelligence, providing information on German oil production. He undertook this assignment from 1941 to 1944 with great success.

6. JOHN HUSTON, movie producer and director

Born in Nevada, Mo., in 1906. Huston made Ireland his permanent home in the 1950s when he purchased a 10th-century monastery, 16 mi. inland from the seaport of Galway, and converted it into a spacious estate. He officially became an Irish citizen in 1964. At an early age, Huston's two children, Tony and Anjelica, also decided to adopt Irish citizenship.

7. HENRY JAMES, novelist

Born in New York, N.Y., in 1843. James traveled extensively as a child, and in 1869 he took the traditional "grand tour" of Europe. In 1876 he settled in London, where he produced his major works. In 1915, a year before his death in London, he became a British subject.

8. LEE HARVEY OSWALD, assassin

Born in New Orleans, La., in 1939. After serving almost three years in the Marine Corps, he traveled to Russia in October, 1959, and immediately applied for Soviet citizenship. On Oct. 31 he went to the U.S. Embassy in Moscow and renounced his U.S. citizenship with a signed note and the oral statement, "I am a Marxist." He returned to the U.S. in June, 1962, with his Russian wife, Marina.

9. HENRY MORTON STANLEY, explorer

Born in Denbigh, Wales, in 1841. In 1858 he boarded ship for New Orleans and worked at a variety of jobs in the U.S. until 1869, when he was commissioned by the New York *Herald* to find Dr. David Livingstone, who had disappeared in Africa. For the next 20 years he undertook an extensive exploration of Africa, particularly the Congo. He had secretly become a U.S. citizen in 1885, to protect his royalties for *In Darkest Africa,* but in 1892 he had reassumed his British citizenship and served in Parliament from 1895 to 1900. He died in London in 1904.

10. ELIZABETH TAYLOR, film star

Born in London, England, in 1932. Because her parents were American citizens, she automatically enjoyed dual citizenship from birth. In October, 1964, seven months after her marriage to Richard Burton, she signed papers to renounce her U.S. citizenship in Paris, saying, "I want to become British more than anything else. I like the British best of all." It was not until 1966 that her renunciation was accepted by the U.S. State Department, making her solely a British subject.

—F.B.

13 SECRET ARMIES OF THE CIA

1. UKRAINIAN PARTISANS

From 1945 to 1952, the CIA trained and aerially supplied Ukrainian partisan units which had originally been organized by the Germans to fight the Soviets during W.W. II. For seven years, the partisans, operating in the Carpathian Mountains, made sporadic attacks. Finally, in 1952, a massive Soviet military force wiped them out.

2. CHINESE BRIGADE IN BURMA

After the Communist victory in China, Nationalist Chinese soldiers fled into northern Burma. During the early 1950s, the CIA used these soldiers to create a 12,000-man brigade which made raids into Red China. However, the Nationalist soldiers found it more profitable to monopolize the local opium trade.

3. GUATEMALAN REBEL ARMY

After Guatemalan president Jacobo Arbenz legalized that country's Communist party and expropriated 400,000 acres of United Fruit banana plantations, the CIA decided to overthrow his government. Guatemalan rebels were trained in Honduras and backed up with a CIA air contingent of bombers and fighter planes. This army invaded Guatemala in 1954, promptly toppling Arbenz's regime.

4. SUMATRAN REBELS

In an attempt to overthrow Indonesian president Sukarno in 1958, the CIA sent paramilitary experts and radio operators to the island of Sumatra to organize a revolt. With CIA air support, the rebel army attacked but was quickly defeated. The American government denied involvement even after a CIA B-26 was shot down and its CIA pilot, Allen Pope, was captured.

5. KHAMBA HORSEMEN

After the 1950 Chinese invasion of Tibet, the CIA began recruiting Khamba horsemen—fierce warriors who supported Tibet's religious leader, the Dalai Lama—as they escaped into India in 1959. These Khambas were trained in modern warfare at Camp Hale, high in the Rocky Mountains near Leadville, Colo. Transported back to Tibet by the CIA-operated Air America, the Khambas organized an army numbering at its peak some 14,000. By the mid-1960s the Khambas had been abandoned by the CIA but they fought on alone into 1970.

6. BAY OF PIGS INVASION FORCE

In 1960, CIA operatives recruited 1,500 Cuban refugees living in Miami and staged a surprise attack on Fidel Castro's Cuba. Trained at a base in Guatemala, this small army—complete with an air force consisting of B-26 bombers—landed at the Bay of Pigs on Apr. 17, 1961. The ill-conceived, poorly planned operation ended in disaster, since all but 150 men of the force were either killed or captured within three days.

7. L'ARMÉE CLANDESTINE

In 1962, CIA agents recruited Meo tribesmen living in the mountains of Laos to fight as guerrillas against Communist Pathet Lao forces. Called l'Armée Clandestine, this unit—paid, trained, and supplied by the CIA—grew into a 30,000-man force. By 1975, the Meos—who had numbered a quarter million in 1962—had been reduced to 10,000 refugees fleeing into Thailand.

8. NUNG MERCENARIES

A Chinese hill people living in Vietnam, the Nungs were hired and organized by the CIA as a mercenary force during the Vietnam War. Fearsome and brutal fighters, the Nungs were employed throughout Vietnam and along the Ho Chi Minh Trail. The Nungs proved costly, since they refused to fight unless constantly supplied with beer and prostitutes.

Troops preparing to defend the holy city of Lhasa in Tibet.

9. PERUVIAN REGIMENT

Unable to quell guerrilla forces in its eastern Amazonian provinces, Peru called on the U.S. for help in the mid-1960s. The CIA responded by establishing a fortified camp in the area and hiring local Peruvians who were trained by Green Beret personnel on loan from the U.S. Army. After crushing the guerrillas, the elite unit was disbanded because of fears it might stage a coup against the government.

10. CONGO MERCENARY FORCE

In 1964 during the Congolese Civil War, the CIA established an army in the Congo to back pro-Western leaders Cyril Adoula and Joseph Mobutu. The CIA imported European mercenaries and Cuban pilots—exiles from Cuba—to pilot the CIA air force, composed of transports and B-26 bombers.

11. THE CAMBODIAN COUP

For over 15 years, the CIA had tried various unsuccessful means of deposing Cambodia's left-leaning Prince Norodom Sihanouk, including assassination attempts. However, in March, 1970, a CIA-backed coup finally did the job. Funded by U.S. tax dollars, armed with U.S. weapons, and trained by American Green Berets, anti-Sihanouk forces called Kampuchea Khmer Krom (KKK) overran the capital of Phnom Penh and took control of the government. With the blessing of the CIA and the Nixon administration, control of Cambodia was placed in the hands of Lon Nol, who would later distinguish himself by dispatching soldiers to butcher tens of thousands of civilians.

12. KURD REBELS

During the early 1970s the CIA moved into eastern Iraq to organize and supply the Kurds of that area, who were rebelling against the pro-Soviet Iraqi government. The real purpose behind this action was to help the shah of Iran settle a border dispute with Iraq favorably. After an Iranian-Iraqi settlement was reached, the CIA withdrew its support from the Kurds, who were then crushed by the Iraqi Army.

13. ANGOLA MERCENARY FORCE

In 1975, after years of bloody fighting and civil unrest in Angola, Portugal resolved to relinquish its hold on the last of its African colonies. The transition was to take place on Nov. 11, with control of the country going to whichever political faction controlled the capital city of Luanda on that date. In the months preceding the change, three groups vied for power: the Popular Movement for the Liberation of Angola (MPLA), the National Front for the Liberation of Angola (FNLA), and the National Union for the Total Independence of Angola (UNITA). By July, 1975, the Marxist MPLA had ousted the moderate FNLA and UNITA from Luanda, so the CIA decided to intervene covertly. Over $30 million was spent on the Angolan operation, the bulk of the money going to buy arms and pay French and South African mercenaries, who aided the FNLA and UNITA in their fight. Despite overwhelming evidence to the contrary, U.S. officials categorically denied any involvement in the Angolan conflict. In the end, it was a fruitless military adventure, for the MPLA assumed power and controls Angola to this day.

—R.J.F.

3
CRIMINAL BEHAVIOR

20 UNDERWORLD NICKNAMES

1. FRANK "THE DASHER" ABBANDANDO

A prolific hit man for Murder, Inc.—organized crime's enforcement arm in the 1930s—and with some 50 killings to his credit, Frank Abbandando once approached a longshoreman on whom there was a "contract." Abbandando fired directly into his victim's face, only to have the weapon misfire. The chagrined executioner dashed off, circling the block so fast that he came up behind his slowly pursuing target, and this time Abbandando managed to shoot him dead, picking up his moniker in the process.

2. TONY "JOE BATTERS" ACCARDO

Tough Tony Accardo, a Chicago syndicate boss since the 1930s, is still called "Joe Batters," harkening back to his earlier days of proficiency with a baseball bat when he was one of Al Capone's most dedicated sluggers.

3. JOSEPH "HA HA" AIUPPA

An old-time Capone muscle man, Joseph Aiuppa is today the Mafia boss of Cicero, Ill., and—according to some law-enforcement officials— the top man in the Chicago mob. Because he is a notorious scowler not given to smiling, he is called "Ha Ha."

4. ISRAEL "ICEPICK WILLIE" ALDERMAN

This Minneapolis gangster liked to brag about the grotesque murder method that earned him his nickname. Israel Alderman (also known as "Little Auldie" and "Izzy Lump Lump") ran a second-story speakeasy where he claimed to have committed 11 murders. In each case he deftly pressed an icepick through his victim's eardrum into the brain; his quick technique made it appear that the dead man had merely slumped in a drunken heap on the bar. "Icepick Willie" would laughingly chide the corpse as he dragged it to a back room, where he dumped the body down a coal chute leading to a truck in the alley below.

5. LOUIS "PRETTY" AMBERG

Louis Amberg, the underworld terror of Brooklyn from the 1920s to 1935—when he was finally rubbed out—was called "Pretty" because he may well have been the ugliest gangster who ever lived. Immortalized by Damon Runyon in several stories as the gangster who stuffed his victims into laundry bags, Amberg was approached when he was 20 by Ringling

"Pretty" Amberg.

Brothers Circus, which wanted him to appear as the missing link. "Pretty" turned the job down but often bragged about the offer afterward.

6. MICHAEL "UMBRELLA MIKE" BOYLE

Business agent of the mob-dominated electrical workers union in Chicago in the 1920s, Michael J. Boyle gained the title of "Umbrella Mike" because of his practice of standing at a bar on certain days of the week with an unfurled umbrella. Building contractors deposited cash levies into this receptacle and then magically were not beset by labor difficulties.

7. LOUIS "LEPKE" BUCHALTER

Louis Buchalter—who died in the electric chair in 1944—was the head of Murder, Inc. He was better known as "Lepke," a form of "Lepkeleh." This was the affectionate Yiddish diminutive, meaning "Little Louis," that his mother had used. Affectionate, "Lepke" was not. As one associate once said, "Lep loves to hurt people."

8. "SCARFACE AL" CAPONE

Al Capone claimed that the huge scar on his cheek was from a

W.W. I wound suffered while fighting with the Lost Battalion in France, but actually he was never in service. He had been knifed while working as a bouncer in a Brooklyn saloon-brothel by a hoodlum named Frank Galluccio during a dispute over a woman. Capone once visited the editorial offices of Hearst's Chicago *American* and convinced that paper to stop referring to him as "Scarface Al."

9. VINCENT "MAD DOG" COLL

Vincent "Mad Dog" Coll was feared by police and rival gangsters alike in the early 1930s because of his utter disregard for human life. Once he shot down several children at play while trying to get an underworld foe. When he was trapped in a phone booth and riddled with bullets in 1932, no one cried over his death, and police made little effort to solve the crime.

10. JOSEPH "JOE ADONIS" DOTO

Racket boss Joseph Doto adopted the name of "Joe Adonis" because he considered his looks the equal of Aphrodite's famous lover.

11. CHARLES "PRETTY BOY" FLOYD

Public enemy Charles Arthur Floyd hated his nickname, which was used by prostitutes of the Midwest whorehouses he patronized, and in fact he killed at least two gangsters for repeatedly calling him "Pretty Boy." When he was shot down by FBI agents in 1934, he refused to identify himself as "Pretty Boy" Floyd and with his dying breath snarled, "I'm Charles Arthur Floyd!"

12. CHARLIE "MONKEY FACE" GENKER

For several decades after the turn of the century a mainstay of the Chicago whorehouse world, Charlie "Monkey Face" Genker achieved his moniker not simply for a countenance lacking in beauty but also for his actions while employed by Mike "de Pike" Heitler (a piker because he ran a 50-cent house). Monkey Face matched the bounciness of his jungle cousins by scampering up doors and peeking over the transoms to get the girls and their customers to speed things up.

13. JAKE "GREASY THUMB" GUZIK

A longtime devoted aide to Al Capone, Jake Guzik continued until his death in 1956 to be the payoff man to the politicians and police for the Chicago mob. He often complained that he handled so much money he could not get the inky grease off his thumb. This explanation of the "Greasy Thumb" sobriquet was such an embarrassment to the police that they concocted their own story, maintaining that Jake had once worked as a waiter and gained his nickname because he constantly stuck his thumb in the soup bowls.

14. "GOLF BAG" SAM HUNT

Notorious Capone mob enforcer "Golf Bag" Sam Hunt was so called because he lugged automatic weapons about in his golf bag to conceal them when on murder missions.

"Creepy" Karpis in 1936.

15. ALVIN "CREEPY" KARPIS

Bank robber Alvin Karpis was tabbed "Creepy" by fellow prison inmates in the 1920s because of his sallow, dour-faced looks. By the time he became public enemy No. 1 in 1935, Karpis's face had become even creepier thanks to a botched plastic surgery job which was supposed to alter his appearance.

16. GEORGE "MACHINE GUN" KELLY

Somehow a blundering bootlegger named George R. Kelly became the feared public enemy "Machine Gun" Kelly of the 1930s. His criminally ambitious wife, Kathryn, forced him to practice with the machine gun she gave him as a birthday present, while she built up his reputation with other criminals. However, Kelly was not a murderer, nor did he ever fire his weapon in anger with intent to kill.

17. CHARLES "LUCKY" LUCIANO

Charles Luciano earned his "Lucky" when he was taken for a ride and came back alive, although a knife wound gave him a permanently drooping right eye. Luciano told many stories over the years about the identity of his abductors—two different criminal gangs were mentioned as well as the police, who were trying to find out about an impending drug shipment, but the most likely version is that he was tortured and mutilated by the family of a cop whose daughter he had seduced. Luciano parlayed his misfortune into a public-relations coup, since he was the one and only underworld figure lucky enough to return alive after being taken for a ride.

18. THOMAS "BUTTERFINGERS" MORAN

The acknowledged king of the pickpockets of the 20th century, Thomas "Butterfingers" Moran picked his first pocket during the 1906 San Francisco earthquake and his last in 1970 at 78, some 50,000 pockets in all. He could, other practitioners acknowledged rather jealously, "slide in and out of a pocket like pure butter."

19. LESTER "BABY FACE" NELSON

The most pathological public enemy of the 1930s, Lester Gillis considered his own name as non*macho* and came up with "Big George" Nelson instead—a ridiculous alias considering the fact that he was just 5 ft. 4 in. tall. He was called "Baby Face" Nelson behind his back and in the press, which constantly enraged him.

20. BENJAMIN "BUGSY" SIEGEL

Alternately the most charming and the most vicious of all syndicate killers, Benjamin Siegel could thus be described as being "bugs." However, no one called him "Bugsy" to his face, since it caused him to fly into a murderous rage. His mistress, Virginia Hall, likewise clobbered newsmen who called her man by this offensive sobriquet.

—C.S.

19 STUPID THIEVES

1. CAUGHT WITH HIS PANTS DOWN

Jay Mitchell, 27, successfully robbed a shop in the Old Town district of Albuquerque, N.M., in March, 1980. However, he encountered trouble during his escape when his pants fell down, causing him to fall. He dropped his pistol and some stolen jewelry but was able to flee the scene in a stolen truck. About an hour later, the pistol was reported stolen by a woman who lived in the same building as Mitchell. When police arrived, they spotted the truck as well as Mitchell himself. Mitchell was taken into custody for questioning, but the police knew they had their man when his pants fell down again on the way to the police car. Mitchell subsequently pleaded guilty to the robbery.

2. WRONG PLACE, WRONG TIME

On Nov. 29, 1978, David Goodhall and two female accomplices entered a home supplies shop in Barnsley, South Yorkshire, intending to engage in a bit of shoplifting. After stuffing a pair of curtains into a plastic carrier bag, the threesome attempted to leave by separate exits. However, they were apprehended immediately by several store detectives. Goodhall and his cohorts had failed to notice that the shop, at that very moment, was hosting a convention of store detectives.

3. DOUBLE-SEXED FORGER

Houston pawnbroker Ted Kipperman knew something was wrong when a man entered his store on Apr. 8, 1982, and attempted to cash a $789 tax-refund check, claiming his name was "Earnestine and Robert Hayes." Noting that the check was made out to two parties, Kipperman asked the customer for identification, whereupon the man produced an ID card with the name "Earnestine and Robert Hayes." He explained that his mother had expected twins. When only one child showed up, she gave him both names. Kipperman took the stolen check and the makeshift ID and then told the man that the police had just come by looking for the check, which caused the would-be customer to flee. Kipperman located the real Earnestine and Robert Hayes, a couple who lived in southeastern Houston, and gave them back their tax-refund check.

4. CHECKING OUT

Eighteen-year-old Charles A. Meriweather broke into a home in Northwest Baltimore on the night of Nov. 22–23, 1978, raped the woman who lived there, and then ransacked the house. When he discovered that she had only $11.50 in cash, he asked her, "How do you pay your bills?"

She replied, "By check," and he ordered her to write out a check for $30. Then he changed his mind and upped it to $50.

"Who shall I make it out to?" asked the woman, a 34-year-old government employee.

"Charles A. Meriweather," said Charles A. Meriweather, adding, "It better not bounce or I'll be back."

Meriweather was arrested several hours later.

5. SELF-INFLICTED CAPITAL PUNISHMENT

On Aug. 7, 1975, John Anthony Gibbs, described by witnesses as "very nervous," entered a restaurant in Newport, R.I., flashed a gun, and demanded cash. After collecting $400, he put the money in a bag and tried to stuff the bag into his shirt pocket. Unfortunately, he was holding his gun in the same hand as the bag. The gun went off under his chin and Gibbs, 22, was killed instantly.

6. JUST REWARDS

Every night, Mrs. Hollis Sharpe of Los Angeles took her miniature poodle, Jonathan, out for a walk so that he could do his duty. A responsible and considerate citizen, Mrs. Sharpe always brought with her a newspaper and a plastic bag to clean up after Jonathan. "You have to think of your neighbors," she explained. On the night of Nov. 13, 1974, Jonathan had finished his business and Mrs. Sharpe was walking home with the bag in her right hand when a mugger attacked her from behind, shoved her to the ground, grabbed her plastic bag, jumped into a car, and drove off with the spoils of his crime. Mrs. Sharpe suffered a broken arm but remained good-humored about the incident. "I only wish there had been a little more in the bag," she said.

7. A MINOR DETAIL

Edward McAlea put on a stocking mask, burst into a jewelry store in Liverpool, and pointed a revolver at the three men inside. "This is a stickup," he said. "Get down." None of them did, since all of them noticed the red plastic stopper in the muzzle of McAlea's toy gun. After a brief scuffle, McAlea escaped, but not before he had pulled off his mask. The jeweler recognized him as a customer from the day before, and McAlea was apprehended.

8. GOLDILOCKS

When Thomas Schimmel of Tawas City, Mich., went home from work for lunch on the afternoon of Nov. 1, 1978, he was surprised to discover that someone had entered his home, eaten a bowl of cereal and some chicken, and left. A sheriff's deputy was called and a report was filed, after which Mr. Schimmel went back to work. Returning home at 6:30 P.M., he immediately fell asleep on the couch and didn't awaken until 11:45 P.M. He then went to his bedroom, where he discovered that the thief had not only returned, but was in fact asleep in Mr. Schimmel's bed. Schimmel called the police, who woke the burglar and charged him with breaking and entering.

9. BARK BIGGER THAN BITE

A 14-year-old would-be burglar in South Phoenix, Ariz., managed to chop his way through a brick wall of the State Market on East Broadway on the night of Apr. 3, 1980. However, he tripped an alarm in the process. The store was soon surrounded by police officers, but the boy refused to surrender. Then Officer Steve Gregory had a stroke of inspiration and called out to the boy that they were about to send in the K-9 Corps. Officer Al Femenia supported this threat by barking loudly.

"Don't let the dog come in," cried the burglar, "I'm coming out!" The young man was greatly disturbed when he learned that a policeman had been doing the barking, not a dog.

10. A PETTY THIEF

Things didn't work out quite the way Clay Weaver had planned on the night of Feb. 16, 1982. The 19-year-old entered Hutchinson's Fine Foods in West Valley City, U., at 9:00 P.M., intending to rob the store. He waved a gun at the clerk, who laughed because she thought it was a toy. The gun was quite small, but it was in fact real—a two-bullet derringer. Weaver cocked the gun, but the bullets dribbled out onto the counter. Weaver then fled but got into an argument with his accomplice, Gary Hendrikson, who pushed Weaver away and drove off without him. Finally, he was chased down and hauled back to Hutchinson's by two store employees who happened to be members of the high school wrestling team. Weaver later confessed to 14 other robberies he had miraculously managed to commit.

11. KEEP THE CHANGE

In 1977 a thief in Southampton, England, came up with a clever method of robbing the cash register at a local supermarket. After collecting a basket full of groceries, he approached the checkout area and placed a £10 note on the counter. The grocery clerk took the bill and opened the cash register, at which point the thief snatched the contents and ran off. It turned out to be a bad deal for the thief, since the till contained only £4.37 and the thief ended up losing £5.63.

12. THE WELD-PLANNED ROBBERY

On the night of Aug. 23–24, 1980, a well-organized gang of thieves began their raid on the safe of the leisure-center office in Chichester, Sussex, by stealing a speedboat. Using water skis to paddle across a lake, they picked up their equipment and paddled on to the office. However, what they thought were cutting tools turned out to be welding gear, and they soon managed to seal the safe completely shut. The next morning it took the office staff an hour to hammer and chisel the safe open again.

13. TO PROTECT AND SERVE

Twenty-two-year-old Michael Schery became a bit confused on the night of Nov. 17, 1981. After a long session of drinking, he managed to climb over a fence and enter the second story of an office building in downtown Tampa, Fla. He then spent three hours trying to get out again. Finally he did what he had been taught to do in times of trouble—he called the police. Arriving officers took him to another building he couldn't get out of—the jail. He was charged with burglary in connection with the theft of one package of M&Ms.

14. THE HAMBURGLAR

During the early morning hours of May 6, 1982, Carlos Aralijo attempted to burglarize a McDonald's restaurant in midtown Los Angeles by sliding down an oven flue. What the 28-year-old Aralijo discovered too late was that although the vent was 14 in. square at the roof, it narrowed to 8 in. square above the stove. Aralijo became stuck in the pipe, which was heavily coated with grease, and spent four or five hours screaming for help before someone heard him. It took fire fighters and paramedics 30 minutes to free him, by which time he had suffered first- and second-degree burns on his feet and lower legs.

15. WHO WAS THAT MASKED MAN?

Clive Bunyan ran into a store in Cayton, near Scarborough, England, and forced the shop assistant to give him £157 from the till. Then he made his getaway on his motorbike. To hide his identity, Bunyan had worn his full-face crash helmet as a mask. It was a smooth and successful heist, except for one detail. He had forgotten that across his helmet, in inch-high letters, were the words, "Clive Bunyan—Driver." Bunyan was arrested and ordered to pay for his crime by doing 200 hours of community service.

16. BURGLARY BY THE NUMBER

Terry Johnson had no trouble identifying the two men who burglarized her Chicago apartment at 2:30 A.M. on Aug. 17, 1981. All she had to do was write down the number on the police badge that one of them was wearing and the identity number on the fender of their squad car. The two officers—Stephen Webster, 33, and Tyrone Pickens, 32—had actually committed the crime in full uniform, while on duty, using police department tools.

17. BELATED COVER-UP

Gregory Lee Cornwell had everything in order when he planned to rob the Continental Bank in Prospect Park, Pa., in 1978: a car for the getaway, a ski mask to conceal his identity, an army knapsack for the money, and a sawed-off shotgun to show he was serious. On Aug. 23, he parked his car in front of the bank and went inside. Displaying his shotgun, he threw the knapsack on the counter and demanded money. Then he put on his mask. Although he managed to leave the bank with $8,100, Cornwell was apprehended quickly and easily identified.

18. THE WORST LAWYER

Twenty-five-year-old Marshall George Cummings, Jr., of Tulsa, Okla., was charged with attempted robbery in connection with a purse-snatching at a shopping center on Oct. 14, 1976. During the trial the following January, Cummings chose to act as his own attorney. While cross-examining the victim, Cummings asked, "Did you get a good look at my face when I took your purse?" Cummings later decided to turn over his defense to a public defender, but it was too late. He was convicted and sentenced to 10 years in prison.

19. STUPID THIEF MAKES GOOD

Just because a person is a stupid thief doesn't mean that he is doomed to a life of failure. A good example is country music singer-songwriter Merle Haggard. In December, 1957, Haggard and a friend named Micky Gorham got very drunk one night in Bakersfield, Calif., and decided at about 3:00 A.M. to break into a local restaurant on Highway 99. After ripping off the screen on the back door, Haggard began prying on the lock with a crowbar. Just as the door opened, he heard the voice of the owner, a man Haggard knew well.

"What are you boys doing? Why don't you boys come around to the front door like everybody else?"

What Haggard and Gorham had failed to realize was that it wasn't 3:00 A.M. at all. In fact, it was barely 10:00 P.M., and the restaurant was still open, with customers inside. Haggard was convicted of burglary and eventually served a prison term at San Quentin. In 1972 he received a full and unconditional pardon from California governor Ronald Reagan.

—D.W.

8 PEOPLE WHO KILLED IN THEIR SLEEP

1. "A.F." (Germany; 1839)

This young man, known to history only by his initials, shared his father's passion for weapons and hunting. Both kept loaded guns in their adjoining bedrooms. At about 1:00 A.M. on Sept. 3, 1839, after a successful day in the field, A.F. was disturbed by the sound of someone colliding with the door that connected the two bedrooms. He shouted "You dog, what do you want here?" Then he jumped out of bed and fired. Since there was a brilliant moon, he could have seen—had he been awake—that the "intruder" he had killed was his father.

2. ESTHER GRIGGS (England; 1859)

The gloomy peace of No. 71 East Street, in London's Marylebone district, was shattered that January night by a woman's cries, "Oh, my children! Save my children!" Three constables pounded up the stairs amid the sound of breaking glass to find that they were too late. Esther Griggs, stumbling around in total darkness, had already thrown her baby into the street. But for the constables' knocking, which wakened her, her other children, aged three and five, would have followed. The young mother had dreamed that her house was on fire.

3. SIMON FRASER (Scotland; 1878)

An inoffensive 28-year-old man who worked as a saw grinder, Fraser often dreamed that his Glasgow tenement home was being invaded by a dangerous beast. Leaping up while sound asleep, he would try to kill it with his bare hands. Shortly before 1:00 A.M. on Apr. 10, 1878, Fraser had—in his own words—dreamed of "a white beast flying through the floor." He seized it, dashed it to the ground, and woke. He had killed his infant son.

4. ROBERT LEDRU (France; 1888)

While recuperating from overwork at Le Havre, this brilliant Paris police detective was asked by his chief to investigate a murder at nearby Sainte Adresse. The victim, a vacationing businessman, had been shot at night on the beach. The only clues were the murder bullet, which was from a Luger, and some blurred footprints, which indicated that the killer had been wearing socks. Ledru noticed that the murderer's right foot lacked a toe. His own right foot also lacked a toe, and his socks—in which he slept—had been damp that morning. He checked his Luger and found that it had been fired. He test-fired it, compared the two bullets—and turned himself in.

5. JO ANN KIGER (U.S.; 1943)

A revolver in each hand, 16-year-old Jo Ann Kiger blazed away at the human monster who was bent on murdering the members of her family as they slept in their summer home near Burlington, in Boone County, Ky. She, too, was asleep, and did not wake until she had slain her little brother with three shots and her father with five. Her mother, wounded in the hip, survived to testify at the trial that Jo Ann had a history of sleepwalking and that she loved her family deeply.

6. WILLIAM POLLARD (U.S.; 1946)

"He always works best in his sleep," neighbors used to say of Pollard, who raised chickens near Little Rock, Ark., and who had once loaded an entire truck with them before he woke up. The Pollards' four-year-old daughter Brenda slept in her parents' room. One November night Pollard fought with a marauding stranger in a dream. His wife's screams jarred him awake. The flashlight he had seized while asleep showed that in defending their child, he had killed her.

7. WASYL GNYPIUK (England; 1960)

Even with some brandy inside him, he was cold at night. Gnypiuk, a Polish-Ukrainian refugee living in a Nottinghamshire tool shed, broke into the house of his former landlady, 63-year-old Louise Surgey. His shouts failed to bring her downstairs, and he fell asleep there after drinking some of her liquor. Nazi internment had left him prey to nightmares, during which he dreamed of fighting back. In the morning Mrs. Surgey lay dead at his feet. He panicked and tried to get rid of the body. He also took some of the money that Mrs. Surgey had left around the house. The police treated this action as evidence that his real motive in coming to the house was theft. In vain he pleaded that he had overlooked a much larger sum, stored by Mrs. Surgey in the bag into which he had stuffed her severed head.

8. WILLIS EUGENE BOSHEARS (England; 1961)

His leave canceled, Staff Sgt. Boshears, a Korean War hero stationed with the U.S. Air Force at Wethersfield, England, was unable to join his wife and three children for New Year's Eve. While drinking in a pub he invited an acquaintance, 20-year-old Jean Constable, to celebrate at his apartment with a young man she had just picked up. Soon after midnight Boshears passed out on the floor; Constable was already sleeping there. The young man, who had had sex with her earlier, briefly roused Boshears and then left. The next thing Boshears was aware of was the girl's body beneath him. He had his hands around her throat. Not until he was fully awake did he realize that it had been Constable and that he had strangled her. Terrified by his act, he hid the body in a ditch some miles away.

HOW THE LAW DEALT WITH THEM: Western legal tradition recognizes sleepwalking as a defense in murder cases but is otherwise quite inconsistent on the subject. Griggs and Pollard were never charged; "A.F.," Kiger, and Boshears were acquitted; Fraser and Ledru were acquitted but ordered by the court to sleep henceforth only by themselves, in locked rooms; while Gnypiuk, denied an appeal to the British House of Lords, was hanged.

—J.M.B.E.

55

11 PEOPLE ARRESTED FOR CRIMES COMMITTED BY THEIR "DOUBLES"

1. LESURQUES (1796)

On Apr. 27, 1796, the Paris–Lyon mail coach was held up near Château-Thierry by four highwaymen, who murdered the postilion and escaped with about 75,000 francs. They then spent the evening at an inn in nearby Mongeron. The authorities promptly checked the lodging houses in Château-Thierry for newcomers from Paris and arrested two men who lived in the same house. M. Guesno had an alibi and was released, but M. Couriol was retained. The next morning, Guesno met his friend M. Lesurques, a young man of independent means and blameless character, who accompanied him to the judge's chambers for his discharge. Here witnesses from the inn at Mongeron positively identified not only Guesno but Lesurques as well, and they were committed for trial along with Couriol. Couriol's mistress Madeleine Breban claimed that Lesurques had been mistaken for a M. Dubosq, whom he greatly resembled, but Lesurques was found guilty nonetheless and sentenced to the guillotine. On Mar. 10, 1797, Lesurques was led to the scaffold while Couriol shouted to the crowd, "I am guilty! Lesurques is innocent!" Four years later, thanks to the efforts of Madeleine Breban, Dubosq was tried and executed for the same crime.

2. THOMAS BERDUE (1851)

Escaped Australian convicts were a menace in Gold Rush California. Berdue, a law-abiding British subject, was found guilty of a San Francisco robbery committed by the most notorious of these "Sydneymen." He was then removed to Marysville in Yuba County, where he was tried as James Stuart for a murder that Stuart had certainly committed. The murderer was known to have a scar on his right cheek and India ink on several fingers. Berdue had these identifying marks, and his hair and eyes were the same color as Stuart's. Berdue would have been hanged if the real Stuart—fortuitously captured by vigilantes in San Francisco—had not confessed to both crimes.

3. ADOLF BECK (1895)

Beck was confronted one afternoon in London by a woman who demanded he return her rings and watches. The shady middle-aged promoter was arrested and identified by 10 more victims. The police decided he must be "John Smith," an aristocratic con man who had served a jail sentence more than 10 years earlier for "borrowing" valuables from women he offered to employ as his housekeeper. Beck was sentenced to a term of seven years. Released early, he was rearrested when the swindles began again. Not until the real "Smith," adventurer Wilhelm Meyer, was caught redhanded did Beck establish his own identity. Beck's fleshy lips and military moustache were very much like Meyer's, and both men habitually dressed and behaved as if they owned half of London.

Adolf Beck (top) was convicted for the crimes committed by his double, William Meyer (below).

4. PAYNE BOYD (1924)

In 1918, Squire H. E. Cook of Mercer County, W. Va., was shot dead by Cleveland Boyd, a black miner, who escaped. Six years later, Payne Boyd, a black W.W. I veteran from Winston-Salem, N.C., was arrested in Richmond, Va., and identified from police records as Cleveland Boyd. Payne, like Cleveland, had a scar over his left eye and another under the left side of his jaw. Twice found guilty on the evidence of eight witnesses from Mercer County, Payne was tried a third time, in Cabell County, but it made no difference. He was not released until the police belatedly checked his fingerprints with the War Dept. in Washington, D.C.

5. LONZO THORNTON (1926)

He only wanted his coat back. Unfortunately, he had lent it to a recently made friend, James Ivory, who was in the Middletown, O., jail charged with mugging an immigrant the previous evening. When Thornton appeared at the jail, he was detained, identified as Ivory's accomplice, and brought to trial. A year later, petty criminal Baby Ruth Williams was arrested, and he admitted to being the second mugger. Thornton, by now serving a 10-to-25-year sentence in the penitentiary at Columbus, O., was pardoned. Contemporary accounts say that Thornton and Williams looked so much alike they could have been twins.

6.–7. FRANK AND NORMA HOWELL (1929)

Newspaper descriptions of the couple who had just held up a gas station in New Martinsville, W. Va., sounded so much like the poverty-stricken Howells, a married couple who lived on nearby Fishing Creek, that Norma Howell remarked jokingly, "Probably me and Frank done it." The police, who disliked Frank Howell anyway, agreed with her. Frank got 15 years; his wife was acquitted—inexplicably, since the woman bandit had held a gun. Fourteen months later, Irene Schroeder and Glenn Dague—two notorious holdup artists awaiting execution in Newcastle, Pa., for murdering a highway patrolman—confessed to the gas station robbery, and Howell was pardoned. Each couple had consisted of a tall, thin man and a short, plump woman.

8. NANCY LOUISE BOTTS (1934)

After cleaning her apartment in Brazil, Ind., Nancy Botts—recently married and now pregnant—called on her neighbor Marjorie Roberts, who was talking with three male visitors. Two of the men yelled, "That's the woman!" The third, who had been questioning Roberts, arrested Botts. She was taken to Kokomo, some 100 mi. away, where seven merchants identified her as the woman who had bilked them out of merchandise and cash using forged checks. Botts spent two years in jail; during this time, she miscarried and her health was ruined. Eventually a married woman named Dorsett was booked, and her handwriting proved that she had committed the crimes for which Botts had been jailed. The two women were physical doubles but Dorsett was the better talker: She convinced the jury that her husband had forced her into a life of crime, and she got off.

9. A. B. CHASTAIN (1936)

His brother Leroy, wanted for holdups throughout Florida, was an escaped convict, but A. B. Chastain was a farmer and solid citizen. The Tampa police nevertheless booked him on suspicion of harboring or helping his brother. Photographed in a lineup, A. B. Chastain impressed one police detective as being a dead ringer for Hugh Grant, supposed leader in the Mar. 3 holdup of the Columbia Bank in the Ybor City section of Tampa. Despite numerous defense witnesses, A. B. Chastain was eventually convicted of armed robbery. He served 17 months of a 20-year sentence before a petition—signed by, among others, the officers who had worked on his case—procured his release.

10. ERNEST MATTICE (1936)

When Canadian-born Mattice arrived in Denver on Oct. 16, 1936, he decided that he would like some female company. Mattice and three like-minded male companions piled into a car, picked up two respectable but not unwilling young women, and took them to a dance. Everybody had a good time, and the women were returned home safely. Unfortunately, Denver had been suffering a well-publicized series of rapes committed by men in automobiles. The nervous parents of Mattice's dancing partners called the police, who traced Mattice to his hotel and arrested him. At 2:00 A.M. on Oct. 17, Margaret Cyckose, 22, had been raped and beaten by two young men, who forced her into their car. Cyckose immediately identified Mattice as one of her attackers. Tried on four counts of rape, Mattice was found guilty and sentenced to prison. Frank Neill, a local car thief, eventually confessed that he had raped Cyckose. The resemblance between the two men must have otherwise been close, since Mattice had a thick moustache at the time, while Neill was clean-shaven. Mattice was released and compensated by the state of Colorado.

11. BERNARD T. PAGANO (1979)

As the Roman Catholic chaplain who ministered to criminals and mental patients, 53-year-old Father Pagano was well known to the police of New Castle County, Del. When a polite, neatly dressed bandit began holding up stores near Wilmington, the police noted that his face, at least, was like Pagano's; the police sketch, however, had to modify the hairline, since Pagano was going bald. Placed on trial, Pagano was identified as the "gentleman bandit" by seven store clerks. His trial was finally halted after Ronald Clouser, a 39-year-old U.S. Postal Service engineer with a full head of hair, confessed to all of the robberies.

—J.M.B.E.

WHAT 12 ASSASSINATION VICTIMS HAD PLANNED FOR THE REST OF THE DAY

1. GAIUS JULIUS CAESAR (100–44 B.C.)

Roman statesman and soldier Julius Caesar was assassinated in a hall of Pompey's Theater in Rome by a group of 60 conspirators led by Marcus Junius Brutus and Gaius Cassius Longinus on Mar. 15, 44 B.C. In the street a few minutes earlier, a Greek logic teacher named Artemidorus had handed Caesar a note, warning him that it should be read immediately. But Caesar put it aside. The unread note cautioned him that assassins planned to attack him as he entered the hall. At the theater, Caesar had expected to attend a meeting of the Roman Senate, where he and his followers were to speak in favor of his being crowned king of Rome.

2. ABRAHAM LINCOLN (1809–1865)

President Lincoln was shot at Ford's Theater in Washington, D.C., by John Wilkes Booth at 10:15 P.M. on Good Friday, Apr. 14, 1865, and died the next day. Lincoln had intended to watch the entire play *Our American Cousin* and then be introduced to the cast. From the theater, he and Mrs. Lincoln, accompanied by two young friends—Major Henry Rathbone and the major's fiancée, Clara Harris—were to return to the White House for a small party at which refreshments would be served, since the president had missed supper that evening.

3. JAMES GARFIELD (1831–1881)

President Garfield was shot at the Baltimore and Potomac train depot in Washington, D.C., by Charles J. Guiteau at 9:30 A.M. on July 2, 1881, and died on Sept. 19. Shot while preparing to leave the capital for the Fourth of July holidays, President Garfield had arranged to take the 9:30 train to Elberon, N.J., where his wife, Lucretia—and their sons Harry and James—were to join him before he proceeded to Williams College in Williamstown, Mass. Garfield was to observe the 25th anniversary of his graduation and enroll his sons in the college's freshman class, after which he expected to spend the evening as an overnight guest at the home of Cyrus Field.

4. WILLIAM MCKINLEY (1843–1901)

President McKinley was shot at the Temple of Music at the Pan-American Exposition in Buffalo, N.Y., by Leon Czolgosz at 4:07 P.M., on Sept. 6, 1901, and died on Sept. 14. Shot during a public handshaking reception, President McKinley had intended to leave three minutes later and take his private carriage to the John Milburn mansion, where he was staying while in Buffalo. That night, McKinley was looking forward to one of those rarities in a president's life, an unscheduled evening of privacy with his wife and a few friends. Before retiring that night, he would have done some packing, since he was returning to his family home in Canton, O., the next morning.

5. EMILIANO ZAPATA (1877–1919)

The Mexican revolutionary leader was assassinated at Chinameca hacienda near Cuautla, Mexico, by soldiers commanded by Col. Jesús Guajardo, at 2:10 P.M. on Apr. 10, 1919. Zapata, who was ambushed while riding into Chinameca hacienda, had planned to share a dinner of tacos and beer with the treacherous Colonel Guajardo who, with his 50th Regiment, had tricked Zapata into believing he was defecting from the Mexican federal government. (Actually, Guajardo's sole purpose was to lure Zapata into a trap.) After dinner, Zapata had intended to negotiate the final details of the new alliance and to obtain 12,000 rounds of ammunition for his men. After officially announcing the new partnership, Zapata would have returned to his guerrilla camp at Sauces, two miles to the south.

6. LEON TROTSKY (1877–1940)

The exiled Russian revolutionary leader was attacked at his home in Mexico City by Jacques Mornard just before 6:00 P.M. on Aug. 20, 1940. Trotsky was attacked while discussing an article on the Fourth International with his assassin and died the next day. Trotsky had expected to have dinner with his wife, Natalia, and possibly would have invited Mornard to join them. After dinner, Trotsky would have studied some recently published French economic statistics and written a few pages of an article on Stalin that was to be published in *Harper's* magazine.

7. MOHANDAS K. GANDHI (1869–1948)

Indian independence leader Mahatma Gandhi was assassinated in New Delhi, India, by Hindu fanatic Nathuram Godse at 5:13 P.M. on Jan. 30, 1948. Gandhi was killed upon arriving in the Birla House gardens, where he was supposed to lead a prayer meeting attended by several hundred of his followers. After the religious ceremonies, he was to return to the home of Ghanshyam Das Birla, his host in New Delhi. That evening, Gandhi had intended to follow his usual evening routine, which consisted of talking to his relatives and followers for a short time, before a session of reading and writing. At about 9:00 P.M., he would have had his nightly enema before going to bed.

8. RAFAEL LEONIDAS TRUJILLO MOLINA (1891–1961)

The dictator of the Dominican Republic was assassinated on the highway between Ciudad Trujillo and San Cristóbal by seven men in two automobiles at approximately 10:15 P.M. on May 30, 1961. When hit by machine-gun bullets, Trujillo was on his way to one of his immense ranches, Estancia Fundacion, where he was to spend the night. Awaiting his arrival was at least one of his mistresses. In fact, he may well have been looking forward to an orgy that night. These frequently involved as many as 40 women, who were supplied by a government official whose fee was 10% of all funds allocated for public works.

9. JOHN F. KENNEDY (1917–1963)

President Kennedy was assassinated in Dealey Plaza in Dallas, Tex., at 12:30 P.M. on Nov. 22, 1963. After the motorcade—during which he was shot—Kennedy was scheduled to speak at the new Trade Mart building and then to fly to Bergstrom Air Force Base near Austin, Tex., where the coach of the University of Texas Longhorns was to present him with a team-autographed football. In Austin, a second motorcade was planned, to be followed by a Democratic fund-raising banquet for which 8,000 steaks had been prepared. Presidential advance man Bill Moyers had found out too late that the menu featured steaks—a highly inappropriate selection for a Catholic president's Friday night dinner. Kennedy had agreed to take a helicopter from Austin to the LBJ Ranch near Johnson City, Tex., where he was to spend the night. To entertain Kennedy that evening, Vice-President Johnson had organized a whipcracking and sheepherding demonstration.

10. MARTIN LUTHER KING, JR. (1929–1968)

Dr. King was assassinated at the Lorraine Motel in Memphis,

Tenn., by James Earl Ray just after 6:00 P.M. on Apr. 4, 1968. When he was shot, King was leaving his room on his way to a soul-food dinner at the home of the Reverend Samuel (Billy) Kyles. Accompanying King were his friends and supporters, including Dr. Ralph Abernathy, the Reverend Jesse Jackson, the Reverend Andrew Young, and lawyer Chauncey Eskridge. King had also promised to attend an evening rally in support of the striking black garbage collectors of Local 1733. He had requested that Ben Branch, the lead singer of the Breadbasket Band, which was providing the evening's entertainment, sing "Precious Lord" at the rally.

11. ROBERT F. KENNEDY (1925–1968)

The Democratic presidential candidate was shot at the Ambassador Hotel in Los Angeles, Calif., by Sirhan Sirhan and possibly a second gunman at 12:15 A.M. on June 5, 1968, and died the following day. Kennedy was shot while walking through a corridor off the kitchen on his way to the hotel's Colonial Room for a press conference following his victory in the California Democratic primary election. After that, he had planned to return to his room, Suite 511, where several dozen celebrities were awaiting him. Once freshened up, he would have gone with his friends and supporters—including Roosevelt "Rosie" Grier, Rafer Johnson, and Pierre Salinger—to The Factory, an exclusive and very chic Los Angeles discotheque.

12. FAISAL IBN 'ABD AL-AZIZ AL SAUD (1906?–1975)

King Faisal was assassinated before noon on Mar. 25, 1975, in the Ri'Assa Palace in Riyadh, Saudi Arabia. The assassin was his nephew, ibn Musad 'Abd al-Aziz. At the time, the king was preparing to meet with a Kuwaiti delegation, which included that nation's oil minister. Matters concerning both nations—such as a territorial dispute over a tract of oil-rich desert—were to be discussed. Also, since it was the birthday of the Prophet Mohammed, Faisal had planned to hold the traditional *majlis,* an open court in which any Saudi Arabian, aristocrat or peasant, could have an audience with the king and ask a personal favor of him.

—R.J.F.

19 CASES OF ANIMALS AND INSECTS THAT WERE BROUGHT BEFORE THE LAW

There has been a long and shocking tradition of punishing, excommunicating, and killing animals for real or supposed crimes. In medieval times, animals were even put on the rack to extort confessions of guilt. Cases have been recorded and documented involving such unlikely creatures as flies, locusts, snakes, mosquitoes, caterpillars, eels, snails, beetles, grasshoppers, dolphins, and most larger mammals. In 17th-century Russia, a goat was banished to Siberia. The belief that animals are morally culpable is happily out of fashion—but not completely, for even now, in the 20th century, these travesties and comedies still occur.

1. CANINE CONVICT NO. C2559

Rarely in American history has an animal served a prison term. Incredibly, it happened as recently as 1924, in Pike County, Pa. Pep, a male Labrador retriever, belonged to neighbors of Governor and Mrs. Gifford Pinchot. A friendly dog, Pep unaccountably went wild one hot summer day and killed Mrs. Pinchot's cat. An enraged Governor Pinchot presided over an immediate hearing and then a trial. Poor Pep had no legal counsel, and the evidence against him was damning. Pinchot sentenced him to life imprisonment. The no doubt bewildered beast was taken to the state penitentiary in Philadelphia. The warden, also bewildered, wondered whether he should assign the mutt an ID number like the rest of the cons. Tradition won out, and Pep became No. C2559. The story has a happy ending: Pep's fellow inmates lavished him with

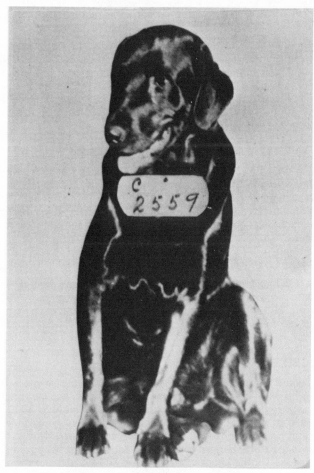

Pep, posing for his prison mug shot.

affection, and he was allowed to switch cellmates at will. The prisoners were building a new penitentiary in Graterford, Pa., and every morning the enthusiastic dog boarded the bus for work upon hearing his number called. When the prison was completed, Pep was one of the first to move in. In 1930, after six years in prison (42 dog years), Pep died of old age.

2. THE RISING COST OF AIR TRAVEL

At Tripoli in 1963, 75 carrier pigeons received the death sentence. A gang of smugglers had trained the birds to carry bank notes from Italy, Greece, and Egypt into Libya. The court ordered the pigeons to be killed because "they were too well trained and dangerous to be let loose." The humans were merely fined.

3. TOO MUCH MONKEY BUSINESS

In 1905 the law against public cigarette smoking was violated in South Bend, Ind. A showman's chimpanzee puffed tobacco in front of a crowd and was hauled before the court, where he was convicted and fined.

4. IT'S A DOG'S LIFE

In 1933 four dogs in McGraw, N.Y., were prosecuted to the full extent of the law for biting six-year-old Joyce Hammond. In a full hearing before an audience of 150, their lawyer failed to save them from execution by the county veterinarian. Proclaimed Justice A. P. McGraw: "I know the value of a good dog. But this is a serious case. . . . The dogs are criminals of the worst kind."

5. A HOOF FOR A HOOF

The Wild West custom of killing a horse responsible for the death of a human was reenacted by a group of Chicago gangsters in 1924. When the infamous Nails Morton died in Lincoln Park after being thrown from a riding horse, his buddies in Dion O'Banion's gang sought revenge. They kidnaped the animal from its stable at gunpoint and took it to the scene of the crime, where they solemnly executed it.

6. YOU REALLY GOT A HOLD ON ME

In 1451 in Lausanne, a number of leeches were brought into an ecclesiastical court. We can only imagine their distress as they listened to the reading of a document demanding that they leave town. When the tenacious leeches stuck to their guns, they were exorcised by the bishop-court.

7. DOGGED BY THE LAW

"Perverts transformed their stables into harems," wrote a French author in his legal history of the province of Lorraine. For centuries, bestiality was a regularly prosecuted crime, and as recently as 1940 a man was burned at the stake in Pont-à-Mousson, France, with three cows. The case of Guillaume Guyart in 1606 contains a surreal twist. Guyart was sentenced to be hanged and burned for sodomy; his accomplice, a female dog, was to be knocked on the head and burned along with him. When Guyart managed to escape, the court decreed that his property be confiscated to pay for the costs of the trial. If the criminal was not caught, the judges ruled, the sentence would still be carried out—a painting of Guyart would be hung from the scaffold. There is no record of the ultimate fate of the man or the dog.

8. THE BARNYARD BORDELLO

Puritan clergyman Cotton Mather left a rare account of an American buggery case. He wrote, "on June 6, 1662, at New Haven, there was a most unparalleled wretch, one Potter by name, about 60 years of age, executed for damnable Beastialities [sic]." Potter, it seems, began sodomizing animals at the age of 10 and never stopped. At the same time, he was a devout churchgoer noted for his piety and for being "zealous in reforming the sins of other people." The man's wife, Mather wrote, "had seen him confounding himself with a bitch 10 years before; and he had excused himself as well as he could, but conjured her to keep it secret." Potter then hanged the animal, presumably as an apology to his wife. Eventually the law caught up with him, and he went to the gallows preceded by a cow, two heifers, three sheep, and two sows. Watching his concubines die one by one, Potter was in tears by the time he approached the scaffold.

9. I'M NOT THAT KIND OF GIRL

In Vanvres, France, in 1750, Jacques Ferron was caught in the act of love with a she-ass and sentenced to hang. Normally, his partner would have died as well—but members of the community took an unprecedented step. They signed a petition that they had known the she-ass for four years, that she had always been well behaved at home and abroad and had never caused a scandal of any kind. She was, they concluded, "in all her habits of life a most honest creature." As the result of this intervention, Ferron was hanged for sodomy, and the she-ass was acquitted.

10. JUVENILE DELINQUENTS?

The vast majority of prosecuted animals were pigs. In the Middle Ages they were frequently left unwatched, and they often harmed small children. Once arrested, they were usually placed in solitary confinement in the same jail with human criminals, registered as "so-and-so's pig," and publicly hung with all the formality of a typical medieval execution. In the annals of animal crime, there are many famous pig cases. One of the most fully documented and most unusual occurred in Savigny, France, in 1457. A sow and her six piglets were accused of "willfully and feloniously" murdering a five-year-old boy, Jean Martin. Found guilty, the sow was eventually hung by its hind legs from the gallows. But the matter was not so simple: Were the six piglets—who had been found stained with blood at the scene of the crime—also guilty? Their owner, Jean Bailly, was asked to post bail for them until a second trial and to take the accused back into his custody. Bailly said he didn't have the money, and furthermore, refused to make any promises about the piglets' future good behavior. Three weeks later "the six little porklets" went to court. Because of their youth and the lack of firm evidence of their guilt, the court was lenient. The piglets were given to a local noblewoman; Bailly didn't have to pay; and the porklets could hold their heads high.

65

11. AN IMPORTANT RULING

A significant pig case occurred in 1846 in Pleternica, Slavonia—it was one of the first times an animal's owner bore responsibility for damages. A pig ate the ears of a one-year-old girl and was given the usual death sentence. Its owner was sentenced to labor in order to provide a dowry for the earless girl, so that, despite her loss, she might someday find a husband.

12. MONKEYING AROUND

As recently as Jan. 23, 1962, an animal was called into the courtroom. Makao, a young cercopithecoid monkey, escaped from his master's apartment in Paris and wandered into an empty studio nearby. He bit into a tube of lipstick, destroyed some expensive knickknacks, and "stole" a box which was later recovered—empty. The victims of Makao's pranks filed a complaint stating that the box had contained a valuable ring. The monkey's owner contended before the judge that his pet could not possibly have opened such a box. Makao was ordered to appear in court, where he deftly opened a series of boxes. His defense ruined, Makao's master was held liable for full damages.

13. A HAPPY TAIL

In 1877 in New York City, Mary Shea, a woman of Celtic origin, was bitten on the finger by Jimmy, an organ-grinder's monkey. Mary demanded retribution, but the judge said he could not commit an animal. Miffed, Mary stormed out of the courtroom, snarling, "This is a nice country for justice!" The monkey, who was dressed in a scarlet coat and velvet cap, showed his appreciation: He curled his tail around the gas fixture on the judge's desk and tried to shake hands with him. The police blotter gave this record of the event: *"Name:* Jimmy Dillio. *Occupation:* Monkey. *Disposition:* Discharged."

14. HARD-BOILED CRIMINAL

One of the most celebrated animal trials was that of the rooster in Basel, Switzerland, who was accused in 1474 of laying an egg (without a yolk, no less). It was a widely held belief that such eggs could be hatched by witches in league with Satan, giving birth to deadly winged snakes. The accused cock was in a tight spot, and even his defense attorney didn't argue that the charges were false. He did argue that his client had no pact with the devil and that laying an egg was an unpremeditated and involuntary act. The judges were not impressed, and after a lengthy trial it was decided that the rooster was possessed by Satan. The bird and the egg were burned at the stake before a huge crowd. The subject was being debated over 200 years later, in 1710, when a Frenchman presented a paper before the Academy of Sciences stating that yolkless eggs were merely the occasional products of an ailing hen.

15. WOMEN AND CHILDREN FIRST

In Stelvio, Italy, in 1519, field mice (referred to in a German account as *Lutmäusse,* they may have been moles) were accused of damaging crops by burrowing. They were granted a defense attorney, Hans Grienebner, so that they could "show cause for their conduct by pleading their exigencies and distress." He claimed that his clients were helpful citizens who ate harmful insects and enriched the soil. The prosecutor, Schwarz Mining, argued that the damage they caused was preventing local tenants from paying their rents. The judge was merciful. Though he exiled the animals, he assured them of safe conduct "and an additional respite of 14 days to all those which are with young, and to such as are yet in their infancy."

16. PUTTING THE BITE ON THE LANDLORD

In the 1700s, an order of Franciscan friars in Brazil was driven to despair by the termites which were devouring not only the food and furniture, but also the very walls of the monastery. The monks pleaded with the bishop for an act of excommunication, and an ecclesiastical trial was held. When the accused defiantly failed to appear in court, they were appointed a lawyer. He made the usual speech about how all of God's creatures deserved to eat, and he praised his clients' industry, which he said was far greater than that of the friars. Further, he argued that the termites had occupied the land long before the monks. The lengthy trial overflowed with complicated legal speeches and much passionate quoting of authorities. In the end, it was decided that the monks should give the termites their own plot of land. The judge's order was read aloud to the termite hills. According to a monk's document dated January, 1713, the termites promptly came out of the hills and marched in columns to their new home. Woodn't you know it?

17. A CAT-ASTROPHIC RULING

It was an ancient Breton belief that tomcats had to be killed before reaching the age of seven, or they would kill their masters. One morning a farmer of Pleyben was found dead in his bed, his throat slit. The local judge had already arrested two servants, when the herdsman noticed the household cat in front of the hearth. Proclaiming, "I for one know who the culprit is!" the herdsman pulled the following stunt: He tied a string to the dead man's wrist, ran the other end through a window, and gave it a tug from outside—thus "shaking" the corpse's arm. Right in front of the judge, the tomcat calmly approached his "revived" master in order to finish him off properly. The guilty cat was burned alive.

18. WHAT'S A MAYOR TO DO?

In Ansbach, Germany, in 1685 it was reported that a vicious wolf was ravaging herds and devouring women and children. The beast was believed to be none other than the town's deceased mayor, who had turned into a werewolf. A typical politician, the wolf/mayor was hard to pin down but was finally captured and killed. The animal's carcass was then dressed in a flesh-colored suit, a brown wig, and a long gray-white beard. Its snout was cut off and replaced with a mask of the mayor. By court order, the creature was hung from a windmill. The weremayor's pelt was then stuffed and displayed in a town official's cabinet, to serve forever as proof of the existence of werewolves.

19. THE CRUEL DEATH OF "FIVE-TON MARY"

There are ancient records of the hangings of bulls and oxen, but there is only one known case of the hanging of an elephant—it happened in Erwin, Tenn., on Sept. 13, 1916. The Sparks Circus was stationed in

"Five-ton Mary" hanging from a 100-ton derrick.

Kingsport, Tenn., when Mary, a veteran circus elephant, was being rid-
den to water by an inexperienced trainer, Walter Eldridge. On the way,
Mary spotted a watermelon rind and headed for this snack. When Eldridge jerked hard on her head with a spear-tipped stick, Mary let out a
loud trumpet, reached behind her with her trunk, and yanked the trainer
off her back. Mary dashed Eldridge against a soft-drink stand and then
walked over and stepped on his head. A Kingsport resident came running
and fired five pistol shots into the huge animal. Mary groaned and shook
but didn't die—in fact, she performed in that night's show. The next day
the circus moved to Erwin, where "authorities" (no one is sure who) decreed that Mary should die on the gallows, to the great sorrow of her
friends in the circus. She was taken to the Clinchfield railroad yards,

68

where a large crowd was gathered. A ⅞-in. chain was slung around her neck, and a 100-ton derrick hoisted her 5 ft. in the air. The chain broke. The next chain held, and Mary died quickly. Her five-ton corpse was buried with a steam shovel.

—A.W.

18 UNUSUAL LAWSUITS

1. PRAY FOR RAIN

In hopes of ending a drought in upstate New York in the 1880s, a Presbyterian minister named Duncan McLeod organized a mass prayer session to take place on a Saturday in August. At noon people throughout the area stopped their activities and prayed for rain. By one o'clock clouds had appeared; by two a gusty wind was blowing; by three the temperature had dropped 20 degrees, and by four a thunderstorm had arrived. The storm, which dropped almost two inches of rain, washed out a bridge and completely destroyed a barn, which burned to the ground after being struck by lightning.

As it happened, the barn belonged to Phineas Dodd, the only farmer in Phelps, N.Y., who had refused to join the collective prayer. Many thought that Dodd had been a victim of divine justice, but Dodd had other ideas: When he heard that Reverend McLeod was accepting congratulations for having ended the drought, he sued the minister for $5,000 to cover the damages to his property. The minister was put in a difficult situation: After repeatedly telling his followers that God had answered their prayers, he could hardly back down and say that the storm was just a coincidence. Fortunately for McLeod, his lawyer was able to convince the judge that the mass prayers had requested only rain and that the thunder and lightning had been a bonus provided by God and for which McLeod and his parishioners were not responsible.

2. A TIGHT SQUEEZE

In the spring of 1888, actress Lillian Russell starred on Broadway in the play *The Queen's Mate*. When producer James Duff decided to take the show on the road, he insisted that Russell wear silk tights in one scene, as she had in New York. Russell refused, saying that what was acceptable in New York might be considered scandalous in smaller cities. She also claimed that theaters out West were drafty and that she might catch cold. While cynics gossiped that Russell's reluctance was due to recent weight gains (she was now 5 ft. 6 in. and 165 lb.), Duff took the issue to court. The judge turned out to be a gallant fellow who ruled in Lillian Russell's favor, observing that her figure was a national asset which needed to be protected at all costs.

3. THE KABOTCHNICKS SPEAK ONLY TO GOD

The elite status of the Cabot family of New England is summarized in the old ditty:

> *Here's to the city of Boston,*
> *The land of the bean and the cod,*
> *Where the Lowells speak only to the Cabots,*
> *And the Cabots speak only to God.*

In August, 1923, the Cabots received a bit of a jolt when Harry and Myrtle Kabotchnick of Philadelphia filed a petition to have their last name changed to Cabot. Immediate objections were raised by several prominent members of the Cabot family as well as by The Pennsylvania Society of the Order of Founders and Patriots of America. However, Judge Audenried ruled in favor of the Kabotchnicks, and a new branch was grafted onto the Cabot family tree.

4. A CABLE CAR NAMED DESIRE

The case of Gloria Sykes caused a sensation in San Francisco throughout the month of April, 1970. A devout Lutheran and college graduate from Dearborn Heights, Mich., the 23-year-old Sykes had been in San Francisco only two weeks when, in September, 1964, she was involved in a cable car accident. The Hyde Street cable car lost its grip and plunged backward, throwing Sykes against a pole. She suffered two black eyes and several bruises, but worst of all, claimed her lawyer, she was transformed into a nymphomaniac. Although she had had sex back in Michigan, she became insatiable after the accident and once engaged in sexual intercourse 50 times in five days. This inconvenience caused her to sue the Municipal Railway for $500,000 for physical and emotional injuries. The jury of eight women and four men was basically sympathetic and awarded Sykes a judgment for $50,000.

5. SUING A FOREIGN PRINCE

In 1971 Gerald Mayo filed suit in Pennsylvania at a U.S. district court against Satan and his servants, claiming they had placed obstacles in his path which had caused his downfall. On Dec. 3, Mayo's complaint was denied on the grounds that the defendant did not reside in Pennsylvania.

6. COUNTING HIS BLESSINGS

On Sept. 7, 1971, Hugh McNatt of Miami donated $800 to the Allapattah Baptist Church after hearing Pastor Donald Manuel promise that "blessings, benefits, and rewards" would come to anyone who tithed 10% of his or her wealth to the church. Three years passed without any blessings, benefits, or rewards, so McNatt, an unemployed electrical worker, sued the church. Before the case could come to trial, a Texas businessman named Alton S. Newell read about McNatt's predicament and sent him a check for $800, whereupon McNatt agreed to drop the suit.

7. THE LOUISIANA PURCHASE RIP-OFF

In 1976 Cecilia M. Pizzo filed suit in New Orleans to nullify the Louisiana Purchase, which had doubled the size of the U.S. in 1803. Pizzo claimed that neither Napoleon nor Thomas Jefferson had the authority to make the deal and that the 8-million-acre parcel still belonged to Spain. Judge Jack M. Gordon ruled that although it might be true that only the French Parliament and the U.S. Congress had had the legal right to engage in negotiations, the fact was that Pizzo had filed her suit 167 years too late, since the statute of limitations on such cases is only six years.

8. SHARPER THAN A SERPENT'S TOOTH IS A THANKLESS CHILD

In April, 1978, 24-year-old Tom Hansen of Boulder, Colo., sued his parents, Richard and Shirley, for "parental malpractice." Young Hansen claimed that his parents had done such a bad job of rearing him that he would be forced to seek psychiatric care for the rest of his life. He asked $250,000 in medical expenses and $100,000 in punitive damages. In explaining his reasons for filing the suit, Hansen said it was an alternative to his desire to kill his father: "I felt like killing my father for a long time. I guess I found a more appropriate way of dealing with it." The suit was subsequently dismissed by the District Court and later by the Colorado Court of Appeals.

9. STANDING UP FOR THE STOOD UP

Tom Horsley, a 41-year-old accountant from Campbell, Calif., was quite upset in May, 1978, when his date for the night, 31-year-old waitress Alyn Chesselet of San Francisco, failed to show up. He was so upset, in fact, that he sued her for "breach of oral contract." His lawyer explained that Mr. Horsley is "not the type of man to take standing up lying down." Horsley asked for $38 in compensation: $17 for time lost at his hourly wage of $8.50, $17 in travel expenses, and $4 in court costs. Chesselet, in her defense, said she had attempted to call Horsley about

Alyn Chesselet and Tom Horsley—"not the type of man to take standing up lying down."

her change in plans, which was due to having to work an extra shift, but he had already left his office. Judge Richard P. Figone ruled against Horsley, who remained philosophical. "I feel good about the whole thing," he said. "It raised people's consciousness about this problem. . . . There's too much of this thing, broken dates. It shows people are not sincere."

10. WORSE THAN CAPITAL PUNISHMENT

In 1978 convicted murderer Ralph E. Dodson claimed that his sentence of life imprisonment in an all-male prison was cruel and unusual punishment because it imposed upon him a lifetime of celibacy. He requested transfer to a women's prison instead. The Indiana Supreme Court rejected Dodson's appeal on the grounds that he had forfeited his right "to pursue his amorous pleasures as if he were a free man" when he was convicted of first-degree murder. Three years later, Dodson was charged with murdering a fellow prisoner.

11. THE MISPLACED CORPSE

Beatrice Daigle, 73, of Woonsocket, R.I., filed a $250,000 suit when she learned that she had been praying at the wrong grave for 17 years. After her husband died on Jan. 28, 1961, The Church of the Precious Blood in Woonsocket sold Mrs. Daigle a plot at St. John the Baptist Cemetery in Bellingham, Mass. Mrs. Daigle visited the grave frequently to pray for the repose of her dead husband's soul. On Apr. 26, 1978, workers opened the grave in order to move Mr. Daigle's body to another plot and discovered instead the body of a woman, Jeanne Champagne. Three more graves had to be dug up before Mr. Daigle's body was located. Mrs. Daigle, who was present at the exhumation, suffered "severe emotional trauma and distress" because of the mistake. In November, 1979, the case was dismissed.

12. PREMATURE DETHRONEMENT

When Julie Wullschleger was chosen Miss Arlington of 1978, she was told that her reign as beauty queen would last for 12 months. Thus it came as a rude shock when she learned that she would be dethroned 2½ months early because the 1979 pageant had been rescheduled in order to give the new Miss Arlington time to prepare for the all-important Miss Texas pageant. Wullschleger, who was also the reigning Miss Miracle Whip, claimed that her career as a model was being harmed, so she sued the city of Arlington for $10,000 in actual losses and $50,000 in punitive damages. District Court Judge H. M. Lattimore ruled against Wullschleger, saying: "The possible injuries to [Miss Wullschleger] do not overbalance the injury to [the city] if the injunction is upheld."

13. DEMON LIQUOR

On Feb. 5, 1979, Woodrow W. Bussey filed a $2 million suit in Oklahoma County District Court claiming that the Adolph Coors Co. and a local tavern had caused him to become an alcoholic by failing to warn him that the 3.2 beer served in Oklahoma is actually an intoxicating beverage. Bussey said that Coors beer had done irreparable damage to his brain, "pickling his mind" and preventing him from thinking clearly. The case has not yet been resolved.

14. THE WANDERING BELLY-BUTTON

Virginia O'Hare, 42, of Poughkeepsie, N.Y., filed a malpractice suit against plastic surgeon Howard Bellin after her navel ended up two inches off-center following surgery in November, 1974, to give her "a flat, sexy belly." Dr. Bellin had previously performed successful operations on O'Hare's nose and eyelids. Bellin argued that O'Hare's navel (which was later returned to its proper position by another plastic surgeon) had only been misplaced by a half inch, which he called "not cosmetically unacceptable." In May, 1979, a State Supreme Court jury awarded O'Hare $854,219, including $100,000 for pain and suffering, $4,219 for the corrective surgery, and $750,000 for loss of earnings. Not surprisingly, Dr. Bellin appealed the verdict but later agreed to pay Mrs. O'Hare $200,000.

15. EXTRASENSORY PAIN

Martha Burke's twin sister, Margaret Fox, was one of the 580 people killed in the plane disaster at Tenerife in the Canary Islands on Mar. 27, 1977. Consequently, Mrs. Burke sued Pan American—not for the wrongful death of her sister, but for her own injuries, which she sustained because of the "extrasensory empathy" which is common among identical twins. At the moment of the collision, Mrs. Burke, sitting at her home in Fremont, Calif., suffered burning sensations in her chest and stomach and a feeling of being split.

On Feb. 21, 1980, Federal Court Judge Robert Ward ruled against Burke, explaining that legally she had to be physically present at the accident to collect damages.

16. THE POORLY TRAINED SPY

Maria del Carmen y Ruiz was married to one of Fidel Castro's intelligence chiefs when, in 1964, she was approached by the CIA in Cuba and asked to be a spy. She worked diligently at her new job, but in January, 1969, she was caught by Cuban counterintelligence agents and sentenced to 20 years in prison. After serving 8½ years, she became the first convicted American spy to be released from Cuban custody. In May, 1980, Ruiz, now remarried and known as Carmen Mackowski, sued the CIA for inadequate training. She also charged that the CIA had misled her into believing that if she was detected, they would arrange for her immediate release. U.S. District Court Judge Dickinson Debevoise of Trenton, N.J., ruled in favor of the CIA because, as one newspaper put it, federal judges "do not have authority to intervene in CIA employment matters that might result in the release of intelligence information."

17. X-RATED SHRUBBERY

In September, 1980, in La Jolla, Calif., the "Grand Old Man of Divorce Law," John T. Holt, and his wife, Phyllis, filed suit against their neighbors, William and Helen Hawkins, claiming that the Hawkins had trimmed their hedges into obscene shapes. The Holts named 20 other neighbors as coconspirators. They asked $250,000 in punitive damages and demanded removal of trees and hedges which had been shaped "to resemble phallic symbols." The case was finally dismissed in January, 1982.

18. THE MUMMY'S CURSE

Police officer George E. La Brash, 56, suffered a stroke on Sept. 23, 1979, while guarding the 3,300-year-old golden mask of King Tutankhamun when it was on display in San Francisco. La Brash claimed that he was a victim of the famous Curse of King Tut, which had caused the sudden death of numerous people involved in the 1923 discovery of Tut's tomb. For this reason he contended that the stroke was job-related and that he was entitled to $18,400 in disability pay for the eight months of his recuperation. On Feb. 9, 1982, Superior Court Judge Richard P. Figone denied La Brash's claim.

—D.W.

10 MEMORABLE U.S. HUNG JURIES

"HUNG JURY: A deadlocked jury
unable to reach a verdict."

1. *DISTRICT OF COLUMBIA* v. *JOHN HARRISON SURRATT* (1867)

Wanted in connection with the assassination of Abraham Lincoln, Surratt fled to Canada and, shortly after his mother was hanged for her part in the conspiracy, he enrolled in the Papal Zouaves under an assumed name. He was recognized and returned to the U.S. to stand trial. From the opening gavel on June 10, 1867, the prosecution maintained that Surratt had been in Washington as an active coconspirator with John Wilkes Booth and others. But the defense produced a haberdasher from Elmira, N.Y., who swore that he had waited on Surratt at his store early on the morning of the day following Lincoln's assassination. The testimony weighed heavily with the jurors. On Aug. 10, 1867, they voted eight Not Guilty and four Guilty. Surratt was released and the government dismissed the case.

2. *NEW YORK* v. *EDWARD S. STOKES* (1872)

"Ned" Stokes had shot "Jubilee Jim" Fisk, the quintessential robber baron, over the affections of a comely actress named Josie Mansfield. Stokes faced the jury for the first time on June 19, 1872, and during the course of the trial succeeded in casting doubt on the district attorney's colorful assertion that the defendant's "hands are stained with blood to the very shoulders." Stokes claimed that Fisk had drawn first and that if anybody had murdered him it was the attending physicians, who pumped Fisk full of morphine and botched the emergency surgery. The jury formally deadlocked on July 15, 1872, with the tally reported at seven for murder in the first degree, five for manslaughter. At his second trial, Stokes was convicted and sentenced to hang. He appealed and at his third trial was convicted of manslaughter. He served four years of a six-year sentence at Sing Sing.

3. *THEODORE TILTON* v. *HENRY WARD BEECHER* (1875)

In a sensational trial, Tilton, a prominent editor, brought suit against the popular preacher charging him with having committed adultery with Mrs. Tilton. The plaintiff asked $100,000 in damages. Beecher bore up well during the long and embarrassing proceedings, never losing his cool. The trial lasted from Jan. 11 to July 2. The jury argued through 52 ballots before giving up. The final vote stood nine to three in favor of Beecher, who returned to his adoring flock at Plymouth [Congregational] Church in Brooklyn. Tilton went into a self-imposed exile abroad.

4. *NEW YORK* v. *NAN PATTERSON* (1904)

Patterson, a shapely Florodora Girl, was charged with murdering her lover, Caesar Young, inside a hansom cab as it inched its way down lower Broadway in New York. Because the angle of the fatal shot seemed too awkward to make a case for suicide, and since the pair were alone in the cab, all fingers pointed to Patterson. Yet her sincere manner and unshakable claim that Young had indeed shot himself created doubt in the minds of enough jurors for her to survive two trials. After two hung juries, the state gave up, and charges against Patterson were dropped.

5. *NEW YORK* v. *HARRY K. THAW* (1907)

Thaw, a wealthy but unstable man with a bad temper and a sadistic affinity for whips, was on trial for the murder of Stanford White, a well-known architect who had designed Madison Square Garden in 1889. What triggered Thaw was the knowledge that White had seduced the future Mrs. Thaw before her marriage. Testifying on her husband's behalf, Mrs. Thaw told a packed courtroom how White had taken advantage of her. Some details seemed to shock her sensibilities so intensely that she could flesh them out only in whispers to the district attorney. The first trial began Feb. 4, 1907, and ended in a hung jury on Apr. 13. A second jury found Thaw Not Guilty by reason of insanity. He was committed to an institution, but his mother used the family wealth to secure his release after seven years.

6. *CALIFORNIA* v. *CLARENCE DARROW* (1913)

The great trial lawyer had just been acquitted on one charge of attempting to bribe a juror. However, the district attorney still hoped to nail him on a second charge. The state claimed that Darrow had directed his staff to bribe jurors to acquit the McNamara brothers, who were accused of blowing up the *Los Angeles Times* building. Although he pleaded eloquently on his own behalf, Darrow alienated some jurors by describing the *Times* bombing as a "social crime" growing out of the class struggle between labor and management. On Mar. 7, 1913, the jury began its deliberation and declared itself at an impasse three days later. According to the foreman, the final tally read eight to four for conviction. Other charges pending against Darrow were subsequently dropped, and he left Los Angeles exhausted, discouraged, and broke. The incident marked the end of his career in labor law.

7. *CALIFORNIA* v. *ROSCOE ARBUCKLE* (1921)

"Fatty" Arbuckle, a $3,000-a-day silent-screen comic, was on trial for the alleged murder of Virginia Rappe, an actress whose cherubic face had appeared on the sheet music of "Let Me Call You Sweetheart." The state claimed that the 300-lb. Arbuckle had raped Rappe during an afternoon party in his San Francisco hotel suite. Rappe's bladder, filled to near capacity, allegedly burst under Fatty's weight. Peritonitis set in, and she died a few days later. One witness testified Arbuckle told friends he shoved a jagged piece of ice into her vagina, and Hollywood gossipmongers whispered he used a champagne bottle, too. Arbuckle denied rape and any responsibility for her death. The first trial began Nov. 14, 1921, only to end with the jury stalled—reportedly at ten to two for acquittal—on Dec. 4. A second jury returned a mirror image, ten to two for conviction. At his third trial, Arbuckle was acquitted of all charges—but his career never recovered from the bad publicity.

8. *UNITED STATES* v. *ALGER HISS* (1949)

On May 31, 1949, Federal Judge Samuel H. Kaufman opened the perjury trial of Alger Hiss, the U.S. diplomat suspected of feeding classified documents to the Soviets. The prosecution contended that Hiss had lied when he testified under oath that he was not a spy. The jury reached an impasse early in its deliberations and on July 8 was discharged with the vote standing eight Guilty, four Not Guilty. Convicted on retrial, Hiss served three years and eight months of two concurrent five-year sentences.

9. *CALIFORNIA* v. *DR. BERNARD FINCH AND CAROLE TREGOFF* (1960)

Dr. Finch, a surgeon, and his mistress were on trial for the 1959 murder of Mrs. Finch, not because the doctor's wife had refused a divorce but, on the contrary, precisely because she wanted a divorce—and half of Dr. Finch's net worth of $750,000, as prescribed under California's community property laws. Despite the large body of evidence compiled against them, the pair drew two hung juries. The first, after 37½ hours of deliberation, was dismissed with the vote ten to two for conviction of Finch for murder, eight to four for acquittal of Finch on conspiracy charges, and eight to four for acquittal of Tregoff on both murder and conspiracy charges. The two holdouts arguing against Finch's murder conviction were a black and a Chicano, who later reported that the majority had treated them as inferiors and more than once yelled racial epithets in the jury room. The second trial began Nov. 20, 1960, and ended similarly. The jury, perhaps resenting the judge's last-minute comment that he saw "a willful and deliberate taking of human life," gave up after 71 hours. The third trial, however, found the defendants guilty of second-degree murder, and on Apr. 5, 1961, the couple was sentenced to life imprisonment. Crime reporter Dorothy Kilgallen, who covered the trials, applauded the ultimate verdict, claiming the two "got what they deserved." Tregoff was paroled in 1969, and Finch was released in 1971.

10. *CALIFORNIA* v. *LESLIE VAN HOUTEN* (1977)

Convicted in 1971 of taking part in the murder of Leno and Rosemary LaBianca, Van Houten, a disciple of Charles Manson, won reversal on appeal on the grounds that her lawyer had died suddenly during the original trial. At the second trial, which opened in March, 1977, and lasted 15 weeks, Van Houten sought to establish that she had acted with "diminished capacity" the night of the murders. By contending that she had acted under the influence of both drugs and Manson's eerie powers, she hoped to avoid a repeat of her earlier first-degree conviction and draw manslaughter instead. On Aug. 4, 1977, the jury of seven women and five men reported that they were deadlocked. Twice ordered to continue deliberations, the jury on Aug. 6 finally convinced the judge that the situation was "hopeless." The vote stood at seven for conviction of first-degree murder, five for manslaughter. Van Houten was released on $200,000 bail pending a third trial. She was finally convicted and sentenced to three concurrent life terms in September, 1978 for conspiracy in the Sharon Tate murders and for first-degree murder in the death of the LaBiancas.

—W.A.D.

7 TRIAL VERDICTS THAT CAUSED RIOTS

1. THE DREYFUS AFFAIR (1894–1906)

The conviction of a Jewish army officer for high treason in 1894 unleashed a tidal wave of anti-Semitism and popular unrest in France. Alfred Dreyfus, the son of a manufacturer who lived in the Alsace, a region annexed by Germany in 1871, had achieved the rank of captain and was the only Jew on the general staff when he was accused of selling military secrets to the Germans. On the basis of forged and falsified evidence, he was court-martialed and sentenced to life imprisonment on Devil's Island, a notorious prison off the coast of French Guiana. His trial polarized French society into two groups—the "revisionists" (liberals and anticlericals) and the "nationalists" (the army and the Catholic Church). Friendships and family ties were broken over the case, duels were fought, strikes occurred, and street fights broke out, bringing France to the verge of civil war. Novelist Émile Zola was convicted of criminal libel for writing a newspaper article that accused the authorities of framing Dreyfus. Retried in 1899—and again found guilty by the army—Dreyfus was pardoned by the president of France that year, but he was not restored to his former rank until 1906.

2. MME. CAILLAUX (July 28, 1914)

In July, 1914, the wife of France's minister of finance was tried for the murder of Gaston Calmette, the editor of *Le Figaro*. Lacking any legal means to stop Calmette's personal and professional attacks upon her husband, Henriette Caillaux had purchased a pistol, presented herself at the editor's office, and shot him to death. During her nine-day trial she wept copiously and was subject to fainting spells, especially when her prenuptial love letters from the then-married Caillaux were read in open court.

After the verdict of acquittal was announced on July 28, pandemonium broke out in the courtroom and in the streets of Paris, reflecting the widespread feeling that power and wealth had subverted justice. Coincidentally, that very day Austria-Hungary declared war on Serbia, swallowing up the Caillaux verdict in the general onrush toward W.W. I.

3. SACCO AND VANZETTI (1921–1927)

In 1921 two Italian-born anarchists were convicted, on the basis of disputed evidence, of murdering a guard and a paymaster in a South Braintree, Mass., payroll robbery. The six-year legal battle for the life of shoemaker Nicola Sacco and his friend Bartolomeo Vanzetti, a fishmonger, became an international *cause célèbre*. There were general strikes in South America, massive demonstrations in Europe, and protest meetings in Asia and Africa to affirm a worldwide belief in their innocence. Despite new evidence, the trial judge refused to reopen the case, sending Sacco and Vanzetti to the electric chair on Aug. 23, 1927, and sparking a new wave of riots all over the world. In the U.S., important people and public facilities were placed under armed guard as a precaution, while thousands of mourners conducted the martyrs to their final resting place.

4. THE SCOTTSBORO BOYS (1931–1950)

Nine young blacks, aged 13–19, were charged with the "rape" of two white prostitutes who had been riding the rails with them. Hurriedly tried and convicted in the Alabama town of Scottsboro, all but the youngest boy received a death sentence in 1931. The case attracted the attention of the Communist party, and workers throughout the U.S. soon demonstrated—at Communist instigation—against the convictions of the "Scottsboro boys." In Dresden, Germany, the U.S. consulate was stoned by a crowd of Communist youths. In New York City's Harlem, 1,500 protestors led by Communists left so many signs and banners after their march that two dump trucks were needed to haul the refuse away. The U.S. Supreme Court twice ordered retrials, citing the inadequacy of defense counsel and the exclusion of blacks from southern juries. The Scottsboro boys were retried three times in all. It was 1950 before the last one—middle-aged by now—was released.

5. THE CHICAGO SEVEN (1969–1970)

The case of the Chicago Seven, spawned in street rioting during the 1968 Democratic national convention in Chicago, triggered a renewed round of protest after the jury verdict was delivered in 1970. The trial itself was chaotic: Black Panther leader Bobby Seale had to be bound and gagged to keep him quiet, and the wife of Yippie leader Abbie Hoffman warned the judge that she would dance on his grave. The seven defendants were acquitted of conspiracy, but five of them received maximum sentences (five years plus fines and court costs) for their intent to incite a riot. The "jury of the streets" registered its immediate disapproval: Some 5,000 marchers protested the verdict in Boston, 3,000 assembled in Chicago, and in Washington, D.C., over 500 demonstrators convened in front of the Watergate residence of U.S. Attorney General John Mitchell. Students at the University of California in Santa Barbara burned down a local bank in protest, prompting Governor Reagan to threaten further antiriot prosecutions.

6. THE DAN WHITE CASE (1979)

At his trial for the murders of San Francisco Mayor George Moscone and Supervisor Harvey Milk, Dan White claimed as a mitigating circumstance that he ate too much junk food. A former policeman and a member of the city's board of supervisors (he was elected with the slogan, "Crime is number one with me"), White had resigned from the board,

The campaign slogan of the "Twinkie Killer" Dan White (left) was, "Crime is number one with me."

then changed his mind. Angered by the mayor's refusal to reappoint him, he shot Moscone and Milk, leader of the city's large gay population, on Nov. 27, 1978. White had suffered from depressions that were compounded by his overconsumption of Twinkies, his attorney argued. On May 21, 1979, when the jury returned a verdict of involuntary manslaughter due to "diminished capacity"—which meant the possibility of parole in five years—thousands of gays and their supporters rioted in the streets of San Francisco, torching 12 police cars and causing $1 million worth of property damage. As one gay leader announced, "Society is going to have to deal with us not as nice little fairies who have hairdressing salons, but as people capable of violence."

7. THE McDUFFIE RIOTS (May 17–19, 1980)

The verdict came down on a Saturday, exonerating four white Miami policemen accused of beating to death a 33-year-old black insurance salesman. Arthur McDuffie, who had been stopped for speeding on his motorcycle, died four days later of injuries. Three police officers testified under immunity that their colleagues, the four men on trial, had beat McDuffie over the head. "Street justice," the prosecutor called it. "They wanted to teach him a lesson. And boy, did they ever. He is not going to run from police any more." The night of the acquittal, violence broke out in Miami's black ghetto, where three white men were dragged from a passing car and beaten to death. By the time the smoke cleared away three days later, there were 14 dead in Miami, 300 injured, and $100 million in property damage.

—C.D.

13 REMARKABLE ESCAPE ATTEMPTS FROM ALCATRAZ

A 12-acre maze of brick, steel, and barbed wire, Alcatraz Island lies a mile and a quarter north of San Francisco. In 1934, Alcatraz, nicknamed "the Rock" by its inmates, became America's ultimate escapeproof federal prison and the new home for the country's most troublesome public enemies. During Alcatraz's 29-year history as a U.S. penitentiary, eight convicts and three guards were killed during escape attempts but, according to the official record, no one ever succeeded in escaping. Actually, whether or not there was a successful escape from Alcatraz remains a mystery, since five convicts who plunged into San Francisco Bay were never seen again. One or all of the five may have swum to freedom.

1. BOWERS (Apr. 27, 1936)

Considered by the guards to be too stupid to escape, Joe Bowers was assigned the job of taking care of the incinerator, which was near the wire fence along the Alcatraz shoreline. An extremely strong man, Bowers worked on the incinerator as he watched the guard in the nearest tower. When the guard looked away, Bowers bolted for the fence. He was descending the far side when the guard spotted him. After two warning shots, the guard fired and hit Bowers, who fell into the bay. By the time the prison launch arrived and pulled him in, he was dead. Bowers had made the first attempt to escape from Alcatraz and became the prison's first casualty.

2. COLE and ROE (Dec. 16, 1937)

Murderer and kidnaper Theodore Cole and bank robber Ralph Roe, who were homosexual lovers, decided to use the fog which often blanketed Alcatraz to cover their escape. Having behaved like model prisoners, the pair had been given jobs in the low-security rubber-mat factory. When a heavy fog rolled over the island on the morning of Dec. 16, they decided the time had come. Cole broke into a nearby machine shop and stole a wrench and a large metal pipe without being detected. Using these tools, they ripped off the steel grille covering the factory window and jumped to a catwalk 20 ft. below. With the tower guards unable to see them because of the fog, they smashed the lock on a gate in the wire fence and leaped from the catwalk onto a pile of discarded rubber tires on the rocky shore. Then they dove into the bay and disappeared. Although a massive police and Coast Guard search was launched, no clue to the fate of Cole and Roe was ever discovered. A few months later, Alcatraz officials declared that the escapees must have drowned.

3. FRANKLIN, LIMERICK, and LUCAS (May 23, 1938)

Bank robbers Whitney Franklin, Sandy Limerick, and Jim Lucas agreed they would make their escape across the prison roofs by killing the guards in the towers and taking their weapons. Working in the furniture shop, the three jumped an unarmed guard and fractured his skull with a claw hammer. Lucas crawled out a window and cut the barbed wire surrounding the roof. The three escapees filled their pockets with metal tools and climbed onto the roof, which had a guard tower in its center. They charged the tower from three directions, hurling wrenches and hammers at the glass windows. Inside the tower, Hal Stites, who was later killed during the "Battle of Alcatraz" breakout, calmly raised his revolver and fired. He shot and killed Limerick and wounded Franklin before he ran out of ammunition. As Lucas tried to open the tower door and as the bleeding Franklin charged again, Stites grabbed his rifle and shot Franklin a second time. Lucas raised his hands as Stites aimed at him. Franklin survived, but he and Lucas were given life without parole for the hammer murder of the guard.

4. BARKER, MARTIN, McCAIN, STAMPHILL, and YOUNG
(Jan. 13, 1939)

During the night of this Friday the 13th, kidnaper Arthur "Doc" Barker, together with convicts William Martin, Rufus McCain, Dale Stamphill, and Henri Young broke out of their cells. How they managed to open the cell doors remains a mystery to this day. The five escapees jumped out a cell-house window into the yard and climbed over the wall. Just as sirens blasted the news that their absence had been discovered, they dove off a cliff on the south end of the island into a small cove below. Guards raced up to the cliff and fired wildly into the dark waters. Martin, McCain, and Young were recaptured by guards in the prison launch. Stamphill and Barker, both wounded, sought refuge on the rocks along the shore but were forced to surrender when guards arrived in a small boat. Stamphill recovered, but Barker died the next morning. His last and only words were, "I was a fool to try it. I'm shot all to hell."

5. CRETZER and SHOCKLEY (May 21, 1941)

As he served his life sentence, gangster Joseph "Dutch" Cretzer carefully planned his getaway. Having secretly informed his gang of the date of his escape, Cretzer enlisted the aid of Sam Shockley, a violent convict who belonged in a mental institution. On the morning of May 21, Cretzer went to the window of the rubber-mat shop where he and Shockley were working and saw two men in a speedboat fishing nearby. They were gang members who planned to rescue him as soon as he appeared on the Alcatraz shore. Confident that the plan was working, the two convicts knocked out and tied up the shop guard. Cretzer found an emery wheel and began working on the window bars. Forty minutes later, he had only polished the steel bars. The emery wheel failed even to nick them. After a last look at the boat that was supposed to take him to freedom, Cretzer turned to Shockley and told him that escape from the rubber-mat shop was impossible. The pair surrendered to a guard who arrived a few minutes later.

6. BAYLESS (Sept. 15, 1941)

On garbage detail at the Alcatraz wharf, bank robber John Bayless was lining up with other prisoners to return to the cell house when he impetuously tried to escape. Because the fog was thick that morning, he was able to leap unnoticed from the wharf to a road below, which led to the shore. He stripped off his coveralls and eased into the water. As soon as his flight was discovered, the alarm was sounded, and guards swarmed over the dock and along the shore. Bayless might have escaped but he splashed too loudly, was spotted by a guard, and was recaptured. For his efforts, Bayless had five years added to his sentence.

7. BOARMAN, BREST, HUNTER, and HAMILTON (Apr.13, 1943)

Bank robber James Boarman, kidnaper Harold Brest, mail robber Fred Hunter, and bank robber Floyd Hamilton (his brother was an associate of Bonnie Parker and Clyde Barrow) attempted to swim to freedom in broad daylight. Assigned to make concrete blocks in the workshop, the four overpowered their two guards and escaped through a broken window. Wearing homemade life preservers and with their bodies greased with thick motor lubricant, they plunged into the bay. A tower guard spotted Boarman and Brest and opened fire. Boarman was killed immediately, while Brest was wounded and picked up by the prison launch. Hunter took refuge in one of the caves that dot Alcatraz and hid under a pile of tires he found there. He surrendered an hour later when a guard fired a shot into the heap of tires. Hamilton also hid in a cave. For two days, he endured the cold and damp without food. Finally, he crawled back through the window he had escaped from and hid in a room near the workshop. On the third day after the escape, a guard found him there, hiding behind some cable reels.

8. WALTERS (Aug. 7, 1943)

After timing the movements of the prison guards, bank robber Ted

Walters slipped out of their view and out of the laundry, where he worked. He managed to climb over the wire fence at a point that was a blind spot for the tower guard. By then, the laundry supervisor noticed that he was missing and sounded the alarm. When Walters finally got to the shore, he found a Coast Guard boat blocking his way and the prison warden waiting for him.

9. GILES (July 31, 1945)

Mail-train robber John Giles's job on Alcatraz, sweeping the dock, gave him access to the incoming laundry from U.S. Army posts. Piece by piece, Giles stole the complete uniform of an army technical sergeant. On the morning of July 31, when the Army steamer arrived, Giles put on his sergeant's uniform and pulled his coveralls over it. He walked down to the wharf with the other convicts and then, at an opportune moment, he crawled under the dock. Here he removed his coveralls before slipping aboard the boat. With a notebook and pencil in hand, he roamed around the ship as it pulled away from Alcatraz. The soldiers thought he was a technician and did not bother him. When the guards discovered Giles had disappeared, prison officials called the army post at Angel Island and requested the detention of any soldier aboard the boat who did not have the proper papers. An Alcatraz guard finally arrived, identified Giles, and took him back to Alcatraz.

10. "BATTLE OF ALCATRAZ" (May 2–4, 1946)

Masterminded by Bernard Coy, the "Battle of Alcatraz," as it was dubbed by the press at the time, was a mass-escape attempt involving most of the island's prisoners. It resulted in a three-day gun battle between a small cadre of armed convicts and prison guards backed up by San Francisco policemen and U.S. Marines. Besides Coy, five other convicts were involved in planning the escape. These were Sam Shockley, Dutch Cretzer, Marvin Hubbard, Buddy Thompson, and 19-year-old Clar-

Alcatraz Island.

ence Carnes. After two years of studying the prison layout and routine, the convicts went into action. On May 2, outside the mess hall, Coy and Hubbard knocked out their guard and took his keys. They released the four ringleaders who were still in their cells and seized the gun gallery, which overlooked the interior of the cellblock. Within 50 minutes, the six convicts were in control of the main cell house, had captured nine guards, and had freed many of the other prisoners. But when Cretzer went to open the door to the recreation yard, through which they could make their break to freedom, he discovered he could not unlock the door—the only door which led directly outside. The escapees were caught inside the cell house. Armed with only a pistol and a rifle, Cretzer, Coy, and Hubbard decided to fight it out to the end, even though the situation was hopeless. To recapture the cell house, more prison guards from San Quentin and Leavenworth were called in, along with San Francisco policemen and two companies of U.S. Marines. At the end of 41 hours of fighting, guards using shotguns, grenades, bazookas, and mortars stormed into the cell house. Cretzer, Hubbard, Coy, and two guards were killed.

11. BURGETT and JOHNSON (Sept. 29, 1958)

While working on the garbage detail, bank robber Clyde Johnson and mail robber Aaron Burgett overpowered their guard using prison-made knives. After tying and gagging him, the pair raced to the shore, put on homemade water wings, and swam away. Johnson's water wings suddenly deflated only 60 yd. offshore. He turned back and was recaptured by a Coast Guard cutter as he was wading ashore at Alcatraz. For 13 days the Coast Guard combed the bay, but no trace was found of Burgett. On Oct. 14, an Alcatraz tower guard saw a body floating 100 yd. from the island. The prison launch recovered the body. Although the bloated face was unrecognizable, the body was dressed in a prison uniform with Burgett's convict number sewn to it.

12. MORRIS, ANGLIN, and ANGLIN (June 12, 1962)

Bank robbers Frank Morris and the brothers Clarence and John Anglin made the most elaborate and successful escape from Alcatraz. Working at night with stolen hammers and chisels and a drill made from an electric fan, they enlarged the air-vent holes running from their cells to the utility corridor. On the night of their escape, they put plaster heads adorned with real hair in their beds to fool the guards. After crawling through the air vents to the utility corridor, the three escapees climbed up pipes to an air vent in the ceiling. Removing the screen, they reached the roof and raced to the south wall. Putting on life preservers made from plastic raincoat sleeves, they swam away, never to be seen again. The next morning, about nine hours after their departure, the guards discovered they were missing. A search of the bay and neighboring San Francisco expanded into a nationwide manhunt. Several months later, prison officials announced that the three men must have drowned. However, on the night of their escape, the ebb and flood tides around Alcatraz were exceptionally mild, making it highly possible that Morris and the Anglin brothers, with their homemade life preservers, did reach safety and escape.

13. PARKER and SCOTT (Dec. 16, 1962)

The last escape attempt from Alcatraz was made by bank robbers Darl Parker and Paul Scott. After escaping from the cell house and reaching the bay, the pair put on water wings made from rubber surgical gloves and dove into the water. At that moment, the alarm was sounded by the guards who realized they were gone. Parker swam as far as a rocky islet called "Little Alcatraz" before he became completely exhausted and could go no farther. The freezing water numbed his legs and arms as he clung to the rocks to keep from drowning. Several hours later, a prison launch picked him up. An excellent swimmer, Scott headed toward the San Francisco skyline. An hour later, he reached the mainland at a point beneath the Golden Gate Bridge. Exhausted, he lay down on the shore and fell asleep. When he awoke, he was surrounded by policemen. Although he failed to escape, Scott had dispelled the myth—maintained by Alcatraz officials—that it was impossible to swim from Alcatraz to the mainland. His success indicated that the five earlier escapees who had disappeared might well have survived.

Note: By order of Attorney General Robert Kennedy, Alcatraz Federal Penitentiary was closed on March 21, 1963.

—R.J.F.

14 LAST MEALS OF THE CONDEMNED

1. CHARLES FREDERICK PEACE, a notorious 19th-century British thief and multiple murderer, was hanged Feb. 25, 1879, at Armley Jail in Leeds. Peace ate a hearty breakfast of eggs and a huge amount of bacon, but he complained bitterly about the quality of the latter. Apparently the bacon was so salty that when the hood was placed over his head, the thirsty murderer demanded a last glass of water. His request was ignored.

2. GORDON FAWCETT HAMBY, a bank robber who killed two clerks in a holdup, was executed in Sing Sing in 1920. He slept a peaceful 10 hours his last night and dressed carefully in a black suit and white shirt for his final meal. Already having eaten a substantial lunch, Hamby shared cigars, candy, and ice cream with his 29 fellow death-row inmates. For his last meal he ordered a lobster salad, reasoning, "I need not worry about indigestion."

3.–4. RUTH SNYDER and JUDD GRAY, the convicted killers in one of America's most famous triangle murders of the 1920s, were electrocuted Jan. 12, 1928, at Sing Sing. Gray, much composed, had a last meal of chicken soup, chicken, mashed potatoes, celery, stuffed olives, and ice cream, which was followed by a cigar. Snyder was so emotional, clinging to the hope of a last-minute reprieve, that Warden Lewis E. Lawes decided that choosing a last meal would only upset her further. Instead, she got the regular fare offered other death-house inmates.

5. FRANCIS "TWO GUN" CROWLEY, the mad-dog killer of the 1930s, was electrocuted at Sing Sing in 1931. For his last meal he ordered steak and onions, french fries, apple pie, and ice cream. Just minutes before he was to pass to the other side of the little green door, Crowley realized that he and a prisoner in a neighboring cell with whom he shared his food had not eaten the quart of ice cream that had been provided. Not enough time remained for them to consume the hard ice cream, but Crowley convinced one of the guards to heat it up, and both prisoners drank a pint of multicolored goo. Then Crowley shook hands with John Resko, his dinnermate, and marched off to face death on a full stomach.

6. PETER KÜRTEN, the notorious German "Monster of Düsseldorf," was convicted of nine murders. Peter Lorre portrayed the Monster in Fritz Lang's classic film *M*. Kürten was beheaded July 2, 1931, at Cologne's Klingelputz Prison, after being given the traditional *Henkers-Mahlzeit,* or the condemned man's last meal. He ordered wiener schnitzel, fried potatoes, and a bottle of white wine—and he enjoyed his meal so much that he requested, and got, a complete serving of seconds.

7. MURL DANIELS, a mass murderer, was electrocuted on Jan. 3, 1949, at Ohio State Penitentiary. Setting what may be a record for last-meal quantity, Daniels ordered and got: orange juice, grape juice, fried chicken, fried oysters, chili, potatoes, Limburger cheese, bread and butter, vanilla ice cream with chocolate syrup, chocolate cake, and coffee. He was also permitted to invite a fellow inmate, whom he had met during a stay in another prison, to share his *bon voyage* meal.

8.–9. MARTHA BECK and RAYMOND FERNANDEZ, New York's infamous "Lonely Hearts killers," victimized and murdered love-starved women. They were electrocuted at Sing Sing on March 8, 1951. Martha Beck consumed a double-helping order of fried chicken, fried potatoes, and salad. Fernandez lost his appetite completely and had his last meal distributed to other prisoners—but did smoke a Havana cigar.

10. DONALD SNYDER was a New York murderer who killed an 11-year-old girl, whom he was holding hostage, even as the police gunned him down. He was electrocuted on July 16, 1953, at Sing Sing, where he had gained the reputation of being the greatest glutton on death row. Weighing a puny 150 lb. upon his arrival, he ate huge portions of food, always demanding seconds and then some. He finally confided to another inmate that he intended to get so fat he wouldn't fit in the electric chair. At the end, he weighed 300 lb., and while eating his last meal, he called for "pork chops and eggs, and plenty of 'em." It was left for a reporter from the *New York Daily News* to summarize the result of Snyder's bizarre effort: "The hot seat fitted him as though it had been made to order."

11. LOWELL LEE ANDREWS, a 300-lb., 18-year-old student at the University of Kansas, shot and killed his father, mother, and sister. He was hanged Nov. 30, 1962, at Kansas State Penitentiary after devouring

two fried chickens with side helpings of mashed potatoes, green beans, and pie à la mode.

12.–13. RICHARD E. HICKOK and PERRY E. SMITH were the Clutter Family murderers profiled by Truman Capote in *In Cold Blood.* They were hanged Apr. 14, 1965, at Kansas State Penitentiary. Both men ordered the following: shrimp, french fried potatoes, garlic bread, ice cream with strawberries and whipped cream. Hickok ate heartily, but Smith barely touched his portion.

14. GARY MARK GILMORE was the first man to be executed in the U.S. since 1967, following the reinstatement of the death penalty by the U.S. Supreme Court in 1976. He faced a firing squad on Jan. 17, 1977, at Utah State Prison. His last meal consisted of hamburger, eggs, potatoes, and two minibottles of contraband Bourbon.

—C.S.

WITTICISMS OF
7 CONDEMNED CRIMINALS

1. GEORGE APPEL (electrocuted in 1952)

As he was being strapped into the electric chair Appel quipped, "Well, folks, you'll soon see a baked Appel."

2. GUY CLARK (hanged in 1832)

On the way to the gallows the sheriff told Clark to speed up the pace. Clark replied, "Nothing will happen until I get there."

3. JAMES DONALD FRENCH (electrocuted in 1966)

Turning to a newsman on his way to the chair, French helpfully suggested, "I have a terrific headline for you in the morning. 'French Fries'."

4. WILLIAM PALMER (hanged in 1856)

As he stepped onto the gallows Palmer looked at the trapdoor and exclaimed, "Are you sure it's safe?"

5. SIR WALTER RALEIGH (beheaded in 1618)

Feeling the edge of the ax soon to be used on him, Raleigh said, "'Tis a sharp remedy but a sure one for all ills."

When asked if he had a last request, James Rodgers replied,
"Why yes—a bulletproof vest."

6. JAMES W. RODGERS (shot in 1960)

Asked if he had a last request, Rodgers stated, "Why yes—a bulletproof vest."

7. FREDERICK CHARLES WOOD (electrocuted in 1963)

Sitting down in the electric chair Wood said, "Gentlemen, you are about to see the effects of electricity upon wood."

—The Eds.

4
CATASTROPHE—
WAR AND DISASTER

9 UNUSUAL DISASTERS

1. ST. PIERRE SNAKE INVASION

Volcanic activity on the "bald mountain" towering over St. Pierre, Martinique, was usually so inconsequential that no one took seriously the fresh steaming ventholes and earth tremors during April, 1902. By early May, however, ash began to rain down continuously, and the nauseating stench of sulphur filled the air. Their homes on the mountainside made uninhabitable, more than 100 fer-de-lance snakes slithered down and invaded the mulatto quarter of St. Pierre. The 6-ft.-long serpents killed 50 people and innumerable animals before they were finally destroyed by the town's giant street cats. But the annihilation had only begun. On May 5, a landslide of boiling mud spilled into the sea, followed by a tsunami that killed hundreds, and three days later, May 8, Mt. Pelee finally exploded, sending a murderous avalanche of white-hot lava straight toward the town. Within three minutes St. Pierre was completely obliterated. Of its 30,000 population, there were only two survivors.

2. THE SHILOH BAPTIST CHURCH PANIC

Two thousand persons, mostly blacks, jammed into the Shiloh Baptist Church in Birmingham, Ala., on Sept. 19, 1902, to hear an address by Booker T. Washington. The brick church was new. A steep flight of stairs, enclosed in brick, led from the entrance doors to the church proper. After Washington's speech, there was an altercation over an unoccupied seat, and the word "fight" was misunderstood as "fire." The congregation rose as if on cue and stampeded for the stairs. Those who reached them first were pushed from behind and fell. Others fell on top of them until the entrance was completely blocked by a pile of screaming humanity 10 ft. high. Efforts by Washington and the churchmen down front to induce calm were fruitless, and they stood by helplessly while their brothers and sisters, mostly the latter, were trampled or suffocated to death. There was no fire—nor even a real fight—but 115 persons died.

3. THE GREAT BOSTON MOLASSES FLOOD

On Jan. 15, 1919, the workers and residents of Boston's North End, mostly Irish and Italian, were out enjoying the noontime sun of an unseasonably warm day. Suddenly, with only a low rumble of warning, the huge cast-iron tank of the Purity Distilling Company burst open and a great wave of raw black molasses, two stories high, poured down Commercial Street and oozed into the adjacent waterfront area. Neither pedestrians nor horse-drawn wagons could outrun it. Two million gallons of

Havoc wreaked by the 1919 Boston Molasses Flood.

molasses, originally destined for rum, engulfed scores of persons—21 men, women, and children died of drowning or suffocation, while another 150 were injured. Buildings crumbled, and an elevated train track collapsed. Those horses not completely swallowed up were so trapped in the goo they had to be shot by the police. Sightseers who came to see the chaos couldn't help but walk in the molasses. On their way home they spread the sticky substance throughout the city. Boston smelled of molasses for a week, and the harbor ran brown until summer.

4. THE PITTSBURGH GASOMETER EXPLOSION

A huge cylindrical gasometer—the largest in the world at that time—located in the heart of the industrial center of Pittsburgh, Pa., developed a leak. On the morning of Nov. 14, 1927, repairmen set out to look for it—with an open-flame blowlamp. At about 10 o'clock they apparently found the leak. The tank, containing 5 million cu. ft. of natural gas, rose in the air like a balloon and exploded. Chunks of metal, some weighing more than 100 lb., were scattered great distances, and the combined effects of air pressure and fire left a square mile of devastation. Twenty-eight people were killed and hundreds were injured.

5. THE GILLINGHAM FIRE "DEMONSTRATION"

Every year the firemen of Gillingham, in Kent, England, would construct a makeshift "house" out of wood and canvas for the popular fire-fighting demonstration at the annual Gillingham Park fête. Every year, too, a few local boys were selected from many aspirants to take part in the charade. On July 11, 1929, nine boys—aged 10 to 14—and six firemen costumed as if for a wedding party, climbed to the third floor of the "house." The plan was to light a smoke fire on the first floor, rescue the "wedding party" with ropes and ladders, and then set the empty house ablaze to demonstrate the use of the fire hoses. By some error, the real fire was lit first. The spectators, assuming the bodies they saw burning were dummies, cheered and clapped, while the firemen outside directed streams of water on what they knew to be a real catastrophe. All 15 persons inside the house died.

6. THE EMPIRE STATE BUILDING CRASH

On Saturday morning, July 28, 1945, a veteran Army pilot took off in a B-25 light bomber from Bedford, Mass., headed for Newark, N.J. The copilot and a young sailor hitching a ride were also aboard. Fog made visibility poor. About an hour later, persons on the streets of midtown Manhattan became aware of the rapidly increasing roar of a plane and watched with horror as a bomber suddenly appeared out of the clouds, dodged between skyscrapers, and then plunged into the side of the Empire State Building. Pieces of plane and building fell like hail. A gaping hole was gouged in the 78th floor, one of the plane's two engines hurtled through seven walls and came out the opposite side of the building, and the other engine shot through an elevator shaft, severing the cables and sending the car plummeting to the basement. When the plane's fuel tank exploded, six floors were engulfed in flame, and burning gasoline streamed down the sides of the building. Fortunately, few offices were open on a Saturday, and only 11 people—plus the three occupants of the plane—died.

7. THE TEXAS CITY CHAIN REACTION EXPLOSIONS

On Apr. 15, 1947, the French freighter *Grandcamp* docked at Texas City, Tex., and took on some 1,400 tons of ammonium nitrate fertilizer. That night a fire broke out in the hold of the ship. By dawn, thick black smoke had port authorities worried because the Monsanto chemical plant was only 700 ft. away. As men stood on the dock watching, tugboats prepared to tow the freighter out to sea. Suddenly a ball of fire enveloped the ship. For many it was the last thing they ever saw. A great wall of flame radiated outward from the wreckage, and within minutes the Monsanto plant exploded, killing and maiming hundreds of workers and any spectators who had survived the initial blast. Most of the business district was devastated, and fires raged along the waterfront, where huge tanks of butane gas stood imperiled. Shortly after midnight, a second freighter—also carrying nitrates—exploded, and the whole sequence began again. Over 500 died, and another 1,000 were badly injured.

8. THE AL-BASRAH MASS POISONING

In September, 1971, a huge shipment of seed grain arrived in the Iraqi port of Al Basrah. The American barley and Mexican wheat—which had been chemically treated to prevent rot—were sprayed a bright pink to indicate their lethal coating, and clear warnings were printed on the bags—but only in English and Spanish. Before they could be distributed to the farmers, the bags were stolen from the docks, and the grain was sold as food to the starving populace. The Iraqi government, embarrassed at its criminal negligence or for other reasons, hushed up the story, and it was not until two years later that an American newsman came up with evidence that 6,530 hospital cases of mercury poisoning were attributable to the unsavory affair. Officials would admit to only 459 deaths, but total fatalities were probably more like 6,000, with another 100,000 suffering such permanent effects as blindness, deafness, and brain damage.

9. THE CHANDKA FOREST ELEPHANT STAMPEDE

In the spring of 1972, the Chandka Forest area in India—already suffering from drought—was hit by a searing heat wave as well. The local elephants, who normally were no problem, became so crazed by the high temperatures and lack of water that the villagers told authorities they were afraid to venture out and to farm their land. By summer the situation had worsened. On July 10, the elephant herds went berserk and stampeded through five villages, leaving general devastation and 24 deaths in their wake.

—N.C.S.

9 TERRIFYING AIRLINER NEAR-CRASHES

1. AMERICAN AIRLINES (Aug. 25, 1975)

A DC-10 taking off from New York's Kennedy International Airport was traveling 173 mph down the runway when the pilot heard two landing-gear tires explode. He aborted the takeoff, skidding to a halt in sandy turf 100 yards short of a blast fence, as 216 passengers watched the incident on the plane's movie screens. It had been captured by a closed-circuit camera located in the cockpit. One passenger was hospitalized with a minor concussion, and 34 others suffered cuts and bruises. Ironically, on the day after the accident occurred, the plane's pilot appeared in a newspaper ad extolling American's DC-10s and their virtue of "taking off promptly."

2. OVERSEAS NATIONAL AIRWAYS (Nov. 12, 1975)

A DC-10 was taking off on a runway at New York's Kennedy International Airport when it ran into a flock of sea gulls. The pilot pulled back on the throttles of his engines and pressed on the brakes. The takeoff was successfully aborted, but an engine on the right wing fell to the ground in the process, and that area of the plane immediately caught on fire. Once the plane had come to a full stop off the runway, the 139 persons on board slid down escape chutes before explosions left the entire plane engulfed in flames.

3. AMERICAN AIRLINES/TRANS WORLD AIRLINES (Nov. 26, 1975)

An air controller admitted that he was distracted by a plane unexpectedly routed into his area, causing him to ignore momentarily an American Airlines DC-10 and a TWA L-1011, which almost collided near

Detroit. Just one minute before the near-collision, the controller was relieved for lunch. His replacement immediately spotted the danger on the radarscope and ordered the American Airlines pilot to descend rapidly. The jets missed each other by a mere 20 to 100 ft. as the American Airlines jetliner plunged into a 2,000-ft. dive. Three passengers on the DC-10 were seriously injured in the dive, and 21 others suffered minor injuries.

4. SWIFT AIRE LINES (Mar. 30, 1977)

Ernesto Agdulos, the 40-year-old pilot of a Swift C-47 plane, was ferrying troops to the southern Philippines when he went berserk and began shooting at passengers with an M-16 automatic rifle carried in the cockpit. Six soldiers and a stewardess were killed by the pilot, after which a copilot took over the controls of the plane and made an emergency landing at Zamboanga City, 500 mi. south of Manila. The pilot later said he had suffered a mental blackout and recalled nothing of the shooting spree.

5. ALL-NIPPON AIRWAYS (Aug. 7, 1977)

A Lockheed Tristar was flying at an altitude of nearly 40,000 ft. over northeastern Japan when Mount Usu—a 2,378-ft., twin-peaked volcano—erupted below. Gray ash and fist-sized rocks shot tens of thousands of feet into the air, engulfing the plane in smoke and cracking two cockpit windows. The jet, carrying 317 passengers and crew members from Sapporo to Nagoya, was kept under control by its pilot, but he was forced to return the plane to Sapporo.

6. TRANS WORLD AIRLINES (Apr. 4, 1979)

Actions by the cockpit crew of a Boeing 727 caused the jet to plunge 6 mi. out of control over Michigan on a flight from New York to Minneapolis. A wing slat had not been properly retracted, leading to a chain of events that provoked a wild spin from an altitude of 39,000 ft. down to 5,000 ft. in 63 seconds before the pilot successfully stabilized the plane. Twice the jet rolled over completely. Minor injuries were suffered by 8 of the 89 persons aboard the flight, and an emergency landing was made at Detroit's Wayne County Airport.

7. AIR CANADA (Sept. 17, 1979)

The rear door and the tail cone of a DC-9 twin-jet airliner were blown out over the Atlantic Ocean on a flight from Boston to Halifax, Nova Scotia. A passenger recalled, "We heard a boom. Everyone turned around. You could see a hole where the tail cone is supposed to be." A food cart and assorted parcels were sucked out through the 5-sq.-ft. opening, but none of the 43 persons on board were seriously injured. The crippled craft, flying at 25,000 ft. when the incident occurred, turned back to Boston's Logan International Airport and made a safe emergency landing.

8. CESSNA 172 (Oct. 9, 1979)

Robert Baudin, a 61-year-old disgruntled pilot-author, rented a single-engine Cessna plane and for more than three hours buzzed the high rises of midtown Manhattan. Baudin made repeated passes over the

Harcourt Brace Jovanovich, Inc. building, sometimes at altitudes as low as 250 ft., to protest that publisher's decision to delete "the raunchy parts" of his autobiography, *Confessions of a Promiscuous Counterfeiter*, before publishing the book. Prior to his flight—which forced the evacuation of the Harcourt building and the nearby United Nations—Baudin had sent the *New York Post* a tape-recorded message demanding that his publisher reedit and reissue his book and promising that if his demands were not met, "I just possibly might fly into the top man's office window and attempt a short landing on his desk." Baudin landed safely at LaGuardia Airport after being promised a meeting with a Harcourt Brace Jovanovich editor.

9. AIR FRANCE/U.S. AIR FORCE F-15s (Oct. 30, 1979)

An Air France Supersonic Concorde jet, beginning a flight from Washington, D.C., to Paris, came within a few feet of a collision with a formation of five U.S. Air Force F-15 fighters over the Atlantic Ocean southeast of New Jersey. The commercial plane, flying southeast at 28,000 ft., passed just 10 ft. above the Air Force leader and 15 ft. in front of the No. 3 plane as the military formation was making a descending left turn to the southwest. The Air Force accepted responsibility for the near-accident, conceding that its fighters deviated from their assigned altitude.

—R.T.

10 U.S. NUCLEAR WEAPONS ACCIDENTS

There has never been an accidental detonation of U.S. nuclear weapons. All detonations reported here were of what is called "conventional high explosives," which are used to trigger the nuclear material. Several of these explosions have damaged the nuclear device, allowing radiation to escape into the air.

1. OFF THE COAST OF BRITISH COLUMBIA, Feb. 13, 1950

A B-36 en route from Alaska to Carswell Air Force Base in Fort Worth, Tex., developed serious mechanical difficulties, complicated by severe icing conditions, leading to the world's first nuclear accident. The crew headed out over the Pacific Ocean and dropped the nuclear weapon from 8,000 ft. The weapon's high-explosive material detonated on impact. The crew parachuted to safety; the nuclear weapon is presumably still in the ocean.

2. 20 MILES NORTHEAST OF CAMBRIDGE, ENGLAND, July 27, 1956

A U.S. B-47 practicing a touch-and-go landing at Lakenheath Royal Air Force Station went out of control and crashed into a storage igloo housing three Mark 6 nuclear bombs, each of which had about

8,000 lb. of TNT in its trigger mechanism. Four crewmen were killed, but fire fighters were able to extinguish the blazing jet fuel before it ignited the TNT. In the words of one Air Force general, "It is possible that a part of eastern England would have become a desert" had the TNT exploded.

3. 100 MILES SOUTHEAST OF POMONA, N.J., July 28, 1957

A C-124 "Glovemaster" transporting three nuclear weapons and a nuclear capsule from Dover Air Force Base in Delaware to Europe experienced loss of power in two engines. The crew jettisoned two of the weapons somewhere east of Reheboth, Del., and Cape May and Wildwood, N.J. A search for the weapons was unsuccessful and it is a fair assumption that they are still there at the bottom of the ocean. Plutonium-239, an isotope used to fuel atomic bombs, has a half-life of 24,000 years and remains poisonous at least 500,000 years.

4. SIDI SLIMANE, MOROCCO, Jan. 31, 1958

Unbeknownst to Moroccan officials, a B-47 loaded with a fully armed nuclear weapon crashed at a U.S. Strategic Air Command base 90 mi. northeast of Rabat. The Air Force evacuated everyone within 1 mi. of the base while the bomber burned for seven hours. During cleanup operations a large number of vehicles and aircraft were contaminated with radiation. Plutonium contamination was subsequently traced to another U.S. base 40 mi. away as well as to other locations around the country.

5. MARS BLUFF, S.C., Mar. 11, 1958

A B-47 on its way from Hunter Air Force Base in Georgia to an overseas base accidentally dropped an unarmed nuclear weapon into the garden of the home of Walter Gregg and his family. The high-explosive detonation injured six family members and destroyed the house, leaving a crater 50–70 ft. in diameter and 25–30 ft. deep. Five other houses and a church were also damaged. Five months later the Air Force paid the Greggs $54,000 in compensation.

6. GOLDSBORO, N.C., Jan. 24, 1961

Four days after John F. Kennedy became president, a B-52 fell apart in midair, killing three out of eight crew members and releasing two 24-megaton nuclear bombs. (All of the bombs dropped on Germany and Japan during W.W. II totaled 2.2 megatons.) One bomb parachuted to the ground and was recovered, but the other fell free and landed in waterlogged farmland, never to be found. When the recovered bomb was studied, it was discovered that five of its six safety devices had failed.

7. PALOMARES, SPAIN, Jan. 17, 1966

A B-52 carrying four nuclear weapons was attempting to refuel in the air above southwestern Spain with the help of a KC-135 tanker. However, the two planes collided, killing eight of the eleven crew members and igniting the KC-135's 40,000 gallons of jet fuel. The planes, valued at $11 million, crashed and burned, scattering wreckage over an area of 100 sq. mi. One of the four hydrogen bombs fell to earth intact, one fell into the ocean, and two released plutonium over the fields of Palomares. It took 2 weeks for the U.S. Navy to locate the bomb in the ocean, 12 mi.

off Palomares, and another 9½ weeks to recover it. Meanwhile, between 1,400 and 1,750 tons of radioactive soil and vegetation were removed from Spain and shipped to a nuclear waste dump at Aiken, S.C. The U.S. eventually settled claims by 522 Palomares residents at a cost of $600,000 and gave the town a gift of a $200,000 desalting plant.

8. THULE, GREENLAND, Jan. 21, 1968

A fire broke out in the navigator's compartment of a B-52 carrying four nuclear weapons, spreading smoke throughout the plane. The crew abandoned the bomber, which veered off and crashed onto the ice 7½ mi. south of Thule Air Force Base. The high explosives in the outer coverings of the four bombs exploded, fracturing the casings of the nuclear bombs, spreading plutonium radiation and fires. The contaminated ice and airplane debris were sent back to the U.S., with the bomb fragment going back to the manufacturer in Amarillo, Tex. The incident outraged the people of Denmark—which owns Greenland and which prohibits nuclear weapons on or over its territory—and led to massive anti-U.S. demonstrations. Total costs of the crash, cleanup, and compensation ran into millions of dollars.

9. 400 MILES SOUTHWEST OF THE AZORES, May, 1968

The U.S.S. *Scorpion,* a nuclear-powered attack submarine, was last heard from on May 21, 1968. It was eventually photographed lying on the bottom of the ocean. Ninety-nine lives were lost. Details of this accident remain classified but the *Scorpion* was assumed to have been carrying four to six nuclear weapons.

10. DAMASCUS, ARK., Sept. 19, 1980

An Air Force repairman doing routine maintenance in a Titan II ICBM silo dropped a wrench socket, which rolled off a work platform and fell to the bottom of the silo. The socket struck the missile, causing a leak from a pressurized fuel tank. The missile complex and surrounding area were evacuated. Eight and a half hours later, fuel vapors ignited, causing an explosion which killed an Air Force specialist and injured 21 others. The explosion also blew off the 740-ton reinforced concrete-and-steel silo door and catapulted the nuclear warhead 600 ft. into the air. The silo has since been filled in with gravel, and operations have been transferred to a similar installation at Rock, Kans.

—D.W.

PRIMARY SOURCE: *The Defense Monitor,* Vol. X, No. 5, published by The Center for Defense Information, 122 Maryland Avenue, NE, Washington, D.C., 20002.

6 UNUSUAL DUELS

1. COMTE JACQUES DE LÉVIS DE QUELUS and SIEUR DE DUNES (1578)

This duel suddenly erupted into a full-fledged battle when the two sets of seconds that the French noblemen had brought along spontaneously joined the fray. The duel had barely begun when one pair of seconds began fighting, and the second, apparently shamed by their noncombatant status, then turned on each other. The final toll: Quelus died, De Dunes was wounded, three of the seconds also died, and the fourth was disfigured for life.

2. JOHANN MATTHESON and GEORGE FREDERICK HANDEL (1704)

During a performance of Handel's opera *Antony and Cleopatra,* Mattheson allowed the visiting composer Handel to take over as conductor for a while. Later in the performance Mattheson wished to resume conducting, but Handel refused to leave the podium. Mattheson immediately challenged Handel to a duel. The performance ceased, and the audience gathered in the street in front of the Hamburg opera house to watch the fight. Mattheson was a skilled swordsman, while Handel was a rank amateur. However, Handel was dressed in a heavy coat featuring large wooden buttons. The point of Mattheson's sword lodged firmly in one of these buttons and remained there until friends separated the composers and sent them on their way.

3. M. DE GRANDPRÉ and M. LE PIQUE (1808)

After quarreling over a lady, the two gentlemen agreed to fight a duel while riding in balloons high over Paris. Two balloons exactly the same size and shape were constructed, and on the designated date each man armed himself with a blunderbuss and then ascended over the Tuileries gardens. M. le Pique missed his shot, but M. de Grandpré punctured his opponent's balloon. Le Pique and his second plunged half a mile to their deaths.

4. HENRI D'EGVILLE and CAPTAIN STEWART (1817)

This unusual encounter was staged in a grave near Kingston, Jamaica. D'Egville, a hot-tempered French Creole duelist, used an imagined slight as an excuse to challenge Stewart to a duel. Stewart, a Scotsman, hated dueling, but nevertheless agreed to fight the arrogant D'Egville on one condition—that the fight be held in an open grave. D'Egville agreed, and the two men entered a large grave which had been freshly dug. But as the two men prepared to fire their pistols, D'Egville's courage deserted him and he fainted. Stewart sneered an insult and walked away.

5. ELLA ZEIGLIN and MRS. DAUGHSON (1902)

The two Newkirk, Okla., neighbors had been feuding for a long time, but when Ella Zeiglin bragged to her neighbor Mrs. Daughson that she could lure her husband away any time she felt like doing so, Mrs.

Daughson decided to take action. She went to court and charged Zeiglin with trespassing and inciting trouble. The court levied a $300 fine against Zeiglin; she paid it and immediately rushed to Mrs. Daughson's house and challenged her to a duel. The two women wasted no time—they faced off with revolvers at 50 ft. Each fired three shots, but none of them found their mark. Then Mrs. Daughson fired again and this time hit her opponent in the breast—twice. Zeiglin was taken to the hospital, and reportedly both women's husbands and friends were seen preparing their own guns to carry on the conflict.

6. SERGE LIFAR and THE MARQUIS DE CUEVAS (1958)

Lifar was a choreographer, the marquis was the head of a ballet company appearing in Paris. Despite a court order and Lifar's strong objections, the marquis' company performed one of Lifar's ballets. The two men argued during the intermission, and Lifar challenged the marquis to a duel with swords. They fought in front of an audience of 50 journalists a few miles outside Paris. Lifar's arm was nicked, and after it was bandaged, the two men embraced and declared their mutual admiration.

—E.F.

The Marquis de Cuevas.

Serge Lifar.

The Marquis de Cuevas and Serge Lifar settling their artistic differences.

11 FAMOUS PEOPLE WHO WERE ONCE INTELLIGENCE AGENTS

1. ROBERT STEPHENSON SMYTH BADEN-POWELL (1857–1941), British founder of the Boy Scouts

Baden-Powell's insatiable thirst for adventure made him ideally suited for espionage. One of his first opportunities to act as a spy came in 1885 when, as a restless young army captain in South Africa, he surveyed and mapped mountain passes while posing as a newspaper correspondent. Over the next two years, on his own initiative, he took to spying on the military in Germany and Russia. In 1890 he was appointed British intelligence officer for the entire Mediterranean area. Baden-Powell affected many disguises, but perhaps his most ingenious was that of butterfly collector. In his sketches of the insects' wings, he would carefully conceal the outlines of military fortifications and weaponry.

2. APHRA BEHN (1640–1689), British playwright and novelist

Aphra Behn sailed to Holland in 1666, during the second Anglo-Dutch war, as a spy for Charles II. She was to employ "all secrecy imaginable" to obtain information on Dutch military plans and the activities of British dissidents in Holland. Although she supplied valuable information, much of it was ignored by Charles, and her mission was continually hampered by lack of funds. She was obliged to pawn her rings to meet expenses and eventually was forced to borrow money to book passage back to England. When Charles proved deaf to her pleas for assistance, Behn was thrown into debtors' prison. After her release from jail, she penned a play and went on to become the first woman in Great Britain to support herself through her writing.

3. MOE BERG (1902–1972), U.S. baseball player

Lawyer, linguist, and superb major league catcher, Berg was involved in clandestine operations for the U.S. throughout the 1930s. In 1934, while on an all-star baseball tour of Japan, he snapped photos which were used in the planning of the first U.S. attack on mainland Japan in W.W. II. In 1943—a year after he retired from baseball—Berg joined the Office of Strategic Services, where he became a key agent and ferreted out important information about German advancements in atomic weaponry. But Berg never lost his love for baseball. His last words were: "How did the Mets do today?"

4. WILLIAM F. BUCKLEY (1925–   ), U.S. author and journalist

After graduating from Yale with honors and teaching Spanish for a year, Buckley joined the CIA and was sent to Mexico, where he worked under E. Howard Hunt in 1951 and 1952. They became such close friends that Buckley is the godfather of three of Hunt's children. In an interview in 1978, Buckley refused to discuss any details of his intelligence mission in Mexico, claiming that it would be boring to do so. When asked why he left the CIA, he replied, "Ennui" (boredom).

5. DANIEL DEFOE (1659?–1731), British author

The author of *Robinson Crusoe* was a master espionage agent for at least a decade. In 1704 he devised an ingenious scheme whereby Queen Anne's ministers could obtain information from around the country. Under the guise of a traveling salesman, Defoe wandered throughout England to work out the details of the scheme—and, incidentally, gather material for his books. During the subsequent reign of George I, he continued his role as domestic spy—working just as effectively for the Whigs as he had for the Tories.

6. IAN FLEMING (1908–1964), British author

The creator of James Bond served as assistant to the director of Naval Intelligence during W.W. II. After D-day, Fleming was put in charge of Assault Unit No. 30, which became known as Fleming's Private Navy. Under his supervision, the special section seized German code books and equipment as attack troops began to sweep through France.

7. E. HOWARD HUNT (1918–   ), U.S. author and presidential adviser

This prominent Watergate figure joined the CIA little more than a year after its creation in 1947 and engaged in "covert political action" in Europe, Asia, Mexico, and South America. He was chief of the CIA operation which led to the toppling of the Guatemalan government in 1954, and he helped plan the Bay of Pigs fiasco. Although he eventually backed out of the Bay of Pigs project because of its "leftist" leanings, Hunt continued to be actively involved in CIA plans for the overthrow of Fidel Castro until his retirement from the organization in 1970. Hunt found his Cuban contacts invaluable in his later role in the Nixon administration.

8. ALFRED EDWARD WOODLEY MASON (1865–1948), British novelist

Mason, a top-notch cloak-and-dagger storyteller, created the 20th century's first important fictional police detective, Inspector Gabriel Hanaud, in a series of stories that began with *At the Villa Rose* (1910). Not content simply writing about detection work, Mason, at age 50, joined the Royal Marine Light Infantry during W.W. I. He performed intelligence tasks in Spain, Morocco, and Mexico (where he posed as a butterfly collector and successfully knocked out a German radio station). He was instrumental in foiling a German plan to ship anthrax-infected shaving brushes from Spain to French troops.

9. W. SOMERSET MAUGHAM (1874–1965), British author

"I told them I was the wrong man for the job, but they wouldn't believe me," bemoaned Maugham after British Intelligence sent him to Russia in 1917 disguised as a reporter writing for American publications. His mission: to support the Mensheviks and retain Russia as an active confederate in the war. Although he had already done undercover work in Switzerland and the Pacific during W.W. I, he considered himself woefully inexperienced for such an important assignment. He was also hampered by ill health and had, in addition, a persistent stammer, which interfered with his transmission of top-secret messages. For the rest of his life, Maugham rued his "complete and utter failure" to prevent the Bolshevik takeover in Russia and Russia's consequent withdrawal from W.W. I.

10. HARRIET TUBMAN (1820?–1913), U.S. abolitionist

During the Civil War, Tubman worked for the Union cause behind enemy lines. In South Carolina, she organized a division of military scouts who reported on the movements of Southern troops. Information gathered by Tubman's scouts led to many Northern assaults, including the highly successful Combahee River raid. Officially credited to Col. James Montgomery, it was actually planned and organized by Tubman. The raid resulted in the destruction of Southern supplies and property worth millions of dollars, and it also freed nearly 800 slaves.

11. BYRON (WHIZZER) WHITE (1917–   ), U.S. justice

Although the color-blind Rhodes scholar was prevented from joining the U.S. Marines during W.W. II, he was accepted by the Navy and sent to the Solomon Islands in 1943 as an intelligence officer. White remained on active duty until 1946, by which time he had earned two Bronze Stars and a presidential unit citation. While serving in the Pacific theater he had, fortuitously, renewed his acquaintance with John F. Kennedy. In 1962, President Kennedy chose White as his first appointee to the U.S. Supreme Court.

—F.B.

10 FAMOUS DRAFT DODGERS AND RESISTERS

1. WILLIAM LLOYD GARRISON (1805–1879)

The famed abolitionist was summoned to the Boston Police Court on June 24, 1829, for refusing to pay a $4.00 fine that had been levied against him two weeks earlier. The reason for the fine was Garrison's failure to enlist in the local militia that May. Though an acquaintance lent him the money to pay the fine, Garrison declared months later that he would "never obey any order to bear arms, but rather cheerfully suffer imprisonment and persecution" since he was "conscientiously opposed to all military exhibitions. . . ."

2. ROBERT TODD LINCOLN (1843–1926)

The son of Abraham Lincoln and Mary Todd Lincoln avoided serving in the U.S. Army in 1859 due to a letter-writing campaign orchestrated by his father. Then the Republican nominee for president, Honest Abe enrolled young Robert in Harvard with the help of a letter written to the school's president by Democratic presidential nominee Stephen A. Douglas, who described Robert as the son of a friend "with whom I have lately been canvassing the State of Illinois." To ensure that his son would remain in school and out of the Army, Lincoln sent Gen. Ulysses S. Grant a separate letter stating that he didn't "wish to put [Robert] in the ranks." Five years later, however, Robert left Harvard Law School after 4½ months' study to join General Grant's Union Army staff prior to pursuing his own political career.

3. JOHN PIERPONT MORGAN (1837–1913)

Morgan, who in 1895 established the most powerful private banking company in the world, hired a substitute to take his place in the Union Army in the Civil War. The Morgan family claimed that even after Morgan's "soldier-employee" completed the term of service, Morgan continued to take an interest in the man, whom he often referred to as the "other Pierpont Morgan."

4. JOHN D. ROCKEFELLER (1839–1937)

During the Civil War, the founder of Standard Oil paid another man to join the Union Army in his place. Rockefeller and a partner had started a commission business in Cleveland, O., a few years before the war, and the business was flourishing. Rockefeller felt that he was more valuable to the war effort by providing employment for people who were involved with supplying food and grain to the military. Rockefeller was also the sole support of his family and had many church responsibilities. However, his brother Frank did join the Army.

5. GROVER CLEVELAND (1837–1908)

Cleveland was working as a lawyer for the firm of Rogers, Bowen, and Rogers in Buffalo, N.Y., in 1863, during the Civil War. Though two of his brothers joined the Union Army, Cleveland insisted on remaining at his job in order to support his mother, sisters, and two other brothers in New Jersey. He was legally permitted to do this by hiring a substitute to take his place in the armed forces. Though it was a common practice at the time, his failure to serve came back to haunt him during his Democratic campaign for the presidency 21 years later. The damage proved minimal, however, when it was learned that his Republican opponent, James Blaine, had done the same thing.

6. ROGER BALDWIN (1884–1981)

Baldwin, a sociology teacher from Missouri, was director of the American Union against Militarism in New York in 1917, and he cited his conscientious-objector status as the reason he would not serve in the Army during W.W. I. He spent a year in prison as a result. On his release he founded the American Civil Liberties Union and served as its director and chairman from 1920 to 1955.

7. ALVIN C. YORK (1887–1964)

Having undergone a religious conversion at a revival meeting in 1911, Alvin Cullum York declared himself a conscientious objector when the U.S. entered W.W. I. With some prompting from his pastor and after the denial of his petition for draft exemption, York reluctantly joined the Army and served in the 82nd Infantry Division in Europe. Ironically, York became the most renowned hero of the war after single-handedly capturing a German major, 132 prisoners, and 35 machine guns—as well as killing 25 enemy troops—on Oct. 8, 1918. He was awarded over 50 decorations, including the Congressional Medal of Honor and the French Croix de Guerre. Though best known as a sergeant, the rank to which he was later promoted, York was in fact a corporal at the time of his heroic deeds. Gary Cooper was awarded a Best Actor Oscar in 1941 for his portrayal of the soldier in the movie *Sergeant York*.

8. DICK CONTINO (1930–   )

After numerous unsuccessful attempts to avoid being drafted due to a neurotic fear of leaving his family, famed 1940s accordion virtuoso Dick Contino was inducted on Apr. 13, 1951, but he disappeared from his Fort Ord, Calif., barracks the eve of his first day in the service. Convicted of draft evasion, Contino surrendered and was sentenced to six months in a Washington State penitentiary and fined $10,000. Though he later spent six years in the Army reserves and won many awards, including a pardon from President Truman, the wave of public dismay caused when Contino went AWOL effectively derailed his career and left scars that remain to this day.

9. MUHAMMAD ALI (1942–   )

Having been reclassified by the Army from his original 1-Y deferred category to 1-A, the legendary heavyweight boxing champ claimed conscientious-objector status on the basis of his membership in the Black Muslims. Notified that he was to report for duty on Apr. 18, 1967, he refused to fight in the Vietnam War. Consequently he was stripped of his title and license by the World Boxing Association and, within two months' time, was convicted by a Texas court of draft evasion, sentenced to five years in prison, and fined $10,000. Free on appeal, Ali turned to the lecture circuit and did not box again until his conviction was overturned by the U.S. Supreme Court on June 20, 1970.

10. DAVID HARRIS (1946–   )

David Harris, the 22-year-old student antiwar activist who married 27-year-old folk/blues balladeer Joan Baez in 1968, was imprisoned for draft refusal during the Vietnam War in 1969. His wife released *David's Album* during the time Harris served his sentence. The couple parted in 1971.

—D.B.

10 CASES OF NONVIOLENT CIVIL DISOBEDIENCE

1. INDIAN CAMPAIGN FOR HUMAN RIGHTS IN THE TRANSVAAL (1906–1914)

By the early 1900s, some 13,000 Indians, who had originally come to South Africa as manual laborers at the invitation of the Europeans there, began to compete with their hosts in farming and trade. The newcomers were subjected to many unjust laws, such as the Asiatic Registration Act—introduced in 1906 and passed in 1907—which required every Indian in the Transvaal to be fingerprinted and always to carry a certificate of registration under threat of fine or deportation. Under the leadership of an Indian lawyer named Mohandas K. Gandhi, Indians organized mass protests, committed acts of nonviolent civil disobedience, and were arrested by the hundreds. The struggle lasted until 1914, when government officials, swayed by Gandhi's tenacity and charisma, finally yielded to the protesters' demands, repealing the Asiatic Registration Act and other discriminatory practices.

2. SUFFRAGISTS PICKET THE WHITE HOUSE (1917)

Led by Alice Paul, Quaker head of the Congressional Union for Woman Suffrage, militant American women fought for the passage of a constitutional amendment giving women the right to vote. On Jan. 10, 1917, they began a silent vigil in front of the White House, picketing it for the first time in U.S. history. When 218 of the women demonstrators were arrested, they demanded to be treated as political prisoners in order to emphasize the political, not criminal, nature of their offense. They asked to be allowed to wear their own clothing instead of prisoners' uniforms, to associate freely with one another while in prison, and to be exempt from prison work. When the Wilson administration refused their demands, the women began a hunger strike and were painfully force-fed by prison officials. Vivid press reports helped win wide support for the movement, and in early 1918 Congress passed the suffrage amendment which was ratified in 1920.

3. THE INDIAN SALT CAMPAIGN (1930)

In colonial India, the British government had effectively monopolized the production and distribution of salt, upon which a heavy tax was levied. "Next to water and air," observed Gandhi, "salt is perhaps the greatest necessity of life. It is the only condiment of the poor." The fact that it was illegal for any Indian to gather salt along the shoreline made the situation all the more galling. Seizing upon the salt issue as a symbol of British oppression, Gandhi led a 241-mi. march to the sea, which culminated with his breaking the salt law by picking up some natural salt lying on the shore. Throughout India, the population was sparked into passive resistance, boycotting British salt and other goods. Numerous protests resulted in the arrests of over 100,000 people for various acts of civil disobedience, and world opinion was slowly swayed in favor of independence for India.

4. NORWAY'S TEACHERS RESIST THE NAZIS (1942)

During the Nazi occupation of Norway, Minister-President Vidkun Quisling set out to reshape the country according to National Socialist party principles. He met with opposition from many quarters—the church and universities in particular. To combat subversion in the schools, he required all educators to join a new union which would be part of his corporate-state system. Between 8,000 and 10,000 of the country's 12,000 teachers refused to join and went on strike in February, 1942. Quisling ordered the arrest of approximately 1,000 male teachers and sent them off to concentration camps to do heavy labor. Reports of their suffering and endurance further strengthened Norwegian resistance and forced Quisling to abandon his plan and release the imprisoned teachers. In Oslo he raged, "You teachers have destroyed everything for me."

5. THE GREENSBORO, N.C., LUNCH-COUNTER SIT-DOWN (1960)

On Feb. 1, 1960, a group of black students quietly filled up every lunch-counter seat at the Woolworth and Kress stores in Greensboro, N.C. The stores had had a policy of serving blacks only if they stood at the counters, reserving the seats for white patrons. The protest was a daily event, interrupted only by periodic bomb threats, and in time the sit-down tactic spread to lunch counters in other cities as well. On the following July 25, Greensboro lunch counters were officially desegregated.

6. THE BIRMINGHAM, ALA., CIVIL RIGHTS CAMPAIGN (1963)

In April, 1963, a drive was launched by civil rights activists to desegregate public facilities in Birmingham, Ala. In the course of three weeks, over 400 protesters were arrested on charges of trespassing, loitering, and parading without a permit. Among those jailed was Dr. Martin Luther King, Jr., who was held for more than a week. The Birmingham campaign was one of many that year which contributed to the strengthening of federal civil rights laws.

7. THE WASHINGTON, D.C., ANTIWAR PROTESTS (1971)

For three weeks in April and May, 1971, anti-Vietnam War activists descended on Washington, D.C., by the hundreds of thousands to lobby for their cause. The most intense protest activity took place May 3 to May 5, during which almost 10,000 arrests were made. With the Nixon administration's blessing, Washington police ran amok, jailing protesters and pedestrians alike, detaining suspects incommunicado, and falsifying arrest reports. The demonstrators' reliance on peaceful civil disobedience was called a "wretched tactic" by Atty. Gen. John Mitchell, who would later gain infamy for his own tactics in the Watergate cover-up.

8. PROTESTING REPRESSION IN SOUTH AFRICA (1977)

Despite a government ban on all political rallies, over 1,500 people gathered and sang black nationalist anthems on the campus of the University of Fort Hare in Alice, South Africa. The rally, one of many, was called to commemorate the death in prison of Black Consciousness Movement leader Stephen Biko, an alumnus of the university. Policemen with attack dogs arrested more than 1,200 black students, who offered no re-

Reverend Martin Luther King, Jr., at Montgomery, Ala., police
headquarters, 1958.

sistance. Protests spread to major cities and university campuses, heightening the controversy surrounding the young black leader's death and focusing international attention on South Africa's racist policies.

9. OPPOSING NUCLEAR POWER AT SEABROOK, N.H. (1977)

Over 2,500 members of the antinuclear power Clamshell Alliance took over the construction site of the proposed Seabrook, N.H., nuclear power plant and occupied it for about two days beginning on April 30. The demonstrators sought to halt construction of the plant, viewing it as a potential threat to the environment. (Their fears were given credence two years later, with the accident at the Three Mile Island nuclear plant in Pennsylvania.) Police arrested and removed 1,414 demonstrators at the Seabrook plant site, jailing them in armories for up to two weeks. As of this writing, the Seabrook nuclear power plant has yet to open.

10. ANTINUCLEAR WAR PROTEST IN NEW YORK CITY (1982)

On June 14, 1982, nonviolent demonstrators erected a human blockade around the United Nations missions of five nations with nuclear arsenals—the U.S., France, China, Great Britain, and the U.S.S.R. The aim of the demonstration was less to disrupt U.N. business than to focus attention on the fact that 30 years of diplomatic rhetoric had done nothing to reduce the worldwide threat of nuclear war. Indeed, the protest was well publicized, since nearly 1,700 were arrested, the largest number ever taken into custody at a political demonstration in New York City. Most were booked for disorderly conduct, an interesting charge considering that the antinuke protesters were on the average better behaved than the crowds at Yankee Stadium.

—THE EDS.

5
TERRA FIRMA

17 MINERALS OUR ECONOMY CAN'T DO WITHOUT—AND WHO CONTROLS THEM

1. BAUXITE

This is the principal ore of aluminum production. The U.S. imports most of its bauxite from Jamaica, Guinea, and Brazil. The International Bauxite Association is a cartel composed of 15 countries that control 79% of the world's annual production. Australia alone accounts for about one fourth of the earth's supply. The U.S. watched with interest as Jamaica's socialist regime, which had taken control of bauxite mining, was unseated in bloody elections in 1980. The new government has begun an intense program to bring back foreign investors to Jamaica. Many had decided to do business elsewhere because of the unstable government policies.

2. BERYLLIUM

Acting as a hardening agent in alloys, beryllium in combination with other metals is used as structural material in missiles and spacecraft. The high-grade beryl from which beryllium is derived is found primarily in Brazil, India, and the U.S.S.R. Since beryllium has special importance and value for space exploration, U.S. business sees a lucrative future for the mineral and has invested in developing products from it for use in the space program.

3. CHROMITE

Chromium, an essential element in the manufacture of stainless steel, is also a necessary ingredient in the chemical and petrochemical industries. Over one third of the world's chromite, the mineral from which chromium is derived, comes from Zimbabwe and the Transvaal of South Africa. The U.S.S.R. also has major reserves, but the U.S. must import almost all the chromite it uses. In 1967 embargoes were placed on all trade with the racist southern African nations, so the U.S. began importing chromite from the Soviet Union. Big business felt it was too risky to depend upon the U.S.S.R. for this vital mineral and successfully lobbied to have the embargo lifted. In 1972 trade was again opened with Rhodesia (now Zimbabwe) and South Africa.

4. COAL

Coal is used in the U.S. mainly for generating electric power and making coke for the steel industry. Without industrial coke to fire blast furnaces or to power generators at factories, most modern alloys could not be made. Although the U.S. controls about 16% of the world's recoverable coal resources, it is not all high grade, and the proposed mining of reserves is cause for ecological controversy. On the other hand, the U.S.S.R. has approximately 68% of the world's recoverable coal. This imbalance between the U.S. and Soviet reserves could weaken or rescind antistrip-mining codes for the American Northwest.

5. COBALT

This tough magnetic element is used chiefly in alloys. In combination with other minerals it can withstand high temperatures and is used in missile and jet aircraft production. An isotope, cobalt 60, is used in treating cancer patients. Mineral-rich Zambia and Zaire have over 40% of the world's reserves. Finland, Cuba, the U.S.S.R., Canada, and Morocco also have reserves, but the U.S. has virtually none. The U.S. imports over 70% of its cobalt—considered strategic because of its military applications—from central Africa. Rebellions there have caused concern, especially in Zaire's cobalt-rich Shaba Province, where Western powers have become involved in the fighting. Continued instability has forced the U.S. to substitute other minerals where possible, but Africa's problems have given impetus to requests from U.S. businesses for government aid in mining cobalt from the ocean floor along the equator.

6. COPPER

Copper is known to be the best low-cost conductor of electricity. It is used widely in electrical wiring as well as in plumbing and has potential importance in solar energy technology. The U.S. and the U.S.S.R. along with Chile, Peru, Zambia, the Congo, and Canada control over 90% of the world's reserves. American oil companies control 40% of the U.S. copper industry, hence American involvement in Chilean politics against former President Salvador Allende, who tried to boost the Chilean economy by driving up copper prices through hoarding.

7. DIAMONDS

The most popular gemstones, diamonds are the hardest naturally occurring substance known. This makes them essential for use in industry as cutting and grinding tools. Gem-quality diamonds make up one fourth of the total supply but bring in three quarters of the revenue. Their price has been kept high by De Beers Consolidated Mines of South Africa, which controls over 80% of the world's diamond business. However, revolutions in diamond countries such as Ghana and Zaire have led to rejection of De Beers' handling their supplies. The U.S.S.R. is also becoming increasingly important as a diamond producer, and it is believed that China has sizable amounts of the mineral. Still, most diamonds come from South Africa, where De Beers has firm control. It would be impossible to mine most other minerals without diamonds to use for drilling bits.

8. GOLD

Major deposits of the mineral upon which the financial systems of the world are based are found in South Africa, the U.S.S.R., and Canada. The U.S., Brazil, New Guinea, Australia, and Ghana have small reserves.

By hoarding gold, a country has the power to undermine the financial structure of the Western world. The higher the price of gold, the lower the value of the dollar. This leads to increased inflation while lessening U.S. buying power overseas. One result is higher prices for those minerals essential to the U.S. economy.

9. IRON

Iron ore is the basic element in steel, which in turn is the basic alloy of modern life. The U.S. has used up most of its high-grade ore. It now requires twice as much crude ore to make a ton of iron than was necessary 30 years ago. The U.S.S.R. has approximately 25% of the world's supply, followed by Brazil with 15%, India with 13%, the U.S. with 12%, and Canada with 7%. Important reserves can also be found in Australia, China, France, and several of the African countries. Japan gets three fourths of Australia's export of iron ore, thus allowing Japan to challenge U.S. steel dominance. Japan as well as West Germany are now able to compete favorably with the U.S. in steel products such as cars and appliances.

10. MANGANESE

Manganese is an essential element in steel since it strengthens it and removes impurities—about 14 lb. of manganese must be added to every ton of steel produced. Most manganese ore is found in the U.S.S.R. and South Africa, which together account for over 50% of the world's supply. Reserves are also found in Brazil, Australia, and Gabon, where U.S. Steel owns 44% of the Moanda mine (the world's largest single producer of manganese ore). The U.S. must import 98% of the manganese that it uses. The Soviets don't export their reserve outside the communist bloc nations, so the U.S. must remain friendly with South Africa in order to compete with Japan and West Germany for supplies.

11. NIOBIUM

This platinum-gray metal is used primarily to toughen and harden steel. It is also of importance in constructing nuclear reactor cores and superconductive magnets. It is found mainly in Brazil, South Africa, the U.S., Australia, and the U.S.S.R. The U.S. looks to Brazil for a stable supply but maintains trade relations with politically tense but mineral-rich South Africa for a share as well.

12. PETROLEUM

Oil is the basis for fuels, plastics, chemicals, medicines, and foods. Middle East supplies account for over 50% of the world's oil reserves. The remainder is concentrated mainly in the U.S.S.R., the U.S., China, and Nigeria. Newly developed Mexican oil fields have provided another source for the U.S., which consumes by far more oil than any other country. Consequently, a stable, friendly Mexican government has become extremely important. The Mexican find, plus U.S. overreaction to OPEC's threats to cut off oil, contributed to world oil gluts in the early 1980s. Threats of future shortages of this vital fluid are used as a rationale to decontrol U.S. oil prices and to attempt to open offshore drilling sites previously considered ecologically unsound.

13. PLATINUM

One of the heaviest metals known, platinum is important as a catalyst in the chemical and petroleum industries. It is also widely used in glass making, dentistry, and jewelry design. The U.S. has very little platinum. It is found mainly in the Transvaal of South Africa, the U.S.S.R., and Canada. Since platinum is so narrowly controlled, any one of these three countries can raise or lower the price by withholding supplies. This happened in 1978, when the Soviet Union suddenly pulled out of the market. The price of platinum more than doubled.

14. TITANIUM

Offering lightweight durability and heat resistance, titanium is essential in the aerospace industry. It is used as structural material in aircraft, rockets, guided missiles, and artillery. Found raw primarily in the U.S.S.R., which is hoarding its supply, titanium comes to free-world countries mainly from Australia and Canada. The U.S. has large ilmenite reserves, an ore which contains deposits of titanium in combination with other minerals, but has not developed a really efficient means of removing the metal from it. The titanium industry in the U.S. is controlled by a small number of companies, and they emphasize the manufacture of jet engine parts rather than research and development for a better refining process. A total of 75% of U.S. jet aircraft production requires the use of titanium, and it is an essential ingredient in the construction of the controversial B-1 bomber.

15. TUNGSTEN

Tungsten lights the world—the filaments in light bulbs are made of it. It is also used in steel to provide resistance to intense heat. The U.S., Australia, Bolivia, Canada, South Korea, and Portugal produce it, but China has the largest tungsten industry. It is estimated that 80% of the world's reserves are located in China. While evincing a hard-line stance against communism in the Soviet Union and the Caribbean, the U.S. continues to develop business interests in China, where cheap labor and mineral resources are potentially vast.

16. URANIUM

A vital ingredient for fuel used in nuclear reactors, uranium is necessary for atomic bombs and nuclear weapons. Beyond its destructive powers it also has uses in medical research. It is believed that the U.S. has the largest supply of uranium—almost 27% of the world's reserve. Australia follows with 18%, Sweden with 16%, South Africa with 15%, and Canada with 9%. Oil companies control 70% of the U.S. uranium industry. In the early 1970s they bought supplies of the metal and hoarded them until prices went up 800% by the end of the decade. The government is allowed to keep information about uranium confidential since it is used by the military, but it is commonly believed that a ban on nuclear arms and nuclear power facilities would markedly decrease the value of uranium.

17. VANADIUM

Vanadium is used widely in the automobile and aerospace industries because of its ability to strengthen many metals when used as an alloy. It is found primarily in the U.S., the U.S.S.R., South Africa, Chile, and Finland. The U.S. has sufficient reserves of vanadium, but foreign supplies are cheaper. It gets most of its imported vanadium from South Africa. If that supply line were ever cut off the U.S. could mine more of its own reserves, but the cost would be higher.

—T.C.

15 CASES OF BIZARRE WEATHER

1. NEW ENGLAND'S DARK DAY

The sun did rise in New England on May 19, 1780, but by midday the sky had turned so dark that it was almost impossible to read or conduct business, and lunch had to be served by candlelight. The phenomenon was noted as far north as Portland, Me., and as far south as northern New Jersey. Gen. George Washington made mention of the spectacle in his diary. At Hartford, Conn., there was great fear that the Day of Judgment had arrived, and at the State Legislature a motion was made to adjourn. Calmer heads prevailed and when the sky cleared the following day, it was generally concluded that the problem had been caused by smoke and ash from a fire "out West."

2. THUNDER AND LIGHTNING DURING SNOWSTORM

During the night of Feb. 13, 1853, the residents of Mt. Desert Island, Me., were frightened by the freak attack of a thunderstorm during a snowstorm. Bolts of purple lightning flashed to the ground and balls of fire entered homes, injuring several people. Fortunately, no one was killed.

3. GIANT SNOWFLAKES

Huge snowflakes, 15 in. across and 8 in. thick, fell on the Coleman ranch at Fort Keogh, Mont., on Jan. 28, 1887. The size of the flakes, which were described as being "bigger than milk pans," was verified by a mail carrier who was caught in the storm.

4. TURTLE HAIL

Included in a severe hailstorm in Mississippi on May 11, 1894, was a 6-in.-by-8-in. gopher turtle, which fell to the ground, completely encased in ice, at Bovina, east of Vicksburg.

5. SUDDEN TEMPERATURE RISE

On Feb. 21, 1918, the temperature in Granville, N.D., rose 83° in 12 hr.—from $-33°F$ in the early morning to 50°F in the late afternoon.

6. FOURTH OF JULY BLIZZARD

Patriotic celebrants were stunned in 1918 when a major blizzard swept across the western plains of the U.S., disrupting Fourth of July festivities in several states. Independence Day began with the usual picnics and parties, but in the afternoon the temperature dropped suddenly and rain began to fall, followed by hail, snow, and gale-force winds.

7. HEAVIEST SNOWFALL

The largest snowfall on record is 76 in. in 24 hr. at Silver Lake, Colo., on Apr. 14–15, 1921.

8. LONGEST HOT SPELL

Marble Bar, Western Australia, experienced 160 consecutive days of 100°F temperatures from Oct. 31, 1923 until Apr. 7, 1924.

9. SUDDEN TEMPERATURE DROP

On Dec. 24, 1924, the temperature in Fairfield, Mont., fell 84° in 12 hr., from 63°F at noon to −21°F at midnight.

10. SLOWEST HAIL

On Apr. 24, 1930, at 2:30 P.M., hail began to fall at Hinaidi, Iraq, at the remarkably slow speed of 9 mph. A clever observer was able to determine the speed by timing the fall of several specimens against the side of a building.

11. GREATEST TEMPERATURE FLUCTUATION

The most bizarre temperature changes in history occurred at Spearfish, S.D., on Jan. 22, 1943. At 7:30 A.M., the thermometer read −4°F. However, by 7:32 A.M. the temperature had risen 49°, to 45°F. By 9:00 A.M. the temperature had drifted up to 54°F. Then, suddenly, it began to plunge, 58° in 27 min., until, at 9:27 A.M., it had returned to −4°F.

12. MOST RAIN IN ONE MINUTE

The most rain ever recorded in one minute was 1.23 in. at Unionville, Md., on July 4, 1956.

13. CURIOUS PRECIPITATION AT THE EMPIRE STATE BUILDING

While rain was falling on the street in front of the Empire State Building on Nov. 3, 1958, guards near the top of the building were making snowballs.

14. POINT RAINFALL

An extreme case of localized rainfall occurred the night of Aug. 2, 1966, 1½ mi. northeast of Greenfield, N.H. Robert H. Stanley reported that rain began to fall at 7:00 P.M., reaching great intensity from 7:45 P.M. until 10:15 P.M. When he awoke the next morning, Mr. Stanley found that his rain gauge had filled to the 5.75-in. mark. However, Stanley's neighbor ³⁄₁₀ mi. away had collected only .5 in. in his rain gauge. Walking around the area, Stanley discovered that the heavy rainfall was limited to ½ mi. in any direction.

15. SNOW IN MIAMI

At 6:10 A.M. on Jan. 19, 1977, West Palm Beach reported its first snowfall ever. By 8:30 A.M. snow was falling in Fort Lauderdale, the farthest south that snow had ever been reported in Florida. The snow continued south to Miami, and some even fell in Homestead, 23 mi. south of Miami International Airport. The cold wave was so unusual that heat lamps had to be brought out to protect the iguanas at Miami's Crandon Park Zoo.

—D.W.

34 U.S. LOCATIONS AND THEIR GRAVITY LEVELS

Most people assume that gravity is the same all over the globe. That would be true if the earth were perfectly round and smooth, but it isn't. Where the earth's radius is shortest—at the poles—the gravitational pull is greatest. Mountains and valleys also make a difference, and there is a definite relationship between the intensity of gravity and the density of the rock underlying the surface; a heavy deposit of ore slows gravity at the surface; a cavern accelerates it. The differences are plotted on gravity anomaly maps, also called Bouguer anomaly maps (named for Pierre Bouguer [1698–1758], a French scientist who was the first to begin charting them). The gravitational values are shown in milligals—1/1,000 of a centimeter per second squared. The positive numbers stand for greater mass; the negative stand for the least. Today the gravity anomalies are measured by a variety of instruments, including satellites, and are used primarily to locate mineral wealth under the ground.

Place	Bouguer Anomaly in Milligals
1. Mauna Loa Volcano, Hawaii	+300
2. Williams, Ia.	+60
3. Yachats, Ore.	+50
4. Washington, D.C.	+40
5. Santa Barbara Island, Calif.	+40
6. New York, N.Y.	+30
7. Philadelphia, Pa.	+30
8. Little Rock, Ark.	+20
9. Miami Beach, Fla.	+20
10. Lincoln, Neb.	+10
11. San Francisco, Calif.	+10
12. Santa Catalina Island, Calif.	+10
13. Boston, Mass.	0
14. Shreveport, La.	0
15. Bangor, Me.	−10
16. Chicago, Ill.	−20

17. Dallas, Tex.	−20
18. Eugene, Ore.	−30
19. Cincinnati, O.	−50
20. Fairbanks, Alaska	−60
21. Phoenix, Ariz.	−60
22. Los Angeles, Calif.	−70
23. Rapid City, S.D.	−80
24. Prineville, Ore.	−110
25. Pecos, Tex.	−140
26. Laramie, Wyo.	−170
27. Salt Lake City, U.	−190
28. Flagstaff, Ariz.	−200
29. Butte, Mont.	−210
30. Boulder, Colo.	−230
31. Taos, N.M.	−260
32. Durango, Colo.	−270
33. Hanna, Wyo.	−280
34. Breckenridge, Colo.	−300

—V.S.

8 OF THE LONGEST PLACE NAMES IN THE WORLD

1. Krung Thep Mahanakhon Bovorn Ratanakosin Mahintharayutthaya Mahadilok pop Noparatratchathani Burirom Udomratchanivetmahasathan Amornpiman Avatarnsathit Sakkathattiyavisnukarmprasit (167 letters)

   Poetic full name for the capital of Thailand. The native Thais shorten it to Krung Thep, meaning "City of Angels." Foreigners know it as Bangkok.

2. Taumatawhakatangihangakoauauotamatea (turipukakapimaungahoronuku) pokaiwhenuakitanatahu (83 letters)

   Native Maori name for a hill in New Zealand. It translates as "The brow of the hill where Tamatea (the man with the big knees who slid, climbed, and swallowed mountains) who traveled all over the land played his flute to his lover." Mapmakers only use the 57 letters preceding and following the parenthetical phrase.

3. Llanfairpwllgwyngyllgogerychwyrndrobwllllantysiliogogogoch (58 letters)

   This town in Wales was originally called Llanfairpwllgwyngyll, which meant "St. Mary's pool of the white hazel." The name was lengthened by an 18th-century cobbler who wanted to pinpoint further its location near St. Tisilio's church and a red cave.

4. El Pueblo de Nuestra Señora la Reina de los Angeles de la Porciuncula
   (57 letters)

The full Spanish name of Los Angeles, Calif., means "The town of our Lady the Queen of the Angels of the Little Portion." It originally referred to the river beside which Franciscan missionaries camped on the Feast of the Porciúncula in 1769 and honors the "little portion" of land in Assisi, Italy, on which the mother church of the Franciscan order is built.

5. Chargoggagoggmanchauggagoggchaubunagungamaugg (45 letters)

Lake in Massachusetts, about 3 mi. long, near the town of Webster. It is an Indian name meaning "fishing place at the boundaries, neutral meeting grounds." More loosely translated it means, "You fish on your side, I'll fish on mine, and no one fishes in the middle."

6. Lower North Branch Little Southwest Miramichi (40 letters)

A river in New Brunswick, Canada, with the distinction of having the longest place name in Canada.

7. Villa Real de la Santa Fé de San Francisco de Asis
   (40 letters)

The official name of Santa Fe, N.M., means "Royal City of the Holy Faith of St. Francis of Assisi."

8. Te Whakatakanga-o-te-ngarehu-o-te-ahi-a-Tamatea (38 letters)

The Maori name for Hanmer Springs, New Zealand. It literally means "the falling of the cinders of the fire of Tamatea" and comes from a legend about how the water in the springs came to be warm.

—V.S.

33 PLACES WHOSE NAMES WE EAT OR DRINK

Place	*Food or Drink*
1. Bologna commune, Italy	bologna or baloney
2. Bordeaux, France	Bordeaux wine
3. Bourbon County, Kentucky	Bourbon whiskey
4. Brie district, France	Brie cheese
5. Brussels, Belgium	brussels sprouts
6. Burgundy region, France	Burgundy wine
7. Camembert, France	Camembert cheese
8. Cantalupo town and papal villa, Italy	cantaloupe
9. Cayenne, French Guiana	cayenne pepper
10. Champagne region, France	champagne
11. Cheddar, England	Cheddar cheese
12. Chianti mountains, Italy	Chianti wine
13. Cognac commune, France	cognac brandy
14. Corinth, Greece	currants
15. Edam commune, the Netherlands	Edam cheese
16. Frankfurt am Main, West Germany	frankfurters
17. Gorgonzola, Italy	Gorgonzola cheese
18. Gouda commune, the Netherlands	Gouda cheese
19. Hamburg, Germany	hamburger
20. Limburg province, Belgium	Limburger cheese
21. Madeira Islands	Madeira wine
22. Mocha, Yemen	mocha coffee
23. Münster, France	Muenster cheese
24. Oporto, Portugal	port wine
25. Parma commune, Italy	Parmesan cheese
26. Plzeň, Czechoslovakia	pilsner beer
27. Roquefort-sur-Soulzon, France	Roquefort cheese
28. Scotland	Scotch whiskey
29. Selters, Germany	seltzer water
30. Tabasco river and state, Mexico	Tabasco sauce
31. Tangier, Morocco	tangerines
32. Turkey	turkey—mistaken for Turkish guinea fowl
33. Worcestershire, England	Worcestershire sauce

—THE EDS.

9 ANOMALIES OF POLITICAL GEOGRAPHY

1. CABINDA

The enclave of Cabinda, 2,807 sq. mi. (7,270 sq. km.), population 80,000, is administered from Angola but is separated from it by a sliver of Zaire and the Zaire (Congo) River. The area is rich in oil.

2. CAMPIONE

This tiny Italian village on Lake Lugano is surrounded by Switzerland. Campione survives on its casino and tourists seeking tax-free goods.

3. FULTON COUNTY, KENTUCKY

Eleven square miles of Fulton County in western Kentucky were cut off from the rest of the state when the meandering Mississippi River changed its course. Today, the detached territory can only be reached by first crossing the river into neighboring Missouri or Tennessee.

4. LLIVIA

The Spanish village of Llivia and the nearby farms are completely surrounded by French territory. The enclave is 6 mi. (10 km.) from the main part of Spain. The nearest city is Bourg Madame.

5. MUSANDAM PENINSULA

The tip of this peninsula, which juts into the Strait of Hormuz and guards the entrance to the Persian Gulf, belongs to Oman. It is separated from the rest of Oman by 42 mi. (70 km.) of the United Arab Emirates.

6. POINT ROBERTS

The tip of a small peninsula extending into the Strait of Georgia, Point Roberts is separated from the rest of Washington State by part of British Columbia and by Boundary Bay.

7. SWISS-GERMAN BORDER

This border is incredibly tortuous. The town of Busingen (on the Rhine near Schaffhausen) is German but completely surrounded by Switzerland.

8. WALVIS BAY

Although Walvis Bay has served as Namibia's (formerly South-West Africa's) main port on the Atlantic Ocean, it has never technically been part of Namibia. The British occupied Walvis Bay while the Germans colonized Namibia in the late 19th century, and the port was later bequeathed to South Africa when the latter became independent in 1910. South Africa's current refusal to give up Walvis Bay is a major issue in the negotiations leading to Namibia's independence from South Africa.

9. WEST BERLIN

The most famous anomaly of all. This city of 2½ million is administered by West Germany but is over 100 mi. (161 km.) inside East Germany. It is connected to West Germany by road, rail, air, and canal corridors.

—W.J.C. & M.J.T.

12 NATIONS WHICH LOST THEIR INDEPENDENCE IN THE 20TH CENTURY

1. AUSTRIA-HUNGARY

Independence: This empire, formed by the unification of the Austrian empire and the kingdom of Hungary, came into existence in 1867. The second largest country in Europe, it was exceeded in size only by Russia.

Disappearance: In 1918, the victorious Allies dismantled Austria-Hungary and dissolved the Hapsburg monarchy which had ruled it.

Today: Because of further divisions following W.W. II, territory it once claimed now belongs to Austria, Hungary, Yugoslavia, Romania, Czechoslovakia, Poland, Italy, and the U.S.S.R.

2. ESTONIA

Independence: After the Russian revolution in November, 1917, Estonia proclaimed itself free and established its own government in 1918. It was not until Estonia routed both German occupation forces and then Soviet Red Army troops that it was truly independent. In 1920, the U.S.S.R. formally recognized the sovereignty of Estonia.

Disappearance: In 1940, when war with Germany threatened the stability of the Baltic nations, complete Soviet occupation occurred and a pro-Soviet Estonian government aligned the nation with the U.S.S.R.

Today: It is a republic of the U.S.S.R.

3. HEJAZ

Independence: The Turks were pushed out of the Arabian land of Hejaz with the help of British Col. T. E. Lawrence, and freedom from Turkish rule was proclaimed in 1916 by Husein ibn-Ali, the sherif of Mecca.

Disappearance: In 1924, when Husein declared himself caliph (head of the Islamic world), ibn-Saud, sultan of neighboring Nejd, declared war and defeated Husein in 1924–1925. Ibn-Saud assumed the title of king of Hejaz in 1926, and the following year Great Britain recognized the independence of Hejaz and Nejd under the leadership of ibn-Saud. In 1932 he consolidated his kingdom, calling it Saudi Arabia.

Today: It is part of Saudi Arabia.

4. LATVIA

Independence: The republic of Latvia, with Karlis Ulmanis (formerly a teacher at the University of Nebraska) as its head, was proclaimed in 1918. It was 1919, however, before both German and Red Army troops left the country, and 1920 before the independence of Latvia was formally recognized by the U.S.S.R.

Disappearance: Latvia was reabsorbed by the U.S.S.R. when a pro-Soviet Latvian parliament voted in favor of joining the Soviet Union in 1940.

Today: It is a republic of the U.S.S.R.

5. LITHUANIA

Independence: This Baltic state also issued a declaration of independence from Russia in 1918. But it was not until August, 1919, that the last Red Army occupation forces were routed. The U.S.S.R. signed a formal pact recognizing Lithuania's independence in 1920.

Disappearance: As in Estonia and Latvia, a pro-Soviet government voted to join the U.S.S.R. in 1940.

Today: It is a republic of the U.S.S.R.

6. MONTENEGRO

Independence: When Serbia lost its war with Turkey in 1389, the principality of Zeto—now Montenegro—continued to resist the Turks. In 1878 Montenegro's freedom was formally recognized at the Congress of Berlin.

Disappearance: After unanimously deposing Nicholas I, the national assembly voted on Nov. 26, 1918 to unite with Serbia and others to form the Kingdom of the Serbs, Croates, and Slovenes. Later the name was changed to Yugoslavia.

Today: It is still part of Yugoslavia.

A stamp from Montenegro.

7. NEWFOUNDLAND

Independence: This British colony was granted representative government in 1832, parliamentary government in 1855, and attained dominion status (equal to but separate from Canada) in 1926.

Disappearance: It voluntarily gave up its independence—becoming the first state to withdraw from the British Commonwealth—and reverted back to colonial status in 1934 in the face of grave economic difficulties. Great Britain then assumed Newfoundland's debts.

Today: In 1949 Newfoundland joined Canada and is now that country's 10th and easternmost province.

8. PRUSSIA

Independence: Achieving its freedom from Poland in the 17th century, Prussia established itself as a kingdom in 1701. During the next two centuries, Prussia expanded its territorial holdings and was the leader in the unification of the German Empire (with William I of Prussia as emperor) in 1871.

Disappearance: After the abdication of William II in 1918, Prussia became a state in the new German republic. Since it was the symbol of German militarism, the Allies formally dissolved Prussia in 1947.

Today: It is part of the U.S.S.R., Poland, and East and West Germany.

9. SOUTH VIETNAM

Independence: South Vietnam withdrew from the French Union in 1954, a few months after a cease-fire line divided Vietnam in half and ended the French-Indochina War.

Disappearance: In spite of U.S. military and financial aid, South Vietnam lost its bid for sovereignty. Formal reunification of North and South Vietnam occurred in 1976.

Today: It is part of the Socialist Republic of Vietnam.

10. TANNU TUVA

Independence: With Russian encouragement, Tannu Tuva broke away from China in 1911, and in 1914 Tannu Tuva became a Russian protectorate. Then, in 1921, it was declared independent.

Disappearance: The nation was annexed by the U.S.S.R. in 1944.

Today: It is the Tuva Autonomous Soviet Socialist Republic.

11. TIBET

Independence: In 1912 the Tibetans, aware that the Manchu Dynasty had been overthrown, expelled the Chinese from their territory. Though it had its own government organization, Tibet was continuously plagued by Chinese interference and territorial claims.

Disappearance: The Chinese Communists invaded Tibet in 1950, and in 1951 forced the Tibetans to recognize Chinese sovereignty in return for severely limited autonomy. Tibetan rebellions—the last major uprising occurred in 1959—were put down by the Chinese, who gradually tightened their control over the country.

Today: The Tibetan Autonomous Region is part of the People's Republic of China.

12. TRANSVAAL

Independence: Internal self-rule was achieved in 1881 after British occupation forces suffered a crushing military defeat at the hands of Afrikaner troops.

Disappearance: The discovery of gold in the new nation in 1886 triggered a war between Great Britain and the Transvaal in 1899, and in 1900 the British officially annexed the land. Hostilities continued until the Treaty of Vereeniging was signed in 1902. The Transvaal lost its independence, becoming a crown colony of the British Empire.

Independence: Great Britain granted the Transvaal full independence on Dec. 6, 1906.

Disappearance: In 1910 the Transvaal became a province of the Union of South Africa (now the Republic of South Africa).

Today: It is part of the Republic of South Africa.

—J.E.W.

6
ANIMAL SHOW

11 WINNERS OF THE DOG HERO OF THE YEAR AWARD

Since 1954, Ken-L Ration has honored canine heroes by awarding a Dog Hero of the Year medal. Each year a panel of judges selects the dog who has shown the greatest courage in saving life or property. Here are the remarkable stories of 11 of the winners. At last count the Ken-L Ration dog heroes had saved the lives of more than 290 humans and 300 animals.

1. TANG (1954)

The first Ken-L Ration Dog Hero of the Year was a collie owned by Air Force Capt. and Mrs. Maurice Dyer of Denison, Tex. While the Dyers were stationed at Air Force bases in Alaska and Texas, the friendly dog saved at least five youngsters from being hit by military vehicles. On another occasion, Tang planted himself in front of a parked truck, howling and barking, until the driver discovered a two-year-old stowaway. Had she not been found, the little girl would have fallen to the pavement the moment the truck began to move. Tang was a familiar and well-loved sight in Denison, and when he was awarded the Ken-L Ration gold medal, the neighborhood children had a parade in his honor.

2. TAFFY (1955)

This cocker spaniel was owned by Mr. and Mrs. Ken Wilson of Coeur d'Alene, Ida. Taffy was selected for saving three-year-old Stevie Wilson from drowning in an icy lake. The boy was supposed to stay with a neighbor while his father was trying out a saddle horse in a corral near a lake. But the child and his dog went out to play, and Stevie fell into the lake and sank to the bottom. Taffy bounded up to the corral barking excitedly and racing about Wilson's horse. When this did not attract the man's attention, Taffy dashed into the lake, barking at the top of her lungs, and then came out and nipped at the horse's legs until Wilson was almost thrown from his mount. The man then leaped off his horse and raced after Taffy to the lake. Wilson saw Stevie's red mackinaw floating on the surface, dove into the four-foot-deep water, and lifted his unconscious son from the bottom. Six hours later, Stevie regained consciousness. The first thing he saw was his dog Taffy, crouched in a prayerful attitude beside his bed. The attending physician said that just a few more moments at the bottom of the lake probably would have proved fatal.

Taffy saved three-year-old Stevie Wilson from drowning.

3. BUDDY (1964)

A collie owned by Mr. and Mrs. Matthew S. Crinkley, Jr., of Budd Lake, N.J., was the only Ken-L Ration Dog Hero of the Year to be chosen because of heroism that led to the saving of animal life. The Crinkleys ran a goat dairy farm, and one cold January morning before dawn a fire broke out in the farm's maternity barn. While his master was sleeping, Buddy took charge and herded the entire flock of 70 pregnant goats out of the barn to safety, suffering severe burns on his paws and nasal damage from smoke inhalation. The Crinkleys were awakened by Buddy's frantic barks and rushed to a window, only to see the walls and roof of the now-empty barn tumble into a flaming pile of ruin. The warning of this dedicated farm dog allowed the Crinkleys just enough time to wet down the roof of a second barn and save the 30 remaining goats.

125

4. RINGO (1968)

The Saint Bernard mix owned by Mrs. Raymond Saleh of Euless, Tex., saved two-year-old Randy Saleh from being hit by traffic on a busy road. Randy wandered away from home one day, and a two-hour police search failed to locate the boy. About three quarters of a mile away from the Saleh home, Harley Jones, a school maintenance employee, came upon a traffic jam which motorists said was caused by a "mad dog in the road ahead." Jones parked his car and went to the head of the line where Ringo, resolutely stationed in the center of the road, was protecting Randy, who was playing in the center of the heavily traveled roadway. Ringo would block the oncoming cars and then rush back to Randy and nudge him to the side of the road. But Randy, thinking it was a game, would immediately return to the center of the road. Jones spoke soothingly to Ringo and finally calmed him down. However, the dog did not relax and allow cars to pass until Randy was safely out of the traffic.

5. TOP (1969)

The Great Dane owned by Axel Patzwaldt of Los Angeles saved two children from death or severe injury by performing two heroic deeds within eight weeks. The dog's exploits began in April when an 11-year-old neighbor girl took him for a walk. A short distance from home, she started across the street, not noticing that a large truck was swiftly approaching. Top barked loudly, jumped in front of her, and pushed her out of the way. She was unhurt, but Top was hit by the truck, which broke his right rear leg. One week after his seven-week stint in a cast, Top found two-year-old Christopher Conley, another neighbor's child, at the bottom of a nearby swimming pool. Top alerted his master by barking wildly and then led him to the scene. A former lifeguard, Patzwaldt pulled Christopher out and began mouth-to-mouth resuscitation on the child, who resumed breathing in a short time.

6. GRIZZLY BEAR (1970)

This Saint Bernard owned by Mr. and Mrs. David Gratias of Denali, Alaska, battled and finally chased away a grizzly bear that had attacked the dog's mistress behind their cabin home. Mrs. Gratias had discovered a young grizzly bear cub in the backyard. Assuming that the mother must be near, the woman raced back to close the front door in an effort to protect her napping two-year-old daughter, Theresa. As she rounded the corner of the house, she came face-to-face with the mother grizzly. The huge beast raised itself up to its eight-foot height and grabbed Mrs. Gratias, who slipped on the icy ground and lay stunned by the fall. Instantly upon her, the grizzly raked her cheek with one paw while it sank the other one deep into her shoulder. Before the bear could inflict a possibly fatal bite, she suddenly staggered backward as the Saint Bernard—aptly named Grizzly Bear—lunged with all of his 180 lb. Maneuvering and slashing at the beast with his teeth and paws, Grizzly Bear protected his helpless owner until the bear wandered off, exhausted.

7. MIMI (1972)

The only miniature poodle to become the Ken-L Ration Dog Hero of the Year, Mimi was owned by Mr. and Mrs. Nicholas Emerito of Danbury, Conn. This tiny canine helped save the lives of eight members of one family when fire broke out in their home. The dog aroused Mr. Emerito at 5:30 A.M. after he had fallen asleep in front of the TV. Wakened by Mimi's barking and scratching at his chest, the man found the living room in flames. While he ran to awaken his wife and small son in a first-floor bedroom, Mimi raced up the stairs and aroused five other children. Two of the teenage boys were trapped by the flaming stairway, but they leaped to safety from the roof. All were saved, but the house was completely destroyed.

8. BUDWEISER (1973)

A Saint Bernard owned by Mr. and Mrs. B. M. Carter of John's Island, S.C., pulled a four-year-old girl from a blazing house and returned to rescue a second child. An explosion had sent flames shooting through the Carter home, where six of their grandchildren were visiting. Budweiser charged into the house, grabbed the youngest child, Linda Lawson, by her shirt and pulled her out. He then raced back and pulled five-year-old Joyce Hinson out of the blazing house. In the meantime, Mrs. Carter rounded up the other four children and herded them to safety. When the dog tried to enter the house a third time to rescue the family's Chihuahua, he was driven back by intense flames that soon caused the roof to collapse.

9. ZORRO (1976)

This German shepherd/wolf owned by Mr. and Mrs. Mark A. Cooper of Orangevale, Calif., twice pulled his master out of a whirlpool after Cooper had fallen 85 ft. into a ravine and had been knocked unconscious. The dog slept on top of Cooper during the night to keep him warm while Cooper's companion left to get help. Cooper was rescued, but the dog was left behind out of necessity. Later, two volunteer searchers from the Sierra Club rescued Zorro, who was still guarding his master's abandoned backpacking equipment.

10. CHESTER (1978)

The 25th Ken-L Ration Dog Hero of the Year was a Chesapeake Bay retriever owned by Mr. and Mrs. Gary Homme of Livingston, Mont. Nicknamed Chessie, the heroic dog pulled five-year-old Kenny Homme from a surging creek. Mrs. Homme was washing dishes at the time and periodically looked out of her kitchen window to check on the boy, who was playing outside. Suddenly Mrs. Homme noticed that Kenny was gone. She ran outside and heard him shouting, "Help me! Save me!" The boy had slid down a steep hill and fallen into a creek that was swollen and surging with a powerful current. Chester was in the water trying to save the child. As the dog swam toward Kenny, the water pulled the boy into a culvert. Chester battled the raging water for 10 minutes. Kenny grabbed onto Chester's fur twice but lost his grip both times. Then Kenny climbed on top of the dog's back and was carried out of the tunnel to safety. "If we didn't have Chessie, we wouldn't have a son," Mrs. Homme said.

11. THUMPER (1979)

The eight-month-old Saint Bernard owned by Mr. and Mrs. Carl Bodie of Lockport, N.Y., stayed close to the Bodies' three-year-old son Benjamin (Benji) after he wandered away from home into an area dotted with farm ponds. The young boy disappeared early in the afternoon, and by midnight some 1,000 people were involved in the search. Finally, at 2:00 A.M., a volunteer heard Thumper barking in a distant field. Following the sound, he came upon Benji—covered with dog hair but safe and warm beside the big puppy. When daylight came, the Bodies traced the steps of child and dog. "They came within a few feet of a pond," says Mrs. Bodie, "but Thumper had the good sense to stay with Benji and keep him out of the water. You don't expect such devotion from a puppy. He's our sweetheart!"

SOURCE: Quaker Oats Company, Pet Foods Division, Chicago, Ill.

10 FAMOUS PEOPLE WHO SLEPT WITH THEIR DOGS

1. ELIZABETH BARRETT BROWNING (1806–1861), British poet

The cocker spaniel Flush has become immortal in literary history through the poem "To Flush, My Dog." His mistress, Elizabeth Barrett, was a semi-invalid when Flush first came to live with her. Elizabeth wrote, "Flush is my constant companion, my friend, my amusement." He generally would eat only from her hand and when occasionally denied his accustomed sleeping place on her bed, he would spend the night moaning. Jealous of Elizabeth's affection, Flush nipped her suitor, Robert Browning, on several occasions. Mr. Browning—who eventually married Elizabeth—soon learned that his presence was made more tolerable when he brought along some tasty tidbits.

2. WINSTON CHURCHILL (1874–1965), British statesman

Fond of all animals, Churchill had a continuous succession of pets. Rufus Two, his poodle, was particularly partial to sleeping at the foot of Sir Winston's bed. The morning would often begin with Rufus Two waking his master by licking his face. Sir Winston would then share his breakfast in bed with Toby, his parakeet. Toby's cage would be placed on the bed and he would be allowed to perch on the tray and peck at the crumbs. The powerful world leader carefully ate his breakfast so as not to disturb the little bird's meal.

3. GEORGE ARMSTRONG CUSTER (1839–1876), U.S. army officer

General Custer doted on his dogs, who generally accompanied him in a clamorous pack. Two of his favorites were Turk, a white bulldog, and Byron, a greyhound. In addition, there were numerous beagles, staghounds, wolfhounds, and foxhounds. They shared his food, his tent, and his bed—much to the chagrin of Custer's wife, Libbie.

4. MARION DAVIES (1897–1961), U.S. actress

While staying at Deske's Grand Hotel in Bad Nauheim, Germany, Marion Davies acquired a dachshund whom she named Gandhi. He had been abandoned by hotel guests who left without paying their bill. William Randolph Hearst, Marion's companion, settled the debt and presented the dog to her. It was love at first sight. Gandhi traveled everywhere with them and at night would sleep on his mistress's feet to keep them warm. When he died, Marion was heartbroken and arranged a funeral service for him complete with an Irish priest. Gandhi is buried at Wyntoon, the Hearst estate on the McCloud River in northern California.

5. DORIS DAY (1924–   ), U.S. actress

Well known for her efforts on behalf of homeless animals, Doris Day always seems to have an entourage of dogs in her home. A case in point is a little gray poodle named El Tigre de Sassafrass. Badly neglected and neurotic when he first went to live with the actress, Tigre would seldom come out from under the bed. However, after some tender loving care, Doris reported that Tigre was soon spending almost all his time on the bed. Believing that her dogs reciprocate the care they receive, the actress credits them with saving her life. One night, Doris awoke because the dogs sleeping in her bedroom were restless. Deciding to take a walk around the pool with them, Doris went to the patio door and opened it to go out, but the dogs stopped, refusing to go farther. Doris hesitated and just then she heard a loud cracking sound. The giant sycamore in her backyard toppled over with a thunderous crash. Had she been in the yard she might have been killed.

6. EDWARD VIII (1894–1972), King of the United Kingdom

Edward VIII—known as the Duke of Windsor after his abdication—always enjoyed the company of dogs. While serving his country as the Prince of Wales, he was particularly fond of cairn terriers, although in later life he switched his allegiance to pugs. One of his favorite cairns was named Cora, and she always slept with the prince. As she grew older, Cora was troubled with rheumatism, but her thoughtful master had steps built so she could more easily get onto the bed.

7. PRINCESS GRACE OF MONACO (1928–1982)

In 1956, when Grace Kelly sailed from New York for Monaco to marry Prince Rainier, she brought along Oliver, her beloved black poodle. Accustomed to sleeping at the foot of his mistress's bed, Oliver saw no need to change his habits even though there was a new member in the family. Therefore, on the royal wedding night the poodle was in his usual spot, and he continued to sleep there until his death some years later. Gamma, Oliver's daughter, then carried on the family tradition.

8. PETER THE GREAT (1672–1725), Czar of Russia

Whenever he was at home, the czar was constantly followed by Lisette, a small Italian greyhound. During Peter's afternoon nap Lisette always slept at his feet. Once the czar's wife, Catherine, unhappy that a member of the court was being falsely accused of corruption, tried to convince the czar of the man's innocence. Peter had a short temper and was so furious with the courtier that he refused to let anyone, even the czarina, petition him to pardon the man. Cleverly, Catherine wrote a sad little petition in the name of Lisette and tied it around the dog's neck. When Peter found it, he smiled and said that since it was a request from Lisette the charge would be dropped.

9. MANFRED VON RICHTHOFEN (1892–1918), German aviator

When the famous W.W. I flying ace, the Red Baron, decided he wanted a dog he went looking for a "little lap dog." He bought a puppy of unknown origin that kept growing until, as Richthofen put it, "my tender little lap dog became a colossal great beast." Moritz—named after a performing monkey—turned out to be a Great Dane. Despite his unexpected size, Moritz and Richthofen became fast friends. They not only slept together but also flew together—with Moritz in the observer's cockpit. Once, when the Great Dane was chasing a rolling airplane, he was struck on the head by the propeller. Moritz suffered minor injuries but the propeller was broken.

10. THE DUCHESS OF WINDSOR (1896–   )

For many years a typical photograph of the Duke and Duchess of Windsor showed each carrying a pug under one arm. Their dogs were much loved and an important part of their lives. After the death of the duke in 1972, two of the pugs—Gin-Seng and Black Diamond—were lonely and insisted on sleeping with the duchess, who remarked, "It is flattering to know that there are creatures who still want to share my bed."

THE 24 MOST POPULAR NAMES FOR CATS

Male	*Female*
1. Tiger or Tigger	1. Samantha
2. Smokey	2. Misty
3. Pepper	3. Patches
4. Max or Maxwell	4. Cali or Calico
5. Simon	5. Muffin
6. Snoopy	6. Angel or Angela
7. Morris	7. Ginger
8. Mickey	8. Tiger or Tigger
9. Rusty or Rusti	9. Princess
10. Boots or Bootsie	10. Punkin or Pumpkin
11. Charles or Charlie	11. Tabitha
12. Puff	12. Shadow

SOURCE: *Cat Fancy*, September, 1981.

10 THINGS TO TRY IN THE MATING SEASON

1. COMPOSTING

The male mallee fowl of Australia and New Guinea builds a mass of leaves to serve as an incubator once his mate lays her eggs. The female is then lured to the nest by the male's crooning sounds. When the eggs are laid, the male works frantically to maintain the optimum hatching temperature—adding more vegetation when the nest grows too cold, digging it up when it gets too hot.

2. EXHIBITIONISM

During the mating season, male squirrel monkeys exchange penile displays and urinate in each other's face. As aggression mounts, they pile on one another and fight violently. The behavior is not related to mating success but rather to a rearrangement of the dominance hierarchy. Male mandrill baboons give a red, white, and blue display of their colorful genital areas.

3. HOMOSEXUALITY

Lesbian mating is practiced by between 8% and 14% of the sea gulls on the Santa Barbara Islands, off the California coast. Lesbian gulls go through all the motions of mating, and they lay sterile eggs. Homosexual behavior is also known in geese, ostriches, cichlid fish, squid, rats, and monkeys.

4. MASTURBATION

Masturbation in the animal kingdom has been observed among deer, lions, apes, monkeys, moose, boars, porcupines, dolphins, and elephants (who use their trunks).

5. MATE-BEATING

The female rhinoceros may ram her bull before mating with him. Ocelots bite their partners around the face and head to stimulate mating. During copulation, nonvenemous snakes often bite their partners.

6. MATE-EATING

The female praying mantis may swallow her mate during the sexual act. (The male may continue to copulate after his head and thorax have been bitten off.) In many species of spiders, the female—the aptly named black widow, for example—eats her smaller male mate during or after copulation.

7. PRESENT-GIVING

The male Adelie penguin must select his mate from a colony of more than a million, and he indicates his choice by rolling a stone at the female's feet. Stones are scarce at mating time because many are needed to build walls around nests. It becomes commonplace for penguins to steal them from one another. If she accepts this gift, they stand belly to belly and sing a mating song.

8. SELF-ABORTION

Newly pregnant mice are biologically stimulated to abort by the scent of urine from a strange male. Rabbit does are known to internally dissolve the cells of their developing fetuses if proper nutrition and environment are not present.

9. SELF-IMPREGNATION (AND OTHER HERMAPHRODITIC GYMNASTICS)

Many species of animals and plants are hermaphroditic, that is, individuals possess both male and female sex organs. In most such animal species, including earthworms and snails, elaborate mating behaviors have evolved which preclude self-copulation. The hermaphroditic European sea hare mollusk, for example, mates in chains of three or more. The animal in front acts only as a female, while others act as males for those in front and females for those behind. Among the few hermaphrodites which self-fertilize are pulmonate mollusks; species of scale insect, perches, and darters; and two black bass species of the Black Sea.

10. TOTAL COLLAPSE

Exhaustion is the frequent fate of the male Uganda kob, an African antelope. Like many species of birds and mammals, the kob roams in a social group until the mating season, when the dominant male establishes a mating territory, or lek. But the females decide which territory they wish to enter and then pick the male they think most attractive. He then mates with all the females until he is too weak to continue (usually due to lack of food) and is replaced by another.

—D.L.

9 LARGE ANIMALS DISCOVERED BY WESTERN SCIENCE SINCE 1900

In 1812, the "Father of Paleontology," Baron Georges Cuvier, rashly pronounced that "there is little hope of discovering new species" of large animals and that naturalists should concentrate on extinct fauna. In 1819 the American tapir was discovered, and since then a long list of "new" animals have disproved Cuvier's dictum. Even within the present century rather astounding zoological finds have been announced, and the fact remains that other animals are out there waiting to be "found" by modern scientists.

The male Uganda kob: a mere sex object.

1. OKAPI

By saving a group of Congolese Pygmies from a German showman who wanted to take them to the 1900 Paris Exhibition, Sir Harry Johnston immediately gained their trust. He then began hearing stories about the okapi, a mule-sized animal with zebra stripes. In 1901, Sir Harry sent a whole skin, two skulls, and a detailed description of the okapi to London, and it was found that the okapi had a close relationship to the giraffe. In 1919 the first live okapi were brought out of the Congo River basin, and in 1941, the Stanleyville Zoo witnessed the first birth of an okapi in captivity. The okapis, striking in appearance, are now rare but popular attractions at the larger, more progressive zoological parks of the world.

2. MOUNTAIN NYALA

First discovered in the high mountains of southern Ethiopia in 1910, the mountain nyala remains a relatively unknown species. The male has gently twisting horns almost 4 ft. long and can weigh up to 450 lb. The coat is a majestically grayish-brown with white vertical stripes on the back. After it was first described by Richard Lydekker, the eminent British naturalist, it was ruthlessly hunted by field biologists and trophy seekers through some of the most inhospitable terrain in existence. The mountain nyala lives at heights above 9,000 ft., where the sun burns hotly in the day and the night temperatures fall to freezing. Its existence is presently threatened by illegal hunting.

3. PYGMY HIPPOPOTAMUS

Karl Hagenbeck, a famous German animal dealer, established a zoological garden near Hamburg that was the prototype of the modern open-air zoo. In 1909, Hagenbeck sent German explorer Hans Schomburgk to Liberia to check on rumors about a "giant black pig." After two years of jungle pursuit Schomburgk finally spotted the animal 30 ft. in front of him. It was big, shiny, and black, but the animal clearly was related to the hippopotamus, not the pig. Unable to catch it, he went home to Hamburg empty-handed. In 1912, Hans Schomburgk returned to Liberia, and to the dismay of his critics, came back with five live pygmy hippos. A full-grown pygmy hippopotamus weighs only about 400 lb., one tenth the weight of the average adult hippopotamus.

4. KOMODO DRAGON

These giant monitor lizards are named for the rugged volcanic island of Komodo, part of the Lesser Sunda Islands of Indonesia. Unknown to science until 1912, the Komodo dragon can be up to 12 ft. long and weigh over 350 lb. The discovery of the giant lizard was made by an airman who landed on Komodo island and brought back incredible stories of monstrous dragons eating goats, pigs and even attacking horses. At first no one believed him, but then the stories were confirmed by Major P. A. Ouwens, director of the Buitenzorg Botanical Gardens in Java, who offered skins and photographs as proof. Soon live specimens were caught and exhibited. The world's largest living lizard is now a popular zoo exhibit.

5. ANDEAN WOLF

The Andean wolf was identified from only one skin obtained by Karl Hagenbeck's son Lorenz, who had inherited his father's zoological business. The Hagenbeck find was made in 1926 when Lorenz bought one of four such skins shown him in Buenos Aires. It was from a large canine, said to be from the Andes. Finally in 1947, Dr. Ingo Krumbiegel of the Munich Museum reconstructed the animal from the skin and announced that it was a large blackish-brown-maned wolf more adapted for a cold climate than the pampas. Thus far, no living specimen of the Andean wolf has been caught.

6. CONGO PEACOCK

Some animal discoveries are made in museums. In 1913, the New York Zoological Society sent an unsuccessful expedition to the Congo in an attempt to bring back a live okapi. Instead one of the team's members, Dr. James P. Chapin, brought back some native headdresses with curious long reddish-brown feathers striped with black. None of the experts could identify them. In 1934, Chapin, on another of his frequent visits to the Congo, noticed similar feathers on two stuffed birds at the Tervueren Museum. They were labeled "Young Indian Peacocks," but Chapin immediately knew that was not what they were. As it turned out, a mining company in the Congo had donated them to the museum and labeled them "Indian peacocks," but Chapin soon discovered that they were a new species. The following year he flew down to the Congo and brought back seven birds. Chapin confirmed them as the first new bird genus discovered in 40 years. They were not peacocks after all, but pheasants. The Congo peacock is now commonly found in European and North American zoos.

7. KOUPREY

The most recent large animal to be discovered in Asia is found along the Mekong River in Cambodia and Laos and has been the source of much controversy. In 1937, the director of the Paris Vincennes Zoo, Professor Achille Urbain, went to North Cambodia and reported that a large wild ox, unlike the gaur and the banteng, was to be seen in Cambodia. Other naturalists felt he was wrong and suggested that the kouprey might be just a hybrid of the gaur and the banteng. Finally in 1961, a detailed anatomical study of the kouprey proved it to be so different from the area's other wild oxen that it might belong in a new genus. Urbain's 1937 discovery was upheld. The Vietnam War was responsible for killing many koupreys, and not more than 200 now exist in the wild. A 1975 New York Zoological Society expedition was unable to capture any, although they did see a herd of 50.

8. COELACANTH

This 5-ft.-long, 127-lb., large-scaled, steel-blue fish was brought up in a net off South Africa in December, 1938. The huge fish crawled around on deck for three hours before it died. The only problem was the coelacanth was supposed extinct for 60 million years. Ms. M. Courtenay-Latimer and ichthyologist James Smith of Rhodes University, South Africa, identified the coelacanth after it already was dead and had begun to decay. Professor Smith then began years of searching for a second living coelacanth and finally was rewarded in December, 1952, when a fishing trawler off the Cormores island of Anjouan, near Africa's east coast, brought up an excellent specimen. Dr. Smith was soon shocked to learn the local inhabitants of the Cormores had been catching and eating the "living fossils" for generations.

9. LONG-NOSED OR CHACOAN PECCARY

This "rangy big pig," as biology professor Dr. Ralph M. Wetzel of the University of Connecticut termed his 1975 discovery, was a big surprise, since it was a Pleistocene Epoch survivor—a species thought to have died out about 2 million years ago. The long-nosed peccary, a relative of pigs, boars, and warthogs, weighed in at over 100 lb. Wetzel found it in the wilds of Paraguay and stated that it differed from other known peccaries by its larger size; longer ears, snout, and legs; and proportionately shorter tail.

—L.C.

8 WORST MONSTER HOAXES

1. THE FEEJEE MERMAID

Phineas Taylor Barnum, master hoaxer, came into possession of the Feejee Mermaid in 1842. In an elaborate scheme to gain wide notoriety for the mermaid, Barnum mailed letters to the New York press from various locations announcing the wonderful discovery of a mermaid taken from the Feejee Islands and preserved in China. Barnum's well-thought-out plans were very successful, and great numbers of people came to his American Museum to pay 25¢ to see the dried, ugly specimen labeled *The Feejee Mermaid*. This single exhibit transformed the American Museum and P. T. Barnum into national institutions, according to Barnum biographer Irving Wallace. Later in his life, Barnum admitted the mermaid was a hoax, having been created by uniting the upper half of a monkey to the lower half of a fish.

2. THE SEA SERPENT OF SILVER LAKE

Perry, N.Y., is a quiet town 50 mi. south of Buffalo, and during the summer of 1855, A. W. Walker hatched a plan to bring in some business. With the help of some trustworthy friends, Walker constructed a 60-ft. serpent covered with waterproof canvas and worked from shore with a series of bellows and ropes. Soon fishermen, residents, and tourists were excitedly witnessing close encounters with the "most horrid and repulsive-looking monster" they had ever seen. A Vigilance Society was formed, armed men prowled the shores, and a tower was built at the north end of Silver Lake to combat the menace. Crowds came to see the beast—and stay in the hotels. The sightings tapered off in 1856. Then, in 1857, just before Walker House burned to the ground, firemen were amazed to find a giant sea monster in the hotel's attic. A. W. Walker took off to Canada. Today he is viewed as a hero, and an annual Sea Serpent Festival is still held in Perry, N.Y.

3. JEFFERIES'S JERSEY DEVIL

Since the mid-1700s, throughout the Pine Barrens of New Jersey, people have reported encounters with a mysterious winged creature. In January, 1906, a wave of sightings spread through eastern Pennsylvania and nearby New Jersey. Publicist Norman Jefferies "caught" the "Jersey Devil" and exhibited it at the Arch Street Museum in Philadelphia for 10¢ a peek. Jefferies's devil was in reality a kangaroo painted with green stripes and bronze wings attached by a rabbit-skin harness. It was set in a cage with previously gnawed bones. For years afterward, Jefferies made money selling the notion he was responsible for all the devil sightings.

4. DE LOYS'S APE

In 1920, François de Loys, a Swiss geologist, reported to the scientific world that while on an expedition into the Venezuelan jungle, he had met some apes. (Apes are not supposed to exist in South America.) These apes, De Loys stated, screamed wildly as they walked about upright. Then they defecated in their hands and hurled their excrement at the explorers. De Loys shot one of the primates, sat it on a box, and took his now famous (or infamous) photograph. *Ameranthropoides loysi,* as Professor Georges Montandon dubbed the "species" on the strength of this one photograph, was a crude hoax—a dead spider monkey perched on a wooden crate. De Loys said that he had removed the skull and preserved it in a box filled with salt so he would have proof of his zoological find. However, the skull of "the find of the century" quickly dried up and was lost bit by bit.

5. THE 1933 LOCH NESS MONSTER

In April, 1933, with the opening of a new road around Loch Ness, Scotland, the long series of "monster" sightings had their modern beginning. *The Daily Mail,* an important British newspaper of the time, launched an expedition. By late December, 1933, the expedition's big-game hunter had found some strange footprints on the loch's shore near Dores. The monster was declared genuine by the press. Plaster casts of its spoor were sent to the British Museum, and the bad news quickly came back. The tracks had been made by a dried hippopotamus foot, perhaps a Victorian umbrella stand from someone's front hall. The Loch Ness monster has been sighted many times since 1933 and has even been filmed. However, the mysterious creature continues to elude capture.

6. GIANT GRASSHOPPERS OF BUTTS ORCHARD

On Sept. 9, 1937, the following headline appeared on the front page of the *Tomah* (Wis.) *Monitor-Herald:* "Giant Grasshoppers Invade Butts Orchard East of City." The accompanying story gave details of the invasion. Apparently, after eating some special plant food that farmer A. L. Butts had sowed on his apple orchard, the grasshoppers grew to an astounding 3 ft. in length—large enough to snap off tree limbs as they leaped about the orchard. Along with the article, there were photographs of the mutant insects being hunted with shotguns. Because the story was continued on page four, many readers never got to the final paragraph, which suggested that it was all a put-on: "If there are those who doubt our story it will not be a new experience, inasmuch as most newspaper writers are thought to be the darndest liars in the world." The elaborate hoax was concocted by Mr. Butts and the *Monitor-Herald* publisher, B. J. Fuller.

7. THE KANGAROO TERROR OF TENNESSEE

Throughout the 1970s and early 1980s, the newest "monster" in America was the phantom kangaroo. Few people know that a famous 1934 hoax involved a giant kangaroo. In January of that year, there were accounts of a mysterious kangaroo that was killing dogs, geese, and ducks in the hills of Tennessee. The news spread to the dailies of New York City. As shotgun-toting farmers took to the fields, the New York City police wired they would send in reinforcements if needed. Later, Horace N. Minnis of South Pittsburg, Tenn.—a stringer for the *Chattanooga Times*—admitted perpetrating the hoax.

8. RANT MULLENS'S BIGFOOT

In May, 1982, 86-year-old Rant Mullens of Toledo, Wash., admit-

Hoaxster A. L. Butts holding a 3-foot grasshopper.

ted to being the father of "bigfoot." Although the huge apelike creature reported to inhabit the forests of the Pacific Northwest had for centuries been a fixture of Indian legends, it was the mischievous Mullens who fabricated the first hard evidence of the beast's existence. In 1928, forest ranger Mullens whittled a pair of oversized wooden feet, put them on, and stomped around the woods near Mt. St. Helens, leaving "bigfoot" prints to be discovered by hikers. Over the years, he carved six more pairs of big feet, and with the help of accomplices made tracks throughout the Northwest. "I tell you, people will believe just about anything," says Rant Mullens.

—L.C.

10 PERSONS WHO WOULD NOT KILL INSECTS

1. MAHAVIRA (599 B.C.–527 B.C.)

A contemporary of Buddha, he was a great prophet and teacher of Jainism, the religion in India that, by recent count, has 2.6 million followers. Mahavira practiced the doctrine of *ahimsa,* meaning nonviolence toward all living creatures. Except in winter, when he wore a robe, Mahavira went about naked. He would allow insects to crawl over him and bite him; removed all manner of vermin from his person and settled them in a shady and safe place; and draped a piece of cloth over his mouth to protect insect life and air life.

2. ST. FRANCIS OF ASSISI (1182–1226)

The son of a rich Italian merchant, he refused his inheritance to spend his life serving the poor. In 1224, he received the stigmata, bleeding from those places on his body where Christ had suffered his five sacred wounds. St. Francis loved the birds and all living creatures, insects among them. When someone caught a fish, he would throw it back into the water. When he walked, he would remove worms from his path. In winter, St. Francis served honey and wine to wild bees. Although he allowed trees to be trimmed, he would not allow one to be cut down. Yet, odd contradiction, St. Francis was not a vegetarian and for his daily fare he greatly relished pig's knuckles and chicken legs.

3. THOMAS DAY (1748–1789)

Day was a British author and social reformer. Raised to be kind to all animals, he respected the lives of insects. Although Day became a lawyer, he never practiced law. One day in 1775, he was having a conversation with a legal friend when the friend spotted a spider nearby and called out, "Day, kill that spider!" Studying the spider, Day replied, "No, I don't know that I have a right. Suppose that a superior being said to a companion, 'Kill that lawyer.' How should you like it? And a lawyer is more noxious to most people than a spider."

4. AMOS BRONSON ALCOTT (1799–1888)

The mystical American philosopher, educator, writer—whose daughter Louisa wrote *Little Women*—was a friend of Thoreau and Emerson. A gentle man, Alcott would not harm a mosquito or any insect. In fact, in his garden, he collected potato bugs, put them in a can, and carefully released them in his neighbor's yard.

5. JANE CLEMENS (1803–1890)

This American lady was notable for being the mother of Samuel Clemens, who gained worldwide renown as the author Mark Twain. Mrs. Clemens refused to kill flies, among other insects. When her pet cat caught and throttled mice, Mrs. Clemens punished the cat. She was even kindly toward ants. Her son, Mark Twain, saw no reason for this, stating that he had never "come across a living ant that seemed to have any more sense than a dead one."

6. LEO TOLSTOI (1828–1910)

For most of his life, the great Russian author of such enduring novels as *War and Peace* and *Anna Karenina* was a wealthy landowner whose passions were sex and hunting ("he killed game mercilessly," wrote his son Sergei). But around the age of 51, Tolstoi endured a crisis of conscience and faith and took up a belief in Christian anarchism. He gave up not only his property but also hunting and sex and became a believer in nonviolence as well as a strict vegetarian. (Tolstoi once tied a live chicken to his sister-in-law's dining room chair and gave her an ax to kill the animal if she wanted meat for dinner.) He renounced the slaughter of all living things, and presumably this vow included insects. When someone wrote to him that it was inconsistent to refuse to kill animals and yet to wear clothing made of fur and leather, Tolstoi replied, "You are quite right that since I renounce the deliberate killing of living creatures, I ought not use parts of their body for clothing. . . . I am so far away from perfection in my own life, not only in the matter of not using the bodies of creatures that have been killed but in many, many other far more important things too, that the efforts which I can direct towards improving my life in a moral sense first of all, I find it more expedient to direct towards correcting my many other failings."

7. PIERRE AUGUSTE RENOIR (1841–1919)

Among the greatest of French Impressionist painters, he avoided harming any living thing. Wrote Renoir's son, Jean, of him: "When he walked through the fields he would do a curious dance to avoid crushing a dandelion. He believed that in destroying an ant one might be upsetting the balance of a whole empire. . . . Renoir always dreamed of a world in which neither animals nor plants had been harmed by man's needs."

8. SHRIMAD RAJACHANDRA (1867–1900)

A short-lived philosopher and writer, he was considered a saint and was the most beloved modern leader of Jainism in India. Later, Mahatma Gandhi looked up to him as a guru. Rajachandra would allow flies, gnats, and other insects to assault him, crawl over him, and not harm them. When he received food infested with insects, he would remove the insects without hurting them. He defended disease germs, insisting that they had been spawned by humans' unsanitary habits and that humans should be sentenced to 10,000 years in hell.

9. MOHANDAS K. (MAHATMA) GANDHI (1869–1948)

Of course, Gandhi was world-renowned for his belief in *ahimsa,* a general policy of nonviolence toward all living things. This Indian political and spiritual leader would not extinguish the life of mosquitoes, scorpions, or snakes. When a poisonous snake appeared in his ashram, Gandhi would pick it up with tongs and free it in a nearby field. Once a snake slithered onto his ankle. He shook it free but apologized because his reaction had not been entirely nonviolent. Gandhi would never pluck fruit from a tree—since that gesture might indicate a minor act of violence—but always gathered fruit after it had fallen to the ground.

140

10. ALBERT SCHWEITZER (1875–1965)

This German genius held doctorates in medicine, theology, philosophy, and music. An authority on the organ, Schweitzer wrote books on Bach and Jesus. Schweitzer was most celebrated for the hospital he established in the heart of French Equatorial Africa (later Gabon). His personality was contradictory. Both a humanitarian and a healer, he was also dictatorial, egotistical, and cranky. The winner of the 1952 Nobel Peace Prize espoused a philosophic reverence for life. He grew up refusing to catch fish or shoot birds and would not harm an animal or step on a flower. Still, his attitude was inconsistent. When he and his wife first moved into their African bungalow and found it infested with cockroaches and spiders, Schweitzer destroyed them all to make his home habitable. British gossips reported that he once kicked a rooster preying on his corn crops. Yet rather than swat a mosquito, he would put it out of his house. When his wife trapped some rats, he set them free. While an operating room was being built for his hospital, he held up construction until an ant's nest could be removed. Schweitzer even favored allowing fever bacillus to survive. As he explained to a visiting journalist, "The important thing is that man should be humane to all living things. He should never take the smallest life, say a fly on this table, without regret and compassion."

—I.W.

16 ANIMALS KILLED FOR THEIR FUR

Behind the silky luster of every luxurious fur coat is the ugly fact that each animal sewn into its elegant lines suffered hours of agony and terror before it was finally killed in the name of fashion.

Fur-bearing animals have long endured a holocaust that grows worse each year. More than 303 million of the world's animals were killed for their fur in the trapping season of 1977–1978; over 18 million of these deaths occurred in the U.S. alone. Species slaughtered nearly to extinction have become even more valuable as pelts, ironically driving up the demand for the skins—and lives—of the few creatures who remain.

In the 1977–1978 season, 211,133 beaver, 587,082 foxes, 2,058 lynx, 255,017 wild mink, 3 million ranched mink, 958,868 opossum, and 3,805,510 raccoons were killed for their fur. Consider these average figures for a woman's fur coat:

1. If you have a beaver coat, you are wearing 15 dead beavers.
2. If you have a bobcat coat, you are wearing 11 dead bobcats.
3. If you have a chinchilla coat, you are wearing 60–100 dead chinchillas.
4. If you have an ermine coat, you are wearing 150 dead ermines.
5. If you have a fox coat, you are wearing 15–25 dead foxes.
6. If you have a leopard coat, you are wearing 4–5 dead leopards.
7. If you have a lynx coat, you are wearing 10 dead lynx.
8. If you have a mink coat, you are wearing 35–65 dead mink.
9. If you have a muskrat coat, you are wearing 60 dead muskrats.

It takes 35 to 65 minks to make a mink coat.

10. If you have an ocelot coat, you are wearing 12–25 dead ocelots.
11. If you have an opossum coat, you are wearing 25 dead opossum.
12. If you have a raccoon coat, you are wearing 20–40 dead raccoons.
13. If you have a river otter coat, you are wearing 18 dead river otters.
14. If you have a sable coat, you are wearing 45–60 dead sables.
15. If you have a Swakara lamb coat, you are wearing 28–30 dead Swakara lambs.
16. If you have a tiger coat, you are wearing 3–10 dead tigers.

—K.P.

142

13 GROUPS OF ANIMALS USED FOR LABORATORY RESEARCH IN THE U.S.

Mice	13,413,813*
Rats	4,358,766*
Rabbits	473,922
Birds	450,352*
Guinea pigs	432,632
Hamsters	397,522
Dogs	188,649
Swine	104,769*
Cats	58,090
Primates	57,515
Wild animals	50,111
Cattle and horses	26,897*
Sheep and goats	12,610*

Figures marked * are for 1978; all others are for 1981.

SOURCES: Institute of Laboratory Animals Resources and Animal and Plant Health Inspection Service.

CLEVELAND AMORY'S 10 COUNTRIES THAT ARE THE CRUELEST TO ANIMALS

The widely syndicated columnist and radio commentator is passionately concerned with the well-being of animals. He is founder and president of The Fund for Animals. Amory's latest books are *Animail* and *The Trouble with Nowadays: A Curmudgeon Strikes Back*.

1. JAPAN

Although the annual slaughter of dolphins off Iki island was recently halted by the combined efforts of The Fund for Animals and The Sea Shepherd Conservation Society, virtually everything Japan does, from the continued slaughter of whales to their treatment of laboratory animals, is on the low end of the cruelty totem pole.

2. TAIWAN

The Taiwanese enjoy pitting all kinds of animals against each other in fights to the death. Among the more exotic—snakes against hawks. They especially prize preparing fish which are cooked *and eaten* alive.

3. INDONESIA

For the "sacrifices" on the island of Bali alone, this country rates a low marking. There, the people gather one of every species of animal on the island, haul them to an appointed spot and, in a Stone Age ritual, cruelly butcher them.

4. THE PHILIPPINES

They eat dogs—not as a relatively inexpensive meat, but for a gourmet cocktail dish. Although the trade is illegal and attempts are being made to stop it, the dogs are still unbelievably cruelly confined before the slaughter—crammed into cages and, in the boiling sun, often left without water or food for five days. They are then slaughtered on top of the cages, with live dogs still underneath.

5. SYRIA

The treatment of camels and donkeys, awful in all Arab countries, is particularly awful here. Only among the Druse Arabs is the situation remotely better. Unfortunately, the reason is not because the Druse are kinder but because they believe in the transmigration of souls—i.e., the camel might be your grandmother or you might come back as a donkey.

6. EGYPT

The treatment of horses, outrageous in so many countries, is particularly evident here—albeit Egypt is no prize with donkeys, camels, or dogs.

7. UGANDA

This country, ironically since Amin, has probably the worst record in Africa for the unchecked poaching of elephants and rhinos for tusks and horns (the latter thought to be aphrodisiacs), as well as for the brutal snaring of other animals and the general destruction of its once magnificent parks for animals.

8. SPAIN

The bullfight alone, a barbaric relic of the old bull- and bear-baiting events, sets this country's cruelty tone. Even if you do not care about the bull, regularly tampered with in the chute before the fight, you should care about the picador's horses. They wear blinders on the side from which the bull will charge, they are drugged, and their vocal cords are cut. As for the supposed padding which they also wear, remember the bull easily gets underneath it, and it has never been favored, in any case, by the Spaniards. It was instituted only to "avoid offending the sensitivities of the tourists."

9. MEXICO

The bullfight is here, if anything, worse than in Spain. And, again, this ethic spreads to other animals, particularly stray dogs. One sight I have never forgotten is that of Mexicans dragging stray dogs into the ocean to see how far they could swim and how long it would take them to drown. Of course, I also have seen Mexican children walk for literally miles, barefoot, bringing their own beloved mongrels to a clinic for a free rabies shot.

10. CANADA

The annual clubbing to death and sometimes skinning alive of some 180,000 infant harp seals off the Magdalene Islands and the coast of Newfoundland is probably the most infamous cruelty in the world—since it involves the killing of a baby beside its mother who, on the ice, is powerless to defend it. Heavily subsidized by the Canadian government, benefiting very few people except the big shippers and the Norwegians, it's all not even for a fur coat but for the lining of a jacket or glove or, most ironically, to make a stuffed animal.

—Exclusive for *The Book of Lists 3*

12 LAWS NEEDED TO PROTECT ANIMALS IN THE UNITED STATES

1. CESSATION OF THE KILL OF MARINE MAMMALS (Federal)

The Marine Mammal Protection Act of 1972 prohibited the "take" of marine mammals (defined broadly by the act as including harassing, hunting, capturing, or killing any marine mammal or attempting to do so) except as permitted by the secretaries of the Commerce and Interior depts. This "loophole" has permitted the bureaucracy to give classic vent to protection of the exploiters rather than the animals. Broad permits have been issued to "take" the mammals incidental to fishing, a process which is rendering various species endangered. The Congress must be called upon to take responsibility by amending this law to prohibit entirely the "take" of marine mammals. Long-term environmental effects must legally be held to take precedence over short-term economic profits.

2. TO DIMINISH HUNTING (Federal)

"Sport hunting" in the conterminous 48 states is entirely dependent upon habitat manipulation—burning and clear-cutting of forests to increase populations of deer, and flooding of land to attract migratory birds for convenient shooting. Such single-species "management" is dangerous to the sensitive interrelationships of animals and habitat and serves to render extinct the "nongame" animals whose food and habitat are eliminated. The funding for such habitat manipulation is known as the Pittman-Robertson Act, which accords to states for this purpose (and for training youngsters to hunt) the excise taxes on guns, ammunition, bows, and arrows. These monies should be put back in the general treasury, and expenditures for wildlife management, including habitat manipulation, should be terminated.

3. ANIMALS IN EXPERIMENTATION (Federal)

"Social lag"—the failure of human patterns of behavior to keep up with technological advance—is classic and nowhere more severe than in the field of research methodology. A whole spectrum of nonanimal methods of teaching, testing, and conducting research is available but little used. Universities and private industries, reliant upon government funding programs, have been denied academic freedom to pursue nonanimal research programs because Congress consigns authority for funding to the National Institutes of Health and the Depts. of Agriculture and Health—and those groups in turn grant money primarily to animal experimentation research. The torture of some 100 million animals per year and the waste of about $1.8 billion in tax funds is primarily attributable to federal law. The Congress must realize its responsibility and force the use of nonanimal research methods by redesignation of funding.

4. WILD ANIMALS MUST BE BARRED FROM INTERSTATE COMMERCE (Federal)

American institutions which subject wildlife to sustained torture and unnatural conditions are the zoos, research laboratories, and private "game" ranches which specialize in guaranteed kills of pen-raised species, both native and foreign (exotic). These groups collaborate to expand the gene pool of various species under the guise of saving endangered species, when in fact the aim is to save the jobs of the people involved and the profit of game ranchers. They trade live animals for breeding purposes, trade the progeny, and overall, warp the animal from a wild, free-roaming creature into an exploited domestic species. With a ban on shipment in interstate commerce, this exploitation can be brought to a halt.

5. HORSE SLAUGHTER (Federal)

There are far more horses in the nation today than there were when the horse was the normal mode of transportation. This is due to the ever-increasing phenomenon of horse racing. One of the major cruelties which must be solved is the fate of the "losers," which are currently trucked to Canada and shipped to Europe, where they are killed and eaten by those who consider horsemeat as digestible as lamb. On the basis that it's better to die quickly than to be subjected to hours and days of fear and abuse, an amendment to the federal Livestock Slaughter Act of 1958 is needed to require states to maintain and/or supervise horse slaughter within close proximity to racetracks.

6. PUPPY MILLS (Federal)

The mass production of puppies in the Midwest to be sold at great profits in metropolitan areas is a business engendering cruelty. To maximize profits the dogs are given minimal attention, female dogs are subjected to lifelong confinement and accelerated reproductive schedules, and puppies are born with genetic defects and health disorders due to overbreeding.

The passage of our model bill to license hobby breeders within a state at about $\frac{1}{10}$ the license required of an out-of-state breeder would effectively render it economically impossible for the Midwest puppy mills to sell in metropolitan areas.

Another model bill hits the bottom line, entitled "net profit," by requiring those selling animals to be responsible for the health of the animal and veterinary costs for a period of 60 days from the date of sale.

7. FACTORY FARMING (Federal)

The production of animals for meat and dairy products has become a profit-maximizing endeavor of major proportions. Intensive "farming" of animals in overcrowded, inhumane conditions requiring heavy doses of hormones and antibiotics to combat diseases has become the norm.

Raising animals in total isolation, darkness, and confinement should be outlawed immediately, and the most cruel practices associated with factory farming such as battery cages for egg-laying hens, debeaking, and docking tails of sheep and pigs should be stopped.

An amendment to the federal Livestock Slaughter Act of 1958 should be proposed which would ban the interstate shipment of animals and products from animals which have been raised in unnaturally confined conditions.

8. BANNING THE LEGHOLD TRAP (Federal and State)

It is past time to ban all trapping. All of it is nonselective (takes all species, female as well as male), and all of it is fantastically cruel, subjecting animals to a slow, torturous death. At the federal and state levels, a first step is to ban the leghold trap; it is the trap most frequently used in the U.S. and has been banned by 63 nations of the world (more than one third of all nations). The federal bill calls for a ban on the interstate shipment of furs by any state or nation which has failed to ban this trap, thereby forcing the states to enact the needed law. We also urge local government to clarify their right to ban *all* trapping within municipal boundaries either to protect wildlife or public safety.

9. ANTICRUELTY STATUTES (State)

A major void in animal protection exists in current state anticruelty laws, almost all of which are over 100 years old. These statutes regard domestic animals as "property" and address the issue with unenforceable and ambiguous verbiage such as "unnecessary suffering." A new approach has been compiled in the form of concern for animal rights, and this first draft of model state legislation is proposed for devil's advocacy by legislatures, lawyers, and law schools. A copy is available for $2.00 from the Committee for Humane Legislation, 11 West 60th Street, New York, N.Y. 10023.

10. INSTIGATION OF ANIMAL FIGHTS (State)

The fact that some humans find pleasure in watching animals (e.g., pit bulldogs or cocks) tear each other to shreds speaks of the insensitivity *Homo sapiens* show to other species. Dog fighting and cock fighting should be outlawed immediately, and in those states where it is already illegal, the classification of the crime of participating in or instigating an animal fight should be raised to a felony.

11. HABITAT PRESERVATION (State)

The exploding human population, both through the birth rate and illegal immigration, must be contained if wildlife is not to lose its habitat

147

through suburban and industrial sprawl. Commissions composed of such experts as demographers, urban planners, naturalists, environmentalists, etc., must be pressed into action by the states to study land-use patterns. Laws must be enacted to preserve wildlife's habit and to integrate the need for natural habitats with the increasing urban sprawl and the complexity of human life-styles. The preservation of forest and open space is essential to the preservation of life, both human and animal.

12. RODEO (State)

The centerpiece of attraction is the bucking-bronco act. Tame, domestic animals are agitated into the advertised "wild horse" frenzy by the placement and tightening of bucking straps in the area of the genitalia and intestines. A ban on the bucking strap would effectively end this act and put rodeos out of business as an entertainment spectacle—thereby sparing calves, steers, and other animals from being harassed, thrown to the ground, and suffering broken legs and horns.

SOURCE: Friends of Animals, 11 West 60th Street, New York, N.Y. 10023.

7
LET'S GO—TRAVEL AND TRANSPORTATION

JAN MORRIS'S 10 MOST FASCINATING CITIES IN THE WORLD

As James Morris, this British journalist traveled throughout the world as special correspondent for the *London Times*. Praised for his "sensuous descriptive prose," Morris developed his experiences into a number of books, including *The World of Venice* and *Cities*. In 1973 Morris became a woman after a sex-change operation in Morocco. She is currently working on *Pax Britannica,* a three-volume study of the British Empire.

1. New York
2. London
3. Venice
4. Cairo
5. Istanbul
6. Rio de Janeiro
7. Chicago
8. Delhi
9. Paris
10. Beirut

—Exclusive for *The Book of Lists 3*

THOR HEYERDAHL'S 10 PLACES IN THE WORLD HE'D LIKE TO GO BACK TO

The Norwegian explorer, ethnologist, and author has led scientific expeditions throughout the world. His 1947 best seller, *Kon-Tiki,* is the story of his journey across the Pacific on a balsa raft to prove the possibility of early contact between ancient Peru and Polynesia. Two decades later he crossed the Atlantic on a boat made of papyrus. Heyerdahl now lives in a small village in Italy.

1. Fatu-Hiva in the Marquesas group
2. Easter Island
3. Kwatna Bay in British Columbia
4. The reed marshes of southern Iraq

Fatu-Hiva.

5. Lake Zwai in Ethiopia
6. Lake Titicaca in Peru and Bolivia
7. Lake Chad in Central Africa
8. San Agustín in Colombia
9. Luxor in Egypt
10. The Rondane Mountains of Norway

—Exclusive for *The Book of Lists 3*

8 COUNTRIES MOST OFTEN VISITED BY THE VIRGIN MARY

Between 1928 and 1975, there were 232 reported visitations by the Virgin Mary (fairly well authenticated, but not recognized by the Catholic Church) in 32 different countries. In that almost half-century period, where was the Virgin Mary seen most frequently?

Country	No. of Times Seen
1. Italy	83
2. France	30
3. Germany	20
4. Belgium	17
5. Spain	12
6. United States	9
7. Canada	6
8. Switzerland	5

SOURCE: Dom Bernard Billet, J. M. Alonso, and René Laurentin, *Vraies et Fausses Apparitions dans l'Église*. Paris: Lethielleux, 1976.

THE 6 SMALLEST COUNTRIES ON EARTH

1. VATICAN CITY Size: .16 sq. mi. Population: 750.
   Location: Rome, Italy.

   The size of a golf course, the Vatican City became the smallest independent country in the world in 1929. Ruled by the pope and a committee of three cardinals, its dimensions may be miniscule but its power is immense. As the seat of the Roman Catholic Church, its constituency consists of 550 million followers. The main buildings are St. Peter's Basilica, largest church in the world covering 163,200 sq. ft. (to Notre Dame's 64,100), and the Vatican Palace, largest residence on earth with 1,400 rooms and 200 staircases. The Vatican's great library has 60,000 ancient manuscripts, and the Vatican Palace contains priceless artworks by Da Vinci, Raphael, and Titian. The ceiling of the Sistine Chapel was done by Michelangelo while lying on his back on a mattress suspended beneath the ceiling for four years. These treasures are protected by 100 Swiss Guards (armed with medieval spears and automatic pistols and attired in uniforms made by the Brooks Costume Company) and 150 Italian police. The Vatican once contained four hard-drink bars (now there is one) and a kosher kitchen. This nation, without a single street address, has a pharmacy (that sells rum), a filling station, a railway depot (but no train), an international newspaper, a modern radio station (reaching almost every country in the world with programs in nearly 30 languages). The Vatican issues its own passports, citizenship papers, airmail stamps (although it has no airport), its own coins (one bore the portrait of a pope and the motto, "This is the root of all evil"). The Vatican is an ecclesiastical paradise—there are no taxes.

2. MONACO Size: .4 sq. mi. Population: 28,000. Location: French Riviera on the Mediterranean.

The second smallest sovereign state in the world is half the size of New York City's Central Park. The Grimaldi family has ruled Monaco for over 670 years. According to a treaty made with France in 1918, Monaco can lose its independence to France if it does not have a male ruler. When the current ruler, Prince Rainier III, took over, he was a bachelor, and most Monegasques were gloomy about Monaco's future as a sovereign state. But then the prince found a bride, Hollywood actress Grace Kelly, in 1956, and the marriage produced a male heir two years later. The big attraction in Monaco, besides the Royal Palace and its 300 rooms, is the ornate gambling casino at Monte Carlo (one ceiling bears a painting of beautiful nude women smoking cigars). Only one sixth of the population is native; the rest of the people are French, Italian, Belgian, Swiss, or English. The citizens are not allowed to enter the casino, but they can derive pleasure from the fact that they do not pay income taxes. Corporations are drawn to Monaco because they too are tax-exempt. Besides Grace Kelly, the most legendary figures in Monaco history are Sergei Diaghilev, who founded the Ballet Russe, and Charles Wells, "the man who broke the bank" at Monte Carlo.

3. NAURU Size: 8 sq. mi. Population: 8,000.
Location: Western Pacific Ocean.

Nauru, which became independent in 1968, has one of the highest per-capita incomes in the world. Its wealth comes from bird droppings. These droppings, rich in phosphate, are exported to Australia, New Zealand, and Japan. Phosphate deposits are expected to be depleted by the 1990s, but happily current profits are invested in Australian trust funds to support the people in the distant future. Nauru was discovered by an American whaler in 1798. For years there was much internal strife on the island among tribes inflamed by drinking alcoholic palm wine. During W.W. II, the Japanese occupied the island and sent 1,200 Nauruans into forced labor camps. Australians freed the island in 1945. Today, half the inhabitants are native Micronesians, most are Christians, all are educated in English to the age of 17, and none pay taxes. The government, a democratic republic, is financed entirely by bird droppings.

4. TUVALU Size: 9 sq. mi. Population: 7,500. Location: South Pacific.

Tuvalu consists of nine low-lying tropical atolls. Originally it was sighted by the Spanish in 1568. The early population was 20,000, but after slavers raided it between 1850 and 1875, the population was reduced to 3,000 persons. Gradually, the British took over Tuvalu, then known as the Ellice Islands, and combined it with the nearby Gilbert Islands, making both a British crown colony in 1915. However, the Ellice Islanders, who were mostly Polynesian, did not like being grouped with the Gilbert Islanders, who were Micronesian. So the Ellice Islanders broke with the Gilberts, and in 1978 they formed an independent state known as Tuvalu. Today, a leading industry is fishing. Life seems ideal. There is no robbery or violence. Tipping and public drinking are not allowed. Wild animals and poisonous insects do not exist.

5. SAN MARINO Size: 24 sq. mi. Population: 19,000.
   Location: North-central Italy near Adriatic coast.

San Marino, 125 miles north of Rome, was founded in the fourth century A.D. and is the world's oldest republic. Once a pope asked, "What does your motto, 'Liberty,' mean?" and a leader of San Marino replied, "It means that we belong to ourselves, that we owe no homage to anyone among ourselves, only to the Master of all things." Conquerors have coveted it. Caesar Borgia took it for a month in 1503, and Cardinal Alberoni took it for a month in 1739. Napoleon refused to take it at all. "Why, it's a model republic!" he exclaimed. When San Marino made Abraham Lincoln an honorary citizen, he wrote its leaders that San Marino proved "that government founded on republican principles is capable of being so administered as to be secure and enduring." George Sand praised the country as an asylum for the oppressed, and indeed San Marino gave refuge to people on the run like Giuseppe Garibaldi, leader of Italy's independence movement, in 1849. During W.W. I, San Marino sided with the Allies and lost two soldiers. During W.W. II, German Nazis occupied the country, which was bombed by Allied planes, killing 63 people. The nation is ruled by an elected Council of 60 (each member serving five years), which appoints a Congress and two captains regent (each serving six months) to administer governmental affairs. Today, a communist-socialist coalition controls the country. Women may vote but cannot hold office. The full-time army consists of 80 soldiers. The greatest source of income is the sale of postage stamps.

6. LIECHTENSTEIN Size: 61 sq. mi. Population: 27,000.
   Location: Between Switzerland and Austria.

This constitutional monarchy, the size of Washington, D.C., one third located in the Rhine Valley, two thirds in the Alps, became an independent nation in 1866. Its capital is Vaduz, a city of 4,600 persons. After W.W. II, the country changed from an agricultural to an industrial nation (although there are still 2.6 cows there per person). With a booming economy, there is no unemployment and low taxes. Liechtenstein exports everything from machinery, precision instruments, glass for space capsules, and textiles to false teeth (the world's biggest supplier), sun-

San Marino.

glasses, and sewing machine needles. It is also a big dealer in fancy stamps. One third of the work force is foreign. Because Liechtenstein offers a favorable tax structure ($10,000 taxes on $10 million holdings—that is, .1 percent—no taxes on interest), over 30,000 international corporations are based there, including Lockheed Aircraft; Synanon Foundation; and ICW Trust, which sold Soviet arms to African guerrillas. The nation's three banks have 3 billion Swiss francs on deposit. Many of these deposits are from U.S. tax evaders and bribe takers, handled by 65 Liechtenstein lawyers who reveal nothing to the U.S. Internal Revenue Service. Says one of these lawyers, "Paying bribes is something entirely normal, and it has been a standard procedure in the world for the last 2,000 years." The most famous royal ruler was Prince Johann, whose reign from 1858 to 1929 covered the terms of 16 U.S. presidents (Buchanan and Lincoln to Harding and Coolidge, through the election of Hoover). Johann paid the taxes of all his citizens for 71 years. His suc-

154

cessor, Franz I, kept his residence in Vienna and ruled Liechtenstein by telephone. The present-day sovereign is Prince Franz Josef II, the first ruler to live inside the country. He and a parliament of 15, elected by male suffrage, hold sway over 11 communes, with order maintained by a 30-man police force. There is no army, no military budget. There is no inflation. The citizens speak a German dialect, and most are Catholic.

—I.W.

5 FORBIDDEN AREAS

1. BADUI INNER VILLAGES

On 14,000 acres of mountainous land in western Java live approximately 4,000 Badui tribesmen. The Outer Badui (Badui Luar) form a protective circle around the Inner Badui (Badui Dalam), who inhabit three villages in the tribe's southernmost region. No one—not even a Badui Luar—may settle on the Badui Dalam's land. Ritual restrictions forbid Badui Dalam to cultivate cash crops, fertilize the soil, eat four-legged beasts, or domesticate any animals except chickens. Their medicines are restricted to herbal preparations which they themselves make. The Badui Dalam are considered a very powerful people, and they are consulted occasionally by Javanese politicians on matters of national importance.

2. MECCA

Every year nearly two million devout Muslims make their way to this most holy of Islamic cities, 45 mi. inland from the Red Sea in southwestern Saudi Arabia, where Mohammed was born. Pilgrims must observe certain restrictions. They are not allowed to clip their nails, cut their hair, raise their voices in anger, or engage in sexual activity. Within the sacred territory around Mecca, no animals may be hunted. Mecca has a resident population of over 300,000, all of them Muslims because nonbelievers are strictly forbidden. Sir Richard Burton, a nonbeliever, disguised himself as an Arab (he even had himself circumcised) to visit Mecca successfully in 1853. He was one of a handful of non-Muslims to manage the feat. The city of Medina, where Mohammed fled in 622, is also off limits to anyone who does not profess the Muslim faith.

3. MOUNT ATHOS

The most sacred spot in the Eastern Orthodox faith, Athos is a 30-mi.-long, heavily wooded peninsula in northern Greece, with the Holy Mountain itself near the southern tip. It has been a monastic republic for a millennium. The Virgin Mary reputedly spent the last years of her life on Athos, but since that time the peninsula has been forbidden to all women, with the prohibition even extending to female animals. Although Greeks may cross the border whenever they choose, outside tourism is strongly discouraged, partly because the crumbling monasteries can provide little in the way of accommodations. A maximum of 10 male foreigners are allowed in per day, and their stay is limited to four days each.

4. NORTH SENTINEL ISLAND

North Sentinel is one of the more than 200 islands that make up the Andaman Islands group in the Bay of Bengal, between India and Burma. Of the nearly 115,000 people who live in the Andamans, only 600 are original islanders—remnants of a race of pygmies who once populated much of Southeast Asia and Oceania. The 150 tribesmen who inhabit the 20 sq. mi. of North Sentinel have had a reputation for fierceness throughout recorded history. The seas around the island are dangerous, and the Stone Age Sentinelese greet visitors with bows and arrows. There is no need to forbid tourists officially; even anthropologists leaving gifts for the Sentinelese have been unable to make contact with them.

5. STAPHORST

The Dutch Calvinist town of Staphorst, situated 120 mi. northeast of Amsterdam, has changed little since the 16th century. Although tourists are grudgingly tolerated, they are forbidden by law to take pictures. This prohibition is enforced most rigidly on Friday nights, when the young women of the village discreetly entertain their lovers, and on Sundays, when the quaintly costumed villagers form long processions to and from church. The village is difficult to find (there are no signs for it on the highway), and if you should by chance offend a villager you are likely to be pelted with mud and harried out of town.

—F.B.

25 AIRLINES RANKED BY NUMBER OF PASSENGER COMPLAINTS

The major categories of complaints were: flight problems (22.1% of the total), baggage (21.8%), and customer service (11.3%).

Airline	*Complaints per 100,000 Passengers (1981)*
1. Southwest	.82
2. Delta	.88
3. Hawaiian	1.34

4. Piedmont	1.39
5. Republic West	1.75
6. Frontier	1.85
7. Ozark	1.99
8. Western	2.06
9. Aloha	2.06
10. PSA	2.11
11. United	2.27
12. Eastern	2.44
13. Continental	2.77
14. Republic	2.77
15. Northwest	2.78
16. US Air	2.89
17. American	2.91
18. TWA	6.51
19. Pan Am	8.78
20. Imperial	17.01
21. Evergreen	21.66
22. World	22.56
23. Rocky Mountain	24.73
24. Golden Gate	29.01
25. Capitol	34.87

SOURCE: Civil Aeronautics Board.

THE 10 BEST PLACES TO HITCHHIKE

Larry Evans, coauthor of *Hey Now, Hitchhikers!* (with his brother Don Evans) estimates he has hitchhiked about 100,000 mi.—since 1979. Often those rides have taken him to a variety of jobs, from tree planter to cook. The Evans brothers were curious about ride-thumbing customs throughout North America, so in 1980 they drew up a questionnaire for distribution to 10,000 hitchhikers. Nearly 1,000 people mailed back their answers. Larry and Don tabulated the data on the University of Montana's computers and found that they had enough interesting and informative material to write a book. Based on length of time it took to get a ride, here are the best and the worst hitchhiking locations. Their facts are direct from the source—the people who have stood on roadsides throughout the U.S. and Canada, waiting for a ride.

1. 101, Oregon–Northern California
2. I-87, Albany–Montreal
3. I-5 through Oregon
4. I-95, Boston–Washington, D.C.
5. I-55/I-57, Chicago–New Orleans

6. I-40/I-44, St. Louis–Flagstaff, Ariz.
7. 285, Taos, N.M.–Colorado
8. I-70, St. Louis–Pennsylvania
9. I-35, Des Moines–Duluth
10. I-80 through Midwest

SOURCE: Larry and Don Evans, *Hey Now, Hitchhikers!* St. Louis, Mo.: Peace Institute Printing, 1982.

THE 10 WORST PLACES TO HITCHHIKE

1. Salt Lake City
2. North Ontario
3. Western Arizona–eastern California
4. New Jersey Turnpike
5. West Texas
6. Northern British Columbia
7. Richmond, Va.
8. Seattle Wash., heading south
9. Northern Ohio
10. Nevada

SOURCE: Larry and Don Evans, *Hey Now, Hitchhikers!* St. Louis, Mo.: Peace Institute Printing, 1982.

PEDESTRIAN DEATHS IN 17 COUNTRIES

Approximately 8,000 pedestrians lose their lives in traffic accidents every year in the U.S.

Country	Pedestrian Fatalities per 100,000 Population
1. Hungary	6.6
2. Yugoslavia	6.4
3. West Germany	6.1
4. Austria	5.9
5. Denmark	5.6

5. Finland	5.6
7. France	5.1
7. Poland	5.1
9. United Kingdom	4.2
10. United States	4.0
11. Italy	3.8
12. Greece	3.7
13. Canada	3.6
13. Norway	3.6
13. Spain	3.6
16. Netherlands	2.8
17. Japan	2.6

SOURCE: Arthur C. Wolfe and James O'Day, *Factbook on U.S. Pedestrian Accidents.* Ann Arbor, Mich.: Highway Safety Research Institute, University of Michigan, February, 1981.

THE 7 MOST UNFRIENDLY AND THE 7 FRIENDLIEST FREIGHT YARDS IN THE U.S.

Edward W. McLane, who has crisscrossed America many times by hopping freight trains, is currently writing *The Hobo's Handbook,* a manual for would-be knights of the road. He finds that most freight yards are wonderful places for meeting nice people and finding a free ride. There are some, however, that make life more difficult for the hobo. In sharing with us the following lists, he hopes to "aid the wary train rider in avoiding the railroad bulls (police) that plague the habitual hobo."

MOST UNFRIENDLY

1. Cheyenne, Wyo. (Union Pacific)
2. Jacksonville, Fla. (Seaboard Coast Line)
3. Tyler, Tex. (Cotton Belt)
4. Pocatello, Ida. (Union Pacific)
5. Lincoln, Neb. (Burlington Northern)
6. Buffalo, N.Y. (Conrail)
7. Minneapolis (Northtown Yards), Minn. (Burlington Northern)

FRIENDLIEST

1. Minot, N.D. (Burlington Northern)
2. Cleveland, O. (Conrail)
3. Milwaukee, Wis. (Milwaukee Road)

4. Nashville, Tenn. (Louisville and Nashville)
5. Spokane, Wash. (Burlington Northern)
6. Cumberland, Md. (Chessie System)
7. Evansville, Ind. (Louisville and Nashville)

—Exclusive for *The Book of Lists 3*

8
WORDS FOR THE WISE—
COMMUNICATIONS

KERMIT SCHAFER'S
20 FAVORITE BLOOPERS

Using as his motto, "To err is divine," multimedia producer Kermit Schafer created a successful business out of human error. Starting in the 1930s, he began collecting slips of the tongue that he heard on the radio. He soon published his first collection of bloopers, titled *Your Slip is Showing*. His last book, *Blooper Tube*, appeared in 1980, the year after Schafer's death. Once asked if people became angry when he pointed out their mistakes, Schafer replied, "For the most part, their feelings are best summed up in the immortal words of Mark Twain, 'I am never more tickled than when I laugh at myself.'"

1. HARRY VON ZELL: "Ladies and gentlemen, the president of the United States, Hoobert Heever."

2. STATION PROMO: "Stay tuned for Charles Dickens's immortal classic, *A Sale of Two Titties*."

3. FOOTBALL COMMENTATOR: "Anderson has injured his nose. It looks like the same nose he injured last year."

4. ANNOUNCER (introducing the great banjoist Eddie Peabody): "Ladies and gentlemen: Mr. Eddie Playbody will now pee for you."

5. COOKING SHOW: "Today we are going to make a spice cake with special emphasis on how to flour your nuts."

6. SPORTSCASTER: "The winner of the Ladies' 54-Hole Tournament, played on three separate courses, is Helen Douglass, the new State Intercourse Champion!"

7. TV HOST: "I'm sorry, our time is up. . . . This is your TV storyteller leaving Don Quixote sitting on his ass till next week."

8. COMMERCIAL: "Visit our Coin-o-Matic Laundry. All ladies who drop off their clothing will receive prompt attention."

9. COMMERCIAL: "So, try 7-UP. . . . You will recognize it with the big seven and U-P after!"

10. GAME SHOW CONTESTANT: "I'm a maid for a large family of four boys, three girls, one adult, and one adulteress."

11. NEWSCASTER: "The collision of the two boats was due to the fog, which was as thick as sea poop."

12. LOCAL COMMERCIAL: "And Friday is poultry night . . . all ladies present will receive a free goose."

13. NEWSCASTER:" Rumor that the President would veto the bill has come from a high White Horse souse."

14. NEWSCASTER: "Murph the Surf was arrested after the bodies of two women were found floating in the bay, tied to concrete and bound with electrical cord and stab wounds on their bodies . . . police suspect foul play."

15. SPORTSCASTER: "McPhearson is anxious to make a good showing. He wants to play in the worst way, and that's just what he's doing!"

16. WEATHERMAN: "That's the weather from Anchorage. Now I'll take a leak out the window to see if it's freezing outside our studio."

17. NEWSCASTER: "President Carter has painful hemorrhoids and is being treated by his physician, Rear Admiral . . . William Lookass . . . Lukash!!!"

18. FOOTBALL COMMENTATOR: "He's at the 40 . . . the 50 . . . the 60 . . . look at that sonovabitch run!"

19. SPORTSCASTER: "Yankee catcher Yogi Berra was hit in the head by a pitched ball. X-rays of the head showed nothing."

20. GAME SHOW CONTESTANT: "I work for the Pittsburgh Gas Company. At least 90 percent of the people in Pittsburgh have gas."

—Exclusive for *The Book of Lists* 3

18 WINNERS OF THE DOUBLESPEAK AWARDS

Each year the Committee on Public Doublespeak of the National Council of Teachers of English pays tribute to public figures who have used language which is "grossly unfactual, deceptive, evasive, euphemistic, confusing, or self-contradictory." Here are some of our favorite examples of doublespeak:

1. COL. DAVID H. E. OPFER, USAF (1974)

After a bombing raid, Colonel Opfer, a press officer in Cambodia, complained to reporters, "You always write it's bombing, bombing, bombing. It's not bombing. It's air support."

2. RON ZIEGLER (1974)

When asked whether a certain batch of Watergate tapes was still intact, a question which would seem to have required a simple answer of "yes" or "no," President Nixon's press secretary gave the following 99-word reply: "I would feel that most of the conversations that took place in those areas of the White House that did have the recording system would in almost their entirety be in existence, but the special prosecutor, the court, and, I think, the American people are sufficiently familiar with the recording system to know where the recording devices existed and to know the situation in terms of the recording process, but I feel, although the process has not been undertaken yet in preparation of the material to abide by the court decision, really, what the answer to that question is."

3. YASSER ARAFAT (1975)

Apparently a believer in the philosophy that "love is hate" and "war is peace," the leader of the Palestine Liberation Organization stated, "We do not want to destroy any people. It is precisely because we have been advocating coexistence that we have shed so much blood."

4. HARRY VOLWEIDER (1975)

When asked why a black person had been rejected for membership in the Springdale Golf Club in Princeton, N.J., Volweider, president of the club, replied, "We didn't turn him down. We didn't accept him."

5. EARL CLINTON BOLTON (1978)

Mr. Bolton, a former executive vice-president of the University of California, wrote a memorandum for the Central Intelligence Agency in which he attempted to deal with the sensitive issue of academics who work for the CIA. He suggested that those aiding the agency "may be on the defensive" and advised academics to defend themselves by explaining their CIA involvement "as a contribution to . . . proper academic goals." Bolton's memo went on to say, "It should also be stressed that when an apologia is necessary it can best be made: (1) by some distant academic who is not under attack, (2) in a 'respectable' publication of general circulation (e.g., Harper's, Saturday Review, Vital Speeches, etc.), and (3) with full use of the jargon of the academy." Bolton suggested that aiding the CIA be defended on grounds of "academic freedom" and "privilege and tenure." He concluded by encouraging the agency to "have an insulator such as Rand or IDA. Such entities have quite good acceptance in academia. . . . Such an independent corporation should of course have a ringing name (e.g., Institute for a Free Society). . . ."

6. THE QUAKER OATS COMPANY (1978)

Quaker Oats' Aunt Jemima frozen "Jumbo Blueberry Waffles" were advertised as being made "With Real Blueberry Buds and Other Natural Flavors." On the back of the package, however, the following ingredients were listed in small type: "Blueberry Buds (sugar, vegetable stearine [a release agent]), blueberry solids with other natural flavors, salt, sodium carboxymethyl cellulose [a thickening agent], silicon dioxide [a flow agent], citric acid, modified soy protein, artificial flavor, artificial coloring maltol)."

7. THE NUCLEAR POWER INDUSTRY (1979)

Following the accident at Three Mile Island, the nuclear power industry came up with an extraordinary array of euphemisms to downplay the dangers of nuclear accidents. An explosion became "energetic disassembly" and a fire "rapid oxidation." The word "accident" was taboo and was replaced with "event," "incident," "abnormal evolution," "normal aberration," or "plant transient." The phrase "plutonium contamination" was another no-no. In its place came the phrases "plutonium infiltration" or "plutonium has taken up residence."

8. DWIGHT WELLS (1979)

Kentucky State Representative Wells told reporters, "You are to the people of Kentucky what a parent is to a child. When the truth is harmful and detrimental to the people of Kentucky, you should not only not tell them the truth, but you have a duty to see they do not know the truth."

9. A. J. SPANO (1979)

In an attempt to downplay Denver's air-pollution problem, Colorado State Representative Spano introduced a bill to change the wording of the state's air-quality scale. Spano suggested that the level of pollution which the federal government called "hazardous" be called "poor" instead. "Dangerous" was to become "acceptable," and "very unhealthful" was to become "fair." The bill, which passed the House Transportation Committee, changed "unhealthful" to "good" and "moderate" to "very good."

10. GEN. JOÃO BAPTISTA FIGUEIREDO (1979)

Upon being elected president of Brazil, Figueiredo told reporters, "I intend to open this country up to democracy, and anyone who is against that, I will jail, I will crush."

11. RONALD REAGAN (1980)

Reagan received the Doublespeak Award for using campaign oratory "filled with inaccurate assertions and statistics and misrepresentations of his past record." For example, Reagan proudly pointed out that while he was governor of California he refunded $5.7 billion in property taxes to Californians. What he failed to mention was that this was made possible because he *raised* taxes by $21 billion. Reagan claimed that General Motors "has to employ 23,300 full-time employees to comply with government-required paperwork." A GM executive pointed out that the actual figure was 4,900 and that was for all its paperwork. Reagan constantly told audiences that Alaska has more oil than Saudi Arabia. When this was proved to be grossly incorrect, he continued to use the line anyway. As *The New York Times* noted, Mr. Reagan "doesn't let the truth spoil a good anecdote . . ."

12. JIMMY CARTER (1980)

President Carter referred to the failed military rescue of the American hostages in Iran as an "incomplete success." He also justified the government bail-out of Chrysler by saying that "this legislation does not violate the principle of letting free enterprise function on its own, because Chrysler is unique in its present circumstances." In addition, Carter proudly stated that his administration never supported "nations which stand for principles with which their people violently disagree, and which are completely antithetical to our principles." Nonetheless, he continued to provide military and financial aid to over 20 governments which systematically violated human rights.

13. NEW JERSEY DIVISION OF GAMING ENFORCEMENT (1980)

In an official report concerning participants in organized crime, the division avoided the terms "mob," "syndicate," "Mafia," and "Cosa Nostra," and instead referred to a "member of a career offender cartel."

14. NUCLEAR REGULATORY COMMISSION (1980)

In a report to Congress on the subject of safety at nuclear power plants, the NRC displayed an unusual method of counting accidents, which they of course referred to as "events." The commission enumerated 400 such accidents, including two "abnormal occurrences." One of these "abnormal occurrences" turned out to be accidents at 19 different reactors. Because the 19 accidents were caused by the same design problem, they were counted only once. Another "abnormal occurrence" occurred so frequently that it was called a "normally expected occurrence."

15. U.S. DEPARTMENT OF AGRICULTURE (1981)

The USDA attempted to classify catsup as a vegetable so that it could be counted as one of the two vegetables required as part of the school lunch program. The department also reclassified chickens which had been chilled to 28°F from "frozen" to "deep chilled" so that they could be sold as fresh chickens.

16. MORAL MAJORITY (1981)

In a letter sent to 500,000 people to raise funds to fight sex education, the Moral Majority condemned a college textbook which it claimed was used in public schools across the U.S. When pressed by reporters, however, members could name only two school districts which actually used the book. Cal Thomas, vice-president for communications for the Moral Majority, defended the letter by saying, "You've got to shock people to get them to act anymore."

17. ENVIRONMENTAL PROTECTION AGENCY (1981)

John Hernandez, deputy administrator of the EPA, announced that words like "hazard" would no longer be used. Instead of using the phrase "degree of hazard," the EPA would now talk about "degree of mitigation of risk." The Office of Hazardous Emergency Response was renamed the Office of Emergency and Remedial Response. The term "cancer-causing" was also to be avoided. As part of this campaign, the EPA decided not to publicize a report that certain wood preservatives might cause cancer and decreed that it would no longer identify toxic chemicals that cause birth defects. An EPA press aide explained, "It might scare too many people."

18. ALEXANDER HAIG (1981)

Former Secretary of State Haig was well known for his bizarre use of the English language, peppering his speech with such phrases as "careful caution," "saddle myself with a statistical fence," "definitizing an answer," "caveat my response," and "epistemologicallywise." What won Haig the Doublespeak Award was a series of statements he made to congressional committees following the murder of three American nuns and a religious lay worker in El Salvador. The four women were shot in the head, and three of them were raped. Testifying before the House Foreign Affairs Committee, Haig said, "I'd like to suggest to you that some of the investigations would lead one to believe that perhaps the vehicle that the nuns were riding in may have tried to run a roadblock, or may accidentally have been perceived to have been doing so, and there'd been an exchange of fire and then perhaps those who inflicted the casualties sought to cover it up. And this could have been at a very low level of both competence and motivation in the context of the issue itself. But the facts on this are not clear enough for anyone to draw a definitive conclusion."

Alexander Haig, winner of the 1981 Doublespeak Award for such phrases as "careful caution" and "definitizing an answer."

The next day, before the Senate Foreign Relations Committee, Haig was asked to clarify his previous statement. Was he suggesting that the nuns might have run a roadblock? "You mean that they tried to violate . . . ? Not at all, no, not at all. My heavens! The dear nuns who raised me in my parochial schooling would forever isolate me from their affections and respect." When he used the phrase "exchange of fire," did he mean to imply that the nuns had fired guns at people? asked Senator Claiborne Pell. Haig replied, "I haven't met any pistol-packing nuns in my day, Senator. What I meant was that if one fellow starts shooting, then the next thing you know they all panic."

—D.W.

15 POPULAR MISQUOTATIONS

1. "A rose is a rose is a rose."

Gertrude Stein (*Sacred Emily*): "Rose is a rose is a rose is a rose."

2. "I have nothing to offer but blood, sweat, and tears."

Winston Churchill (first statement as Prime Minister, House of Commons, May 13, 1940): "I have nothing to offer but blood, toil, tears, and sweat."

3. "Alas! poor Yorick. I knew him well."

William Shakespeare (*Hamlet,* Act V, scene 1): "Alas! poor Yorick. I knew him, Horatio."

4. "Music has charms to soothe the savage *beast.*"

William Congreve (*The Mourning Bride*, Act I, scene 1): "Music hath charms to soothe a savage *breast.*"

5. "Git thar fustest with the mostest."

Nathan Bedford Forrest: "Get there first with the most men." (He was a well-educated and literate Civil War soldier.)

6. "Fourscore and seven years ago our *forefathers* brought *unto* this continent a new nation . . ."

Abraham Lincoln (Gettysburg Address, Nov. 19, 1863): "Fourscore and seven years ago our *fathers* brought forth *on* this continent a new nation . . ."

7. "A little *knowledge* is a dangerous thing."

Alexander Pope (*An Essay on Criticism*, Part II, line 15): "A little *learning* is a dangerous thing;/Drink deep, or taste not the Pierian spring:/There shallow draughts intoxicate the brain,/And drinking largely sobers us again."

8. "Hell hath no fury like a woman scorned."

William Congreve (*The Mourning Bride*, Act III, scene 8): "Heaven has no rage like love to hatred turned,/Nor hell a fury like a woman scorned."

9. "Money is the root of all evil."

I Tim. 6:10: "*The love of money* is the root of all evil."

10. "Pride goeth before a fall."

Prov. 16:18: "Pride goeth before destruction, and an haughty spirit before a fall."

11. "Every man has his price."

Sir Robert Walpole: "All those men [referring to a particular group of political enemies] have their price."

12. "Build a better mousetrap, and the world will beat a path to your door." (attributed to Emerson by Mrs. Sarah S. B. Yule)

Ralph Waldo Emerson (*Journal*): "I trust a good deal to common fame, as well we all must. If a man has good corn, or wood, or boards, or pigs, to sell, or can make better chairs or knives, crucibles or church organs, than anybody else, you will find a hard-beaten road to his house, though it be in the woods."

13. "I disapprove of what you say, but I will defend to the death your right to say it."

Voltaire (*Essay on Tolerance*): "Think for yourselves and let others enjoy the privilege to do so too."

14. "I escaped by the skin of my teeth."

Job (Job 19:20): "I am escaped with the skin of my teeth."

15. "In the sweat of thy brow shalt thou eat bread."

God to Adam (Gen. 3:19): "In the sweat of thy face shalt thou eat bread."

—K.A.

GEORGE SELDES'S
15 GREATEST QUOTATIONS

Author and newspaperman George Seldes has written numerous books, including *Facts and Fascism, 1,000 Americans,* and *The Great Quotations*. His varied experience as a news correspondent includes covering the French campaign in Syria in 1926–1927 and the Spanish Civil War in 1936–1937.

1. "Do not that to thy neighbor that thou wouldst not suffer from him." Pittacus of Mytilene (650?–570? B.C.)

2. "The unexamined life is not worth living." Socrates (470?–399 B.C.)

3. "Know thyself." Thales (640?-546 B.C.)

4. "Live every day as if it were your last." Marcus Aurelius (121–180 A.D.)

5. "Until philosophers are kings, or the kings and princes of this world have the spirit and power of philosophy, and political greatness and wisdom meet in one . . . cities will never have any rest from their evils, no, nor the human race, as I believe, and then only will this State have a possibility of life and behold the light of day." Plato (427?–347 B.C.)

6. "Give me the liberty to know, to utter, and to argue freely according to conscience, above all liberties." John Milton (1608–1674)

7. *"I teach you the Superman.* Man is something that is to be surpassed." Friedrich Nietzsche (1844–1900)

8. "Whoso would be a man must be a nonconformist. . . . Nothing is at last sacred but the integrity of your own mind." Ralph Waldo Emerson (1803–1882)

9. "Power tends to corrupt; absolute power corrupts absolutely." Lord John Emerich Edward Acton (1834–1902)

10. "$E = mc^2$." Albert Einstein (1879–1955)

11. "Sex is the central problem of life." Havelock Ellis (1859–1939)

12. "Our liberty depends on the freedom of the press, and that cannot be limited without being lost." Thomas Jefferson (1743–1826)

13. "Government is essentially immoral." Herbert Spencer (1820–1903)

14. *"Homo sum et nihil humani a me alienum puto."* (I am a human being and nothing pertaining to mankind is alien to me.) Terence (185–159 B.C.)

15. "Doubt is the key to knowledge." Persian proverb.

—Exclusive for *The Book of Lists 3*

10 COMMONLY USED FIGURES OF SPEECH

Everybody uses these figures of speech, but not everybody can define what they are using. The etymology of all these words is ultimately Greek, probably because the Greeks had a word for everything.

1. TMESIS (root word meaning a "cutting")

The most ardent adherents of this figure of speech would be the last to know what it's called. Tmesis is the separation, by inserting an additional word or words, of a word or phrase to give strong emphasis. Thus, instead of saying "Adolf Hitler," some British often said, "Adolf-bloody-Hitler." Use of tmesis makes the common phrase "No good" into "No damn good!" and "independent" into "inde-bloody-pendent." It is probably one of the most widespread figures, used by all classes of people.

2. PARONOMASIA (punning)

It is unnecessary to go into detail about punning, or playing with words, since it is so popular. Most puns are clever and amusing, as in these twists on the phrase "to leave no stone unturned": Nudists enjoying a sunbath "left no stern untoned." And the gallery gods in a theater are said to have left "no turn unstoned."

3. EPENTHESIS (from the Greek, "to put or set in")

This is a distortion of pronunciation that adds an extra sound or letter to a word. Outstanding popular examples are calling the prostate gland the "prostrate" gland and calling asparagus "asparagrass."

4. ANAPTYXIS (Greek for "an unfolding")

A form of epenthesis in which an extra vowel distorts the pronunciation of a word. The foremost examples are arthritis and athlete, which become "arthuritis" and "athalete," used by less literate people. But even the literate commit this fault when they say "mischievious" for mischievous.

5. HYPERBOLE (Greek roots, "an overshooting, or excess")

Extravagant overstatement used for emphasis and not meant to be taken literally, as in "a thousand thanks." The publishing world and movie studios are guilty of using hyperbole when they describe a product as, "The greatest novel [or film] of the year." Since this has been said all too often, people do have their doubts. Used ironically, hyperbole can cut to the quick, as when someone who has just made an expensive blunder hears the boss say, "You're an absolute genius, aren't you!"

6. LITOTES (Greek root meaning "plain, simple")

A figure of speech equivalent to understatement, used negatively. A superior who is sparing of his praise may call a helper's brilliant plan "Not a bad idea." According to the speaker, this may be understood to be the highest praise. Thus it becomes hyperbole inverted. So when certain people tell you your work is not "half bad," you may be sure it's quite good.

7. CATACHRESIS (Greek root "to misuse")

Application of a word in the wrong context. There is a story of Yogi Berra in a ball park that had an outfield wall, part wood and part brick. If a fly ball hit the brick, it was a home run. If it hit the wood, it was still in play; Yogi thought a ball hit the brick part of the wall, a home run. The umpire said it hit the wood. Incensed, Yogi burst out with a classic example of catachresis. He cried, "If you can't hear the difference, you must be blind!" Deliberate catachresis is used in a phrase like: "I was so close to winning I could taste it."

8. OXYMORON (Greek root for "pointedly foolish")

A paradoxical term, such as "a rich pauper," is an oxymoron. Other examples: "cruel kindness," "a cheerful pessimist," "terribly pleased," "an honest crook," "sweet sorrow," and "wise fool." Oxymorons can be amusing enough to be a party game.

9. PROSOPOPOEIA (Greek roots, "a face," "a person," "to make")

A figure of speech in which an imaginary or absent person is said to be speaking or doing something. The ever-resourceful Yogi Berra is said to have uttered this statement when things were going badly for the Yankee ball team, "If Miller Huggins was alive today, he'd be turning over in his grave." (Miller Huggins was the Yankee manager in the great Babe Ruth era.) In the case of an imaginary being doing something, one can say, "The Devil made me do it," or "My guardian angel is watching over me."

10. APOSIOPESIS (Greek root, "to be quite silent")

This is a particularly widespread figure of speech in which a statement is left incomplete, usually by a breaking off of one's thought. An example is, "If you don't pay me back, I'll, I'll—!" and there are no further words.

—J.L.

EDWIN NEWMAN'S 10 WORDS MOST OFTEN MISUSED

Newman has been reporting news for over 40 years and has been with NBC since 1952. He has headed news bureaus in London, Paris, and Rome. He has also narrated many television specials, which have won him half a dozen Emmys, and is the author of *Strictly Speaking, A Civil Tongue,* and *Sunday Punch.*

1. *Hopefully* (as in "Hopefully, it won't rain.")
2. *Destiny* (as in "The Forty-niners still control their own destiny.")
3. *Good* (as in "His fast ball is sinking pretty good.")
4. *Evacuate* (as in "Three thousand people were evacuated.")
5. *Rhetoric* (as in "It's nothing but rhetoric.")
6. *Comprise* (as in "The team was comprised of nine players.")
7. *Impact* (as in "The harsh winter impacted our profits.")
8. *Unique* (as in "We offer you the most unique weekend of the year.")
9. *I* (as in "They invited my wife and I to dinner.")
10. *Convinced* (as in "They convinced me to do it.")

Note: Hopefully—to aspire expectantly to become or achieve something. *Destiny*—predetermined state. *Good*—something that possesses desirable qualities and is beneficial. *Evacuate*—empty out. *Rhetoric*—the art of expressive speech. *Comprise*—to include in a particular scope, to sum up. *Impact*—to fix firmly, or a forceful contact. *Unique*—being the only one. *Convince*—to overcome by argument.

—Exclusive for *The Book of Lists 3*

10 COLORFUL "ANIVERBS"

Human behavior can often be described most vividly by using a verb derived from the name of an animal. The following is a list of 10 animals which have become "aniverbs."

1. APE. To mimic.

A small child sometimes will ape his parents' worst actions, much to their chagrin.

2. BADGER. To harry or pester.

The housewife finally badgered her husband into taking out the garbage by dumping it in his lap.

3. DOG. To track or trail persistently.

Whenever he appears in public, the president is always dogged by reporters.

4. FOX. To trick by using ingenuity or cunning.

The 15-year-old boy foxed his way into the theater to see the X-rated movie by wearing a fake moustache and beard.

5. HORSE. To engage in rowdy, prankish play.

The children horsed around the pool all day and succeeded in getting the adults thoroughly wet.

6. MONKEY. To play or tamper with something.

The two little boys monkeyed with their mother's watch until it was damaged beyond repair.

7. SNAKE. To move, crawl, or drag with a snakelike movement.

The peeping Tom snaked his way through the bushes in order to get a better view.

8. WEASEL. To be evasive.

Politicians often weasel their way out of answering tough questions by asking another question.

9. WHALE. To thrash.

The young lady whaled her boyfriend for making improper advances on the first date.

10. WOLF. To eat voraciously.

He overslept this morning, so he wolfed down a doughnut and a cup of coffee before leaving for work.

—F.H.

"Wolfing" down a meal.

OUR 26 FAVORITE ACRONYMS

An acronym is a word formed of the initial letter or letters of other words.

1. BOPEEP—Bangor Orange Position Estimating Equipment for Pastures. Shepherds in Bangor, Wales, attach this electronic beeper to their sheep to keep track of them.
2. BOSWASH—Boston to Washington. Proposed name for possible "supercity" encompassing the area between these two cities.
3. BUSTOP—Breathers United to Stop Standing Time of Passenger Buses. Student legal action organization.
4. CINCUS—Commander in Chief, U.S. Fleet. Created by the Navy during W.W. II, this unfortunate acronym was hastily abandoned after Pearl Harbor.
5. COMSUBCOMNELMCOMHEDSUPPACT—This is the longest acronym in the English language, weighing in at 26 letters. It stands for Commander, Subordinate Command, U.S. Naval Forces Eastern Atlantic and Mediterranean, Commander Headquarters Support Activities.
6. CREEP—Committee for the Reelection of the President, much publicized during the Watergate scandal.
7. EGADS—Electronic Ground Automatic Destruct System. This is the signal given to destroy a missile in flight.
8. FOE—Females Opposed to Equality.
9. GASP—Greater (Washington, D.C.) Alliance to Stop Pollution; Group Against Smog and Pollution.
10. GIMPY—Growing, Improving, Maturing—Puppy of the Year. Canine award.
11. GOO—Get Oil Out. Citizens' group founded after 1969 Santa Barbara, Calif., oil spill.
12. HMHMH—His/Her Majesty's Household Master of the Horse. A rare palindromic acronym (it can be spelled the same backward and forward).
13. LPG—Lousy Paying Guest. Hotel slang.
14. MADDAM—Macromodule and Digital Differential Analyzer Machine This computer term has the distinction of being the only six-letter palindromic acronym.
15. NIIOMTPIABOPARMBETZHELBETRABSBOMONIMONIMONKO-NOTDTEKHSTROMONT—This Russian whopper is the *Guinness Book of World Records* winner for the world's longest acronym. It consists of 60 letters in English, 54 in Cyrillic. The *Concise Dictionary of Soviet Terminology* gives its meaning as: The laboratory for stuttering, reinforcement, concrete, and ferro-concrete operations for composite-monolithic and monolithic constructions of the Department of the Technology of Building—assembly operations of the Scientific Research Institute of the Organization for building mechanization and technical aid of the Academy of Building and Architecture of the U.S.S.R.
16. POCO—Physiology of Chimpanzees in Orbit (NASA term).
17. SCOOP—Stop Crapping on Our Premises. A New York City project

opposing the litter caused by dog dirt. SCOOP also had a more digni-fied meaning: Strategic Confirmation of Optical Phenomenology.

18.–23. SNAFU—This military slang acronym for Situation Normal; All Fouled Up, is well known. But it has spawned several surprising bed-fellows: TARFU—Things Are Really Fouled Up; FUMTU—Fouled Up More Than Usual; FUBB—Fouled Up Beyond Belief; FUBAR—Fouled Up Beyond All Recognition; and JANFU—Joint Army-Navy Foul-Up.

24. VAMP—The Voluntary Association of Master Pumpers was an early organization of volunteer firemen.

25. VIOLENT—Viewers Intent on Listing Violent Episodes on Nation-wide Television. Student legal action organization.

26. WASP—White Ashkenazi Sabra with Pull (Israeli variation on White Anglo-Saxon Protestant).

—A.W.

6 WORDS IN WHICH ALL THE VOWELS APPEAR IN ALPHABETICAL ORDER

1. *Abstemious:* adj., practicing temperance in living.
2. *Abstentious:* adj., characterized by abstinence.
3. *Arsenious:* adj., of, relating to, or containing arsenic.
4. *Caesious:* adj., having a blue color.
5. *Facetious:* adj., straining to be funny, especially at the wrong time.
6. *Fracedinous:* adj., productive of heat through putrefaction.

—C.R.M.

3 WORDS IN WHICH ALL THE VOWELS APPEAR IN REVERSE ALPHABETICAL ORDER

1. *Duoliteral:* adj., in two languages in the same volume.
2. *Quodlibetal:* adj., having to do with quodlibet (quodlibet is any ques-tion in philosophy or theology proposed as an exercise in argument).
3. *Quodlibetary:* n., a quodlibetical argument.

—C.R.M.

3 WORDS IN WHICH 1 LETTER IS REPEATED 6 TIMES

1. Degenerescence (six e's): n., tendency to degenerate, or the process of degenerating.
2. Nonannouncement (six n's): n., the failure to announce.
3. Indivisibility (six i's): n., the quality or state of being indivisible.

—C.R.M.

6 PANGRAMS: SENTENCES THAT USE ALL THE LETTERS IN THE ALPHABET

1. Waltz, nymph, for quick jigs vex Bud.
2. Quick wafting zephyrs vex bold Jim.
3. The five boxing wizards jump quickly.
4. Jackdaws love my big sphinx of quartz.
5. Pack my box with five dozen liquor jugs.
6. The quick brown fox jumps over a lazy dog.

—THE EDS.

4 FAMOUS COMMAS

1. THE FATAL COMMA

Czarina Maria Fyodorovna once saved the life of a man by transposing a single comma in a warrant signed by her husband, Alexander III, which exiled a criminal to imprisonment and death in Siberia. On the bottom of the warrant the czar had written: "Pardon impossible, to be sent to Siberia." The czarina changed the punctuation so that her husband's instructions read: "Pardon, impossible to be sent to Siberia." The man was set free.

2. THE BLASPHEMOUS COMMA

In several editions of the King James Bible, Luke 23:32 is changed entirely by the absence of a comma. In the passage which describes the other men crucified with Christ, the erroneous editions read: "And there were also two other malefactors." Instead of counting Christ as a malefactor, the passage should read: "And there were also two other, malefactors."

3. THE MILLION-DOLLAR COMMA

The U.S. government lost at least a million dollars through the slip of a comma. In the tariff act passed on June 6, 1872, a list of duty-free items included: "Fruit plants, tropical and semitropical." A government clerk accidentally altered the line to read: "Fruit, plants tropical and semitropical." Importers successfully contended that the passage, as written, exempted all tropical and semitropical plants from duty fees. This cost the U.S. a fortune until May 9, 1874, when the passage was amended to plug the hole.

4. THE WHISKEY COMMA

In 1900, when copper magnate William Andrews Clark waged his campaign for U.S. senator from Montana, he promised free whiskey to the entire population of Butte—which he believed was 450,000—if he were elected. (An earlier distribution of cigars and whiskey throughout Montana's lumber camps had resulted in a popular mandate for his choice of Helena as the state capital.) However, a misplaced comma and an extra zero (Butte had only 45,000 citizens) forced Clark to be more generous than he had originally planned. Upon election, he felt duty bound to distribute among the voters the amount of whiskey calculated on the incorrect population figure.

—F.B.

9
THE ARTISTIC LIFE

10 FAMOUS CARTOONISTS SELECT THEIR OWN FAVORITE CARTOONS

1. CHARLES ADDAMS

"It doesn't take much to collect a crowd in New York."

2. RON COBB

3. PAUL CONRAD

4. JULES FEIFFER

5. HANK KETCHAM

179

6. B. KLIBAN

7. MELL LAZARUS

8. CHARLES SCHULZ

9. RALPH STEADMAN

10. GAHAN WILSON

"WELL, WE FOUND WHAT'S BEEN CLOGGING YOUR CHIMNEY"

—Exclusive for *The Book of Lists 3*

10 POPULAR SONGS THAT WERE ORIGINALLY COMMISSIONED BY BIG BUSINESS

1. "FRIENDSHIP IS FOR KEEPS"

This 1974 song had two sets of lyrics—one to sell Bell Telephone, and the other for popular release. Among the artists who recorded both versions were Tony Bennett, the Carpenters, and Valerie Harper.

2. "I'D LIKE TO TEACH THE WORLD TO SING"

Another Coca-Cola-created hit, this song didn't start out as a commercial. The New Seekers, a British band, introduced it in 1971—without much success—under the title "True Love and Apple Pie." The Coca-Cola people discovered it, fashioned a new arrangement and lyrics, and made it their theme. That's when it became popular, and the British group's newly titled version became a hit in 1972. The song was so popular that a second group, The Hillside Singers, had a hit with their recording of it in the same year.

3. "WE'VE ONLY JUST BEGUN"

This 1970 smash was originally written by Paul Williams and Roger Nichols to celebrate the joys of California's Crocker Bank. But The Carpenters recognized the ballad's potential and recorded it. The result was a no. 2 hit record for four weeks.

4. "NO MATTER WHAT SHAPE (YOUR STOMACH'S IN)"

Was a Top 10 hit for the T-Bones in 1966. But they recorded this instrumental only after it had achieved a different kind of national fame as the theme of an Alka-Seltzer advertising campaign.

5. "THE JOLLY GREEN GIANT"

The Kingsmen successfully transformed this familiar Green Giant Co. vegetable jingle into a 1965 hit about a very large and lustful man.

6. "THE TEABERRY SHUFFLE"

This Herb Alpert tune began life as "The Mexican Shuffle." It lingered in relative obscurity until it attracted the notice of the Clark Teaberry Gum Company. They bought the song, gave it a new title, "The Teaberry Shuffle," and made it the theme of their ad campaign. The result was a 1964 hit.

7. "BOOK OF LOVE"

This 1958 hit by The Monotones is a good example of the romantic growing out of the mundane. It borrowed a Pepsodent toothpaste commercial for its melody.

8. "SEE THE U.S.A. IN YOUR CHEVROLET"

This began, not surprisingly, as a Chevrolet advertising jingle. Later it became the theme of Dinah Shore's "Chevrolet Hour" television show. In 1948, Leon Carr and Leo Corday recognized its commercial possibilities and adapted it into a popular song.

9. "THE GRAND COULEE DAM"

In 1941, the Bonneville Power Administration in Oregon put Woody Guthrie on the payroll for a month and assigned him to make music about the dams it was building on the Columbia River. About 26 songs resulted, among them the well-known folk song, "The Grand Coulee Dam."

10. "ROLL ON COLUMBIA"

Another of the products of Guthrie's 1941 stint on the Bonneville Power Administration's payroll. This classic song was inspired by the Columbia River's majesty and beauty.

—E.F.

11 BLIND MUSICIANS

1. THOMAS (BLIND TOM) BETHUNE (1849–1908)

A natural mimic who learned to play the piano by ear and committed over 700 songs to memory, Bethune was born blind to slaves in Georgia. Purchased by a Colonel Bethune, Tom played (and imitated machine and animal noises) for audiences throughout Europe and the U.S.

2. RAY CHARLES (1930–   )

The 1950s mix of gospel melodies and love lyrics by this renowned composer-singer-pianist was the birth of "soul." Blinded by glaucoma at age six, Grammy winner Charles remembers his mother's advice: "Just because you've lost your eyesight, you're not stupid."

3. JOSÉ FELICIANO (1945–   )

A victim of congenital glaucoma, Puerto Rican-born Feliciano gained fame for his 1968 Latin-soul version of "Light My Fire." He taught himself guitar because "I didn't want to make chairs and mops and brooms."

4. ALLAN (BLIND BOY) FULLER (1903?–1940)

Blinded by a jealous girlfriend who put lye in the water in his washbasin, Fuller sometimes played his fast blues guitar with Blind Blake and Blind Gary Davis, although Fuller is best known for his work with prominent bluesmen Sonny Terry and Brownie McGee. McGee was sometimes called Blind Boy Fuller's No. 2.

5. (BLIND) LEMON JEFFERSON (1897–1930)

Sightless from birth, Jefferson was one of the first to call his rough guitar stylings and high, loud singing the "blues." A blind street singer's bitterness shows in "Tin Cup Blues," but often he was bawdy, as in "Black Snake Moan." He recorded in Chicago, where he froze to death in a snowstorm.

6. WILLIAM (BLIND WILLIE) JOHNSON (1902–1949)

An itinerant guitar-playing gospel minstrel who went blind at age seven, Johnson used a rich blend of gospel tunes and blues style which is often copied. His prominent recordings are "Dark Was the Night" and "Lord, I Just Can't Keep from Crying."

7. RONNIE MILSAP (1945–   )

An award-winning country-and-western vocalist and composer, Milsap isn't bitter about his lifelong blindness, sometimes quipping, "I remember names better than I do faces." His style is that of the honky-tonk love song.

8. GEORGE SHEARING (1919–   )

Blind from birth, jazz pianist-composer Shearing is a British émigré known as a master of the "locked hands" style. His best-known composition is "Lullaby of Birdland." When people offered to bequeath their eyes to him, he refused, saying, "I am a completely happy man. My life today suits me."

9. TOM SULLIVAN (1947–   )

Undeterred by a lifetime blindness, Sullivan is not only a singer-composer-writer but also an actor and an athlete. He is also known for his book (and subsequent movie) *If You Could See What I Hear,* about two years of his young adulthood.

10. ARTHEL (DOC) WATSON (1923–   )

Born blind in Deep Gap, N.C., Watson is a virtual walking history of Southern folk music. A master of flat-picking and finger-picking on guitar, he also plays banjo and fiddle at campus concerts and music festivals where he is a regular. One of his most popular works is a version of "Tennessee Stud."

11. STEVIE WONDER (1950–   )

A premature baby, Wonder blames his blindness on "too much oxygen in the incubator." One of the outstanding composers and performers in soul-rock music, he catapulted to success at age 13 with his first hit, "Fingertips." In the recording studio, Wonder often takes on all the vocal, instrumental, and production responsibilities himself.

—T.C.

8 SURPRISING PEOPLE WHO MADE BILLBOARD'S TOP 100 RECORDS LISTS

	Artist	Record	Year	Position on Chart	Weeks on Chart
1.	Sen. Everett Dirksen	"Gallant Men"	1966	29	6
2.	Mike Douglas	"The Men in My Little Girl's Life"	1965	6	9
3.	José Ferrer	"Woman (Uh-Huh)"	1954	18	4
4.	Sally Field	"Felicidad"	1967	94	4
5.	Merv Griffin	"The Charanga"	1961	69	4
6.	Buddy Hackett	"Chinese Rock & Egg Roll"	1956	87	2
7.	Silvana Mangano	"Anna"	1953	6	17
8.	Pete Seeger	"Little Boxes"	1964	70	8

—K.C.

DIZZY GILLESPIE'S 10 GREATEST JAZZ MUSICIANS IN HISTORY

A star trumpeter with an infectious sense of humor, John Brinks "Dizzy" Gillespie has been called "the perfect jazz musician" by André Previn. Gillespie and Charlie Parker gave birth to the style of jazz known as bop, and over the years Gillespie has played with virtually all the top names in his field, including Miles Davis, Duke Ellington, and Oscar Peterson.

1. Charlie Parker
2. Art Tatum
3. Coleman Hawkins
4. Benny Carter
5. Lester Young
6. Roy Eldridge
7. J. J. Johnson
8. Kenny Clarke
9. Oscar Pettiford
10. Miles Davis

—Exclusive for *The Book of Lists 3*

QUINCY JONES'S 10 FAVORITE JAZZ RECORDINGS OF ALL TIME

Master musician Quincy Jones first teamed up with Ray Charles to form a combo in Seattle, then went on to steal the spotlight as trumpeter with Dizzy Gillespie and Lionel Hampton. He has arranged and conducted music for the likes of Count Basie, Sarah Vaughan, and Aretha Franklin. Also to his credit are numerous award-winning television scores and more than 50 film scores.

1. "Body and Soul" (Coleman Hawkins)
2. "Just Friends" (Charlie Parker)

Charlie Parker.

3. "Miles Ahead" (Miles Davis)
4. "Rockin' in Rhythm" (Duke Ellington)
5. "Love You Madly" (Oscar Peterson)
6. "Giant Steps" (John Coltrane)
7. "I Can't Get Started" (Dizzy Gillespie)
8. "Sleep" (Benny Carter)
9. "The Midnight Sun Will Never Set" (Phil Woods)
10. "Anything" (Count Basie)

—Exclusive for *The Book of Lists 3*

YEHUDI MENUHIN'S 10 GREATEST VIOLINISTS IN HISTORY

The celebrated violinist made his debut at Carnegie Hall at age 11 and had toured the world before his 20th birthday. Winner of scores of awards and honorary degrees, he sponsors annual music festivals in Switzerland and in England where he operates a school for the musically gifted. Menuhin is president of the International Musical Council of UNESCO.

1. Arcangelo Corelli (1653–1713), Italian
2. Antonio Vivaldi (1669?–1741), Italian
3. Pietro Locatelli (1695–1764), Italian
4. Nicolò Paganini (1782–1840), Italian
5. Jean Marie Leclair (1697–1764), French
6. Giuseppe Tartini (1692–1770), Italian
7. Ludwig Spohr (1784–1859), German
8. Henri Vieuxtemps (1820–1881), Belgian
9. Henryk Wieniawski (1835–1880), Polish
10. Pablo de Sarasate (1844–1908), Spanish

—Exclusive for *The Book of Lists 3*

YEHUDI MENUHIN'S 10 GREATEST VIOLINISTS IN LIVING MEMORY

1. Mischa Elman (1891–1967), Russian
2. Jan Kubelík (1880–1940), Czechoslovakian
3. Jascha Heifetz (1901–   ), U.S. (Russian-born)

4. Eugène Ysaye (1858–1931), Belgian
5. David Oistrakh (1908–1974), Russian
6. Fritz Kreisler (1875–1962), French (Austrian-born)
7. Georges Enesco (1881–1955), Romanian
8. Grigoras Dinicu (1889–1949), Romanian
9. Joseph Joachim (1831–1907), Hungarian
10. Ole Bull (1810–1880), Norwegian

—Exclusive for *The Book of Lists 3*

ANDRÉ PREVIN'S 10 GREATEST MODERN COMPOSERS (NOT IN ORDER OF MERIT)

A musical jack-of-all-trades, Previn began his career as a jazz pianist in the 1950s. In the 1960s he switched his primary allegiance to conducting and is the principal conductor of the London Symphony Orchestra as well as the music director for the Pittsburgh Symphony Orchestra. The composer of much classical music, Previn also has more than 50 movie credits to his name. He has adapted numerous Broadway musicals for the screen, winning Academy Awards for his scoring of *Gigi, Porgy and Bess, Irma La Douce,* and *My Fair Lady.*

1. Mozart (will always be modern)
2. Shostakovich
3. Britten
4. Prokofiev
5. Bartók
6. Tippett
7. Copland
8. Walton
9. Messiaen
10. Stravinsky

—Exclusive for *The Book of Lists 3*

13 ENTERTAINERS WHO PLAYED LAS VEGAS JUST ONCE

	Performer	Hotel	Date
1.	Édith Piaf	Sands	January, 1953
2.–4.	The Three Stooges	Flamingo	October, 1953

5.	Shelley Winters	Flamingo	October, 1953
6.	Bela Lugosi	Silver Slipper	February, 1954
7.	Ronald Reagan	Last Frontier	February, 1954
8.	Orson Welles	Riviera	February, 1956
9.	June Allyson	Sahara	October, 1967
10.	Tony Curtis	Caesar's Palace	November, 1967
11.	Don Knotts	Caesar's Palace	July, 1968
12.	Monty Hall	Sahara	April, 1971
13.	David Frost	Riviera	August, 1971

—D.F. & N.F.

15 PLAYS MOST PRODUCED BY HIGH SCHOOL THEATER GROUPS

Each year, the International Thespian Society, an honorary society for high school theater arts students, surveys member schools (approximately 3,500) on the year's productions. The results are published in *Dramatics,* the magazine of the society. Here are the most produced plays in 1972–1973 and 1980–1981.

1972–1973

1. *You're a Good Man, Charlie Brown* (1967), Clark Gesner
2. *Our Town* (1938), Thornton Wilder
3. *Fiddler on the Roof* (1964), Joseph Stein, Jerry Bock, and Sheldon Harnick
4. *Bel Kaufman's Up the Down Staircase* (1969), Christopher Sergel
5. *You Can't Take It With You* (1936), George S. Kaufman and Moss Hart
6. *Arsenic and Old Lace* (1941), Joseph Kesselring
7. *Oklahoma!* (1943), Richard Rodgers and Oscar Hammerstein II
8. *Guys and Dolls* (1950), Frank Loesser, Jo Swerling, and Abe Burrows
9. *The Miracle Worker* (1959), William Gibson
10. *The Curious Savage* (1950), John Patrick
11. *The Crucible* (1958), Arthur Miller
12. *The Wizard of Oz* (1928), Elizabeth F. Goodspeed (based on the book by L. Frank Baum)
13. *Diary of Anne Frank* (1955), Frances Goodrich and Albert Hackett
14. *The Music Man* (1957), Meredith Willson
15. *Harvey* (1944), Mary Coyle Chase

1980–1981

1. *You Can't Take It With You* (1936), George S. Kaufman and Moss Hart
2. *Arsenic and Old Lace* (1941), Joseph Kesselring

3. *Bye, Bye Birdie* (1960), Michael Stewart, Charles Strouse, and Lee Adams
4. *Oklahoma!* (1943), Richard Rodgers and Oscar Hammerstein II
5. *The Miracle Worker* (1959), William Gibson
6. *You're a Good Man, Charlie Brown* (1967), Clark Gesner
7. *Harvey* (1944), Mary Coyle Chase
8. *The Music Man* (1957), Meredith Willson
9. *Fiddler on the Roof* (1964), Joseph Stein, Jerry Bock, and Sheldon Harnick
10. *Our Town* (1938), Thornton Wilder
11. *The Curious Savage* (1950), John Patrick
12. *Guys and Dolls* (1950), Frank Loesser, Jo Swerling, and Abe Burrows
13. *Dracula* (1927), Hamilton Deane and John Balderston (from Bram Stoker's novel *Dracula*)
14. *Godspell* (1971), Michael Tevelak and Steven Schwartz
15. *Grease* (1972), Jim Jacobs and Warren Casey

10 PEOPLE WHO HATED PORTRAITS OF THEMSELVES

1.–5. JACOB VON LOON, VOLCKERT JANSZ, WILLEM VON DOEYENBURG, JACHEM DE NEVE, AERNOUT VAN DER MEIJE

Rembrandt's group portrait of the board of directors of the cloth-makers guild, although judged by modern critics to be a great painting, was thought by its conservative subjects to be too radical in approach. Today it serves as a trademark for a cigar company.

6. MME. MICHEL LÉVY (1857–1919), French publisher's wife

Impressionist Edouard Manet painted Mme. Lévy in the last year of his life. Later she sold the portrait because she felt it didn't do justice to her beauty.

7. WINSTON CHURCHILL (1874–1965), British statesman

"Disgusting," said Lord Hailsham, Churchill's good friend, of Graham Sutherland's portrait. "A beautiful work," said Nye Bevan, Churchill's bitter foe. Churchill called it "a remarkable example of modern art." Churchill hated modern art. So did Lady Churchill. In 1955 she retrieved the portrait, valued at $200,000, from its hiding place behind a cellar boiler, smashed it to the floor, and then tossed it in the incinerator. Another portrait of Sir Winston, done by his painting instructor, Sir Walter Sikert, also met with her disfavor. She put her foot through it.

This portrait of Winston Churchill, valued at $200,000, was
smashed by Lady Churchill, who then threw it in the incinerator.

8. LYNDON JOHNSON (1908–1973), U.S. president

LBJ called Peter Hurd's portrait "the ugliest thing I ever saw in my
whole life." Lady Bird Johnson hoped she would never see another like it
if she "lived to be 1,000." Nevertheless, the Johnsons were unable to
prevent its hanging in the Smithsonian Portrait Gallery in Washington,
D.C.

Lyndon Johnson called this portrait "the ugliest thing that I ever saw in my whole life."

9. PHILIP MOUNTBATTEN (1921–), British prince consort

The prince was not pleased with Pietro Annigoni's portrait. One observer who looked at it said: "If he is really like that, I shouldn't like to meet him in the dark."

10. HENRY KISSINGER (1923–), U.S. secretary of state

Gardner Cox's portrait was to have hung in the State Department, but Kissinger felt he had been "reduced." A spokesman at State said it "made him look something like a dwarf." Cox rejected the offer to rework the portrait, forfeiting his $12,000 commission, saying he liked the painting the way it was.

—R.W.S.

7 ARTISTS WHOSE WORKS WERE PAINTED OVER

1. UNKNOWN ARTIST (10th century), *Kuan Lin Holding Lotus Blossom*

In 1953, officials of the esteemed Nelson Gallery of Art in Kansas City received a valuable 12th-century Chinese wall painting that had been damaged during shipping. The horror of the officials was to be short-lived, for as restorer James Roth worked on the mural, he discovered a trace of blue paint underneath a layer of mud and rice husks. After careful, detailed work, a gracious goddess was exposed and identified as a unique example of 10th-century painting. It had been hailed as one of the greatest Oriental art discoveries in recent years.

2. GIOVANNI BELLINI (1430?–1516); TITIAN (1477–1576), *Feast of the Gods*

It had long been known that the renowned Renaissance painter Titian altered *Feast of the Gods,* a painting by his teacher, Giovanni Bellini. When the painting was X-rayed in the 1950s, it was discovered that Titian had also painted over several principal figures, altered the composition, and in essence changed the very content of the masterpiece. Art historians now view the two masters' artistry as enhancing the value of the canvas and now consider the painting as two original works in one.

3. SANDRO BOTTICELLI (1444?–1510), *Three Miracles of St. Zenobius*

During the cleaning of this 15th-century masterpiece, restorers at the New York Metropolitan Museum of Art noted that a central portion of the painting had been painted over. Technicians using X-rays to examine the area discovered an image of two preserved skeletons lying in a coffin. As the painting had previously been owned by Sir William Abdy of London, it is believed that he had the skeletons painted over in deference to Victorian tastes.

4. LUCAS CRANACH (1472–1553), *Charity*

In this painting of a nude woman nursing her child, puritanical sentiments triumphed over the artist's intentions when a restorer painted a complete set of clothes on the woman. Later the clothing was removed, leaving the painting in its original state.

5. MICHELANGELO (1475–1564), charcoal drawings

The world's only group of mural sketches by the great Renaissance painter, sculptor, and architect was found in late 1975 while chapel director Paolo Dal Poggetto was trying to devise an alternate route for moving tourist traffic through Florence's Medici Chapel. Before opening up a storeroom as an exit to the street, restorer Sabino Giovannoni performed tests on the walls. Under several layers of whitewash and grime, he discovered more than 50 large drawings of the human form and one of a horse's head, evidently Michelangelo's record of past works and preliminary sketches of future projects. Art historians believe that Michelangelo, an outspoken Republican, may have rendered the sketches while hiding out from an assassin hired by the Medicis, who were purging Florence of any political opposition.

6. PAUL CÉZANNE (1839–1906), *Portrait of a Peasant*

After recovering a stolen Cézanne, *The Artist's Sister,* in 1962, the St. Louis City Art Museum decided to have the painting cleaned and re-lined. Art conservator James Roth discovered another portrait on the back of the canvas. Painted while Cézanne was in his early 20s, the new portrait of a peasant raised the value of the original by $75,000. The canvas is mounted so that both portraits may be viewed.

7. ARSHILE GORKI (1905–1948), aviation murals

Two murals of an original 10 painted by Armenian-born artist Arshile Gorki were recovered in 1973 due to the efforts of Mrs. Ruth Bowman, a Newark, N.J., art historian. Five years after the completion of the 10 murals—commissioned by the Works Progress Administration in 1937—the Army Air Corps took over Newark Airport, which housed the murals, and put the first of 14 coats of whitewash over them. Every major art text published since 1948 claimed the murals had been lost, but Mrs. Bowman decided to investigate the walls further and found two murals intact. The other eight paintings were destroyed when walls were torn down to expedite the installation of new radiators.

—E.H.C.

YOUSUF KARSH'S 10 PERSONS IN HISTORY HE WOULD MOST LIKE TO HAVE PHOTOGRAPHED

Karsh is a Canadian photographer whose work has been displayed internationally and has been collected into a dozen books, among them *Karsh Portraits* and *Faces of Our Time.* He, more than any other man, has made a visual history of the latter half of the 20th century through his photos of the world's artistic and political notables. Perhaps his most famous photo is his W.W. II portrait of Winston Churchill.

1. Hippocrates, the father of medicine
2. St. Francis of Assisi
3. Alexander the Great
4. William Shakespeare
5. Leonardo da Vinci

6. Marcus Aurelius
7. Abraham Lincoln
8. Queen Elizabeth I
9. Helen of Troy
10. Cleopatra of Egypt

—Exclusive for *The Book of Lists 3*

10
NO BUSINESS LIKE
SHOW BUSINESS

PATRICK ROBERTSON'S 10 FAVORITE
MOVIE ODDITIES

Robertson worked in the news department of the British Broadcasting Corp. before turning his full attention to writing. He traveled extensively, gathering information for his initial effort, *The Book of Firsts*. Robertson's most recent work is *Movie Facts and Feats: A Guinness Record Book*.

1. MR. PRESIDENT, SUPERSTAR!

Ronald Reagan is not the first U.S. president who acted in films. Theodore Roosevelt played himself in a one-reeler Matty Roubert comedy in 1908, and both Teddy and Woodrow Wilson made guest appearances in the 1917 flag-waver *Womanhood: The Glory of a Nation*. Another movie-minded president was Franklin Delano Roosevelt, who conceived the idea for a 1936 thriller, *The President's Mystery*.

2. THE MOST REMAKES

The story which has been filmed the most times is *Cinderella*. The 58 productions since the first in 1898 have included cartoon, modern, ballet, operatic, parody, communist, and pornographic versions—and one in which Cinderella was played by a black (Billie Daniels). The 53 versions of *Hamlet* include one with a black lead (Ghana's Kofi Middleton-Mends), three with Indians, another in which twins played the role interchangeably, and four in which the prince was portrayed by a woman.

3. MARY PICKFORD—SOVIET STAR

Mary Pickford, the "World's Sweetheart," starred in a Soviet movie without being aware she was in it. During her visit to Moscow in 1926, director Sergei Komorov posed as a newsreel cameraman, and he followed her around with a camera, shooting enough footage to piece together a full-length comedy feature. Titled *The Kiss of Mary Pickford*, it has a climactic sequence in which she was seen in a close embrace with the Soviet hero. To this day no one has been able to explain how Komorov contrived the scene.

4. THE LONGEST SCREEN CAREER

The movie star with the longest career is French actor Charles

Vanel, who has appeared in over 200 films since his debut at the age of 16 in 1908. He declares that he has no intention of retiring early.

5. DEAR RODENT . . .

No mere human star has ever provoked the volume of fan mail received by the world's best-loved rodent. A record number of 800,000 letters were addressed to Mickey Mouse during 1933, a figure well ahead of the best achieved by a flesh-and-blood performer—730,000 letters written to Shirley Temple in 1936.

6. THE LONG AND SHORT OF IT

The longest title of an American film is *Cafeteria, or How Are You Going to Keep Her Down on the Farm After She's Seen Paris Twice.* It runs precisely one minute.

7. DON'T CALL US . . .

Bette Davis, Clark Gable, Maurice Chevalier, Shirley Temple, Brigitte Bardot, and Laurence Olivier had more than success in common. They all failed screen tests.

8. THE YOUNGEST STAR

The youngest performer to receive star billing was Baby Leroy, chosen at the age of six months to play opposite Maurice Chevalier in Paramount's 1933 comedy *A Bedtime Story.* Leroy's contract had to be signed by his grandfather, because not only the star but also his 16-year-old mother were underage.

Baby Leroy was six months old when he received star billing in
A Bedtime Story.

Napoleon's cavalry charging in *Kolberg*, a Nazi-made epic with the largest cast in movie history.

9. THE BIGGEST EPIC

The largest cast ever assembled for a motion picture was the 187,000 performers who appeared in the last Nazi-made epic, *Kolberg*. Whole army divisions were diverted from the front to play Napoleonic soldiers at a time when Germany was on the verge of defeat. Released in 1945 with few Berlin movie theaters still functioning, *Kolberg* was actually seen by less people than had acted in it.

10. CINÉMA CLICHÉ

The most hackneyed line in movie scripts is "Let's get outta here." A recent survey showed that it is used at least once in 84% of Hollywood productions and more than once in 17%.

—Exclusive for *The Book of Lists 3*

20 MAJOR BOX OFFICE FAILURES

Every producer's nightmare is that his film will meet with public indifference. And since movies are getting more expensive to make, it's crucial that they pull in customers and make money—lots of it. If a movie bombs at the box office, even years of TV sales and marketing in other countries will rarely succeed in bringing it out of the red.

		Negative cost: $m	Rental from U.S. and Canada: $m	Loss: $m
1.	Heaven's Gate (1980)	36	1.5	34.5
2.	Raise the Titanic (1980)	36	6.8	29.2
3.	Waterloo (1969)	25	1.4	23.6
4.	Honky Tonk Freeway (1981)	24	.5	23.5
5.	Darling Lili (1970)	22	3.3	18.7
6.	The Fall of the Roman Empire (1964)	20	1.9	18.1
7.	Cleopatra (1962)	44	26	18
8.	Hurricane (1975)	22	4.5	17.5
9.	Sorcerer (1977)	22	5.9	16.1
10.	Meteor (1979)	20	4.2	15.8
11.	Dr. Doolittle (1967)	20	6.2	13.8
12.	The Greatest Story Ever Told (1965)	20	6.9	13.1
13.	The Island (1980)	22	9.6	12.4
14.	Star! (1968)	15	4.2	10.8
15.	Tora! Tora! Tora! (1970)	25	14.5	10.5
16.	The Wiz (1978)	24	13.6	10.4
17.	Mutiny on the Bounty (1962)	20	9.8	10.2
18.	Battle of Britain (1969)	12	2.0	10.0
19.	The Molly Maguires (1970)	11	1.1	9.9
20.	The Brinks Job (1978)	15	5.1	9.9

SOURCE: David Pirie, *Anatomy of the Movies*. New York: The Macmillan Company, 1981; Copyright © Shuckburgh Reynolds, Ltd., London.

12 MOVIES WITH DIFFERENT ENDINGS

1. *THE GODLESS GIRL* (1929)

Cecil B. De Mille's tale of a young atheist ends with Lina Basquette as Judy finally gaining faith in God. De Mille was confused upon hearing of the film's tremendous popularity in Russia, but understood better when he realized that it was being screened without the redeeming final reel.

2. *A FAREWELL TO ARMS* (1932)

After much controversy as to how the film should end, Paramount decided to follow Ernest Hemingway's novel and fade out after Catherine Barkley's death. Although this version played the European and initial U.S. runs, a new ending was filmed for U.S. general release in which Catherine, played by Helen Hayes, lives through the last scene.

3. *MEET JOHN DOE* (1941)

An undecided Frank Capra played his film around the U.S. with four different endings. In one Gary Cooper as John Willoughby commits suicide, while in another a lovelorn Ann Mitchell, portrayed by Barbara Stanwyck, convinces Willoughby not to leap off City Hall. Inspired by the contents of a letter signed "John Doe," Capra filmed a fifth and final ending in which Ann talks some sense into the suicidal Willoughby, then promptly faints into his arms.

4. *THE MAGNIFICENT AMBERSONS* (1942)

In Orson Welles' original ending, Eugene (Joseph Cotten) visits George (Tim Holt) in the hospital. Eugene then goes to the boarding-house—which had been the Ambersons' home—to discuss Lucy (Ann Baxter) and George with Fanny (Agnes Moorehead), and finally gets in his car and looks back at Fanny. Following a poor preview response, Robert Wise, standing in for an absent Welles, cut the 131-minute film down to about 88 minutes and substituted a new ending in which Eugene goes to the hospital with Lucy, then consoles Fanny in the hospital corridor.

5. *DOUBLE INDEMNITY* (1944)

In the original two-hour print screened for preview audiences, Fred MacMurray's Walter Neff is put on trial, then executed in the gas chamber. Those two scenes, which had taken five days to shoot at a cost of $150,000, were lopped off the end of the film for its general release. Director Billy Wilder called the missing 15 minutes "one of the two best sequences I ever did."

6. *THE INVASION OF THE BODY SNATCHERS* (1956)

Don Siegal's politically allegorical science-fiction film about the takeover of a small town by alien pods originally ended with Kevin McCarthy, as Dr. Miles Bennell, running through street traffic and vainly warning motorists of the impending invasion. In the final shot, he turned to the audience and yelled, "You're next!" Finding that ending "too upsetting" and confusing for preview audiences, Allied Artists forced Siegal to add a prologue, narration, and epilogue so that—as Bennell recounts his horrifying experience to a hospital psychiatrist—the entire story becomes a flashback. The new ending has the disbelieving doctor about to have Bennell taken away when a man enters to report that a truck full of pods has been discovered. The audience is left with a ray of hope as the doctor—now convinced of Bennell's story—telephones the FBI. Siegal did not like the studio's version and commented: "What they never understood was that the film was about them."

7. 8½ (1962)

Fellini's film originally ended with a scene in which all the characters, dressed in white, gathered aboard a dining car. Within two weeks of the movie's opening, a new ending was substituted in which Guido Anselmi, played by Marcello Mastroianni, joins hands with his friends and dances happily around the set of a rocket launch pad while a circus band plays on.

8. DR. STRANGELOVE OR: HOW I LEARNED TO STOP WORRYING AND LOVE THE BOMB (1963)

Originally the movie ended with a giant pie-throwing scene in the Pentagon's War Room, concluding with President Muffley (Peter Sellers) and Ambassador de Sadesky (Peter Bull) sitting waist deep in the remains of 2,000 custard pies, singing, "For He's a Jolly Good Fellow." Concerned that such a farcity might detract from the concluding sequence in which the Doomsday Device explodes, director Stanley Kubrick cut the scene from the film.

9. THE SOUND OF MUSIC (1965)

While the film ran its full 174 minutes the world over, a truncated version was featured in Munich, Germany. Missing was the final third of the film, in which the Nazis nearly prevent the Von Trapp family from escaping Austria.

10. ROCKY (1976)

Originally the film featured a rather downbeat ending in which Sylvester Stallone as Rocky enters the empty boxing arena, is consoled by a fellow fighter, takes Adrian's (Talia Shire's) hand, and walks off with her. Test screenings convinced director John Avildsen that a more upbeat finish was needed, so he shot a new scene in which Rocky and Adrian push through the crowded arena to reach each other and then embrace.

11. CLOSE ENCOUNTERS OF THE THIRD KIND (1977)

When the release date drew near for his sci-fi epic, director Steven Spielberg was obliged to make do with a version he considered less than perfect. Flawed or not, the movie grossed well over $100 million, enough to afford Spielberg the rare opportunity of shooting some additional footage for the film's rerelease in 1980. For the revised *Close Encounters,* 16 minutes were cut from the original version, while seven minutes of outtakes and six minutes of new footage were added. The first version ended with earthling Richard Dreyfuss disappearing into the alien spacecraft. The second was expanded to show Dreyfuss's view of the ship's interior—a cross between a cathedral and the Las Vegas Strip at midnight.

12. APOCALYPSE NOW (1979)

After three years of filming and a total cost of over $30 million, director Francis Ford Coppola's Vietnam statement *Apocalypse Now* was still incomplete. Coppola had filmed four different endings and on the eve of release had not yet settled on one. So he solved his dilemma by choosing two—one for the 70 mm version and another for the 35 mm version.

People who saw the film in 70 mm watched Martin Sheen as Captain Willard assassinate mad Colonel Kurtz, played by Marlon Brando, and then ponder the idea of remaining in Kurtz's place before finally sailing back to civilization. The 35 mm version has Willard assassinate Kurtz and then call in an air strike to napalm the colonel's jungle camp, destroying the evil once and for all. Coppola referred to this latter version as his "Mom and apple pie" ending.

—D.B.

WALTER MATTHAU'S 10 FAVORITE COMEDIES OF ALL TIME

An amazingly versatile actor who "can play anything from Scarlett O'Hara to Rhett Butler," Matthau was a smash hit in Neil Simon's play *The Odd Couple,* received an Academy Award for Best Supporting Actor in *The Fortune Cookie,* and was nominated for Best Actor in *Kotch* and *The Sunshine Boys.* His most recent films are *First Monday in October* and *Buddy Buddy.*

1. *The Odd Couple*
2. *The Producers*
3. *A New Leaf*
4. *Macbeth*
5. *City Lights*
6. *Wuthering Heights*
7. *Death of a Salesman*
8. *A Streetcar Named Desire*
9. *Horse Feathers*
10. *Hamlet*

—Exclusive for *The Book of Lists 3*

ROBERT DUVALL'S 10 FAVORITE MOVIES OF ALL TIME

The versatile Duvall has been called "the premier American actor." His stage work won him an Obie for *A View from the Bridge,* and he has played a variety of highly praised dramatic parts on television. For his role in *The Godfather,* he was named Best Supporting Actor by the New York Film Critics. Other screen credits include *To Kill a Mockingbird, M*A*S*H, Network,* and *Apocalypse Now.*

Akira Kurosawa's *The Seven Samurai.*

1. *The Seven Samurai*
2. *Kes*
3. *The Godfather*
4. *Tomorrow*
5. *Pixote*
6. *The 400 Blows*
7. *Gunga Din*
8. *Alambrista*
9. *The Great Dictator*
10. *Kagemusha*

Note: Director Kenneth Loach directed *Kes* (1970), a film about a young boy who trains a hawk. *Tomorrow,* a 1972 film directed by Joseph Anthony, stars Duvall in the story (adapted from William Faulkner) of a Mississippi cotton farmer who raises a child. *Pixote,* a 1981 movie by Brazilian director Hector Babenco, depicts the desperate lives of reform school boys who escape only to find that survival in the city is a lonely and dangerous business. *Alambrista,* first shown on TV in 1977, describes the plight of a Mexican farmworker who immigrates illegally to California but then is forced to return to Mexico. It was written, directed, and photographed by Robert M. Young.

—Exclusive for *The Book of Lists 3*

SEAN CONNERY'S 10 FAVORITE MOVIES OF ALL TIME

A native of Scotland, Connery began his acting career with a bit part in a touring production of *South Pacific*. In the 1960s he became a box-office sensation with a half-dozen films which featured him as the charismatic superspy James Bond in such thrillers as *Goldfinger* and *From Russia with Love*. Nonetheless, Connery admitted that Bond was "not my kind of chap at all." More recent films include *The Great Train Robbery* and *Outland*.

1. *The Seven Samurai*
2. *Seven Brides for Seven Brothers*
3. *Persona*
4. *The Best Years of Our Lives*
5. *Never on Sunday*
6. *On the Waterfront*
7. *African Queen*
8. *Umberto D*
9. *The Gold Rush*
10. *Battleship Potemkin*

—Exclusive for *The Book of Lists 3*

RICHARD D. ZANUCK'S 10 FAVORITE MOVIES OF ALL TIME

Zanuck has followed in the footsteps of his illustrious father to become a respected producer in his own right. After an association with 20th Century-Fox and Warner Brothers, he founded Zanuck-Brown Production Company, Universal Pictures, in 1972. The following year his company made *The Sting,* which walked away with seven Academy Awards, including Best Picture. Other Zanuck productions include *Jaws* and *Jaws II*.

1. *Citizen Kane*
2. *Sunset Boulevard*
3. *Treasure of the Sierra Madre*
4. *Gone with the Wind*
5. *Butch Cassidy and the Sundance Kid*
6. *The Godfather*
7. *The Sting*
8. *The Best Years of Our Lives*

9. *On the Waterfront*
10. *From Here to Eternity*

—Exclusive for *The Book of Lists 3*

IRWIN ALLEN'S 10 FAVORITE MOVIES OF ALL TIME

Allen began his motion-picture career with semidocumentaries, winning an Oscar for *The Sea Around Us* in 1952. Later he took up the challenge of producing dramatic films such as *Towering Inferno* and *The Poseidon Adventure*. Allen has had a number of successful television series, including *Voyage to the Bottom of the Sea* and *Lost in Space*.

1. *The Scoundrel*
2. *Citizen Kane*
3. *Here Comes Mr. Jordan* (original)
4. *Star Wars*
5. *Towering Inferno*
6. *The Poseidon Adventure*
7. *Bridge on the River Kwai*
8. *It's a Wonderful Life*
9. *Hospital*
10. *On Golden Pond*

—Exclusive for *The Book of Lists 3*

ROGER CORMAN'S 10 FAVORITE MOVIES OF ALL TIME

Corman is an author, producer, and director who has transferred many Edgar Allan Poe classics to the screen. He has been a prolific film-maker, producing many films, including *I Never Promised You a Rose Garden* and *The Pit and the Pendulum* and has launched the careers of several young directors, including Francis Ford Coppola and Peter Bogdanovich. Corman is president of New World Pictures.

1. *Battleship Potemkin*
2. *Grand Illusion*
3. *The Seventh Seal*
4. *I Vitelloni*
5. *Citizen Kane*

6. *Lawrence of Arabia*
7. *The 400 Blows*
8. *The Grapes of Wrath*
9. *Star Wars*
10. *The Third Man*

Note: Italian director Federico Fellini made *I Vitelloni* in 1953. It explores the boredom and frustration in the lives of five idle young men living in a small town.

—Exclusive for *The Book of Lists 3*

8 OF THE LONGEST FILMS EVER MADE

1. *COMMENT YUKONG DÉPLAÇE LES MONTAGNES (HOW YUKONG MOVED THE MOUNTAINS)* (France, 1976)

Seventy-eight-year-old Dutch-born filmmaker Joris Ivens and his wife, Marceline Loridan, traveled to China in 1973 with the intent of making a 3-hour documentary about the Chinese people. They remained in China for 1½ years, during which time they shot 120 hours of 16mm film. The result, after editing, was a 12-hour, 43-minute epic.

Joris Ivens, director of the 12-hour, 43-minute epic,
How Yukong Moved the Mountains.

2. *NINGEN NO JOKEN (THE HUMAN CONDITION)* (Japan,
   1958–1961)

   Ningen No Joken, the six-volume Japanese best-selling novel by
Jumpei Gomikawa, was made into a 9-hour, 29-minute motion-picture
trilogy by Shochiku Films. It is the tale of a young Japanese idealist during W.W. II who is forced into military service and tries in vain to improve conditions for army recruits. Eventually captured by the Russians,
he escapes but dies before reaching home. The first part of the trilogy
was cut to 138 minutes and released in the U.S. in 1959.

3. *VOINA I MIR (WAR AND PEACE)* (U.S.S.R., 1967)

   The longest and most faithful motion-picture adaptation of Leo
Tolstoi's epic novel was produced by the Soviet government in commem-
oration of the 50th anniversary of the Revolution. Filmed in three versions simultaneously over a five-year period at a reported cost of $100
million, the original, in the Russian language, runs 8 hours, 27 minutes.
A 6-hour, 13-minute version dubbed in English was named Best Foreign
Film during the 41st Motion Picture Academy Awards ceremony.

4. *ISKRY PLAMJA (SPARKS OF THE FLAME)* (U.S.S.R., 1925)

   Iskry Plamja, the second-longest motion picture made in the
U.S.S.R., was completed in 1925. The silent film runs 7 hours, 58
minutes.

5. *FRANÇAIS SI VOUS SAVIEZ (FRENCH PEOPLE, IF YOU KNEW)*
   (France, 1973)

   This 3-part documentary about the history of modern France,
filmed in both color and black-and-white, runs 7 hours, 45 minutes.
Gaullists were reluctant to cooperate with directors André Harris and Al-
ain de Sédouy, so the two men were forced to threaten a lawsuit before
W.W. II newsreels and postwar newsclips were released for their use.

6. *HITLER: A FILM FROM GERMANY* (West Germany, 1977)

   Hans-Jürgen Syberberg's 22-chapter psychological essay about
Adolf Hitler clocks in at 7 hours. In preparation for four years, the movie
was filmed in 20 days on a budget of $500,000. It played continuously for
six months in a Paris theater and was distributed in the U.S. in 1980 by
Omni Zoetrope.

7. *NAPOLEON VU PAR ABEL GANCE* (France, 1927)

   The only movie ever to have been shown at the famed Paris Opéra
was Abel Gance's *Napoleon,* which premiered there in 1927. Gance originally filmed 12½ hours of scenes that included both color and 3-D se-
quences. This he edited into a 6-hour, 18-minute black-and-white epic
that employed, during a two-hour segment, an innovative triple-screen
effect called Polyvision. Though Gance, in a fit of rage, destroyed the
"triptych" footage when the introduction of sound to movies robbed his
invention of its thunder, Polyvision in fact inspired Henri Chrétien to
later invent the CinemaScope lens, responsible for the wide-screen look
of today's cinema. Though various shortened versions of *Napoleon* have
been released during the past half century (including a 1934 stereo-

phonic-sound print created by Gance), a 4½-hour approximation of the original work containing a 70mm reconstruction of the "triptych" sequence was completed in 1973 and distributed internationally by French director Claude Lelouch in 1981. Gance's epic was obtained by Francis Ford Coppola for limited exhibition in the U.S. These showings were accompanied by a live orchestra, which played an original score composed by Coppola's father, Carmine. Gance lived long enough to hear his masterpiece applauded by sellout crowds.

8. *LES MISÉRABLES* (France, 1934)

This French adaptation of the Victor Hugo novel runs 6 hours, 15 minutes. Because of its length, the film was exhibited in Paris in three parts, shown simultaneously in three different theaters. A 162-minute export version was kept off the U.S. market for two years by 20th Century-Fox, which had just completed its own American adaptation of the book and wanted a fair run for its money.

—D.B.

6 FOOTNOTE FILMS: VERY LONG FILMS NEVER SHOWN IN THEIR FULL VERSION MORE THAN ONCE

1. *FOOLISH WIVES* (U.S., 1921)

Erich von Stroheim's $1-million extravaganza ran 6 hours, 24 minutes in its original form but was cut by Universal to 3½ hours for its New York première and to 2½ hours for national release. Protests from various censorship groups later resulted in the film's shortening to a mere 73 minutes. A 1972 reconstruction effort has restored the print to 120 minutes.

2. *LA ROUE (THE WHEEL)* (France, 1921)

Grief-stricken by the deaths of his lover, Ida Danis, and Séverin Mars, the star of his new movie, *La Roue,* French director Abel Gance fled to America immediately after the film was completed to "escape from myself." He returned five months later to edit an 8-hour, 32-minute version of the production, which the public was never allowed to view since the picture's running time was a little over 5 hours at the time of its first general showing. Though a print of the original version is said to exist in Moscow, only 2½-hour truncations are currently available for viewing.

3. *GREED* (U.S., 1924)

Erich von Stroheim's epic adaptation of Frank Norris's novel *McTeague* was shown only once, at a 9-hour screening at MGM Studios on Jan. 12, 1924. The studio chopped the picture down to 10 reels from its original 42 for general release. The remaining film negative was melted down for its silver nitrate content.

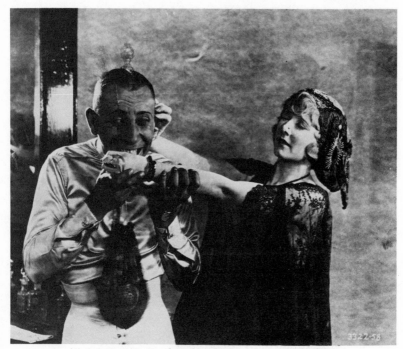

Foolish Wives by Erich von Stroheim was only shown once
in its entirety.

4. *THE BURNING OF THE RED LOTUS TEMPLE* (China, 1928–1931)

The Star Film Company's 27-hour film adaptation of Shang K'ai-jan's newspaper serial *Strange Tales of the Adventurer in the Wild Country* has never been publicly screened in its entirety. The mammoth production was instead exhibited in the form of 18 separate features.

5. ***** (FOUR STARS)* (U.S., 1967)

Also known as *The Twenty-four-hour Movie*, this Andy Warhol film was shown only once in its original 25-hour form and then reedited into two shorter features: a 102-minute condensation of ****, and an 86-minute movie titled *The Loves of Ondine* (1968).

6. *NOLI ME TANGERE* (France, 1971)

Shown only once in its original 13-hour length, this French production was recut to 4½ hours and screened at international festivals under the title *Out 1: Spectre*.

—D.B.

13 TEACHERS WHO BECAME MOVIE STARS

1. MADELEINE CARROLL (1906–   )

Carroll, the beautiful blond star of Alfred Hitchcock's *The 39 Steps* (1935), in which she played opposite Robert Donat, also starred in *The Prisoner of Zenda* (1937). Educated at Great Britain's University of Birmingham, Carroll was a French teacher before making her stage debut in London in 1927.

2. WILL GEER (1902–1978)

Best known as the grandfather on TV's *The Waltons,* Geer was especially noted for his ability to alternate between avuncular and gruff characterizations in films such as *Intruder in the Dust* (1949), *Seconds* (1966), and *In Cold Blood* (1967). Blacklisted in the 1950s, Geer fell back on his degree in plant and animal husbandry from the University of Chicago and gave private classes in vegetable gardening in various parts of the country—as he'd done during W.W. I and W.W. II—in order to make ends meet.

3. MARGARET HAMILTON (1902–   )

As the Wicked Witch of the West in *The Wizard of Oz* (1939), she has terrified generations of small children. Ironically, Miss Hamilton was a kindergarten teacher in Ohio and at the Rye Country Day School in New York. She also ran a nursery school in Cleveland during the 1920s before finally making her film debut in 1933.

4. SAM JAFFE (1891–   )

Acclaimed for his portrayal of the deranged Grand Duke Peter in *The Scarlet Empress* (1934) and nominated for an Oscar for his role as a criminal mastermind in *The Asphalt Jungle* (1950), Jaffe later played Dr. Zorba on television's *Ben Casey.* Jaffe also was once a teacher and dean of mathematics at the Bronx Cultural Institute. He was educated at City College of New York and Columbia University.

5. MADELINE KAHN (1942–   )

Following her graduation from Hofstra University as a speech therapy major, Miss Kahn did "practice teaching" at a public school in Levittown, Long Island, in 1964. She did not, however, "like anything about it. It's a boring job. You don't get interesting problems. At a speech clinic, you get a higher level of work." There is nothing boring about the zany characters she has portrayed in such films as *Paper Moon* (1973) and *Blazing Saddles* (1974).

6. KRIS KRISTOFFERSON (1936–   )

A creative-writing major at Pomona College and a Rhodes Scholar at Oxford, Kristofferson taught English to West Point cadets before becoming a singer/songwriter. Broadening his career into acting, he played a musician in *Blume in Love* (1973), a rancher in *Alice Doesn't Live Here Anymore* (1975), and a football player in *Semi-Tough* (1977).

7. AGNES MOOREHEAD (1906–1974)

In addition to five Oscar nominations, the esteemed character actress had an M.A. and a Ph.D. in English literature. She was an honor student at the American Academy of Dramatic Arts. Moorehead also taught speech and dramatics at the Dalton School in New York City. She joined Orson Welles in establishing the Mercury Theater Company in 1940 and played Welles' mother in *Citizen Kane* (1941), her first movie role.

8. RAMON NOVARRO (1899–1968)

The star of the silent-screen rendition of *Ben-Hur* (1925) was a piano teacher in Los Angeles before breaking into movies as a dashing Latin-lover type.

9. CARROLL O'CONNOR (1925–   )

From 1954 to 1956, O'Connor and his wife lived in a series of cold-water flats in New York while he was substitute teaching. O'Connor taught English. He has played a variety of roles during his film career, but he is best known for slaughtering the English language in his television role as the bigoted Archie Bunker.

10. SIR MICHAEL REDGRAVE (1908–   )

Educated at Cambridge, where he did some acting, Sir Michael taught modern languages for three years. Although celebrated for his Shakespearean roles, he gave one of his greatest film performances as the failed, embittered teacher in *The Browning Version* (1951), for which he was chosen Best Actor at the Cannes Film Festival.

11. GEORGE C. SCOTT (1927–   )

In order to act in school productions Scott agreed to teach mastery of Western literature at Stephens College in Missouri. With a new play every three weeks, he was too busy acting to devote much energy to teaching. One of his students, Tammy Grimes, recalled him as "handsome, strange, and moody, like a Heathcliff."

12. LOUIS WOLHEIM (1880–1931)

Best remembered for one of his few sympathetic roles—Katczinsky in *All Quiet on the Western Front* (1930)—Wolheim usually was typecast as a thug because he had a broken nose and crude, ugly features. His looks belied his actual intelligence—he had an engineering degree from Cornell and taught mathematics there for six years.

13. MONTY WOOLLEY (1888–1963)

Twice nominated for an Oscar, the acerbic character actor was educated at Harvard and Yale. He taught English and coached graduate dramatics at Yale. His students there included Thornton Wilder and Stephen Vincent Benét. Woolley stopped teaching after his Broadway debut in 1936 and was a sensation in *The Man Who Came to Dinner* (1939). He also played in the 1942 film version.

—M.E.P.

GLENDA JACKSON'S 10 ACTRESSES WHO MOST INFLUENCED HER

The internationally famous actress first gained prominence in the Royal Shakespeare Company's 1964 production of *Marat/Sade*. Her transition from stage to screen led to two motion-picture Academy Awards for Best Actress for her performances in *Women in Love* and *A Touch of Class*. Television audiences know her through her portrayal of Queen Elizabeth I in the BBC series *Elizabeth R*.

1. Bette Davis
2. Joan Crawford
3. Barbara Stanwyck
4. Arletty
5. Marie Bell
6. Greta Garbo
7. Sybil Thorndike
8. Simone Signoret
9. Thelma Ritter
10. Kim Stanley

—Exclusive for *The Book of Lists 3*

MARY ASTOR'S 10 GREATEST MOVIE ACTRESSES OF ALL TIME (NOT NECESSARILY IN THIS ORDER)

Since her first screen role at age 14, Astor has appeared in more than 100 films, including *The Prisoner of Zenda, The Great Lie* (for which she received a Best Supporting Actress Oscar), *The Maltese Falcon,* and *Hush, Hush, Sweet Charlotte*. After mastering screen, stage, radio, and television, she published an autobiography, children's books, and several novels.

1. Greta Garbo
2. Lillian Gish
3. Sophia Loren

4. Jane Fonda
5. Vanessa Redgrave
6. Wendy Hiller
7. Maria Ouspenskaya
8. Bette Davis
9. Katharine Hepburn
10. Ingrid Bergman

—Exclusive for *The Book of Lists 3*

THE 7 FILMS IN WHICH JOHN WAYNE DIED

1. *Reap the Wild Wind* (1942)
2. *The Fighting Seabees* (1944)
3. *Wake of the Red Witch* (1949)

John Wayne in *The Shootist*.

4. *Sands of Iwo Jima* (1949)
5. *The Alamo* (1960)
6. *The Cowboys* (1972)
7. *The Shootist* (1976)

John Wayne also played the role of a corpse in *The Deceiver* (1931).

—M.J.H.

8 MEMORABLE LINES ERRONEOUSLY ATTRIBUTED TO FILM STARS

1. "Smile when you say that, pardner."

What Gary Cooper actually said to Walter Huston in *The Virginian* (1929) was, "If you want to call me that, smile."

2. "Me Tarzan, you Jane."

Johnny Weismuller's first Tarzan role was in *Tarzan, the Ape Man* (1932). He introduced himself to costar Maureen O'Sullivan by thumping his chest and announcing, "Tarzan." He then gingerly tapped *her* chest and said, "Jane."

3. "You dirty rat."

In fact, James Cagney never uttered this line in any of his roles as a hard-boiled gangster. It has often been used by impersonators, however, to typify Cagney's tough-guy image.

4. "Come with me to the Casbah."

Charles Boyer cast seductive glances at Hedy Lamarr throughout *Algiers* (1938), but he never did make this suggestion. Delivered with a French accent, the line appeals to many Boyer imitators who enjoy saying, "Come weez mee . . ."

5. "Why don't you come up and see me sometime?"

Cary Grant found himself the recipient of Mae West's lusty invitation, "Why don't you come up sometime and see me?" in *She Done Him Wrong* (1933).

6. "Play it again, Sam."

In *Casablanca* (1942) Ingrid Bergman dropped in unexpectedly at old lover Humphrey Bogart's nightclub, where she asked the piano player to "Play it, Sam," referring to the song "As Time Goes By." Although Bogart was shocked at hearing the song that reminded him so painfully of his lost love, he also made Sam play it again—but the words he used were, "You played it for her, you can play it for me . . . play it."

Humphrey Bogart told Sam, "Play it."

7. "Judy, Judy, Judy."

Cary Grant has never exclaimed this line in any film, but imitators often use it to display their Cary Grant-like accents.

8. "I want to be alone."

In 1955, retired film star Greta Garbo—despairing of ever being free of publicity—said, "I want to be let alone." The melodramatic misinterpretation, however, is the way most people have heard and quoted it.

—K.P.

7 SCREEN PERFORMERS WHO WERE NOT KNOWN AS ACTORS

1. GEORGE HERMAN "BABE" RUTH (1895–1948)

It was fitting that the "Sultan of Swat" should make his film debut in a movie about baseball. *Headin' Home,* an independent production of 1920, starred Ruth as a country bumpkin whose first home run breaks a church window. He joins a big-league team, becomes a champ, and returns home a hero. The reviews gave Ruth credit for his attempts at comedy, but he scored better in the baseball scenes.

2. GERTRUDE EDERLE (1906–   )

Ederle, well-known U.S. sports figure of the 1920s and first woman to swim the English Channel, starred with Bebe Daniels in the 1927 release, *Swim, Girl, Swim*. In the film, Ederle plays a college swim coach who saves an absentminded professor from drowning and coaches Daniels, who is the star of the school team. Ederle's performance was described as "emphatically graceful" so long as she was in the water.

3. JOMO KENYATTA (1894–1978)

The president of Kenya from 1963 to 1978 owned one shirt during the Depression. Living in London at that time, he was barely making ends meet by teaching the Kikuyu language to missionaries about to leave for Kenya. Consequently, he jumped at the chance to earn a bit of extra money playing one of many minor African chiefs in the film *Sanders of the River*, which went into production at Shepperton Studios in 1934. Kenyatta was in only one scene, but he enjoyed the experience, and it gave him an opportunity to meet the star of the film, Paul Robeson.

4. HUGH WALPOLE (1884–1941)

Walpole, New Zealand-born, Cambridge-educated novelist, wrote the screen adaptation for the 1935 version of *David Copperfield*, which starred W. C. Fields—who turned in a critically acclaimed performance as Mr. Micawber—and Lionel Barrymore, as Dan Peggotty. The author also played the role of the vicar in the film.

5. MICKEY SPILLANE (1918–   )

Mystery writer Mickey Spillane played the part of a straw-chewing sleuth trying to solve a string of murders in *Ring of Fear* (1954). The Clyde Beatty Circus was the scene of the crimes, and Beatty himself played the circus master. Spillane also wrote the screenplay for and starred in *The Girl Hunters* (1963). He portrayed the detective of his own creation—Mike Hammer.

6. MANDY RICE-DAVIES (1944–   )

As a key figure, along with Christine Keeler, in Great Britain's 1963 John Profumo sex scandal, Mandy Rice-Davies became internationally known. She later owned three restaurants and a disco in Israel, and in the mid-1970s she starred in a hit play in Tel Aviv. In 1976 the busy lady finished filming an Israeli musical comedy called *Kuni Lemel in Tel Aviv*.

7. YEVGENY YEVTUSHENKO (1933–   )

This popular Soviet poet of the post-Stalin era made his film debut as a space explorer. During the early 1960s, Yevtushenko had fallen out of favor with his government because of some of his writings, but *Flight* (1979), in which he played the lead, was shown at the Moscow Film Festival.

—V.S.

Mickey Spillane playing Mike Hammer in *The Girl Hunters*.

LUCILLE BALL'S 10 FAVORITE TV SERIES OF ALL TIME

The madcap comedienne is perhaps one of the best-known women in the world. Her hugely successful 1950s television show, *I Love Lucy*, received a total of 200 awards, including five Emmys. Her popularity continued with *The Lucy Show* and *Here's Lucy*. The famous redhead has also appeared in nearly 80 feature films and is the president of Lucille Ball Productions.

1. *M*A*S*H*
2. *The Carol Burnett Show*
3. *The Honeymooners*
4. *The Dick Van Dyke Show*
5. *Mary Tyler Moore Show*
6. *The Jack Benny Show*
7. *National Geographic Shows*
8. *Milton Berle Show*
9. *Hallmark Theatre*
10. And, of course, *I Love Lucy*

—Exclusive for *The Book of Lists 3*

DICK VAN DYKE'S 10 FAVORITE
TV SERIES OF ALL TIME

The popular comedian's highly acclaimed *Dick Van Dyke Show* screened on CBS from 1961 to 1966 and was followed in the early 1970s by the *New Dick Van Dyke Show*. Van Dyke has appeared on the stage (most notably in *Bye Bye Birdie*) and has made many television guest appearances. His movies include *Mary Poppins, Divorce American Style, Some Kind of Nut*, and *The Comic*.

1. *Your Show of Shows*
2. *Omnibus*
3. *Twilight Zone*
4. *Monty Python*
5. *Playhouse 90*
6. *Studio One*
7. *Person to Person*
8. *M*A*S*H*
9. *You Are There*
10. *The Dick Van Dyke Show*

—Exclusive for *The Book of Lists 3*

Sid Caesar and Imogene Coca in their version of *A Streetcar Named Desire* from *Your Show of Shows*.

PHIL SILVERS'S 10 FAVORITE TV SERIES OF ALL TIME

The multitalented Silvers has been a star of vaudeville, stage, films, television, and nightclubs. He received a host of awards for his title performance in *Sergeant Bilko* and won Tonys for Best Actor in *Top Banana* and *A Funny Thing Happened on the Way to the Forum*. His films include *The Chicken Chronicles* and *The Cheap Detective*.

1. *Taxi*
2. *Sergeant Bilko*
3. *Jackie Gleason Show*
4. *Carol Burnett Show*
5. *Mary Tyler Moore*
6. *The Dick Cavett Show*
7. *M*A*S*H*
8. *You Are There*
9. *60 Minutes*
10. *All in the Family*

—Exclusive for *The Book of Lists 3*

ARTHUR GODFREY'S 10 BEST TV PERFORMERS OF ALL TIME

The well-known radio and TV personality has been on the air since the 1930s and is the star of the nationally broadcast *Arthur Godfrey Time*. He is an international trustee of the World Wildlife Fund and is a member of the Citizen's Advisory Committee on Environmental Quality and the National Advisory Committee on Oceans and Atmospheres.

1. Art Carney
2. Tim Conway
3. Minnie Pearl
4. Phil Silvers
5. Carol Burnett
6. Lucille Ball
7. Bob Crane
8. Alan Alda
9. Jean Stapleton
10. Benny Hill

—Exclusive for *The Book of Lists 3*

7 PERFORMERS WHO HAVE
WON THE MOST EMMYS

1. DINAH SHORE (8)

Best Female Singer (1954); Best Female Singer (1955); Best Female Personality—Continuing Performance (1956); Best Continuing Performance (Female) in a Series by a Comedienne, Singer, Hostess, Dancer, MC, Narrator, Panelist or any Person Who Essentially Plays Her-

Ed Asner and Mary Tyler Moore in the final episode of
The Mary Tyler Moore Show.

self (1957, *The Dinah Shore Chevy Show*); Best Performance by an Actress (Continuing Character) in a Musical or Variety Series (1958–1959, *The Dinah Shore Chevy Show*); Outstanding Program Achievement in Daytime (1972–1973, *Dinah's Place*); Best Host or Hostess in a Talk, Service, or Variety Show (1973–1974, *Dinah's Place*); Outstanding Host or Hostess in a Talk, Service, or Variety Show (1975–1976, *Dinah!*).

2. EDWARD ASNER (7)

Outstanding Performance by an Actor in a Supporting Role in Comedy (1970–1971, *The Mary Tyler Moore Show*); Outstanding Performance by an Actor in a Supporting Role in Comedy (1971–1972, *The Mary Tyler Moore Show*); Outstanding Continued Performance by a Supporting Actor in a Comedy Series (1974–1975, *The Mary Tyler Moore Show*); Outstanding Lead Actor for a Single Appearance in a Drama or Comedy Series (1975–1976, *Rich Man, Poor Man*); Outstanding Single Performance by a Supporting Actor in a Comedy or Drama Series (1976–1977, *Roots*, Part One); Outstanding Lead Actor in a Drama Series (1977–1978, *Lou Grant*); Outstanding Lead Actor in a Dramatic Series (1979–1980, *Lou Grant*).

3. MARY TYLER MOORE (6)

Outstanding Continued Performance by an Actress in a Series—Lead (1963–1964, *The Dick Van Dyke Show*); Outstanding Continued Performance by an Actress in a Leading Role in a Comedy Series (1965–1966, *The Dick Van Dyke Show*); Outstanding Continued Performance by an Actress in a Leading Role in a Comedy Series (1972–1973, *The Mary Tyler Moore Show*); Best Lead Actress in a Comedy Series (1973–1974, *The Mary Tyler Moore Show*); Actress of the Year—Series (1973–1974, *The Mary Tyler Moore Show*); Outstanding Lead Actress in a Comedy Series (1975–1976, *The Mary Tyler Moore Show*).

4. CAROL BURNETT (5)

Outstanding Performance in a Variety or Musical Program or Series (1961–1962, *Garry Moore Show*); Outstanding Performance in a Variety or Musical Program or Series (1962–1963, *Julie and Carol at Carnegie Hall*); Outstanding Variety Series—Musical (1971–1972, *The Carol Burnett Show*); Outstanding Music or Variety Series ((1973–1974, *The Carol Burnett Show*); Outstanding Comedy-Variety or Music Series (1974–1975, *The Carol Burnett Show*).

5. ART CARNEY (5)

Best Series Supporting Actor (1953, *The Jackie Gleason Show*); Best Supporting Actor in a Regular Series (1954, *The Jackie Gleason Show*); Best Actor in a Supporting Role (1955, *The Honeymooners*); Special Classification of Individual Achievement (1966–1967, *The Jackie Gleason Show*); Special Classification of Individual Achievement (1967–1968, *The Jackie Gleason Show*).

6. PERRY COMO (5)

Best Male Singer (1954); Best Male Singer (1955); Best MC or Program Host—Male or Female (1955); Best Male Personality—Continuing Performance (1956); Best Performance by an Actor in a Musical or Variety Series (Continuing Character) (1958–1959, *The Perry Como Show*).

7. DON KNOTTS (5)

Outstanding Performance in a Supporting Role by an Actor or Actress in a Series (1960–1961, *The Andy Griffith Show*); Outstanding Performance in a Supporting Role by an Actor (1961–1962, *The Andy Griffith Show*); Outstanding Performance by an Actor in a Supporting Role (1962–1963, *The Andy Griffith Show*); Outstanding Performance by an Actor in a Supporting Role in a Comedy (1965–1966, *The Andy Griffith Show*); Outstanding Performance by an Actor in a Supporting Role in a Comedy (1966–1967, *The Andy Griffith Show*).

—J.S.A.

AMERICA'S 30 MOST LISTENED TO RADIO STATIONS

	Station	Market	Number of People Listening*	Format	Owner	1981 Ranking
1.	WOR	New York	172,900	Talk	RKO	2
2.	WKTU-FM	New York	167,400	Urban	Infinity	3
3.	WRKS-FM	New York	162,200	Urban	RKO	74
4.	WBLS-FM	New York	143,400	Black	Inner City	1
5.	WCBS	New York	135,700	News	CBS	5
6.	WYNY-FM	New York	129,600	Adult contemporary	NBC	17
7.	WPLJ-FM	New York	127,700	Album-oriented rock	ABC	10
8.	WNBC	New York	125,300	Contemporary	NBC	4
9.	WGN	Chicago	120,500	Middle-of-the-road/talk	Tribune Co.	9
10.	WINS	New York	117,700	News	Westinghouse	11
11.	WRFM-FM	New York	113,800	Beautiful	Bonneville	8
12.	KABC	Los Angeles	108,000	Talk	ABC	7
13.	WJR	Detroit	106,600	Middle-of-the-road/talk	Capital Cities	14
14.	WLS	Chicago	101,900	Rock	ABC	18
15.	KDKA	Pittsburgh	96,100	Middle-of-the-road	Westinghouse	13
16.	WCCO	Minneapolis	94,700	Middle-of-the-road	Midwest Radio-RV	25

17. WPAT-FM	New York	90,400	Beautiful	Capital Cities	20
18. WNEW	New York	90,300	Nostalgia	Metro-media	15
19. KMOX	St. Louis	89,000	News/talk	CBS	16
20. KGO	San Francisco	85,100	News/talk	ABC	22
21. WMAQ	Chicago	83,300	Country	NBC	12
22. WABC	New York	82,000	Talk	ABC	6
23. KBIG-FM	Los Angeles	82,000	Beautiful	Bonne-ville	21
24. WHN	New York	80,500	Country	Mutual	28
25. WNEW-FM	New York	79,700	Album-oriented rock	Metro-media	27
26. WGCI-FM	Chicago	78,000	Urban	Gannett	72
27. KMET-FM	Los Angeles	77,500	Album-oriented rock	Metro-media	26
28. KYW	Phila-delphia	77,400	News	Westing-house	23
29. WCBS-FM	New York	76,600	Oldies	CBS	39
30. WBAP	Fort Worth/ Dallas	71,600	Country	Capital Cities	32

*Based on average number of people listening during ¼-hour period over a total survey area, Monday through Sunday, 6:00 A.M. to midnight.

SOURCE: James Duncan, Jr., *American Radio*. Privately published semi-annually in Kalamazoo, Mich. Statistics from Arbitron, Fall, 1982.

8 INCREDIBLE LIPOGRAMS

A form of verbal gymnastics, lipograms are written works that deliberately omit a certain letter of the alphabet by avoiding all words that include that letter. "Lipo" actually means "lacking"—in this case lacking a letter. An example of a contemporary lipogram is the nursery rhyme, "Mary Had a Little Lamb," rewritten without the letter *s*:

> *Mary had a little lamb*
> *With fleece a pale white hue,*
> *And everywhere that Mary went*
> *The lamb kept her in view;*
> *To academe he went with her,*
> *Illegal, and quite rare;*
> *It made the children laugh and play*
> *To view a lamb in there.*

—A. Ross Eckler

1. JACQUES ARAGO—AN *A*-LESS BOOK

The French author's book *Voyage Autour du Monde Sans la Lettre A* debuted in Paris in 1853. However, 30 years later in another edition, he admitted letting one letter *a* sneak by him in the book—he had overlooked the word *serait*.

2. GYLES BRANDRETH—*HAMLET* WITHOUT ANY *I*'s

A contemporary British lipogrammarian, Brandreth specializes in dropping a different letter from each of Shakespeare's plays. All *i*'s were excluded from *Hamlet*, rendering the famous soliloquy: "To be or not to be; that's the query." He proceeded to rewrite *Twelfth Night* without the letters *l* and *o*, *Othello* without any *o*'s, and *Macbeth* without any *a*'s or *e*'s.

3. GOTTLOB BURMANN—*R*-LESS POETRY (1737–1805)

Bearing an obsessive dislike for the letter *r*, Burmann not only wrote 130 poems without using that letter, but he also omitted the letter *r* from his daily conversation for 17 years. This practice meant the eccentric 18th-century German poet never said his own last name.

4. A. ROSS ECKLER—LIPOGRAM NURSERY RHYMES

Eckler's specialty is rewriting well-known nursery rhymes such as "Little Jack Horner," excluding certain letters. His masterpiece was "Mary Had a Little Lamb," which he re-created in several versions, omitting in turn the letters *s, a, h, e,* and *t* (as in the *t*-less "Mary Had a Pygmy Lamb").

5. PETER DE RIGA—A LIPOGRAM BIBLE

Summarizing the entire Bible in Latin, the 16th-century canon of Rheims Cathedral in France omitted a different letter of the alphabet from each of the 23 chapters he produced.

6. TRYPHIODORUS—A LIPOGRAM ODYSSEY

The Greek poet Tryphiodorus wrote his epic poem *Odyssey*, chronicling the adventures of Ulysses, excluding a different letter of the alphabet from each of the 24 books. Thus, the first book was written without alpha, the second book contained no betas, etc.

7. LOPE DE VEGA CARPIO—5 NOVELS WITHOUT VOWELS (1562–1635)

Also known as Spain's first great dramatist who reputedly wrote 2,200 plays, this 16th-century author wrote five novels that were lipograms. Each book omitted one of the five vowels *a, e, i, o,* and *u* in turn.

8. ERNEST VINCENT WRIGHT—NOVEL WITHOUT AN *E* (1939)

Tying down the *e* key on his typewriter to make sure one didn't slip in, Wright, a graduate of M.I.T., wrote a credible 50,110-word novel, *Gadsby*, totally excluding the most frequently used letter of the English alphabet. "Try to write a single ten-word sentence without an *e*," said the

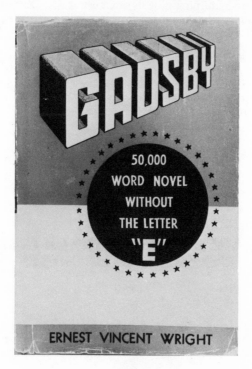

GADSBY

"Oh, how's that old corn of yours? Can't I put a balm——"

"*No!* You cannot! Mary, bring your pup; I'm going along."

As a happy tot was passing out that big, kindly front door, Sarah said:—

"Was Councilman Simpkins always so grouchy, Lady Standish?"

"No. Not until John Gadsby 'cut him out' and won Lady Gadsby."

"Aha!! And a Ho, Ho!!" said Sarah, laughing gayly. "So folks had what you call 'affairs' way back, just as today!" and also laughing inwardly, at what Lucy had said about this kindly Lady Standish and His Honor.

Ah! That good old schoolday, now so long past! How it bobs up, now-a-days, if you watch a young lad and a happy, giggling lass holding hands or laughing uproariously at youthful witticisms. And how diaphanous and almost imaginary that far-back day looks, if that girl with whom you stood up and said "I do," laughs, if you try a bit of romantic kissing, and says:—

"Why, John! How silly! You act actually childish!!"

* * * *

And now it won't do any harm to hark back

[147]

Ernest Vincent Wright, author of *Gadsby*.　　　A page from *Gadsby*.

Los Angeles *Times*, "and you will get some idea of the task he set himself." Wright's novel concerned the effort of a middle-aged man named John Gadsby to make his home town of Branton Hills more progressive and prosperous by turning over its administration to an Organization of Youth. Wright, a 67-year-old Californian, undertook his *e*-less novel to prove such a feat could be done. He wrote the book in 165 days. He employed no tricks, such as coining words or substituting apostrophes for *e*'s. His greatest difficulty, he stated, was in avoiding the use of verbs ending with *ed*, being forced to use "said" for "replied" or "asked," and in avoiding all pronouns such as "he," "she," or "they." Wright died on the day of his book's publication—but the $3.00 novel remains his monument. Today it sells at rare-book dealers for $1,000 a copy with a jacket.

—L.K.S.

17 NOTABLE BOOKS BANNED IN RECENT CENSORSHIP EPISODES

The conservative wave that followed the election of Ronald Reagan as U.S. President in 1980 has made itself felt in libraries across the country. According to Judith Krug, director of the American Library Associa-

226

tion's Office for Intellectual Freedom, censorship reports have tripled since the election. Some of the complaints come from the political left, but by and large, the increase in attempts at censorship are from the right. Of the 253 books reported to be under attack in a recent school library survey, most dealt with the subject of birth and sex.

1.–2. SLAUGHTERHOUSE-FIVE and DELIVERANCE (1973)

In Drake, N.D., novels by Kurt Vonnegut, Jr., and James Dickey were removed from the public schools because they allegedly contained profanity. All 32 copies of the Vonnegut book were consigned to a school furnace. The five school board members who voted for the ban had not read either book.

3. BEST SHORT STORIES BY NEGRO WRITERS (1976)

This collection of stories, edited by Langston Hughes, was one of 11 "objectionable" books (along with Desmond Morris's *The Naked Ape* and Bernard Malamud's *The Fixer*) that were banned from the Island Trees Union Free School District in Nassau County, New York. A parents' group had complained that they "were anti-American, anti-Christian, anti-Semitic, and just plain filthy."

4. THE AMERICAN HERITAGE DICTIONARY (1976, 1977)

The Cedar Lake, Ind., and Eldon, Mo., school boards ordered this dictionary removed from their high schools after parents singled out at least 80 offensive definitions. The criticized entries included such words as "bed," "shack," "rubber," "hot," "horny," and "slut." One Eldon parent made a sincere albeit mind-boggling comment: "If people learn words like that, it ought to be where you and I learned it—in the street and in the gutter."

5. AMERICA IN LEGEND (1977)

The school board of Cobb County, Ga., banned this Richard Dorson book from school libraries because it is "terrible for children," it "condones draft dodging," and it includes stanzas from "Casey Jones" which are related to his sexual prowess.

6. THE BELL JAR (1977)

Sylvia Plath's book was only one of the volumes banned by the Warsaw, Ind., school board. (Others included *The Stepford Wives* and *Go Ask Alice*.) Copies of these books were burned by members of the Warsaw Senior Citizens Club, who applauded the school board's decision to rid the high school of "filth."

7. DADDY WAS A NUMBERS RUNNER (1977)

The superintendent of schools in Oakland, Calif., removed this highly acclaimed autobiographical novel by Louise Meriwether from junior high school library shelves after a black father complained about it. The book describes a 12-year-old black girl growing up in a Harlem tenement. Ironically, the school superintendent formerly was a national director of the National Right to Read program.

8. *IN THE NIGHT KITCHEN* (1977)

Copies of the Maurice Sendak storybook, available in kindergarten classes in Springfield, Mo., were doctored with a felt-tip pen. A pair of shorts were placed on a drawing of a naked boy. The director of elementary education explained, "We felt [the book] was a good story. . . . As far as nudity is concerned I guess I'm an old fogey, but I think it should be covered."

9. *OF MICE AND MEN* (1977)

In Oil City, Pa., the school board removed copies of John Steinbeck's classic from the school library and had the books burned. This action was inspired by parental contentions that the novel "uses the Lord's name in vain, refers to prostitution, and takes a retarded person and makes a big issue of it."

10. *CATCHER IN THE RYE* (1978)

The school board of Issaquah, Wash., voted to remove the J. D. Salinger classic from the optional reading list of a high school literature class after an elderly citizen complained that the book "brainwashes students" and represents "part of an overall Communist plot." She testified that the book "has 222 'hells,' 27 'Chrissakes,' and 7 'hornys.'"

11. *OUR BODIES OURSELVES* (1978)

This women's health book was permanently removed from school libraries in Helena, Mont., after Marc Racicot, a member of the state attorney general's staff, informed the school board that ". . . any person distributing it to a child under the age of 16 could be subject to criminal charges." The Helena chapter of the Eagle Forum had first brought the book to Racicot's attention. They felt, and he agreed, that the book by the Boston Women's Health Collective ". . . assists, promotes, and encourages the reader to engage in sexual conduct." Racicot stated to the press, "I'm sick and tired of hearing the cry of censorship. We've genuflected at the altar of free speech far too long."

12. *THE BIBLE* (1980)

In North Carolina, the Columbus County library forbade children to check out the Bible unless they had obtained parental permission to bring home "adult books." The librarian said the Bible was classified as "adult" not because it was considered racy, but because it was thought to be too difficult for children to read easily.

13. *DEENIE* (1980)

This Judy Blume book was one of four titles (including Elia Kazan's *Acts of Love*, Tom Sullivan's *If You Could See What I Hear*, and Mora Stirling's *You Would if You Love Me*) removed from the state library's bookmobile in Brigham City, U. A member of the Citizens for True Freedom claimed that the books contained "the vilest sexual descriptions" and if read by "the wrong kid at the wrong time [they would] ruin his life."

14. *THE GRAPES OF WRATH* (1980)

John Steinbeck's novel was banished from sophomore English classes at two Kanawha, Ia., high schools after a parent complained that the book was "profane, vulgar, and obscene." The president of the local school board taking the action said that the U.S. was "going pell mell downhill" morally and that Kanawha was reversing the trend by banning the book.

15. *DEATH OF A SALESMAN* (1981)

The principal of Springs Valley High School in French Lick, Ind., proscribed reading this Arthur Miller play in an English class after some ministers complained that the drama included the words "bastard," "goddamn," and "son-of-a-bitch." Students became so curious about the play's contents that they quickly checked out all the local public library copies.

16.–17. *THE BOOK OF LISTS* and *THE BOOK OF LISTS 2* (1981)

Adhering to complaints about *The Book of Lists* from several parents in Glen Rose, Ark., a faculty committee at Glen Rose High School recommended removing only those portions dealing with "sexual perversion." The rest of the best seller by David Wallechinsky, Irving Wallace, and Amy Wallace was allowed to remain intact on the library shelf. Superintendent Don Henson insisted that the action was not censorship, since the book was available—unedited—outside the school. Henson said, "If people want to read these books—fine. But we're not going to provide them." During 1981 Saudi Arabia dealt more severely with *The Book of Lists* 2. The entire book was banned because it contained critical comments about the Saudi government.

—R.T.

16 WELL-KNOWN BOOKS THAT WERE GHOSTWRITTEN

1. *PERSONAL MEMOIRS OF U. S. GRANT* (1885–86)

While Ulysses S. Grant was dying of throat cancer, he dictated the story of his life to a stenographer, sometimes 10,000 words at a sitting, often after taking large doses of cocaine for pain. Mark Twain contracted to publish the two-volume autobiography of the former president of the U.S., and—because of his close involvement in the project—is believed by some historians to have rewritten and polished the manuscript himself.

2. THE NORTH POLE (1910)

A. E. Thomas, dramatist and novelist, wrote Peary's account of his successful expedition to the North Pole. Thomas later said, "It is perfectly true that I wrote the bulk of Peary's *North Pole*. I should think 80% would be about right." It was not an entirely happy collaboration. According to Thomas, "It was a dull book, because Peary was a dull man and it was impossible to get much lively human material out of him."

3. PROFILES IN COURAGE (1956)

In the book's preface, John F. Kennedy ackowledged that his "greatest debt" was to special counsel and speechwriter Theodore C. Sorensen for "his invaluable assistance in the assembly and preparation of the material upon which this book is based." Sorensen and Kennedy, however, both denied that anyone but Kennedy did the actual writing, although the *Los Angeles Times* reported that this Pulitzer Prize-winning book "is widely regarded in publishing (and political) circles to have been largely written by . . . Sorensen."

4. SIX CRISES (1962)

Richard Nixon once said that writing this political memoir was a maturing experience. However, the book—except for the last chapter, about the 1960 presidential campaign—was actually ghosted by former Associated Press reporter Alvin Moscow. Nixon wrote the final chapter himself while Moscow worked on other sections. Doubleday editor Kenneth McCormick commented, "He [Nixon] had read all the stuff that had been written already and had assimilated Al's approach to the figure of Richard Nixon. So he wrote the chapter alone. It actually needed very little editing."

5. THE SENATOR (1968)

Drew Pearson—who was the first reporter to accuse John F. Kennedy of using a ghostwriter for *Profiles in Courage*—turned to Gerald Green when writing his own novel. Green, author of *Holocaust* and *The Last Angry Man*, was casually acknowledged by Pearson for his "assistance in the preparation of this book."

6. THE FRENCH CONNECTION (1969)

Writer Ed Keyes told *The New York Times*, "Actually I wrote most of *[The French Connection]*. But I have a good feeling about Robin, and I don't like to see anybody take anything away from him." The publisher apparently felt the same way, since the title page of the book named Robin Moore as the sole author.

7. HOW TO TALK WITH PRACTICALLY ANYBODY ABOUT PRACTICALLY ANYTHING (1970)

Canadian journalist June Callwood apparently did her job too well when ghosting Barbara Walters' book. Upon seeing the finished manuscript, Barbara complained, "People who know me will know I can't write so well." So she and her ghost spent four days at the Plaza Hotel in New York scaling down the book. Doubleday editor Kenneth McCormick recalled, "They went through it and changed a lot of very hard journalism, which June is capable of, and made it a little more rough-hewn."

8. *OUR ENVIRONMENT CAN BE SAVED* (1970)

Published while Nelson Rockefeller was the governor of New York, the book includes three pages of acknowledgments, thanking no fewer than 63 individuals and institutions. The name of Rodney Campbell appears at the top of the list. A researcher and writer, Campbell finished the book in just a few weeks, but Rockefeller never read the manuscript, explaining to his publisher, "I just don't have time to read it." After the book was released, Rockefeller spoke to a group of conservationists, and his prepared text included the line: "I've just written a book on the environment." During the address, he changed it to: "I've just put out a book . . ."

9. *THE HAPPY HOOKER* (1972)

Writer Yvonne Dunleavy received $100,000 for ghosting this book for Xaviera Hollander. Dunleavy later reported that while taping interviews with Hollander in her Manhattan brothel, they were frequently interrupted by phone calls from the madam's clients.

10. *THE LOVO-MANIACS* (1972)

Although the book jacket called this novel "so wicked only . . . Rona Barrett could write it," publishing sources credit Ted Thackrey, Jr.—a *Los Angeles Times* reporter—with ghosting the book based on Barrett's original concept, ideas, and written material.

11. *COSELL* (1973)

Mickey Herskowitz—who has coauthored books with Dan Rather, Leon Jaworski, and Gene Autry—received no cover credit on *Cosell*. He says that Howard Cosell chose to use a collaborator because "Howard works best in front of an audience."

12. *THE RELAXATION RESPONSE* (1975)

The first editions of this book on meditative techniques had only Dr. Herbert Benson's name on the cover. But once the book became a best seller, writer Miriam Z. Klipper threatened a lawsuit. She wanted to share the royalties as well as get cover credit for helping to write the book. Subsequent editions of the book read "Herbert Benson, M.D., with Miriam Z. Klipper."

13. *BLIND AMBITION* (1976)

Taylor Branch, a contributor to *Harper's* and *Esquire*, was paid $20,000 to rewrite thoroughly the first draft of John Dean's book, which one prepublication reader had found "as interesting as a laundry list."

14. *HONORABLE MEN: MY LIFE IN THE CIA* (1978)

In 1978 Peter Forbath wrote two books. *The River Congo* appeared under his own name, but *Honorable Men* was credited to William Colby. It was the Colby book that received the most attention. Describing his daily sessions with the ex-CIA chief at the Intrigue Hotel in Washington,

D.C., Forbath recalled: "Here was a man who had spent his entire adult life learning to keep his mouth shut and withhold information. And I had to get him to talk. I'd scream at him, scold him, have temper tantrums, and we'd gain a little ground. Still, he was overcautious and I think the book shows it."

15. *A TIME TO HEAL* (1979)

On the acknowledgments page of his book, Gerald R. Ford warmly thanks Trevor Armbrister—a *Reader's Digest* roving editor—whose "writing skills and fierce devotion to excellence made my association with him one of the highlights of my days since leaving the White House." But Armbrister's name didn't appear on the book's cover or title page because Ford's editor at Harper & Row believed that doing so "would not be presidential."

16. *TO SET THE RECORD STRAIGHT* (1979)

Although *Time* magazine described John Sirica as "dotting the i's" on his book about Watergate, *Time*'s own correspondent John Stacks wrote the actual manuscript. When Sirica was asked why he didn't give Stacks credit on the book jacket, he responded, "It's my story, and I saw no reason I should have anyone else's name on the cover."

—R.T.

16 AUTHORS WHO WROTE NOVELS IN LESS THAN 6 WEEKS

1. LOUISA MAY ALCOTT

Alcott wrote *Little Men* (1871) in three weeks while she was on vacation in Rome. She had been notified that her brother-in-law, John Pratt, had died. By this time, Alcott was the family's main source of financial support, and her sister and nephew had an immediate need for money to live on. *Eight Cousins* (New York, 1874) was written in approximately six weeks while Alcott was taking drugs, especially morphine, in order to sleep. She was afflicted with both mental depressions and poor physical health, caused at least partially by the demands of her family. Later she rented a room away from home in order to be able to sleep without the use of drugs.

2. HONORÉ DE BALZAC

Le Père Goriot (1834) was written in one month, 10 days so Balzac could pay his mounting debts. He labored 24 hours a day, drinking large cups of strong coffee and eating sparingly while writing it. His behavior at this time was so fanatical that his doctor diagnosed "brain fever" and insisted he take a complete rest.

3. JOHN CREASEY

Creasey learned to write fast when he was earning about one tenth of a cent per word. Over four decades he wrote 564 novels under his own name as well as many pen names; he probably wrote almost all of these in less than six weeks. His personal record was two books in six days, but he preferred to spend about 12 days on one book.

4. ALEISTER CROWLEY

Crowley, a British writer who called himself "The Great Beast," is better known for his decadent life-style than his writings. *The Diary of a Drug Fiend* (1923) was written at the height of his dabblings in black magic, sex rituals, and drugs. It describes a passionate love affair and the two lovers' growing addiction to heroin and cocaine. Despite his own prodigious daily intake of heroin and other drugs, Crowley's brain and constitution remained, for a period, unaffected. Averaging 5,000 words a day, he finished the book in less than a month, despite a mysterious fever contracted in the last week. The book caused an enormous scandal and was vehemently attacked by the press.

5. DANIEL DEFOE

One of the earliest of the British novelists, Defoe became an instant success with *The Life and Strange Surprising Adventures of Robinson Crusoe, of York, the Mariner*. Eager to capitalize on his luck, he wrote part two—*The Further Adventures of Robinson Crusoe*—the month following the publication of the first volume.

6. ERLE STANLEY GARDNER

Gardner dictated his first Perry Mason novel, *The Case of the Velvet Claws* (1933) in three and a half days, while devoting half of each day to his Ventura, Calif., law practice. In the 80-plus Perry Mason novels that Gardner cranked out, only one error of law was ever detected.

7. H. RIDER HAGGARD

Challenged by his brother to write an adventure story as good as Stevenson's *Treasure Island*, Haggard turned out *King Solomon's Mines* (London, 1885) in exactly six weeks. Because of several prior publishing failures, Haggard was tempted to accept a flat £100 for his quickie book, but at the last minute he signed a 10% royalty contract instead. The book proved an instant success and made him rich. A year later he wrote his second great best seller, *She* (London, 1887), in another six-week period.

8. JAMES HILTON

Hilton had a deadline but no ideas for a British magazine story. After a sleepless night and a morning bicycle ride, he was ready to write. In four days he finished *Good-bye, Mr. Chips* (1934), his story of the kindly schoolmaster. The story went unnoticed in Britain, but after book publication in America, it became an international best seller, guaranteeing Hilton a lifetime reputation as an author.

9. SAMUEL JOHNSON

Johnson wrote *The History of Rasselas, Prince of Abyssinia* (1759) during the evenings in just one week to pay for his mother's funeral expenses. It has often been compared with Voltaire's *Candide*. Both books attack the optimism of the 18th century, and they were published only a few weeks apart.

10. EDWARD ZANE CARROLL JUDSON ("NED BUNTLINE")

One of the originators of the "dime novel" and the man who gave Buffalo Bill his name and made him famous, Judson wrote over 400 adventure novels. He claimed he had written one 610-page book in 62 hours, while not stopping to eat or sleep during that time.

11. ANNE RICE

After writing for 10 years without making a substantial sale, Rice turned out *Interview with the Vampire* (1977), her eerie vampire story, in five weeks in order to meet a contest deadline. She didn't win a prize but did get the book published, and within a year it became a highly profitable best seller.

12. WALTER SCOTT

Written in six weeks partly to pay the bills that had been accumulated by his book-selling business, *Guy Mannering* (1815) is considered one of his best works.

13. GEORGES SIMENON

The prolific Belgian novelist trained himself to write fast. At 17 he wrote his first novel, *Au Pont des Arches* (1920), in 10 days; his personal record for a book was just 25 hours. As he turned to more serious fiction, he developed a system for writing each of the 200-page Inspector Maigret mysteries in precisely 11 days, at a chapter a day. Any time his 11-day pattern was interrupted, he would abandon the book and then start the next one fresh.

14. ROBERT LOUIS STEVENSON

Stevenson wrote *The Strange Case of Dr. Jekyll and Mr. Hyde* (1886) in three days after he had had a nightmare which depicted the plot. His wife, Fanny, however, criticized the results harshly. Instead of a thriller, she said, the story should be an allegory. Stevenson angrily disagreed with her but later admitted that she was right, burned the first manuscript, and—in the next three days—rewrote the story.

15. GORE VIDAL

Writing as "Edgar Box," Vidal turned out three 70,000-word murder mysteries in about a week each. (His house burned down while he was writing the third book, and when he returned to his work he couldn't remember who the murderer was, and he couldn't follow his own clues.) Vidal has generally spent about a year on each of his more serious novels, but he wrote *Myra Breckinridge* (1968), which earned him a million dollars, in one month (not counting rewriting).

16. EVELYN WAUGH

Waugh wrote each of his early satires, such as *Scoop*, in about six weeks, but as he matured he wrote increasingly slowly. However, after the prodigious effort he put into *Brideshead Revisited* (1945), he reverted to his old form and wrote *Scott-King's Modern Europe* (1947), another satire, in five weeks.

—R.B., M.MC., & R.K.R.

9 NOVELS—EACH WRITTEN BY 4 OR MORE AUTHORS

1. *SIX OF ONE BY HALF A DOZEN OF THE OTHER* by Harriet Beecher Stowe, Adeline D. T. Whitney, Lucretia P. Hale, Frederic W. Loring, Frederic B. Perkins, Edward E. Hale. Boston: Roberts Brothers, 1872.

   The "Six of One" in the title refers to six characters in the book—three men and three women—who come together and move apart, both physically and emotionally. Their original names were simplified to show that they were "common-place, not very high-flying, people," according to one of the unsigned prefaces to the book. The "Half a Dozen of the Other" refers to the six authors, of whom Stowe and the Hale siblings are perhaps best known to today's readers, Stowe for *Uncle Tom's Cabin*, brother Hale for *The Man Without a Country*, and sister Hale for the children's book *The Peterkin Papers*. Each of the authors selected the part he or she wished to write. Only five were able to complete the project. Loring was killed—perhaps by Apaches—during a trip to the West. *Six of One* was first serialized in the magazine *Old and New* and later published in book form. It is not usually mentioned in biographies of Stowe.

2. *LA CROIX DE BERNY* by Charles de Launay (pseudonym of Mme. Émile de Girardin), Théophile Gautier, Jules Sandeau, Joseph Méry. Paris: Pétion, 1846.

   Each of the authors—recognized, says the editor of the original edition, "as the four most brilliant of our celebrated contemporaneous authors"—was responsible for one of the characters in this strongly plotted novel—written in epistolary form—about a woman and her lovers. In real life, Sandeau was one of writer George Sand's lovers.

3. *THE MIZ MAZE, OR THE WINKWORTH PUZZLE: A STORY IN LETTERS, BY NINE AUTHORS* by Charlotte Mary Yonge, Christabel Coleridge, Mary M. Bramston, Frances M. Peard, Frances Awdry, Florence Wilford, Eleanor Price, Mary S. Lee, A. E. Mary Anderson Morshead. London: Macmillan, 1883.

The nine British women who wrote this very dull epistolary novel invented 19 characters, which were divided up among them, then wove interlocking correspondences among these characters. Yonge is the most famous of the nine authors. She wrote more than 160 books but is usually remembered for *The Heir of Redclyffe*. Coleridge was Yonge's biographer.

4. *THE WHOLE FAMILY* by William Dean Howells, Mary E. Wilkins Freeman, Mary Heaton Vorse, Mary Stewart Cutting, Elizabeth Jordan, John Kendrick Bangs, Henry James, Elizabeth Stuart Phelps, Edith Wyatt, Mary R. Shipman Andrews, Alice Brown, Henry van Dyke. New York: Harper & Brothers, 1908.

The Whole Family is about a young man who falls in love with his fiancée's maiden aunt and the subsequent reactions of the girl's relatives to this bizarre situation. Each of the twelve authors took the point of view of a different family member in writing his or her chapter. Critics of the day praised the book for its wit and insight into the complexities of human nature.

5. *BOBBED HAIR* by 19 authors, among them: Louis Bromfield, Sophie Kerr, George Agnew Chamberlin, Bernice Brown, John V. A. Weaver, Alexander Woollcott, George Barr McCutcheon, Carolyn Wells, Rube Goldberg, Edward Streeter, Kermit Roosevelt, Frank Craven. New York: G. P. Putnam's Sons, 1925.

For this standard mystery novel, conceived by publisher George Putnam, 19 authors—9 men and 10 women—were commissioned to write one chapter each. Putnam himself also wrote one chapter. They had no detailed story outline but instead simply adhered to Putnam's basic idea, each writer building on the chapter of the previous writer. Moderately successful, the book was serialized in *Collier's* and eventually was made into a movie.

6. *THE FLOATING ADMIRAL* by Dorothy L. Sayers, G. K. Chesterton, Victor L. Whitechurch, G. D. H. Cole, M. Cole, Henry Wade, Agatha Christie, John Rhode, Milward Kennedy, Ronald A. Knox, Freeman Wills Crofts, Edgar Jepson, Clemence Dane, Anthony Berkeley. Garden City, N.Y.: Doubleday, Doran, 1931.

The Floating Admiral was a group effort by 14 associates in "The Detection Club." The club's members pledged to keep the art of detective fiction pure by taking an oath to "detect by their wits, without the help of accident or coincidence," and not to "invent impossible death rays and poisons." Within these guidelines, the authors produced a classic example of detective fiction.

7. *THE PRESIDENT'S MYSTERY STORY* propounded by Franklin Delano Roosevelt and solved by Rupert Hughes, Samuel Hopkins Adams, Anthony Abbot (pseudonym of Fulton Oursler), Rita Weiman, S. S. Van Dine (pseudonym of W. H. Wright), John Erskine. New York: Farrar & Rinehart, 1935.

At a White House dinner in 1935, President Franklin D. Roosevelt described to *Liberty* magazine editor Fulton Oursler a rudimentary plot: A man with several million dollars experiences a midlife crisis, precipitated by a stale marriage and boring work; he dreams of starting over as a wealthy, single man with a new identity. Roosevelt had been unable to follow his story through to completion because he could not resolve one crucial problem: "How can a man disappear with $5 million in any negotiable form and not be traced?" Oursler engaged six mystery writers to solve the problem and flesh out the sketchy plot. He wrote one chapter himself, under a pseudonym. *The President's Mystery Story* ran as a serial in *Liberty*, was published as a book, and was made into a movie.

8. *NAKED CAME THE STRANGER* by Penelope Ashe (pseudonym of 25 journalists on the Long Island paper *Newsday*). New York: Lyle Stuart, Inc., 1969.

Written as a spoof on pulp sex novels, *Naked Came the Stranger* tells in torrid detail the sexual adventures of Gillian Blake—Gilly of the *Billy and Gilly Show,* a husband-and-wife radio program reflecting a supposedly ideal marriage, which is in actuality in very bad shape. *The New York Times Book Review,* its reviewer unaware of the book's real authorship, gave it a C. "The passing grade is for the author's attempt to twine a few thin strands of humor into her wishful thinking." Other reviews weren't much better. Nonetheless, the book sold out instantly everywhere.

9. *MURDER MYSTERY 1* by Sheldon Klein, J. F. Aeschlimann, D. F. Balsiger, S. L. Converse, C. Court, M. Foster, R. Lao, J. D. Oakley, J. Smith. Minneapolis: Distributed at the International Conference on Computers in the Humanities, 1973.

Although computers have proven more competent than human beings in many jobs, there is little chance that the machines will replace living authors. At the University of Wisconsin, nine programmers decided to create the Novel Writer Simulation Program. The result was *Murder Mystery 1*, a 2,100-word story written in 19 seconds by a UNIVAC 1108 computer. The tale begins unceremoniously: "Wonderful smart Lady Buxley was rich. Ugly oversexed Lady Buxley was single. John was Lady Buxley's nephew. Impoverished irritable John was evil. Handsome oversexed John Buxley was single. John hated Edward. John Buxley hated Dr. Bartholomew Hume. Brilliant Hume was evil. Hume was oversexed." Exciting stuff, no? When it comes to producing literature, the computer chip is currently in a class with the cow chip.

—A.E. & M.J.T.

STEPHEN KING'S 10 FAVORITE HORROR BOOKS OR SHORT STORIES

Creator of the horror story *par excellence,* King scored his first success in 1974 with *Carrie.* Six more best sellers followed, including his latest novel, *Cujo.* Both *Carrie* and *The Shining* have been made into movies. Recently King collaborated on a movie entitled *Creepshow.*

1. *Ghost Story* by Peter Straub
2. *Dracula* by Bram Stoker
3. *The Haunting* by Shirley Jackson
4. *Dr. Jekyll and Mr. Hyde* by R. L. Stevenson
5. *Burnt Offerings* by Robert Marosco
6. *Casting the Runes* by M. R. James
7. *Two Bottles of Relish* by Lord Dunsany
8. *The Great God Pan* by Arthur Machen
9. *The Colour Out of Space* by H. P. Lovecraft
10. *The Upper Berth* by F. Marion Crawford

—Exclusive for *The Book of Lists 3*

THE 15 GREATEST
LOCKED ROOM MYSTERIES

Inside a room someone has been murdered. Every door, window, means of entry has been locked from the inside. There is no human in the room except the corpse. How did the murder happen? That's your classical puzzle, the locked room mystery. In 1981, for his *All but Impossible!: An Anthology of Locked Room & Impossible Crime Stories*, author Edward D. Hoch took a poll of 17 mystery story experts—among them Jacques Barzun, Ellery Queen, Howard Haycraft, and Julian Symons—and asked each one for "a list of their favorite locked room or impossible crime novels." Hock awarded 10 points to the first-place choice, 9 to the second, 8 to the third, and so on. Here are the results of the poll.

Title, Author, and Year	*Points*
1. *The Three Coffins*, John Dickson Carr (1935) (British title: *The Hollow Man*)	104
2. *Rim of the Pit*, Hake Talbot (1944)	59
3. *The Mystery of the Yellow Room*, Gaston Leroux (1908)	57
4. *The Crooked Hinge*, John Dickson Carr (1938)	55
5. *The Judas Window*, Carter Dickson (John Dickson Carr) (1938)	51
6. *The Big Bow Mystery*, Israel Zangwill (1892)	47
7. *Death from a Top Hat*, Clayton Rawson (1938)	39
8. *The Chinese Orange Mystery*, Ellery Queen (1934)	35
9. *Nine Times Nine*, H. H. Holmes (Anthony Boucher) (1940)	30
10. *The Peacock Feather Murders*, Carter Dickson (John Dickson Carr) (1937) (British title: *The Ten Teacups*)	22
11. *The King Is Dead*, Ellery Queen (1952)	20
12. *Through a Glass, Darkly*, Helen McCloy (1950)	19
13. *He Wouldn't Kill Patience*, Carter Dickson (John Dickson Carr) (1944)	18

—Copyright 1981 by Mystery Writers of America. Reprinted by permission of Edward D. Hoch.

DORIS LESSING'S 10 FAVORITE WRITERS OF ALL TIME (NOT NECESSARILY IN THIS ORDER)

British novelist Lessing was born in Persia and reared on a farm in Southern Rhodesia. Her childhood experiences provided her with material for many books, including her first published novel, *The Grass Is Singing,* and a five-volume series entitled *Children of Violence.* Many critics consider her greatest work to be *The Golden Notebook.*

1. The sage Mahmud Shabestari
2. Marcel Proust
3. Anton Chekov
4. Idries Shah
5. Henry David Thoreau
6. Gerald Manley Hopkins
7. al-Ghazali of Persia
8. Leo Tolstoy
9. Jalal-ud-din Rumi
10. Ibn al-Arabi

Note: Mahmud Shabestari (c. 1250–c. 1320) was a Persian writer whose poetical work *Golshan-e raz (The Mystic Rose Garden)* is considered by many Europeans to be the classic expression of Sufism (Islamic mysticism). Al-Ghazali (1058–1111), a Muslim jurist and theologian, incorporated Sufism into orthodox Islam largely through his great work, *The Revival of the Religious Sciences.* Jalal-ud-din Rumi (1207–1273), still called "Our Master," is considered to be the greatest Islamic mystic poet in the Persian language. Ibn al-Arabi (1165–1240), one of the giants in the history of Muslim theosophy, was the first to give Islamic thought mature philosophic expression, as evidenced in his work *Fusus al-hikam (The Bezels of Wisdom).*

—Exclusive for *The Book of Lists 3*

AUTHORS OF 11 FAMOUS LOST OR DESTROYED MANUSCRIPTS

1. JEAN-BAPTISTE MOLIÈRE (1622–1673)

The French actor-playwright was also an accomplished classical scholar. He toiled for many years translating a work by the first-century Latin poet Lucretius, entitled *On the Nature of Things*. When a bumbling servant used some pages of the translation as curl papers for Molière's wig, the temperamental author flew into a rage and threw the rest of the manuscript into the fire.

2. ISAAC NEWTON (1642–1727)

No one knows the precise content of the manuscript which Newton lost while teaching at Cambridge University, but its destruction caused the scientist deep distress. The work may have been a study of colors and light, or the result of years of chemistry experiments. It is believed that Newton left his rooms, forgetting on his desk a burning candle which was overturned by his beloved dog Diamond. Returning to find the precious papers burned to a crisp, Newton is supposed to have

Sir Isaac Newton.

said, "Ah, Diamond, Diamond, thou little knowest what damage thou hast done." A number of Newton's surviving manuscripts are scorch-marked, suggesting that the genius who discovered the laws of gravity, motion, and calculus was an absentminded professor.

3. ROBERT AINSWORTH (1660–1743)

A schoolmaster who pursued classical studies on the side, Ainsworth began preparation of his Latin-English dictionary in 1714. It took 22 years to complete the work, due in part to the author's advancing age and his failing eyesight. However, much of the delay was due to the fact that he had to rewrite one whole section, which his wife threw into the fire during a domestic squabble. The dictionary was finally published in 1736.

4. LORD BYRON (1788–1824)

In 1819 Byron gave the only draft of his memoirs to his friend and fellow poet Thomas Moore, with the instruction that it be published posthumously. Read only by a chosen few, reports varied as to the raciness of the contents. One reader saw nothing shameful in it, while another said it was fit for a brothel. Byron's lifelong friend John Cam Hobhouse was jealous of Moore, and when Byron died, Hobhouse urged that the manuscript be destroyed to save Byron's family from a scandal. With Moore and Hobhouse in attendance, all 400 pages of *My Life and Adventures* were torn up and burned in the offices of Byron's intimidated publisher.

5. THOMAS CARLYLE (1795–1881)

Writing was a painful process for this Scottish historian; after five torturous months he completed the first volume of his magnum opus, *The History of the French Revolution*, in February, 1835. Carlyle gave the manuscript to his friend John Stuart Mill, who then lent it to his intimate friend, Mrs. Harriet Taylor—whom he later married. Mrs. Taylor read late into the night, leaving the manuscript on a table. In the morning, her maid spotted a messy-looking pile of paper—167 sheets crammed with 600 words per page. Assuming it was trash, she lit the fire with the entire *History of the French Revolution*. Mill was devastated. He staggered to Carlyle's house, pale, shaking, and at first unable to speak. It took Carlyle and his wife, Jane, three hours to console him. Not until midnight, when Mill finally left, could Carlyle express his true despair. He had not earned a penny from writing in two years and had not saved a single note on the book he'd written in "a kind of blaze." With Jane's support, Carlyle recovered and resolved to start from scratch, rereading a staggering mountain of research. Mill tried to give Carlyle £200, but he would accept only £100. In three months the author had reproduced Volume I, and by 1837 the book was finished. Though he wrote that the task "had nearly choked the life out of me," the book was a dazzling success, immediately hailed as a masterpiece.

6. SIR RICHARD BURTON (1821–1890)

The unconventional explorer and scholar completed an annotated translation of *The Scented Garden*, a 16th-century Arabic sex manual. It included salient information on such matters as "how Eunuchs are made and are married," female circumcision, copulation with crocodiles, a man cuckolded by his donkey, etc. "Mrs. Grundy will howl till she almosts bursts," Sir Richard predicted. Unfortunately, this was not to be—Burton died, and his religious wife rejected a $30,000 offer for the manuscript. She consulted a priest, who confirmed her fears that *The Scented Garden* would corrupt all who read it and ruin her husband's reputation. "Sorrowfully and reverently" she burned every page as well as 40 years' worth of Burton's journals, letters, and papers.

7. SIR ARTHUR CONAN DOYLE (1859–1930)

The first novel by the creator of Sherlock Holmes was lost in the mail on its way to a publisher. *The Narrative of John Smith* was autobiographical in nature and "steered perilously near to the libelous," wrote Doyle. He later observed, "My shock at its disappearance would be as nothing to my horror if it were suddenly to appear again—in print."

8. T. E. LAWRENCE (1888–1935)

The first version of "Lawrence of Arabia's" famous epic account of the Arab revolt was lost forever. In 1919, Lawrence took a train trip from London to Oxford, carrying with him eight of the 10 volumes of his master work in "a bank messenger's bag." He changed trains at Reading, where he entered the station refreshment room. Absentmindedly, he left the precious piece of luggage under a table. An hour later he phoned from Oxford, but the bag was gone. Though Lawrence had destroyed most of his notes, friends persuaded him to rewrite the entire book the following year. In fact, before the first copies were printed in 1922, he rewrote the book a second time.

9. ERNEST HEMINGWAY (1899–1961)

In 1922, Hemingway was working as a correspondent in Switzerland. His first wife, Hadley, who was to join him for Christmas, decided to surprise her husband by bringing him as many of his early manuscripts as she could find—along with carbon copies. She packed them in a valise that she handed to a porter at the Gare de Lyon in Paris. The valise was stolen, resulting in the loss of Hemingway's untitled first novel—written at age 23—and some short stories. (Two stories from that period survived to become classics.) Hadley was inconsolable over the tragedy, Hemingway wrote. He took it manfully and soon left her for another woman.

10. JOHN STEINBECK (1902–1968)

In 1936 Steinbeck's progress on his novella *Of Mice and Men* was delayed when his setter puppy chewed up half the manuscript. There was no other draft, so two months were consumed rewriting the section. Later, when critics panned the work, Steinbeck thought better of the setter's literary taste. "I have promoted Toby-dog to be lieutenant-colonel in charge of literature," he wrote.

11. MARGERIE BONNER (1905–   )

It was only one chapter of the manuscript of Bonner's *The Last Twist of the Knife* (1946), and it was not really lost—merely stuffed away in an editor's bottom drawer. But the "loss" was not discovered until the mystery novel was already in its first printing, lacking a final chapter as well as a sense of mystery. The publisher offered readers a pamphlet version of the chapter but claimed that few even noticed the omission. Bonner, a former movie actress married to writer Malcolm Lowry, did not take the matter quite so lightly. Subsequent printings of the book did include the last chapter.

—M.B.T., C.D., & A.W.

BOOKS THAT FAMOUS WRITERS WOULD TAKE TO A NEW PLANET

We asked a group of well-known authors what books they would take along if they were forced to abandon Earth and travel to another planet. We asked each of them: "If you were one of those chosen to inhabit a livable new planet, real or artificial, and you were allowed to take along any five books ever published, which five books would you put in your luggage? The planet's English-language library already has the Bible, collected works of Shakespeare, an encyclopedia, a dictionary, and Bartlett's *Familiar Quotations*. What 5 books, for your pleasure or reference and that of others, would you take to supplement this library?"

KEN FOLLETT'S 5 BOOKS TO TAKE TO A NEW PLANET

Follett is a young Welsh novelist and playwright who loves music and medieval cathedrals. His first suspense thriller published in the U.S., *The Eye of the Needle*, was an immediate best seller, praised as "a triumph of invention over convention." It has been followed by *Triple, The Key to Rebecca*, and *The Man from St. Petersburg*.

1. *The Uses of Enchantment* by Bruno Bettelheim

Reason: Contains more insight into the nature of fiction than any work of criticism I've ever read.

2. *Remembrance of Things Past* by Marcel Proust

Reason: Sorry to be predictable, but I plan to be reading this book for the rest of my life.

243

3. *The Dream Merchants* by Harold Robbins

Reason: My favorite among the novels of the world's greatest story-teller (and it's time he started paying me for all the publicity I give him).

4. *Philosophical Investigations* by Ludwig Wittgenstein

Reason: On this new planet I might have time to figure out why he's wrong.

5. *The Romance of Lust* (anonymous)

Reason: This is the best pornographic novel ever written.

—Exclusive for *The Book of Lists 3*

VICTORIA HOLT'S 6 BOOKS TO TAKE TO A NEW PLANET

The prolific London-born author has more than a dozen international best sellers to her name. Since the publication of *The Mistress of Mellyn* in 1960, she has become the recognized queen of romantic suspense novels, with sales running in excess of 50 million copies. Holt's latest books are *My Enemy the Queen, The Spring of the Tiger*, and *The Mask of the Enchantress*.

1. *Jane Eyre* by Charlotte Brontë

Reason: It is a book I never tire of reading. It has had a great influence on other writers. It is exciting and moving as a novel and revealing as a picture of its times.

2.–3. *I, Claudius* and *Claudius the God* by Robert Graves

Reason: They give a wonderful insight into the manners and customs of ancient Rome, and reading them is an education as well as a superb entertainment.

4. *The King Must Die* by Mary Renault

Reason: The same reason as above—though ancient Greece instead of Rome.

5. *The Dictionary of National Biography* edited by Sir Leslie Stephen and Sir Sidney Lee

Reason: I know this is an encyclopedia of a kind but I couldn't exist without it if I were to carry on working, and that is a necessity for me. In this I get potted biographies of people who interest me and of whom I might want to read at any moment.

6. *The Oxford Book of English Verse* chosen by Arthur Quiller-Couch

Reason: I must have some poetry and here I should find most of my favorite pieces and something from the greatest of poets from the year 1250 onward.

—Exclusive for *The Book of Lists 3*

ROALD DAHL'S 5 BOOKS TO TAKE TO A NEW PLANET

This Welsh-born author has written plays, screenplays, nearly 50 short stories, and eight highly successful juvenile books, including *Charlie and the Chocolate Factory* and *The Enormous Crocodile*. Although Dahl had his first adult novel, *My Uncle Oswald*, published in 1980, he prefers writing for children because, he says, "adults are much too serious for me."

1. Price's *Textbook of the Practice of Medicine* (Oxford University Press)

Reason: A professional medical textbook covering the description, diagnoses, and treatment of virtually every known disease or illness.

2. *The Greater Oxford Dictionary*

3. *The Pickwick Papers*—Dickens

4. A book containing all of Beethoven's piano sonatas

5. Johann Sebastian Bach's B minor Mass

—Exclusive for *The Book of Lists 3*

DANIELLE STEEL'S 4 BOOKS TO TAKE TO A NEW PLANET

Born in New York and educated in France, Danielle Steel is a writer whose prose and poetry have appeared in such magazines as *Cosmopolitan, Ladies' Home Journal*, and *McCall's*. During the past decade her best-selling romantic novels include *Summer's End, The Ring*, and *A Perfect Stranger*.

1. *Science & Health with Key to the Scriptures* by Mary Baker Eddy

    Reason: This is a must for me and a source of constant inspiration.

2. My appointment book

    Reason: I am compulsively well organized and would be lost without it, anywhere, even on a new planet.

3. Any book by Colette

    Reason: She is a delight to read, and I enjoy her immensely.

4. Something funny

    Reason: I imagine one could use a good laugh on a new planet.

—Exclusive for *The Book of Lists 3*

MARILYN FRENCH'S 5 BOOKS TO TAKE TO A NEW PLANET

Author Marilyn French focuses on the moral and ethical dilemmas of modern life. Her critical studies include *The Book as World: James Joyce's* Ulysses; and *Shakespeare's Division of Experience*. However, the book which made her famous is *The Women's Room*, the story of a traditional woman's slow and painful liberation. Her most recent novel is *The Bleeding Heart*, a love story set in England.

1. *The Poetry and Prose of William Blake*

    Reason: To give us the vision needed to create a decent culture.

2. Friedrich Nieztche: *The Genealogy of Morals, The Gay Science, Beyond Good and Evil*, in a one-volume edition of my own devising

    Reason: To keep us honest in creating that culture.

3. Doris Lessing's trilogy (again in a devised one-volume edition) *Shikasta; The Marriages Between Zones Three, Four, and Five*; and *The Sirian Chronicles*

    Reason: To keep us from forgetting the mistakes of other cultures.

4. *The Complete Poetry of Emily Dickinson*

    Reason: To remind us of the beauties and griefs that appertain to humanness above and beyond any culture.

5. A blank book for myself.

—Exclusive for *The Book of Lists 3*

BENJAMIN SPOCK'S 10 GREATEST CHILDREN'S BOOKS OF ALL TIME

Dr. Spock had been a pediatrician for 17 years when his best-selling *Baby and Child Care* was published in 1946—in time to become a bible to the new mothers of the postwar baby boom. Besides his medical career, he has been an activist in peace movements. In 1972, Dr. Spock was the People's Party candidate for the U.S. presidency.

1. *Tom Sawyer* by Mark Twain
2. *Huckleberry Finn* by Mark Twain
3. *Treasure Island* by Robert Louis Stevenson
4. *Black Arrow* by Robert Louis Stevenson
5. *A Tale of Two Cities* by Charles Dickens
6. *Oliver Twist* by Charles Dickens
7. *Nicholas Nickleby* by Charles Dickens
8. *Westward Ho!* by Charles Kingsley
9. *Ivanhoe* by Sir Walter Scott
10. The Babar books

—Exclusive for *The Book of Lists 3*

THE 21 MOST UNUSUAL TITLES FROM THE LIBRARY OF *THE PEOPLE'S ALMANAC*

1. *THE MAGIC OF TELEPHONE EVANGELISM* by Harold E. Metcalf. Atlanta, Ga.: Southern Union Conference, 1967.

2. *THE BRIGHT SIDE OF PRISON LIFE* by Captain S. A. Swiggett. Baltimore, Md.: Fleet, McGinley & Co., 1897.

3. *WHO'S WHO IN BATON TWIRLING* by Don Sartell. Janesville, Wisc., 1967.

4. *LATER CRIMINAL CAREERS* by Sheldon and Eleanor Glueck. New York: The Commonwealth Fund, 1937.

5. *OLD AGE: ITS CAUSE AND PREVENTION* by Sanford Bennett. New York: Physical Culture Publishing Co., 1912.

Mr. Bennett, "the man who grew young at 70," also authored the book *Exercising in Bed*.

247

enjoy your
CHAMELEON

THE PET LIBRARY LTD

6. *HEROIC VIRGINS* by Alfonso P. Santos. Quezon City, Philippines: National Book Store, Inc., 1977.

7. *GAY BULGARIA* by Stowers Johnson. London: Robert Hall, 1964.

8. *CARNIVOROUS BUTTERFLIES* by Austin H. Clark. Washington, D.C.: U.S. Government Printing Office, 1926.

9. *FOLDING TABLE NAPKINS* by Marianne von Bornstedt and Ulla Prytz. New York: Sterling Publishing Co., 1972. Originally published by ICA Förlaget, Sweden, 1968.

10. *TRADITIONAL ASPECTS OF HELL* by James Mew. London: Swan, Sonneschein & Co., 1903.

11. *PRACTICAL CANDLE BURNING* by Raymond Buckland. St. Paul, Minn.: Llewellyn Publications, 1970.

12. *HOW TO FILL MENTAL CAVITIES* by Bill Maltz. Beverly Hills, Calif.: Malbro, Inc., 1978.

This collection of puns was one of the least successful books of 1978. In a letter to *The Book of Lists,* the author claimed that he had sold five copies—"three to my family, one to my mother-in-law, and the balance to friends." Unfortunately, two of the copies were returned anonymously.

13. *WOULD CHRIST BELONG TO A LABOR UNION?* by Rev. Cortland Myers. New York: Street & Smith, 1900.

14. *ENJOY YOUR CHAMELEON* by Earl Schneider. New York: The Pet Library.

15. *TO KNOW A FLY* by Vincent G. Dethier. San Francisco: Holden-Day, 1962.

16. *SHOUTING: GENUINE AND SPURIOUS, IN ALL AGES OF THE CHURCH, FROM THE BIRTH OF CREATION, WHEN THE SONS OF GOD SHOUTED FOR JOY, UNTIL THE SHOUT OF THE ARCHANGEL: WITH NUMEROUS EXTRACTS FROM THE OLD AND NEW TESTAMENT, AND FROM THE WORKS OF WESLEY, EVANS, EDWARDS, ABBOTT, CARTWRIGHT, AND FINLEY. GIVING A HISTORY OF THE OUTWARD DEMONSTRATIONS OF THE*

G. W. Henry, the author of *Shouting*.

SPIRIT, SUCH AS LAUGHING, SCREAMING, SHOUTING, LEAP-
ING, JERKING, AND FALLING UNDER THE POWER &C.* by G. W.
Henry. Oneida, N.Y., 1859.

17. *YOUR DESTINY IN THUMB: INDIAN SCIENCE OF THUMB READ-
ING* by R. G. Rao. Bangalore, India: The Astrological Office, 1971.

18. *THE PRACTICAL EMBALMER*, third ed., by A. Johnson Dodge.
1920.

19. *CAREERS IN DOPE* by Dan Waldorf. Englewood Cliffs, N.J.: Pren-
tice-Hall, 1973.

20. *THE DYNAMICS OF PSYCHOSOMATIC DENTISTRY* by Joseph S.
Landa. Brooklyn, N.Y.: Dental Items of Interest Publishing Co.,
1953.

21. *I KNEW 3,000 LUNATICS* by Victor R. Small. New York: Farrar &
Rinehart, 1935.

—D.W.

25 CURIOUS HISTORIES AND ESOTERIC STUDIES FROM THE LIBRARY OF THE PEOPLE'S ALMANAC

1. *MOVIE STARS IN BATHTUBS* by Jack Scagnetti. Middle Village,
N.Y.: Jonathan David Publishers, 1975.

One hundred and fifty-six photographs of movie stars in bathtubs.
There are also numerous shots of actors, actresses, and animals in showers and steambaths.

2. *ABBOTT'S ENCYCLOPEDIA OF ROPE TRICKS* by Stewart James.
Colon, Mich.: Abbott's Magic Novelty Co., 1945.

Four hundred and ninety-eight pages of rope tricks including Le-
Roy's Hindoo Yarn Mystery, Scotty Lang's Sucker Rope Trick, and Bur-
ling Hull's Miracle Restoration.

3. *PAINTINGS AND DRAWINGS ON THE BACKS OF NATIONAL GAL-
LERY PICTURES* by Martin Davies. London, 1946.

A rare opportunity to view the flip side of 42 famous works of art.

4. *MANUALE DI CONVERSAZIONE: ITALIANO-GROENLANDESE* by
Ciro Sozio and Mario Fantin. Bologna, Italy: Tamari Editori, 1962.

One of the least-used dictionaries in the world, this slim 62-page
booklet translates Italian into the language of the Greenland Eskimos.

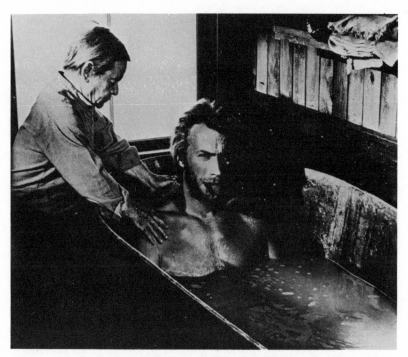

Clint Eastwood in *High Plains Drifter* from
Movie Stars in Bathtubs.

5. *THE ANTS OF COLORADO* by Robert E. Gregg. Boulder, Colo.: University of Colorado Press, 1963.

The author traveled 15,500 mi. over a 16-year period in his search for the 165 forms of ants which can be found within the borders of the state of Colorado. The book is 792 pages long and contains a locator map for each species and subspecies.

6. *STURGEON HOOKS OF EURASIA* by Géza de Rohan-Csermak. Chicago: Aldine Publishing Co., 1963.

An important contribution to the history of fishhooks. Some of the chapter titles: II. "The Character of Sturgeon Hooks"; IV. "Hooks in Eastern Europe"; and VII. "Life Story of Hooks of the Samolov Type."

7. *THE EVOKED VOCAL RESPONSE OF THE BULLFROG: A STUDY OF COMMUNICATION BY SOUND* by Robert R. Capranica. Cambridge, Mass.: The MIT Press, 1965.

This monograph details the responses of caged bullfrogs to the recorded sound of the mating calls of 34 kinds of frogs and toads. The author's academic career was made possible by a fellowship awarded by Bell Telephone Laboratories.

8. *HISTORY OF DENTISTRY IN OREGON* by W. Claude Adams. Portland, Ore.: Binfords and Mort, 1956.

9. *THE SADDLE OF QUEENS* by Lida Fleitmann Bloodgood. London: J. A. Allen & Co., 1959.

A history of sidesaddle horseback riding.

10. *A STUDY OF SPLASHES* by A. M. Worthington. London: Longmans, Green, & Co., 1908.

This pioneering classic makes use of 200 photographs to help answer the question, "What actually happens when a drop falls and splashes?" Worthington's book was considered so valuable to students of physics that it was reissued as recently as 1963.

11. *THE PEOPLE MACHINE* by Dennis R. Cooper. Tampa, Fla.: General Telephone Company of Florida, 1971.

An illustrated history of the telephone on the central west coast of Florida.

12. *WHY BRING THAT UP?* by Dr. J. F. Montague. New York: Home Health Library, 1936.

A guide to and from seasickness by the medical director of the New York Intestinal Sanitarium.

13. *THE DIRECTION OF HAIR IN ANIMALS AND MAN* by Walter Kidd. London: Adam and Charles Black, 1903.

In his preface, Dr. Kidd states, "No doubt many of the phenomena here described are intrinsically uninteresting and unimportant." However, if you have ever yearned for a book that analyzes the direction in which hair grows on lions, oxen, dogs, apes, tapirs, humans, asses, anteaters, sloths, and other animals, you won't be disappointed.

14. *AMERICA IN WAX* by Gene Gurney. New York: Crown Publishers, 1977.

A complete guidebook to wax museums in the U.S. with 678 illustrations, including Brigitte Bardot, Nikita Khrushchev, and the Battle of Yorktown.

15. *EARLY UNITED STATES BARBED WIRE PATENTS* by Jesse S. James. Maywood, Calif., 1966.

A definitive listing of 401 barbed wire patents filed between the years 1867 and 1897.

16. *CLUCK!: THE TRUE STORY OF CHICKENS IN THE CINEMA* by Jon-Stephen Fink. London: Virgin Books, 1981.

At last, a fully illustrated filmography of every movie in which a chicken—living, dead, or cooked—appears. Films in which the words "chicken," "hen," or "rooster" are mentioned are also included.

17. *MANHOLE COVERS OF LOS ANGELES* by Robert and Mimi Melnick. Los Angeles: Dawson's Book Shop, 1974.

Pat and Dick Nixon from *America in Wax*.

18. *ON THE SKULL AND PORTRAITS OF GEORGE BUCHANAN* by Karl Pearson. Edinburgh: Oliver and Boyd, 1926.

Buchanan, one of Scotland's greatest scholars and historians, died in poverty in 1582. This publication was part of a series which included *Phrenological Studies of the Skull and Endocranial Cast of Sir Thomas Browne of Norwich* by Sir Arthur Keith and *The Relations of Shoulder Blade Types to Problems of Mental and Physical Adaptability* by William Washington Graves.

19. *COMMUNISM, HYPNOTISM, AND THE BEATLES* by David A. Noebel. Tulsa, Okla.: Christian Crusade, 1965.

This 15-page diatribe contends that the Beatles were agents of communism, sent to America to subvert its youth through mass hypnosis. "The Beatles' ability to make teenagers take off their clothes and riot is laboratory tested and approved," states Noebel. He supports his theory with no less than 168 footnotes.

20. *ENCYCLOPEDIA OF TURTLES* by Dr. Peter C. H. Pritchard. Neptune, N.J.: T. F. H. Publications, 1979.

An 895-page survey of all living turtle species.

21. *ENGLISH PICNICS* by Georgina Battiscombe. London: The Harvill Press, 1949.

A history of picnicking in England, with a chapter on picnics in fiction and another on picnics in children's literature.

22. *CAMEL BRANDS AND GRAFFITI FROM IRAQ, SYRIA, JORDAN, IRAN, AND ARABIA* by Henry Field. Baltimore, Md.: American Oriental Society, 1952.

The publication of this study was made possible by the generosity of an anonymous donor.

23. *ICE CARVING PROFESSIONALLY* by George P. Weising. Fairfield, Conn., 1954.

An excellent textbook by a master ice sculptor. Weising gives instructions for carving such items as Tablets of the Ten Commandments Delivered by Moses (for bar mitzvahs); Rudolph, the Red-Nosed Reindeer; and the Travelers Insurance Company Tower in Hartford, Conn.

24. *USE OF HUMAN SKULLS AND BONES IN TIBET* by Berthold Laufer. Chicago: Field Museum of Natural History, 1923.

25. *THE HISTORY OF THE SELF-WINDING WATCH: 1770–1931* by Alfred Chapuis and Eugène Jaquet. Neuchâtel, Switzerland: Éditions du Griffon, 1952. English adaptation by Renée Savarè Grandvoinet.

—D.W.

The author of *Ice Carving Professionally* touching up "Mrs. Duck."

10 PEOPLE WHO BECAME BOOKS

1. MORE THAN ONE WAY TO SKIN AN ARISTOCRAT

The tannery at Meudon was kept busy with the hides of beheaded nobles during the French Reign of Terror, which began in 1793. In an extreme case of *noblesse oblige,* the skin of one French aristocrat went to bind a copy of the Revolution's constitution.

255

2. "DO YOU HAVE IT IN PAPERBACK?"

In 1837 outlaw James Allen died in a Massachusetts prison, leaving behind an account of his life. The book, now in possession of the Boston Athenaeum, was, according to Allen's request, bound in his own skin and presented to one of his robbery victims as a token of Allen's esteem.

3. POETIC JUSTICE

George Cudmore, executed in 1830 at Devon County Jail for the murder of his wife, went on to a useful career as a book cover when his hide was used to bind a copy of Milton's *Poetical Works*. The book was last reported to be residing in England's Albert Memorial Library in Exeter.

4. GIVING HIS RIGHT ARM TO GET PUBLISHED

An anonymous but no doubt ardent young Russian poet is said to have lost a limb as a result of a horse-riding accident. He had a collection of his sonnets bound in the skin of his dismembered part and presented to a lady friend.

5. "GIVE US SOME SKIN, MAN"

The skin of one black man, measuring 25 in. by 29 in. before shrinking in the tanning process, was used by a Berlin bookbinder, Paul Kersten, to bind three quarto-sized books in 1910. One of the volumes, containing a dissertation on racial pigmentation, is said to be located in California at Stanford University's Lane Medical Library.

6. THE NAZI FAMILY ALBUM

At the war trial of Ilse Koch, widow of the Buchenwald camp commandant, former inmate Herbert Froboess testified that the skin of a fellow inmate named Jean had been used to bind the Koch family album.

7. POETIC JUSTICE, THE FRENCH EDITION

In the 1880s the skin of an executed murderer named Campi was used to bind the documents relating to his case, including his own postmortem.

8. THEN CAME SKIN MAGS

A copy of *Terres du Ciel* by French astronomer Camille Flammarion bears the following inscription:

PIOUS FULFILLMENT OF AN ANONYMOUS WISH,

BINDING IN HUMAN SKIN (WOMAN) 1882.

The woman, a young countess who died of tuberculosis, was said to be a secret admirer of Flammarion's. She was apparently extremely flattered by a compliment he once paid her on the loveliness of her shoulders.

9. THE DESIGNER LOOK

Hans Holbein's *Dance of Death* has inspired a number of human-hide bound copies, the most notable being an 1891 edition ordered by a physician who wanted a copy bound in the skin of a woman. Tanning was done by Sweeting of Shaftsbury Avenue and the bindery work by Zaehnsdorf.

10. A CHANGE OF PASTE

At the Taktsang Monastery in Bhutan in the Himalayas there's a small volume consisting of black pages written alternately in gold and white. The gold ink comes from real gold. The white comes from the skeleton of one of the monastery's former inhabitants, a great lama whose bones were crushed into a fine paste.

—D.R.

16 BODY PARTS: WHAT THEY COST TO REPLACE

In recent years, advances in medical technology have enabled doctors to replace almost every human organ and bone with a synthetic substitute. New surgical techniques and marvelous endoprosthetics (artificial organs) make possible the elimination of many crippling effects of illness and injury. Though we don't know what breakthroughs to expect

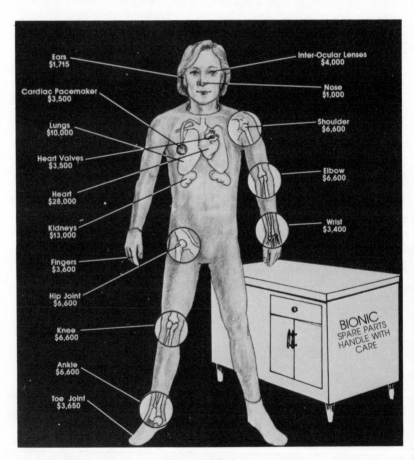

in bionic medicine in the future, we can be reasonably sure of one fact: The spare parts will be expensive. Here are some average costs:

1. Ankle: $6,600
2. Ear: $1,715
3. Elbow: $6,600
4. Finger: $3,600
5. Heart: $28,000
6. Heart pacemaker: $3,500
7. Heart valve: $3,500
8. Hip joint: $9,500
9. Interocular lens: $4,000
10. Kidney: $13,000
11. Knee: $6,600
12. Lung: $10,000
13. Nose: $1,000
14. Shoulder: $6,600
15. Toe joint: $3,650
16. Wrist: $3,400

SOURCE: *Federation of American Hospitals Review*, September/October, 1980.

15 EMINENT SCIENTISTS WHO DID NOT WIN A NOBEL PRIZE

Any world scientist, alive from 1901 onward, was eligible for a Nobel Prize in Physics, Chemistry, Physiology, or Medicine. Almost all of the following were nominated for a Nobel Prize and were voted down.

1. PIERRE EUGÈNE MARCELLIN BERTHELOT (1827–1907), France. Chemistry.

Repeatedly nominated for the prize, Berthelot made important contributions to organic and physical chemistry, and in the history of chemistry as well. He published alchemical works based on his studies of ancient and medieval texts, and his analysis of ancient metallic objects laid the foundations of chemical archaeology.

2. WILLIAM WALLACE CAMPBELL (1862–1938), U.S. Physics.

By far the most influential astronomer of this century, Campbell determined the velocities of the stars in relation to the motion of the earth and sun, laying the foundation for the new science of astrophysics.

3. HARVEY W. CUSHING (1869–1939), U.S. Physiology/Medicine.

Renowned neurosurgeon who revolutionized the techniques of intracranial and spinal surgery. His investigations of the pituitary gland proved that this seemingly inaccessible body could benefit from successful corrective surgery.

4. HUGO DE VRIES (1848–1935), the Netherlands. Physiology/Medicine.

Renowned plant physiologist whose research into the phenomenon of mutation proved valuable in the study of heredity and classical genetics.

5. THOMAS ALVA EDISON (1847–1931), U.S. Physics.

The U.S. Congress once decreed that Edison's inventions "revolutionized civilization." He was nominated for the Nobel Prize only one time. He obtained over 1,000 patents for inventions, including the electric light, the phonograph, printing telegraph, and talking motion pictures. He certainly merited the Physics Prize for his discovery known as thermionic emission or the Edison Effect, which established that a vacuum lamp, acting as a valve, permits electric currents to pass into the vacuum.

6. JOSIAH WILLARD GIBBS (1839–1903), U.S. Chemistry.

Gibbs was a pioneer in the field of chemical thermodynamics (the application of mathematics to chemical subjects), laying the groundwork for modern physical chemistry.

7. WILLIAM CRAWFORD GORGAS (1854–1920), U.S. Physiology/Medicine.

With Walter Reed and Jesse W. Lazear, Gorgas confirmed that yellow fever is transmitted by mosquitoes. The combined efforts of these men rid the Panama Isthmus of yellow fever, which had been one of the main obstacles to the completion of the Panama Canal.

8. JOSEPH LISTER (1827–1912), Great Britain. Physiology/Medicine.

Inspired by Pasteur's research concerning the transmission of microorganisms by air, Lister introduced antiseptics, making possible all later advances in surgery.

9. DMITRI MENDELEEV (1834–1907), Russia. Chemistry.

Formulated the Periodic Law of the elements, which arranged all known elements in a table according to their atomic weights. This table proved that related elements appear at regular intervals, thus predicting the discovery of unknown elements.

10. ALBERT SABIN (1906–   ), U.S. Physiology/Medicine.

Renowned virologist who developed an oral vaccine to immunize against the infection and subsequent paralysis of polio (about 1959).

11. JONAS SALK (1914–   ), U.S. Physiology/Medicine.

This well-known microbiologist developed the first vaccine to immunize against the paralysis of polio. The vaccine was first tested pub-

Dmitri Ivanovich Mendeleev.

licly in 1954. Sabin improved upon his work five years later. Neither man
was nominated for a Nobel Prize.

12. FRITZ RICHARD SCHAUDINN (1871–1906), Germany. Physiol-
ogy/Medicine.

Discovered the causal organism of syphilis with Erich Hoffmann in
1905. Schaudinn was nominated, while Hoffmann was not.

261

13. JEAN-BAPTISTE SENDERENS (1856–1936), France. Chemistry.

With Paul Sabatier, Senderens studied the hydrogenation of oils through catalysis, leading to discoveries which had revolutionary applications in industry. Sabatier received the Chemistry Prize in 1912 for his work, while Senderens, his pupil, was not nominated.

14. ERNEST HENRY STARLING (1866–1927), Great Britain. Physiology/Medicine.

Renowned physiologist and pioneer in the study of the pumping action of the heart. With Sir William M. Bayliss, he coined the term "hormone" for the active substance secreted by the endocrine glands, as well as identifying the hormone secretion secretin.

15. EDWARD TELLER (1908–   ), U.S. Physics.

Known as "the father of the H-bomb," this leading theoretical physicist and advocate of U.S. nuclear defense has, in recent years, urged the declassification of scientific research to encourage debate on the effects of technology on society. He has not been nominated for a Nobel Prize.

—I.W. & L.O.

10 SCIENTIFIC OBJECTS THAT HAVE NEVER BEEN SEEN

1. ANTIMATTER

Physicists have demonstrated the existence of subatomic particles which are oppositely charged but otherwise identical to their counterparts. In principle, then, it is possible that oppositely charged atoms and visible pieces of antimatter exist. However, any antimatter entering our world immediately clashes with ordinary matter in a mutual annihilation. Great masses of antimatter might exist in the vacuum of space. Possibly some of the observable galaxies are antimatter, but this cannot be determined at present.

2. BARNARD'S STAR B

Barnard's Star B is the name given to the planetlike object detected in 1963 whose gravity affects the motion of the red dwarf Barnard's Star. At a distance of six light-years, this is the second nearest star system to our own, but its dark companion is far too faint to spot with any telescope. By measuring displacements in the star's motion, astronomers estimate the planet to be more massive than Jupiter and possibly 100,000 mi. in diameter.

3. BLACK HOLES

By definition, these collapsed, burned-out stars are invisible, since their enormous gravitational fields permit no light to escape. Scientists are increasingly confident they exist, however, because of the strong effects detected in the motions and X-ray emissions of companion stars. Cygnus X-1, a supergiant star, is believed to have a black hole nearby sucking up its substance. Recent developments suggest the existence of mini-black holes (objects of atomic particle size having the mass of a mountain) and supergiant black holes (5 billion times the mass of our sun, at the center of certain galaxies).

4. BROWN DWARFS

Dwarf stars are much smaller than our sun, which is average-sized. Red dwarfs and white dwarfs, while faint, are visible through telescopes. A brown dwarf, however, cannot be seen, being a ball of gas that failed to ignite. Its mass is too small, and its central temperature never reaches the critical point necessary for a star's nuclear burning. While it radiates a very dim light from its heat of contraction, the dwarf is too faint to be seen in a telescope.

5. COSMIC RAYS

The earth is under a constant rain of high-energy-charged particles from space called cosmic rays. Consisting mostly of fast-moving atomic nuclei, probably expelled from supernova explosions, the rays can endanger earthly life by causing mutations in body cells. Fortunately, the rays are deflected by the earth's magnetic field and also partly blocked by the atmosphere. Cosmic rays leave observable tracks in bubble chambers and cloud chambers, but they are too tiny to be seen directly or photographed.

6. EARTH'S CORE

The deepest human penetration into our planet's surface is about 6 mi. by deep drilling. The core, which begins 1,800 mi. below us, is very hot, perhaps 9,000°F (5,000°C) at the center. It is probably made of nickel and iron, with a liquid outer section and a solid innermost area, squeezed to a fantastic pressure of 50 million lb. per sq. in. at the very center.

7. THE COMPLETE ELECTROMAGNETIC SPECTRUM

The band of colors our eyes can perceive as visible light constitutes only a narrow window in a large continuum of radiation called the electromagnetic spectrum. Invisible radiation surrounds us all the time, ranging from the low-frequency, long-wavelength radio waves, into microwaves, infrared (heat radiation), ultraviolet (black light), X-rays, and gamma rays, which have short wavelengths, high frequencies, and high energy.

8. FRANCIUM

Short-lived francium, discovered in 1939 by Marguerite Perey, is the most unstable of the naturally found elements, being formed by the decay of the radioactive element actinium. Francium, too, is radioactive, with its longest-lived isotope having a half-life of 21 min. Quantities of francium that have been isolated in laboratories are too minute to be weighed, much less seen. Probably less than an ounce of francium exists at any given time in the entire crust of the earth.

9. GRAVITONS

Einstein's relativity theory predicts that any gravitational activity should give rise to entities that sometimes behave as waves and sometimes as particles. As particles, they are called gravitons. Gravitons have no mass, no charge, and travel at the speed of light. Because they are relatively weak, they have proved extremely difficult to detect, and any detectable source will probably lie in space, in a supermassive object such as a black hole or a neutron star.

10. QUARKS

The protons, neutrons, and other particles in an atomic nucleus are theorized to be composed of subparticles called quarks, which would thus be among the most basic building blocks of matter. A discrete quark has never been observed, even indirectly, but its proposed electric charge and other characteristics seem to explain tidily particle interactions and collisions. Taking their name, whimsically, from a line in James Joyce's *Finnegan's Wake,* varieties of quarks are distinguished by traits called "color" and "flavor."

—J.A.

10 FUNGUSES THAT CHANGED HISTORY

1. THE YELLOW PLAGUE (*Aspergillus flavus*)

A. flavus is an innocent-looking but deadly yellowish mold also called aflatoxin. Undoubtedly the cause of countless deaths throughout history, it was not suspected of being poisonous until 1960. That year, a mysterious disease killed 100,000 young turkeys in England, and medical researchers traced the "turkey-X disease" to *A. flavus* growing on the birds' peanut meal feed. Hardy, widespread, and lethal, aflatoxin is a powerful liver cancer agent. Even so, people have long cultivated *A. flavus*—in small amounts—as part of the manufacturing process of soy sauce and sake. But *A. flavus* can get out of control easily. It thrives on warm, damp conditions, and as it breeds—sometimes to lethal proportions within 24 hours—the mold produces its own heat, which spurs even faster growth. Some of *A. flavus'* favorite dishes are stored peanuts, rice, corn, wheat, potatoes, peas, cocoa, cured hams, and sausage.

2. THE MOLD THAT TOPPLED AN INDUSTRY (*Aspergillus niger*)

This common black mold, most often found on rotting vegetation, played a key role in the collapse of a major industry. Until the early

1920s, Italy produced about 90% of the world's citric acid, using low-grade lemons. Exported mainly to the U.S. as calcium citrate, this citric acid was a costly ingredient—about a dollar per lb.—used in food, pharmaceutical, and industrial processing. When American chemists discovered that *A. niger*, the most ordinary of molds, secreted citric acid as it grew in a culture medium, they seized the opportunity to perfect citric-acid production using the easily grown mold. Charles Pfizer & Co., of Brooklyn, N.Y., became known as the "world's largest lemon grove"—without a lemon in sight. Hardworking acres of *A. niger* were soon squirting out such quantities of citric acid that by 1923 the price was down to 25¢ per lb., and the Italians were out of business.

3. ST. ANTHONY'S FIRE (*Claviceps purpurea*)

A purplish-black, spur-shaped mass, *C. purpurea* is a formidable and even frightening fungus which has long plagued mankind. But in addition to its horrible effects, *C. purpurea* also has valuable medical uses if the greatest care is taken to use tiny amounts. The fungus is a powerful muscle contractor and can control bleeding, speed up childbirth, and even induce abortion. It is also the source of the hallucinogen LSD-25. In doses larger than microscopic, *C. purpurea*—commonly called ergot—produces ergotamine poisoning, a grisly condition known in the Middle Ages as St. Anthony's fire. There is still no cure for this hideous, often fatal disease caused by eating fungus-infected rye. The victim suffers convulsions and performs a frenzied "dance." This is often accompanied by a burning sensation in the limbs, which turn gangrenously black and fall off. Some victims of medieval ergotism went insane, and many died. In 994 A.D., over 40,000 people in two French provinces died of ergotism, and in 1722 the powerful fungus forced Peter the Great of Russia to abandon his plan to conquer Turkey when, on the eve of the Battle of Astrakhan, his entire cavalry and 20,000 others were stricken with ergotism. The last recorded instance of ergot poisoning was in the French village of Pont-Saint-Esprit in 1951.

4. THE NOBEL MOLD (*Neurospora crassa*)

The humble bread mold *N. crassa* provided the means for scientists to explore the most exciting biological discovery of our century: DNA. As anyone with an old loaf of bread in the bread box knows, *N. crassa* needs only a simple growing medium, and it has a short life cycle. With such cooperative qualities, this reddish mold enabled George Beadle and Edward Tatum to win the Nobel Prize in Medicine/Physiology in 1958 for discovering the role that genes play in passing on hereditary traits from one generation to the next. By X-raying *N. crassa*, the researchers produced mutations of the genes, or components of DNA, and then found which genes corresponded with which traits.

5. THE BLUISH-GREEN LIFESAVER (*Penicillium notatumchrysogenum*)

A few dots of a rather pretty bluish-green mold were Dr. Alexander Fleming's first clue to finding one of the most valuable lifesaving drugs ever developed. In 1928 he noticed that his petri dish of staphylococcus bacteria had become contaminated with symmetrically growing, circular colonies of *P. notatum*. Around each speck, all the bacteria were dead. Fleming further found that the mold also killed pneumonia, gonorrhea, and diphtheria germs—without harming human cells. The unassuming bluish-green mold was beginning to look more interesting, but Fleming could not isolate the active element. Not until 1939 did Howard Florey and Ernst Chain identify penicillin, a secretion of the growing mold, as the bacteria-killer. The first important antibiotic, penicillin revolutionized treatment of many diseases. Fleming, Florey, and Chain won the Nobel Prize in Physiology/Medicine in 1945 for their pioneering work with the common fruit mold which yielded the first "miracle drug."

6. THE GOURMET'S DELIGHT (*Penicillium roquefortii*)

According to an old legend, a French shepherd forgot his lunch in a cave near the town of Roquefort, and when he found his lunch weeks later, the cheese had become blue-veined and was richly flavored. No one knew why this happened until American mycologists discovered the common blue mold *P. roquefortii* in 1918. All blue cheeses—English stilton, Italian gorgonzola, Norwegian gammelost, Greek kopanisti, and Swiss paglia—derive their tangy flavor from the energetic blue mold, which grows rapidly in the cheese, partially digesting it and eventually turning the entire cheese into mold. Of course, it's more appetizing to say that *P. roquefortii* ripens the cheese instead of rotting it, but it's the same process.

7. THE FAMINE-MAKER (*Phytophthona infestans*)

The political history of the world changed as a result of the unsavory activity of *P. infestans*, a microscopically small fungus which reduced Ireland to desperate famine in 1845. Hot, rainy July weather provided perfect conditions for the white fungus to flourish on the green potato plants—most of Ireland's food crop—and the bushes withered to brown, moldy, stinking clumps within days. The entire crop was devastated, causing half a million people to starve to death, while nearly two million emigrated, mostly to the U.S. *P. infestans* dusted a powdery white death over Ireland for six years. The fungus spread rapidly, and just one bad potato could infect and ruin a barrel of sound ones. British Prime Minister Robert Peel tried to get Parliament to repeal tariffs on imported grain, and while the MP's debated, Ireland starved. Relief came so slowly and inadequately that Peel's government toppled the next year, in 1846.

8. THE TEMPERANCE FIGHTER (*Plasmopara viticola*)

A soft, downy mildew infecting American-grown grapes was responsible for nearly ruining the French wine industry. In 1872 the French unwittingly imported *P. viticola* on grafting stock of wine grapes grown in the U.S. Within 10 years, the mild-mannered mildew had quietly decimated much of France's finest old vineyards. But in 1882 botanist Pierre-Marie-Alexis Millardet discovered a miraculous cure for the ravages of *P. viticola*. He noticed that Médoc farmers painted their grape leaves with an ugly paste of copper sulphate, lime, and water—to prevent theft. Called Bordeaux mixture, this paste was the first modern fungicide. The vineyards of France recovered as the entire world sighed with relief.

9. MERCHANT OF DEATH (*Saccharomyces cerevisiae*)

Ordinary brewers' yeast, *S. cerevisiae*, used to leaven bread and make ale, was once employed as a wartime agent of death. During W.W. I, the Germans ran short of both nitroglycerin and the fat used in its manufacture. Then they discovered that the usually friendly fungus *S. cerevisiae* could be used to produce glycerin, a necessary ingredient in explosives. Fermenting the fungus together with sucrose, nitrates, phosphates, and sodium sulphite, the Germans produced over 1,000 tons of glycerin per month. According to some military sources, this enabled them to keep their war effort going for an additional year.

10. THE TB KILLER (*Streptomyces griseus*)

A lowly mold found in dirt and manure piles, *S. griseus* nevertheless had its moment of glory in 1943, when Dr. Selman Waksman discovered that it yields the antibiotic streptomycin, which can cure tuberculosis. Waksman came to the U.S. in 1910 as a Russian refugee, and by 1918 he had earned his doctorate in soil microbiology. He had worked with *S. griseus* before, but not until a crash program to develop antibiotics (a word coined by Dr. Waksman himself) was launched did he perceive the humble mold's possibilities for greatness. Streptomycin was first used successfully on a human being in 1945, and in 1952 Dr. Waksman was awarded the Nobel Prize in Physiology/Medicine.

—K.P.

15 THINGS DISCOVERED OR TRACKED BY SATELLITES

1. FAR SIDE OF THE MOON

The first successful photographs of the dark side of the moon were taken by the Soviet Lunik 3 satellite launched in 1959. Unlike the visible portion of the moon, the dark side was found to have a regular pattern of craters, fewer dark areas known as "seas," and generally more rugged features. In addition to discovering the Soviet Mountains, which stretch over 1,000 mi., Lunik 3 also located the Sea of Moscow (200 mi. in diameter), as well as the Humboldt Sea, the Sea of Crises, the Marginal Sea, the Sea of Waves, the Smyth Sea, the Sea of Fertility, and the Southern Sea.

2. GRAVITY DENTS

One of America's first satellites, Transit 4B, surprised scientists in the early 1960s when it found bumps and indentations in the gravitational field around the equator which interfered with the satellite's speed. In time, other fluctuations in the earth's gravitational field became apparent, leading to the discovery of oil and mineral deposits, such as a major nickel lode near Manitoba, Canada. The gravitational variations noted by Transit 4B were of major concern to the military, who found that they also affected the speed and trajectory of ICBM's.

3. VIETNAM WAR PROTESTERS

During the sociopolitical upheaval of the late 1960s, the Central Intelligence Agency employed satellites to spy on Americans participating in anti-Vietnam War demonstrations. At altitudes of 100 mi., the satellites could easily estimate the size of crowds and even identify individuals. According to the Center for National Security Studies, the request to spy on American citizens had come directly from Lyndon Johnson's White House, allegedly to check for a "possible foreign connection with the U.S. antiwar movement."

4. WALNUT WORMS ET AL.

The Skylab missions of the early 1970s, essentially manned-satellite flights, uncovered a wealth of information. Skylab's six-instrument group, called the Earth Resources Experimental Package, combined radar, infrared, and photographic equipment, plus a 24-in. mirror-system telescope to survey 75% of the earth, 90% of its population, and 80% of its food-bearing environment. EREP produced more than 40,000 photos and filled 45 mi. of magnetic tape, supplying scientists with data about walnut-worm attacks on pecan groves; population shifts; water sources in drought-stricken Africa; hot springs and volcanoes around the world; air and water pollution; wind, hurricane, and ocean-current patterns; areas suffering from corn blight; and new copper, tin, and oil deposits. EREP also proved that space technology will not change human nature—after one copper lode near Ely, Nev., had been verified by ground crews, prospectors rushed to stake their claims.

5. THE AMAZON RIVER

Not the most precise of satellites, the ERTS 1, launched on July 23, 1972, nevertheless provided some valuable information. It found that the longest river in the world, the Amazon, had for years been depicted on maps incorrectly, in some areas by as much as 20 mi. Moreover, ERTS (which stands for "earth resources technology satellite") found some of the river's tributaries to be following different courses than what was indicated on maps.

6. PHOENIX, ARIZONA

After establishing itself in orbit in 1972, the $176 million ERTS 1 satellite took photographs of Phoenix. The pictures revealed that many land tracts had been surveyed improperly. This new information resulted in immediate tax reassessments for local residents.

7. WATER POLLUTION

To the dismay of industry, ERTS 1 was invaluable in pinpointing polluted waters. From an altitude of 560 mi., the satellite spotted waste pumped into Lake Champlain by an International Paper Company plant at Ticonderoga, N.Y. The satellite photographs also played a key evidential role in a lawsuit initiated by the state of Vermont. The case went to the U.S. Supreme Court but was finally settled out of court in 1974—International Paper Company paid $500,000 to Vermont (less than it cost to prosecute the case) and promised to limit pollution from its plant.

8. AGUAJE PALMS

ERTS satellites launched in 1975 and 1978 still survey the earth's form and structure, or geomorphology, and gather data about its vegetation. These two sophisticated pieces of equipment replaced ERTS 1 and are referred to as Landsats. One of the more interesting uses of a Landsat was in spotting jungle aguaje palm stands in Peru, one of that country's most valuable natural food sources rich in vitamin C. The Peruvian government had planned to resettle some of its population living in marginally productive regions to the more productive rain forests, which were known to contain sizable stands of the palm. Landsat not only located unknown stands but also showed how large they were. Landsat satellites have helped countries such as the Dominican Republic, Jamaica, Costa Rica, Bolivia, Ecuador, Morocco, the Philippines, Indonesia, and Thailand predict their crop yields with 95% accuracy.

9. A 1914 DODGE

In 1976, a vintage Dodge competing in the New York to San Francisco leg of the U.S. Bicentennial World Antique Auto Race was tracked by Nimbus 6, a sophisticated weather research satellite. Owner and driver Ed Schuler of Morrison, Ill., designed and constructed a special windshield mount for an antenna which allowed NASA to follow the car. "The world race offered us the opportunity to evaluate and demonstrate the instrument for ground-tracking applications over a long distance at a cost which is negligible," said Charles Cote of NASA's Goddard Space Flight Center.

10. A 33-FOOT SLOOP

In 1977, a Nimbus 6 meteorological satellite successfully monitored the whereabouts of a sloop on a 30-day, 600-mi. trip through the Bermuda Triangle area. The boat was equipped with a $275 battery-operated transmitter that emitted a signal once every minute to the satellite, which had for more than a decade been positioned in a stationary orbit 22,300 mi. above the equator just south of Hawaii. Once the Goddard Space Flight Center had received the satellite's information, scientists could pinpoint the boat's location within 1 or 2 mi.

11. IMPENDING EARTHQUAKE

In 1978, researchers at the Goddard Space Flight Center in Greenbelt, Md., speculated that satellite information indicated a pending major earthquake along California's San Andreas Fault. The satellite had located shifts in the fault that scientists said were "50% larger than we would have guessed from geological history." Geologists had previously speculated that the fault would produce a major quake before the year 2025. However, the satellite data seemed to indicate that the quake would be larger and occur sooner than expected.

12. NUCLEAR BLAST

In the fall of 1979 and again in late 1980, a U.S. VELA early-warning satellite detected what government officials thought were nuclear explosions in the South Atlantic. Suspicion about the source of the blasts immediately centered on South Africa, though the South African government vehemently denied any involvement. The 1980 flash is now generally believed to have been caused by a meteor entering the atmosphere, but there is still some disagreement as to what caused the 1979 flash. The Pentagon maintains that it had the "signature" of a nuclear explosion—the recorded variations in light intensity were similar to those caused by a nuclear blast. However, a White House panel assembled to study the two events noted that no evidence of radioactivity could be found and concluded that the flash was probably a "zoo event"—a signal of unknown origin, perhaps caused by a small meteorite striking the satellite.

13. A LOGGERHEAD TURTLE

From late 1979 to mid-1980, the meteorological satellite Nimbus tracked a 212-lb. loggerhead turtle named Dianne. The loggerhead's odyssey through the Gulf of Mexico to Brownsville, Tex., provided crucial information about the feeding, nesting, and mating habits of this threatened species via a 7-lb. transmitter affixed to its shell. When Dianne was near Texas, the signal suddenly ceased. When it resumed, the turtle seemed to be taking an inland route, winding up in Kansas. The solution to the mystery: The transmitter had been picked up by a fisherman, who took it to his home in Kansas and used it as a doorstop.

14. HOT AND COLD WATER

From 23,000 mi. above the earth, the 1981 NOAA 6 satellite uses infrared sensors to locate shifts in ocean temperature. Where cold spots are detected, plankton abounds, and scientists know that commercially valuable fish, such as salmon, tuna, and Pacific whiting will feed there. The information is relayed to fishermen approximately twice a week. On the other hand, information about warm water currents is passed on to the captains of oil tankers. Warm water raises the temperature of a tanker's cargo as well as that of its hull, and this warmer, thinner oil is easier to pump at destination points.

15. NICARAGUAN MILITARY BASES

The greatest numbers of man-made objects orbiting the earth are spy satellites, carrying sophisticated cameras capable of spotting objects the size of a suitcase. For years, under the rubric "national security," the U.S. military has kept its spy satellite capabilities secret. However, in early 1982, the government tipped its hand in order to show evidence of a military buildup in Nicaragua. High-resolution photographs were released, showing airstrips, antiaircraft batteries, barracks, commando training facilities, and armored vehicles.

—Z.J.K.

13
IT'S HOME AGAIN

10 NOTABLE MARRIAGE PROPOSALS

1. QUEEN VICTORIA and PRINCE ALBERT

Victoria was only 18 years old when she was crowned queen of the United Kingdom in 1837. Faced with the duty of producing an heir, and as yet unmarried, she resolved to wed her German cousin, Prince Albert. With characteristic directness, Her Majesty summoned him one afternoon and bluntly proposed marriage, saying it would make her "too happy" if he consented. In a letter to her aunt, the Duchess of Gloucester, Victoria wrote that she had taken the initiative because Albert would "never have presumed to take such a liberty as to propose to the queen of England."

2. MARK TWAIN and OLIVIA LANGDON

When author Sam Clemens, alias Mark Twain, proposed marriage to Olivia Langdon, her acceptance hinged on her father's approval of the match. Because the Langdons were an upper-class New York family and Clemens was a rough-hewn Westerner, they had no acquaintances in common. So Mr. Langdon asked for references, which Clemens provided. To the prospective bridegroom's dismay, the letters Langdon received gave Clemens a unanimous and enthusiastic thumbs-down. Two even predicted that the author would fill a drunkard's grave.

"Haven't you a friend in the world?" Langdon asked.

"Apparently not," Clemens replied.

"I'll be your friend myself," Langdon said. "Take the girl. I know you better than they do."

His instincts were correct, since Clemens proved a loyal and loving husband to Olivia.

3. LILLIAN RUSSELL and "DIAMOND JIM" BRADY

At the turn of the century, actress and singer Lillian Russell and multimillionaire salesman "Diamond Jim" Brady were a well-matched pair. The buxom Russell was the only woman Brady had ever met whose hearty appetite rivaled his own, and they were frequent dinner companions at Manhattan's finest restaurants. Together, they would deplete whole pantries, eating, for example, buttered sweet corn by the bushel. It was perhaps inevitable that Brady would propose marriage to his ideal "tablemate," and he did so by dumping $1 million cash into her lap. However, Russell declined the offer on the grounds that it would ruin a beautiful friendship.

4. GEORGE BERNARD SHAW and ANNIE BESANT

After separating from her clergyman husband and causing a scandal in a divorce attempt which failed, Annie Besant became an atheist, socialist, and thorn in the side of the Victorian establishment. She frequently kept company with a fellow radical, playwright George Bernard Shaw, and in time the two decided to marry. A private contract which both parties would sign would replace the traditional religious or civil ceremony. Owing to Annie's expertise in the matter—she had authored a pamphlet titled *Marriage—As It Was, Is, and Ought to Be*—she elected to draw up the agreement. Annie labored long and hard on the document. When she finally presented it to Shaw for his approval, he soberly read it through, then burst out laughing and said, "Good God! This is worse than all the vows exacted by all the churches on earth." He refused to sign; Annie refused to rewrite the contract. They never came to terms.

5. WILLIAM BOYD and ELINOR FAIRE

In Cecil B. De Mille's 1926 silent film *The Volga Boatman*, Boyd as Feodor is awaiting execution when he professes his love for Elinor as Vera. Few moviegoers realized that Boyd's onscreen declaration of love was in fact a real-life marriage proposal, which Elinor accepted.

6. LUCILLE BALL and DESI ARNAZ

Like the characters they played in the television series *I Love Lucy*,

William Boyd proposed to Elinor Faire in Cecil B. De Mille's 1926 silent film, *The Volga Boatman*. Audiences didn't know the proposal was real—and was accepted.

Lucy and Desi were a volatile pair, prone to frequent, heated arguments, followed by intense reconciliations. Author F. Scott Fitzgerald, who lived in the same Hollywood apartment building as Lucy, observed the couple's stormy courtship from his balcony. Scott and Sheilah Graham would sometimes bet on the outcome of Lucy and Desi's quarrels. Commented Graham, "No matter which of us lost, we were both pleased when Lucille won."

One night at New York's El Morocco nightclub, Desi blurted out, "Why wait around like this? Let's do it and get it over with." This abrupt proposal was not well received, so Desi apologized and rephrased the question: "Honey, I don't know your language so good. I mean, I can't wait any longer to get married." On Nov. 30, 1940, Lucy and Desi were wed in Greenwich, Conn., at the Byram River Beagle Club.

7. RONALD REAGAN and NANCY DAVIS

When her name turned up on a list of film industry Communist sympathizers, Nancy Davis, debutante-turned-actress, was appalled. Why, she was no more a Commie than Kate Smith! Nancy's friend, director Mervyn LeRoy, referred her to a man who could help her clear her name—Screen Actors Guild president Ronald Reagan. According to Nancy in *Nancy Reagan* by Roger Elwood, "Mervyn assured me that Ronnie was a nice young man and I was a nice young woman, and it might be nice if we met . . . so I, too, said I thought that would be very nice." They met over dinner and got along very nicely indeed. The red-sympathizer misunderstanding was quickly cleared up, and they began dating steadily. Nancy wrote of their courtship, "How can you resist someone who sends flowers to your mother on your birthday, thanking her for making him the happiest man in the world?

"Soon our friends were taking it for granted we'd marry and we did, too—it was just a matter of when. There was never a really formal proposal as I remember, although Ronnie did call my father and ask him for my hand in marriage—the old-fashioned way. . . . [My father] was delighted to say 'Yes, indeed.'

"I was so excited, I went through the ceremony in a daze. . . . I don't even remember saying our 'I do's' or the minister saying he pronounced us man and wife. Ronnie says he did, so I guess we're legal."

8. WILLIAM O. DOUGLAS and CATHY HEFFERNAN

In 1965, 22-year-old Cathy Heffernan was working as a cocktail waitress in Portland, Ore., when she met 66-year-old U.S. Supreme Court Justice William O. Douglas, who stopped by with a friend for a drink. Afterward, Douglas startled his friend by saying he wanted to marry the young waitress. "I loved her the first time I saw her," Douglas later recalled. The two began dating, and a year later in Los Angeles, while shopping for a dress for Cathy to wear to the wedding of Luci Johnson, President Lyndon Johnson's daughter, Douglas and Cathy impulsively decided to marry. While the mood was on them, they hurriedly obtained a license and bought a pair of gold wedding bands. But as zero hour approached, Cathy suddenly balked. "I don't want to get married," she said, sobbing. The compassionate jurist just laughed at her. At this crucial moment there was a knock at the hotel room door; reporters had gotten wind of the marriage plans and were clamoring for a statement. "What are we going to do?" Douglas asked her. Cathy stopped crying and composed herself. Then she walked to the door and boldly announced that she would indeed become the justice's fourth wife.

9. ELVIS PRESLEY and GINGER ALDEN

By age 42, Elvis was a pudgy, drug-addled, emotional wreck, but he was still the king of rock 'n' roll, and 20-year-old Ginger Alden was awed by his attentions: "I was in a daze." According to *Elvis* by Albert Goldman, Presley had known Ginger only nine weeks when he suddenly decided to marry her and consulted *Cheiro's Book of Numbers* for the ideal date on which to propose. According to the book, it was that very day, so preparations were hurriedly made. It was impossible to obtain an engagement ring with a diamond large enough for a queen on such short notice, so Elvis sacrificed the 11½-carat stone from his own ring and had it reset for her. As a fitting site for the proposal, the king chose his throne room—the bathroom. He seated Ginger in his reading chair next to the toilet. Kneeling before her, he declared his love and asked her to marry him. The scene was so overwhelmingly romantic—with the beautiful ring, the flowery speech, the glistening bathroom fixtures—that all Ginger could answer was, "Yes." Sadly, the marriage was not to be. Weeks later, a heart attack (perhaps brought on by a king-sized dose of drugs) ended Elvis's life in that same bathroom.

10. BOB CASTON and GAYLE WELLING

Marriage proposals normally are private affairs, but newsman Caston wanted to ensure a "yes" from Welling. So he proposed to her in his weekly column in the *Saratoga* (Wyo.) *Sun* in 1982. "She couldn't turn me down in front of all our readers," he said. The paper's 2,300 subscribers also had the opportunity of learning the young lady's reply—she accepted him in a letter to the editor.

—M.J.T.

11 FAMOUS WOMEN WHO MARRIED BEFORE THE AGE OF 16

1. THE VIRGIN MARY

Women customarily married at a very young age in biblical times. The mother of Jesus Christ would not have been an exception. Historians of the period feel she was about 14 when she was espoused to Joseph the Carpenter.

2. ELEANOR OF AQUITAINE (1122?–1204)

Perhaps the most powerful woman of the 12th century, Eleanor was 15 when her marriage to Louis VII made her queen of France in

1137. The union wasn't happy, but it lasted 15 years. Two months after an annulment was granted, Eleanor married Henry Curtmantle, who was to become King Henry II of England.

3. MARY, QUEEN OF SCOTS (1542–1587)

Although she was born in Scotland—and later ruled this country—Mary was raised in the French court. It was there, at age 15, that she married the sickly young heir to the French throne in 1558. Upon his death two years later, Mary returned to her native land and began the violent reign that ended with her beheading.

4. MARY II (1662–1694)

The consort of William III was a kind woman who was much loved by her British subjects. She was 15 at the time of her royal marriage to the stadtholder of Holland.

5. MARIE ANTOINETTE (1755–1793)

Diplomacy—not love—was the impetus when 14-year-old Marie Antoinette married the heir to the French throne in 1770. Their union was intended to strengthen Austria's alliance with France. Instead, Marie's Austrian birth was one of the factors that sparked the French Revolution.

6. VICTORIA CLAFLIN WOODHULL (1838–1927)

A feminist, a radical, and an advocate of free love in an era when none of those things were fashionable, Woodhull in 1872 became the first woman to run for president of the U.S. Her personal life was equally unconventional—at 15, she married a physician.

7. ANNIE OAKLEY (1860–1926)

The internationally famous sharpshooter was 15 when she married professional marksman Frank E. Butler in 1876. Appropriately enough, they'd met when the then-unknown teenager beat Butler in a Cincinnati shooting match.

8. KASTURBA GANDHI (1869–1944)

She loyally supported her husband, Mahatma Gandhi, and sometimes shared his imprisonments. Their 62-year marriage began in 1882, when both partners were 13.

9. JUNE HAVOC (1916–   )

This stage and screen actress, the sister of Gypsy Rose Lee, did everything early. "Baby June" was dancing onstage at age 2½, a vaudeville star at 8. And at 13 (according to her mother), she secretly married an 18-year-old member of an entertainment troupe.

10. JIHAN SADAT (1934–   )

Egypt's former first lady, certainly the best known feminist in the Islamic world, was 15 when she married Anwar Sadat in 1949. The man who eventually became president was a penniless 31-year-old military officer.

11. LORETTA LYNN (1935–   )

The coal miner's daughter who eventually became a country music superstar was married at age 13 to Oliver "Mooney" Lynn, who became the most important person in her life. By the time she was 18, Lynn had four children.

—E.F.

THE 16 WORST HOUSEHOLD TASKS

This is an exclusive poll we had the Gallup Organization of Princeton, N.J., conduct for us. To learn the most disliked household tasks, the pollsters interviewed 1,325 persons.

1. Washing dishes	17.0%
2. Cleaning the bathroom	8.8%
3. Ironing	8.5%
4. Scrubbing floors	7.5%
5. Cleaning (nonspecific)	7.3%
6. Vacuuming	6.2%
7. Washing windows	4.9%
8. Cooking	4.8%
9. Dusting	4.7%
9. Laundry	4.7%
9. Cleaning oven	4.7%
12. Cleaning refrigerator	1.7%
13. Making beds	.7%
13. Grocery shopping	.7%
15. Cleaning the carpet	.4%
15. Yardwork	.4%
Miscellaneous	7.2%
Don't know	9.8%

14 FAMOUS COUPLES WHOSE MARRIAGES BROKE UP IN LESS THAN A MONTH

1. JOHN MILTON (poet) and MARY POWELL

Bored, Milton's 16-year-old bride returned home to visit her family a month after their June, 1642, wedding and failed to return as agreed. Milton, heartbroken, wrote his famous essays on divorce during the next four years.

2. GIUSEPPE GARIBALDI (Italian revolutionary) and GIUSEPPINA RAIMONDI

In the midst of his courtship of Esperance von Schwartz, a German baroness who had already twice refused his offers of marriage, the 52-year-old widower married 17-year-old Giuseppina Raimondi in 1860. But their union was short-lived. After the ceremony he was handed a letter containing evidence that Giuseppina was pregnant by one of his officers. Infuriated by what appeared to be a plot to disgrace him, Garibaldi immediately left his second wife and never saw her again. Two years later he obtained a decree of annulment that freed him for a third marriage, to Francesca Armosino.

3. KATHERINE MANSFIELD (writer) and GEORGE BOWDEN (musician)

Mansfield was pregnant by a previous lover at the time of her marriage to Bowden in London on Mar. 2, 1909. Regretting her hasty action, she abandoned her husband the morning after the ceremony and retreated to Bavaria, where her child was stillborn.

4. GLORIA SWANSON (actress) and WALLACE BEERY (actor)

Married in Hollywood in March, 1916, Swanson and Beery separated three weeks later. Said Beery: "She wanted the fancy life—to put on airs and all of that. Me, I like huntin' and fishin' and the simple life." Said Swanson: "There were many reasons, but the chief one was that I wanted to have a baby and Wally didn't want that responsibility."

5. RUDOLPH VALENTINO (actor) and JEAN ACKER (actress)

Married Nov. 5, 1919, Hollywood's smoldering Great Lover was locked out on his wedding night by his lovely bride. His first marriage lasted less than six hours.

6. KATHARINE HEPBURN (actress) and LUDLOW OGDEN SMITH (Philadelphia socialite)

By Jan. 2, 1929—three weeks after her wedding on Dec. 12, 1928, at West Hartford, Conn.—Katharine Hepburn knew the domestic life wasn't for her. She left her husband and returned to the theater. But she and "Luddie" remained close platonic friends for the rest of his life.

Wallace Beery and Gloria Swanson were married in 1916,
for three weeks.

7. BURT LANCASTER (actor/acrobat) and JUNE ERNST (circus
aerialist)

Married in 1935 while on a carnival tour, the two separated immediately. Lancaster complimented his short-term marriage partner by describing her as the "only woman in America who could do horizontal bar
tricks."

8.–10. TOMMY MANVILLE (asbestos heir and "career bridegroom")

A. and BONITA FRANCINE EDWARDS (actress)
One of Tommy's 11 wives, Bonita married him in Ridgefield,

Conn., on Nov. 18, 1941. She arrived in Reno 21 days later, on Dec. 9, to establish residency for divorce, charging incompatibility.

B. and MACIE MARIE (SUNNY) AINSWORTH

Sunny married Tommy Aug. 25, 1943, at the Supreme Court Building in New York City, but separated from him a record 7 hours, 45 minutes later.

C. and ANITA FRANCES RODDY-EDEN (songwriter)

Married to Anita on July 10, 1952, Tommy had announced that his marriage was "all busted up" by July 23. After 13 days, 5 hours of marriage, they had had a row—which Tommy said could never be "patched up"—when she tried to prevent him from leaving their suite at the Waldorf-Astoria.

11. GERMAINE GREER (writer/feminist) and PAUL DE FEU (model)

The first male nude centerfold model for the London edition of *Cosmopolitan* magazine did lure Greer into marriage in May, 1968, in London, but she later said, "It seems that it didn't exist. . . . I'd take the train down on weekends . . . and be all worn out, and the next morning he'd be up at six. . . . The marriage lasted three weeks. Three weekends, to be precise."

12. DENNIS HOPPER (actor/director) and MICHELLE PHILLIPS (singer/actress)

After an eight-month relationship, Dennis Hopper and Michelle Phillips were married on Halloween, 1970. They got married because Hopper wanted to prove to Phillips that they could be married while she still maintained her career. According to Hopper: "She went off to work with Leonard Cohen and called me eight days later. I said, 'I love you, I need you.' She said, 'Have you ever thought of suicide?'" That was the end of the eight-day marriage.

13. BUCK OWENS (musician) and JANA GRIEF (fiddle player)

Buck Owens turned chicken and disappeared less than two days after his wedding to Jana Grief, a fiddle player in his band, in May, 1977. Although he later changed his mind and asked Jana to forgive him, she refused and filed for divorce. It was an expensive marriage for Buck, as the court ruled that he had to pay Jana $25,000 and still allow her to remain in his band.

14. DENNIS WILSON (pop singer) and KAREN LAMM (actress)

This member of the popular Beach Boys first married TV commercial actress Karen Lamm in 1976, but that union lasted a mere seven months. They decided to try it again in July, 1978, but after only two weeks Wilson realized that he'd had enough. The final breakup of her minimarriage drove Lamm into court, suing Wilson for a divorce settlement of $10,000 per month, his Santa Barbara property, and his 68-ft. boat.

—R.S.

9 TEACHERS WHO MARRIED THEIR STUDENTS

1. PETER ABELARD (1079–1144), French theologian-philosopher

After a stormy early career as a teacher, Peter Abelard joined the ranks of the Church hierarchy as an influential lecturer and canon of the cathedral of Paris. He became enamored of a beautiful and intelligent girl about 16 or 17 years old. Héloïse was the niece of Fulbert, another Church canon. Abelard managed to become a lodger at Fulbert's house as well as Héloïse's tutor. Instead of teaching her, he seduced her.. They became lovers, a situation eventually discovered by her uncle. After Héloïse gave birth to a son, the pair were secretly married. Fulbert later mistook Héloïse's residence in the convent of Argenteuil for an attempt by Abelard to "get rid of her." Incensed, he hired thugs to castrate Abelard. Héloïse went on to become an abbess; Abelard resumed his controversial teaching. They are buried beside each other in Père-Lachaise Cemetery in Paris.

2. GEORGE BALANCHINE (1904–   ), Russian-born U.S. choreographer

Organizer of both the American Ballet Company and the School of American Ballet, George Balanchine had an eye for a comely student. He married two of them: Maria Tallchief in 1946 and Tanaquil LeClercq in 1952. Both women were very young when they began to study ballet under Balanchine; Tallchief was 21 at the time of their marriage, and LeClercq was 23. Balanchine's marriage to Tallchief was annulled after five years on the pretext that she wanted children and he did not. "Any woman can become a mother," he said, "but not every woman can become a ballerina." Not long after the annulment, Balanchine married LeClercq. In 1956, at the age of 27, she was stricken with polio and lost the use of her legs. They were divorced in 1969.

3. THOMAS HART BENTON (1889–1975), U.S. artist

Following a stint in the navy during W.W. I, Thomas Hart Benton moved to New York. There, five years earlier, he had met Rita Piacenza while he was teaching a free art class for the Chelsea Neighborhood Association. Her family spoke no English, so Benton rarely tried to communicate with them. After the couple had dated for a few years, the question of marriage came up. Rita's father, dressed in his Sunday best, appeared at Benton's studio one day. Since they couldn't converse, the father sat hour after hour, silently watching Thomas work. When night fell, he rose, shook Thomas's hand, and left. Benton and Rita were married soon afterward, on Feb. 19, 1922.

4. PABLO CASALS (1876–1973), Spanish cellist

Marta Montanez was a promising young cellist who had won musical competitions and prizes in 1954 and then gone to study with Casals—one of the world's premier musicians—at his home in Prades, France. Over the course of three years, and despite the 60-year difference in their ages, their relationship grew on a number of levels. She became indispensable to him and, in 1957, helped nurse him back to health after a massive heart attack. A few months after his recovery, they were married.

5. WILL DURANT (1885–1981), U.S. historian

Partly through circumstance and partly through economic necessity, Will Durant became the "sole teacher and chief learner" of the Ferrer Modern School, founded by an anarchist group in New York. He fell in love with the oldest (though still young enough to cause a scandal) of his students, Ida Kaufman, whom he called Ariel. He was 27, she was 14; he was of French-Canadian extraction and an apostate Catholic, she a Russian Jew. They were married a year later, in 1913. They lived, loved, and worked together for 68 years, completing 11 volumes of their monumental work, *The Story of Civilization*. Ariel died at the age of 83, while Will was hospitalized in intensive care. He died two weeks later, unaware of her passing.

6. MARY BAKER EDDY (1821–1910), U.S. originator of Christian Science

In 1843, Mary Baker married George W. Glover. He died before the birth of their son, George. In 1853, Mary married Dr. Daniel Patterson, a dentist who shared her interest in homeopathy. They were divorced in 1873. By that time, Mary had developed the principles of Christian Science, which espouses healing without medication. In March, 1876, Asa Eddy, who was suffering from heart problems, paid two visits to the self-styled "practitioner" in Boston. Feeling markedly better, Eddy became a regular student. Mary began to rely more and more on Eddy and, despite the persistent courtship of a longtime follower, married Eddy on Jan. 1, 1877. He died in 1882.

7. BENITO MUSSOLINI (1883–1945), Italian dictator

Mussolini married Rachele Guidi on Dec. 16, 1915, but their relationship began in 1909 after Mussolini, a well-known womanizer, spotted her working as a barmaid and waitress at his father's wine shop. She had also been a goatherd and farmhand and had been one of his pupils when he had taken over his mother's class in the village school. In October, 1909, he stormed the farmhouse of Rachele's sister and took Rachele away to live with him. Faced with parental objections, Mussolini overcame them by drawing a pistol and saying, "Here are six bullets—one for Rachele, five for me." They were still married when *Il Duce* and his mistress, Clara Petacci, were executed by Italian partisans.

8. PËTR ILICH TCHAIKOVSKY (1840–1893), Russian composer

Though a homosexual, Tchaikovsky decided to marry Antonina Ivanova Milyukova, an adoring—if not particularly bright—pupil of his at the Moscow Conservatory of Music. After the wedding in 1877, he found his wife more and more loathsome. He attempted suicide, considered murdering her, and finally admitted to nonexistent adulterous relationships—but she would not divorce him. He eventually discovered *her* affairs (some of which produced children) but did not pursue divorce for fear of having his homosexuality exposed publicly. She died in an asylum in 1917.

9. HERBERT GEORGE WELLS (1866–1946), British writer

In the autumn of 1892, H. G. Wells noticed an attractive young woman in the biology class he was teaching at a tutorial college in London. Amy Catherine Robbins, six years younger than Wells, was considerably more emancipated in her thinking than Wells's wife (and cousin), Isabel. What began as a friendship between Wells and Miss Robbins escalated in emotional intensity until Wells suggested that Isabel join him in spending a weekend with Miss Robbins and her mother. Isabel probably realized the situation and, on the trip home, gave Wells an ultimatum—choose between his marriage and his burgeoning affair. At any rate, within days he had arranged to leave his wife. He married Amy on Oct. 27, 1895. She bore Wells two sons and was with him until her death in 1927.

—J.N.

6 BOSSES WHO MARRIED THEIR SECRETARIES

1. FËDOR DOSTOEVSKI

In 1866, widower Dostoevski hired stenographer Anna Grigorievna Snitkina and dictated his short novel, *The Gambler*, to her. A year after the book's publication, he married the efficient and practical secretary, who is credited with making the Russian author's life more serene by relieving him of worldly day-to-day chores. During his most productive period—when he wrote *Crime and Punishment, The Idiot,* and *The Brothers Karamazov*—he was married to Anna.

2. T. S. ELIOT

The first wife of this influential American-born British poet died in 1947, and a decade later he eloped with his private secretary, Valerie Fletcher. (He was then 68, she 30.) One of Eliot's biographers, T. S. Matthews, wrote, "Eliot's second marriage . . . was as happy as his first had been miserable. . . . He acted like a man who had been starved all his life of physical affection, and could not get enough of it."

3. FIORELLO LA GUARDIA

The New York mayor and Depression-era political reformer married his secretary, Marie Fischer, in 1929. He later explained, "Files are the curse of modern civilization. I had a young secretary once. Just out of school. I told her, 'If you can keep these files straight, I'll marry you.' She did, and so I married her."

4. PAUL LAXALT

In 1966, Carol Wilson, then a recent divorcée, became the private secretary of Nevada Governor Laxalt. Ten years later, after the conservative Laxalt successfully weathered the anti-Republican sentiment of the Watergate era and was elected to the U.S. Senate, the millionaire Reno property developer married her.

5. BERTRAND RUSSELL

The third of philosopher-educator Russell's four wives was Patricia Helen Spence, his red-haired, youthful secretary, whom he wed in 1936. In *Marriage and Morals*, Russell had advocated temporary marriages for college students; that pronouncement, and perhaps his own multiple marriages, prompted a New York Supreme Court judge to void Russell's appointment to teach at City College in New York, on the grounds that he was an alien and a supporter of "sexual immorality."

6. SUN YAT-SEN

Dr. Sun, the "George Washington of China," hired Soong Chingling as his secretary and her own sister's successor. Although Sun was already married and twice the age of his new secretary, he fell in love with the girl and announced his plans to marry her after he obtained a divorce. Her parents were horrified, but the couple were married in 1915 at the home of a prominent Japanese lawyer. Soong acted as Sun's secretary and assistant throughout his life, and as one journalist wrote, she was "stared at, mobbed by enthusiastic crowds, and photographed within an inch of her life."

—R.T.

20 INTERRACIAL MARRIAGES

1. WILL ADAMS and BIKUNI SAN

The real-life prototype of "John Blackthorne" in James Clavell's novel *Shōgun*, Adams (1564–1620) was the first Englishman to visit Japan. Known there as Anjin Sama—Mr. Pilot—he became an influential government adviser and was given an estate at Hemi, near Yokosuka. He married a Japanese woman named Bikuni San, daughter of a samurai, and today their graves are marked by a monument.

2. POCAHONTAS and JOHN ROLFE

The legendary Indian princess who was said to have saved Capt. John Smith from execution married British colonist John Rolfe in 1614. Rolfe had petitioned the governor of Virginia for permission to marry, stressing the supposed benefits of Christianizing the Indians. When the couple visited England in 1616, Pocahontas was a model of civilized decorum. She died before their scheduled return to America.

3. PIETER VAN MEERHOFF and EVA

South Africa's equivalent of Pocahontas, Eva was a Hottentot woman who attached herself to the first Dutch settlers at the Cape of Good Hope in 1652. She adopted Western ways and married explorer Pieter van Meerhoff in 1666. This marriage might have encouraged interracial unions in South Africa, but after her husband's death in 1667, Eva lapsed into a dissolute life. The Dutch were offended by her behavior and saw it as proof of the inherent moral degeneracy of Africans. In South Africa today, her name still invokes the supposed dangers of miscegenation.

4. FLETCHER CHRISTIAN and MI'MITTI

In 1981, 54 people lived on tiny Pitcairn Island. Forty-seven of those inhabitants were descendants of nine British sailors (who seized control of H.M.S. *Bounty* in 1789) and 12 Tahitian women. Fletcher Christian, who led the mutiny, took as his wife a tall, proud Tahitian named Mi'Mitti. By 1800, only one of the original nine sailors was still alive. That man, Alexander Smith (afterward known as John Adams), lived until 1829, becoming the true patriarch of the Pitcairn community.

5.–6. CHANG and ENG BUNKER and ADELAIDE and SARAH YATES

After a successful career as traveling showmen, the original Siamese twins became American citizens and married two white Southern belles, the Yates sisters, in 1843. Their complex and largely tranquil marriages lasted until the twins' death in 1874. Between them, the twins fathered 21 children and today have over a thousand descendants spread throughout the U.S.

7.–9. JACK JOHNSON and HIS THREE BLOND BRIDES

The world's first black heavyweight boxing champion (1908–1915), Johnson shocked America by marrying three white women. Etta Terry Duryea—his wife from 1909 to 1912—suffered enormously from the unfavorable publicity, refused to bear his children, and finally committed suicide. His second mixed marriage was to Lucille Cameron, and this lasted from 1912 to 1924. It also created a national stir and led to Johnson's being convicted under the Mann Act for "transporting a woman across state lines for immoral purposes." Johnson and Cameron skipped the country, but he later returned and served a jail sentence. His third interracial marriage was to Irene Marie Pineau in 1925. Surprisingly, there was no public fuss this time.

10. LEONARD RHINELANDER and ALICE JONES

"Kip" Rhinelander—the undistinguished, stammering son of a wealthy and powerful white Eastern family—and Jones, who was one quarter black and the daughter of an obscure working-class family, married secretly in 1924. Rhinelander's outraged father spirited his son away and initiated annulment proceedings the next year, on the grounds that Jones had misled Rhinelander into believing she was a "white" woman. The resulting court case was a national sensation. After a long and bitter trial, the jury decided that in view of the couple's intimate, three-year-courtship, Rhinelander must have known Jones was "nonwhite." Therefore it ruled in her favor, enabling her to win a large cash settlement when Rhinelander divorced her five years later.

11. LENA HORNE and LENNIE HAYTON

This black American singer and actress married white musician Lennie Hayton in Paris in 1947, but the couple waited several years before publicly revealing their marriage. They stayed together until Hayton's death 24 years later. Horne once told an interviewer, "When I look at Daddy, I don't think, 'He's white.' I think, 'He's a man who's been kind to me.'"

12. SERETSE KHAMA and RUTH WILLIAMS

Khama was the hereditary chief of the Bamangwato people of Botswana (then British-ruled Bechuanaland) when he married Williams, a British secretary, in 1948. Khama won Bamangwato support for his marriage, but he still had to contend with the outrage of Great Britain and the racist government of neighboring South Africa. The British banished him from Botswana until 1956, when he finally renounced his chieftaincy. Ironically, his courageous and principled stand for non-racialism helped propel him to leadership of his country's independence movement, and he became Botswana's first president after it gained independence in 1966.

13. PEARL BAILEY and LOUIS BELLSON

Black singer Pearl Bailey and white drummer Bellson have been married since 1952.

14. JAMES MICHENER and MARI YORIKO SABUSAWA

One of the principal themes running through the works of this white American novelist is interracial relations. Michener's own third marriage, in 1955, was to Japanese American Mari Yoriko Sabusawa.

15. SAMMY DAVIS, JR., and MAY BRITT

Davis, the black American entertainer who first stunned the world by converting to Judaism and who later shocked many by publicly supporting and embracing Richard Nixon, created perhaps his biggest public flap by marrying white Swedish actress May Britt in 1960. Their marriage generated a stream of hate mail and ended in divorce in 1968.

16. HOPE COOKE and PALDEN THONDUP NAMGYAL

White American socialite Hope Cooke married the crown prince of the tiny Asian kingdom of Sikkim in 1963, two years before he was crowned king. Cooke, who was philosophically sympathetic to Asian cultures, appeared to have adapted well to her new role as queen, but her nationality became an issue when the Sikkimese rioted against the government, and she fled the country in 1973. Sikkim was annexed by India in 1975. Cooke and her husband officially separated in 1978.

17. DEBRA PAGET and LOUIS C. KUNG

White American film star Debra Paget married Chinese oil tycoon

Louis C. Kung in 1964. She then retired from films and has since lived reclusively with her family in Texas.

18. JOHN LENNON and YOKO ONO

The marriage of British rock star John Lennon and the Japanese-born singer in 1969 is widely credited as a major factor in the breakup of the Beatles the following year. Lennon and Ono held similar philosophical and political views and frequently collaborated on their music until his death in 1980.

John Lennon and Yoko Ono.

19. ROD CAREW and MARILYNN LEVY

Black Panamanian baseball star Rod Carew married Levy, a white Minneapolis girl, in 1970, while he was playing for the Minnesota Twins.

20. DIANA ROSS and ROBERT SILBERSTEIN

Black singing star Ross and Silberstein, a white public-relations executive, were married from 1971 to 1976.

—R.K.R.

9 NOTABLE WOMEN WHO WERE PREGNANT WHEN THEIR HUSBANDS DIED

1. SARAH YOUNG CHATTERTON (1731–1791)

At the age of 17, this pretty young girl from Stapleton, England, married a writing master from Bristol. Her son Thomas was born in November, 1752, shortly after her husband's death. Sarah endeavored to be a good mother and encouraged the boy in his studies, though he remained a backward student until his 10th year. While he was still a teenager, his abilities as a forger of literary works awoke his confidence, and in 1770 he left home for London, where he expected to find sudden fame. He didn't, and though he continued to write cheerfully to Sarah, he died by his own hand three months before his 18th birthday. Sarah survived him by more than 20 years, dying on Christmas Day, 1791.

2. ELIZABETH HUTCHINSON JACKSON (1741–1781)

In 1765 Andrew Jackson, his wife, Betty, and their two small sons sailed from Ireland to the U.S., where they settled in Waxhaw, a frontier settlement on the border between the Carolinas. Less than two years later, Andrew was injured while clearing land; he died within a few hours. A few days following the funeral, which took place in a sleetstorm, his wife gave birth to a son, whom she named Andrew Jackson, Jr. The fatherless family suffered greatly during the Revolution, and in 1781 Betty died of a fever while nursing American soldiers. Her son became the seventh president of the United States.

3. JEAN ARMOUR BURNS (1765–1834)

Although there were many women in his life, Jean was Robert Burns's only wife. They were married in 1788 when the poet was 29 and she 22, but her father disapproved of the union and refused to recognize it. Ill and hounded by a creditor, Burns died on July 21, 1796. His last letter was written to his father-in-law, begging him to care for Jean, who was about to deliver her sixth child. She bore their son Maxwell on July 25, during her husband's funeral. The child died in infancy.

4. AIMEE KENNEDY SEMPLE McPHERSON (1890–1944)

As a girl she'd dreamed of an acting career, but when she met Robert Semple—a linen salesman turned evangelist—in 1907, she fell in love with him and became a convert to Christ. After she and Robert were married, they went to China as missionaries. There, in the summer of 1910, Robert developed typhoid fever and died on August 4. Their daughter Roberta was born one month later. Roberta helped in the work of Aimee's Los Angeles-based Angelus Temple in later years, as did her half brother Rolf McPherson, born in 1913.

5. MADELEINE TALMADGE FORCE ASTOR (1893–1937)

She married divorced millionaire John Jacob Astor in September, 1911, but when New York society refused to let a Brooklyn shipping clerk's daughter usurp the position of Astor's first wife, Ava, the newlyweds fled to Egypt for a protracted honeymoon. By March Madeleine had discovered she was pregnant, and they booked passage home on the *Titanic*. The ship hit an iceberg in the early hours of Apr. 15, 1912. Madeleine was saved, but Astor went down with the ship "like a gentleman." John Jacob Astor VI was born several months later. The thrice-married Madeleine killed herself with sleeping pills in 1937.

6. LINA VON OSTEN HEYDRICH (1912–)

Married to Reinhard Tristan Heydrich in the early 1930s, Lina encouraged his blossoming career within the Nazi party. He soon became Himmler's right-hand man and in 1941 was nominated acting Reich Protector of Bohemia and Moravia. Heydrich and Lina lived like Renaissance royalty in Prague (where she beat the servants and he beat her), but *Der Henker* ("The hangman") was assassinated by four Czech patriots in May, 1942. Hitler accorded Heydrich a lavish state funeral in which Lina, pregnant with her fourth child, participated with dignity. In the fall of that year Heydrich's posthumous daughter Marte was born.

7. KATHLEEN (KAY) WILLIAMS GABLE (1917–)

After a brief fling with Clark Gable in 1944, she married millionaire Adolph Spreckels while Clark married socialite Sylvia Ashley. By 1954 they were both divorced again, and Kay soon became Gable's fifth wife. The blond bride, who bore more than a passing resemblance to his true love and third wife, Carole Lombard, dedicated herself to making him happy. Gable suffered a heart attack in November, 1960, brought on by the physical ordeal of making *The Misfits*, and died 10 days later. Kay gave birth to their son John Clark by Caesarian section on Mar. 20, 1961.

8. ETHEL SKECKEL KENNEDY (1928–)

She might have become the First Lady of the land, but Robert F. Kennedy was assassinated on June 5, 1968, following his victory in the California Democratic presidential primary. At the time, Ethel was expecting her 11th child, who was delivered by Caesarian section on Dec. 12, 1968, at Georgetown University Hospital in Washington, D.C. When the grieving widow left the hospital on Dec. 19 she took her infant daughter Rory Elizabeth Katherine Kennedy directly to Arlington National Cemetery, where she knelt and prayed at her murdered husband's grave.

9. DEBBIE MONTGOMERY MINARDOS POWER (1931–)

She was the 26-year-old divorced mother of one when she met handsome movie star Tyrone Power, himself twice divorced and soured on marriage. During the ardent affair that followed, Debbie became pregnant. Power married her in May, 1958. That summer they traveled to Spain where he worked on the film *Solomon and Sheba*; he collapsed on the set and died of a heart attack in November. Debbie sat alongside Power's coffin during the funeral service, holding his hand. She gave birth to Tyrone Power IV on Jan. 22, 1959.

—J.M.P.

14 FAMOUS PEOPLE WHO WERE ADOPTED

1. Edward Albee (1928–   ), U.S. playwright
2. David Berkowitz (1953–   ), New York's "Son of Sam" killer
3. Robert Byrd (1917–   ), U.S. senator
4. Christina Crawford (1939–   ), U.S. author and daughter of Joan Crawford
5. David Farragut (1801–1870), U.S. naval hero
6. Deborah Harry (1945–   ), U.S. lead singer for rock group "Blondie"
7. Art Linkletter (1912–   ), U.S. TV emcee
8. James MacArthur (1937–   ), U.S. actor
9. James Michener (1907–   ), U.S. author
10. Moses (c. 14th–13th centuries B.C.), Jewish religious leader
11. Karen Ann Quinlan (1954–   ), U.S. woman whose comatose condition led to a legal battle over whether doctors can remove people with hopeless illnesses from artificial life-support systems
12. King Sargon of Akkad (c. 2637 B.C.–2582 B.C.), Mesopotamian ruler, the first recorded adoptee
13. Henry Morton Stanley (1841–1904), British explorer and journalist
14. Edgar Wallace (1875–1932), British author best known for his detective stories

—A.Ti

13 MEN WITH MOTHER FIXATIONS

1. J. M. BARRIE (1860–1937)

Sir James Matthew Barrie was a prolific and sentimental author. His mother, née Margaret Ogilvy, raised him on tales of Scottish village life and her own difficult girlhood. Margaret was orphaned and obliged to raise a younger brother while still a child herself. Barrie often exploited this "little mother" theme in his work, using it particularly for Wendy in *Peter Pan*. At age 36, he wrote a memoir of his mother's life, *Margaret Ogilvy*, which was so adoring that one critic called it "a positive act of indecency."

2. ANDREW CARNEGIE (1835–1919)

Carnegie always credited his mother, Margaret Hodge Carnegie, as being the inspiration for his enormous financial success. To him she was "the power that never failed in any emergency," and he dubbed her his "favorite heroine." Reflecting on his own humble family circumstances, he advanced a theory that poor mothers were intrinsically more virtuous than mothers of means. He vowed never to marry while his mother lived, and he was as good as his word. He remained a bachelor until after her death, which occurred when he was 51 years old.

3. GUSTAVE FLAUBERT (1821–1880)

Anne Justine-Caroline Fleuriot Flaubert, the mother of novelist Flaubert, was an emotional extortionist and a martyr. She could make life a hell for her sensitive son by merely letting tears appear in her eyes. She lived with him until her death in 1872 and distorted his view of other women so effectively that he remained a lifelong bachelor. He once wrote to her, "I know very well that I shall never love another as I do you. . . . Some will perhaps mount to the threshold of the temple, but none will enter." Except, perhaps, a woman named Madame Bovary.

4. J. EDGAR HOOVER (1895–1972)

Annie M. Scheitlin Hoover was the product of a long line of Swiss mercenary soldiers. She ran her household with martial severity and a strong emphasis on moral rectitude. Annie lived with her son, "J.E.," until she died at age 78. The gap left by her death was filled by Clyde Tolson, for many years Hoover's inseparable companion and the no. 2 man at the FBI. Hoover often opined that America's consistently rising crime rate was the result of a general breakdown of parental example. Like Tolson, he was never known to take an interest in the opposite sex.

5. HARRY HOUDINI (1874–1926)

The foremost escape artist the world has ever known was absorbed with his mother even after her death at age 72. Staunchly determined to contact her spirit, he spent his final years patronizing (and exposing) one medium after another. He lay face down on his mother's grave and held long one-sided conversations with her in the hope that he could somehow make contact. Presumably he never did. Psychoanalysts have speculated that Houdini's prowess at breaking out of dark, enclosed spaces into the light stemmed from his need to reenact symbolically the birth process.

6. D. H. LAWRENCE (1885–1930)

Lydia Beardsall Lawrence was disappointed in her husband and possessive of her five children—especially "Bertie," the youngest and most vulnerable of the three boys. "I loved my mother like a lover," the author later wrote. After her death, Lawrence devoted a major portion of his literary energies to excising her Victorian influence from his life and replacing it with a personal credo of sexual indulgence. Ironically, this high priest of the erotic was often impotent and unexpectedly prudish in ways which suggested that his mother's specter was unshakable.

7. WLADZIU VALENTINO LIBERACE (1919–)

Liberace's musical education was provided by his father, a former member of John Philip Sousa's band. Yet his mother, a Wisconsin farmgirl of Polish ancestry, made a more fundamental contribution to her son's career. One of Liberace's fingers was badly infected when he was young and would have been amputated but for a home remedy applied by Frances Zuchowski Liberace. After he achieved success, she shared his celebrity. He is always generous with praise for her and once said: "There are so many little things about my mother that I hold precious.

Liberace with his mother, Frances Zuchowski Liberace.

... I feel terrible sometimes that my appreciation and admiration of her as a lovable and very special person has been ridiculed."

8. YUKIO MISHIMA (1925–1970)

The Japanese author's early childhood was a virtual tug-of-war between two mother figures—his actual mother, Shizue, and his grandmother, a strong-willed traditional Japanese matriarch. This struggle helped to instill in the boy a dual personality: His public face, courtesy of his grandmother, was that of a redoubtable samurai; in private, he reflected his mother's upbringing, acting in an insecure and emotional manner. He lost his grandmother just as he reached puberty, and he thereafter devoted himself completely to his mother. Upon receiving the news of her son's spectacular public *hara-kiri* suicide in 1970, Shizue said only, "Now my lover has been returned to me."

9. ELVIS PRESLEY (1935–1977)

If the king of rock 'n' roll ever had a queen, it was certainly his mother, Gladys Presley. When Elvis was a boy, Gladys accompanied him everywhere, watching over him like a guardian angel. She forbade her precious only son to go swimming or to do anything the least bit dangerous and slept beside him, sharing his bed until he reached puberty. She was his confidante, his adviser, and his alter ego who often communicated with him in bizarre baby talk that was baffling to strangers. Like Elvis, she gobbled amphetamines, or diet pills, and like her son, she was fated to die young. When she died in August, 1958, Elvis was devastated. It took several men to pry him from her casket at graveside.

10. MARCEL PROUST (1871–1922)

Early in life, Marcel Proust noticed that he received extra attention from his beautiful mother, Jeanne Weil Proust, when he was ill. His mother fixation was so strong that he remained sickly for all the years he lived with her, until her death in 1905. Asked as a child what he wanted for a New Year's present, he told his mother, "Your affection." One of the most famous passages from his novel *Swann's Way* deals with the ritual of his good-night kiss: "Sometimes, when after kissing me, she opened the door to go, I longed to call her back, to say to her, 'Kiss me just once more.'" He suffered bitter anguish when she forgot this kiss.

11. STENDHAL (1783–1842)

Although Marie Henri Beyle came from a solidly bourgeois family in Grenoble, France, his mother, Henriette Gagnon Beyle, prided herself on her illustrious Italian forebears. In rejecting the hated taint of his father's middle-class ancestry, author Stendhal became enamored of all things Italian, including women. His mother, who died when he was seven, was his foremost fantasy image. He wrote, "I wanted to cover my mother with kisses, and that there not be any clothing. . . . I always wanted to give them to her on the breast."

12. WILLIAM TILDEN, JR. (1893–1953)

In 1950, an Associated Press poll of sportswriters named Big Bill Tilden the greatest tennis player the century had thus far produced, and many respondents flatly termed him America's greatest athlete ever. Seven years before Tilden's birth, his mother, Selena Hey Tilden, lost her first three children within a two-week period during a diphtheria epidemic. As a result, "June"—short for Junior—was sheltered and insulated from the harsher aspects of life, with one notable exception: Selena constantly harangued him on the horrors of venereal disease. Tilden grew up to be a closet homosexual, and it seems unlikely that he was ever able to consummate a physical relationship with a member of either sex.

13. CLIFTON WEBB (1893–1966)

Clifton Webb, the actor best remembered as "Mr. Belvedere," was the creation of a prototypical stage mother. Mabelle Webb made life difficult for producers and directors on her son's behalf for over 60 years. She is remembered as a tireless hostess who remained an exhibitionist well into her 90th year. At that age, she often jazzed up Hollywood parties with her version of the cancan. Webb was so attached to her that he entered into a decline shortly after her death, which prompted friend Noel Coward to remark, "Poor Clifton! It must be tough to be orphaned at 71."

—M.S.

ERMA BOMBECK'S 10 TIPS ON RAISING CHILDREN

Bombeck's syndicated humor column appears in 800 newspapers. She regularly appears on *Good Morning, America* and is the author of six best-selling books, including *The Grass Is Always Greener over the Septic Tank* and *Aunt Erma's Cope Book*. The mother of three, Bombeck draws much of her material from the trials and tribulations of life in the suburbs.

1. Never turn your back on a two-year-old.
2. Never pick out a Mother's Day gift that you cannot afford.
3. When traveling on an airline, check the children and sit next to your baggage.
4. Never take your child to a pediatrician who has dead tropical fish in the aquarium of his waiting room.
5. Never threaten them with things you can't deliver. (Example: "If you don't open that bathroom door now, I am running away with Warren Beatty and you will never see Mommy again!")
6. Never help your children with their homework, or they won't graduate until they're 35.
7. Never stand in the middle of a kitchen and say to a daughter, "Someday, all of this will be yours."
8. Clean fewer toilet bowls and spend more time eating popcorn in the living room and laughing.
9. Love the child . . . even as you punish the deed.
10. Tell them at least once a day that they are driving you crazy . . . but you cannot imagine a life without them.

—Exclusive for *The Book of Lists 3*

19 RENOWNED RUNAWAYS

1. DAVY CROCKETT (1786–1836), frontiersman

After being whipped at school for fighting an older boy and fearing worse punishment from his father, 13-year-old Davy ran away and hired out with a cattle drive to Virginia. When the drive ended, Davy worked at a variety of jobs for two years while making his way back home.

2. SAMUEL HOUSTON (1793–1863), soldier and politician

Rather than work as a clerk at a local store, 15-year-old Houston, who was to become a leader in Texas's fight for independence, went off to live with the Cherokee Indians for three years. He said, "I prefer measuring deer tracks to measuring tape."

3. DOROTHEA DIX (1802–1887), social reformer

Ten-year-old Dorothea left home in Hampden, Me., where her father was a fundamentalist preacher, and went to live with her wealthy grandmother in Boston, where Dorothea remained through adolescence.

4. ANDREW JOHNSON (1808–1875), U.S. president

At age 14, Andrew and his brother were apprenticed to a tailor in Raleigh, S.C. After two years of bondage, the boys ran away. This was in violation of the contract, and a reward of $10 was offered for their capture. After a time Andrew returned to Raleigh, but the threat of legal action remained, so he again left town. In 1826 he settled in Greenville, Tenn., where he opened up a tailor shop.

5. WILLIAM CODY (1846–1917), Western showman

Better known as Buffalo Bill, he ran away at age 12 when his mother insisted that he go to school rather than become a herder. He returned home two months later with $50.

6. MATTHEW A. HENSON (1866–1955), North Pole explorer

No longer able to tolerate his stepmother, 11-year-old Matthew headed for Washington, D.C., where he became a dishwasher in a lunchroom. At age 12 he decided to become a sailor and walked to Baltimore to sign on with a ship.

7. W. C. FIELDS (1880–1946), actor

When Fields's father, a fruit and vegetable peddler, hit his son on the head with a shovel, the boy planned revenge. Fields hid in a stable and dropped a large wooden box on his father's head. After the incident, Fields—then 11—left home in Philadelphia, Pa., and became a vaudeville and amusement park juggler.

8. DAMON RUNYON (1880–1946), author and journalist

Runyon ran away from his family's home in Manhattan, Kans.

Lying about his age—he was only 14—Runyon joined the Army and fought in the Spanish-American War.

9. HEDDA HOPPER (1885–1966), actress and columnist

Hedda fled from the home of her strict Quaker parents in Hollidaysburg, Pa., at the age of 18, and went to New York City, where she got a job in the chorus of an opera company.

10. ROBERT STROUD (1890–1963), criminal and ornithologist

"The Bird Man of Alcatraz" ran away from his mother's home in Seattle, Wash., at the age of 13 and became a hobo.

11. CLARE BOOTHE LUCE (1903–   ), author and U.S. ambassador

Following graduation from high school, Clare—then 16—abandoned her family in New York and found a job with a company that manufactured paper novelties. However, an attack of appendicitis forced her to cut her adventure short.

12. MIKE MANSFIELD (1903–   ), U.S. senator and ambassador

Mansfield was not yet 15 when the U.S. entered W.W. I, but he ran away from home, lied about his age, and got into the Navy. By the time he was 19, he had also served in the Army and the Marines. Forty years later, Senator Mansfield was still wearing his Marine discharge button.

13. CARY GRANT (1904–   ), actor

Grant (then Archie Leach) was 13 when he bade a silent farewell to his parents and joined an acrobatic troupe that specialized in pantomime, clown routines, stilt-walking, and comic dances. His father found him and took Grant back home, but the boy ran away again about a year and a half later and rejoined the troupe. This time his father allowed him to remain.

14. LYNDON JOHNSON (1908–1973), U.S. president

At the age of 15, Lyndon and a group of friends hopped into a Model T Ford and drove from his home in Johnson City, Tex., to California. During his two years as a runaway, the future president worked as a grape picker, dishwasher, auto mechanic, and law clerk.

15. DANNY KAYE (1913–   ), actor and comedian

With $1.50 to his name, Kaye left his home in Brooklyn at about the age of 16 and went to Florida, where he sang for resort hotel guests.

16. ROD McKUEN (1933–   ), poet, singer, and composer

McKuen dropped out of school when he was 11, left home, and wandered throughout the Western states. He worked at a multitude of jobs, including ranch hand, lumberjack, and shoe salesman.

17. FLIP WILSON (1933–   ), comedian

Unhappy in a foster home, Flip asked to be sent to the reformatory

Lyndon Johnson (left) ran away from home at the age of 15 and worked as a grape picker, dishwasher, and auto mechanic.

where one of his older brothers had been placed. Wilson's request was granted, but he escaped from the reformatory eight times.

18. NEIL DIAMOND (1941–   ), singer and composer

Diamond ran away from his home in Brooklyn at the age of 13 and journeyed to the Midwest, where he formed a musical group called the Roadrunners. They performed in coffeehouses for two years, after which Neil returned home.

19. BOB DYLAN (1941–   ), singer and songwriter

In search of adventure, Dylan decided to leave his parents' home in Hibbing, Minn. He did so seven times between the ages of 10 and 18.

—R.J.F. & T.H.

14
YOU'RE IN THE MONEY

20 OCCUPATIONS WITH THE HIGHEST UNEMPLOYMENT RATES (1981 ANNUAL AVERAGES)

Occupation	Unemployment Rate
1. Grader and sorter in manufacturing	30.6%
2. Enumerator and interviewer	23.2%
3. Construction laborer, including carpenters' helper	22.7%
4. Dishwasher	19.3%
5. Dry-wall installer and lather	18.5%
6. Punch and stamping press operator	18.2%
7. Brickmason and stonemason	17.6%
8. Roofer and slater	16.5%
9. Cement and concrete finisher	16.3%
10. Assembler	16.0%
10. Packer and wrapper, except meat and produce	16.0%
10. Waiters' assistant	16.0%
13. Lodging quarters' cleaner, except private household	15.9%
14. Filer, polisher, sander, and buffer	15.8%
15. Boiling and canning operative	15.4%
16. Recreation and amusement attendant	15.2%
17. Structural metal operative	15.0%
18. Freight and material handler	14.9%
19. Carpenter	14.7%
20. Excavating, grading, and road machinery operative	14.6%

Note: Only those occupations with employment levels of 35,000 or more were considered.

SOURCE: U.S. Department of Labor, Bureau of Labor Statistics, April, 1982.

20 OCCUPATIONS WITH THE LOWEST UNEMPLOYMENT RATES (1981 ANNUAL AVERAGES)

Occupation	*Unemployment Rate*
1. Real-estate appraiser	0.0%
2. Farmer and farm manager	0.2%
3. Funeral director	0.4%
4. Fire fighter	0.6%
4. Physician, dentist, and related practitioner	0.6%
6. Lawyer and judge	0.7%
7. Pattern and model maker, except paper	0.8%
8. Mail carrier, post office	1.0%
9. Assessor, controller, and treasurer; local public administrator	1.1%
9. Computer specialist	1.1%
9. Data processing machine repairer	1.1%
12. Police and detective	1.3%
12. Sales manager, except retail trade	1.3%
14. Religious worker	1.4%
14. Telephone installer and repairer	1.4%
16. Engineer	1.5%
16. Insurance agent, broker, and underwriter	1.5%
18. Bank officer and financial manager	1.6%
18. Real-estate agent and broker	1.6%
18. School administrator, college	1.6%

Note: Only those occupations with employment levels of 35,000 or more were considered.

SOURCE: U.S. Department of Labor, Bureau of Labor Statistics, April, 1982.

15 FAMOUS PEOPLE WHO WORKED IN BED

1. KING LOUIS XI (1423–1483)

This French king was ugly, fat, and sickly but also ruthless and clever, earning the title of the "universal spider." He introduced the custom of the *lit de justice* (bed of justice), a ceremonial appearance of the monarch, in bed, before *le parlement* with the princes of the realm on stools, the greater officials standing, and the lesser ones kneeling. No one is sure exactly why he began the practice, but it caught on and lasted until the French Revolution. Fontanelle, a critic of Louis XV, was asked on the eve of the Revolution, "What, sir, is a 'bed of justice'?" He replied, "It is the place where justice lies asleep."

2. LEONARDO DA VINCI (1452–1519)

Leonardo earned a unique fame as an artist and scientist, and according to his *Notebooks*, he spent some time each night ". . . in bed in the dark to go over again in the imagination the main outlines of the forms previously studied . . . it is useful in fixing things in the memory."

3. CARDINAL DE RICHELIEU (1585–1642)

In the last year of his life the diabolically clever and scheming cardinal took to his bed and stayed there because of his rapidly deteriorating health. This didn't prevent him from working—he directed his highly efficient secret police in exposing the treasonous machinations of the youthful royal favorite Cinq-Mars. Nor did it hinder the peripatetic cardinal from traveling—his servants carried him about in his bed, and if the door of a house he wanted to stay in was too narrow, they would break open the walls.

4. THOMAS HOBBES (1588–1679)

Hobbes, the great British political philosopher, was renowned for his mathematical approach to natural philosophy and found bed a comfortable and handy place to work on his formulas. He wrote the numbers on the sheets and, when he ran out of room, on his thighs. He wrote his 1661 *Dialogue on Physics, or On the Nature of Air* entirely in bed. Hobbes also sang in bed because (according to Aubrey's *Brief Lives*) ". . . he did beleeve [sic] it did his lungs good, and conduced much to prolong his life."

5. HENRY WADSWORTH LONGFELLOW (1807–1882)

Throughout his life Longfellow suffered from periodic bouts of severe insomnia. Out of desperation he decided to put his sleepless nights to some good use, and he began to write poetry in bed—including his 1842 classic "The Wreck of the *Hesperus*."

6. MARK TWAIN (1835–1910)

He loved the luxurious comfort of writing in bed and there composed large portions of *Huckleberry Finn, The Adventures of Tom Sawyer,* and *A Connecticut Yankee in King Arthur's Court.* He seems to have been the only person ever to point out that working in bed must be a very dangerous occupation, since so many deaths occur there.

7. IGNACE FANTIN-LATOUR (1836–1904)

Best known for his portrait groups, especially *Homage à Delacroix,* this French painter worked in bed out of necessity when he could not afford wood for a fire. William Gaunt, in *The Aesthetic Adventure,* describes him propped up in bed, "Shivering, mournful, persistent . . . in a threadbare overcoat, a top hat over his eyes and a scarf round his mouth,

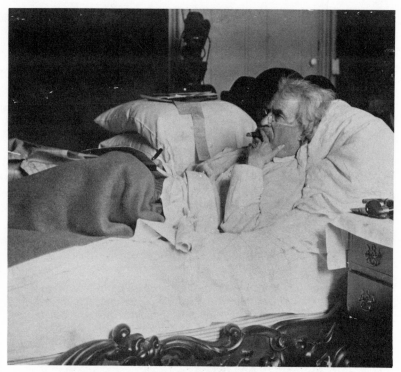

Mark Twain wrote *Huckleberry Finn* and *The Adventures of Tom Sawyer* in bed.

balancing a candle on the edge of his drawing board and sketching with numbed, gloved hand."

8. ROBERT LOUIS STEVENSON (1850–1894)

For years Stevenson was wracked by coughing spells caused by tuberculosis, and consequently he wrote most of *Kidnapped* and *A Child's Garden of Verses* in bed at his home in Bournemouth, England. Bed sometimes brought him inspiration in the form of dreams. One night his subconscious mind spun "a fine bogey tale," as he called it, based on a real-life criminal he had read about. Stevenson's dream became *Dr. Jekyll and Mr. Hyde.*

9. EDITH WHARTON (1862–1937)

Pulitzer Prize-winning author (*Age of Innocence*, 1920) Edith Wharton wrote primarily about the upper class into which she was born. Her perspective on the good life was no doubt sharpened by her work habits—she wrote in the mornings, finding inspiration in the comfort of her bed. So accustomed was she to this routine that she once suffered a fit of hysterics because her hotel room bed did not face the light so she could work.

10. MARCEL PROUST (1871–1922)

Bundled in sweaters, a hot-water bottle at his feet, the French author worked to refine his series of novels called *À la Recherche du Temps Perdu (Remembrance of Things Past)* while lying virtually flat in bed in a cork-lined room. He had all the necessities within arm's reach—more than a dozen pens (if he dropped one, he refused to pick it up because of dust); all of his notes, notebooks, and manuscripts; even fumigation powder, which he believed helped his asthma. In spite of all his precautions, he died of pneumonia at age 51.

11. WINSTON CHURCHILL (1874–1965)

Churchill loved to lie abed in comfort while dictating letters and going through the boxes of official state papers for several hours each morning. Although he much preferred to write his books while standing up, declining health in his later years forced him to write and correct most of *The Second World War* and *A History of the English-Speaking Peoples* in bed.

12. MAE WEST (1892–1980)

The legendary sex queen with the hourglass figure was famous for her *double-entendre* lines. She wrote several of her own screenplays, including *Diamond Lil*, and in 1959 she published her autobiography, *Goodness Had Nothing to Do with It*. She did all her writing in bed, she reported, noting that "Everybody knows I do my best work in bed."

13. MAMIE EISENHOWER (1896–1979)

While in the White House, First Lady Mamie Eisenhower did away with an office but not with the office routine. She held bedside conferences, dictated to her secretary, paid the bills, and signed letters while ensconced in her pink-ruffled bed.

14. F. SCOTT FITZGERALD (1896–1940)

During the last two years of his life, while writing *The Last Tycoon*, Fitzgerald found that he could work longer hours by staying in bed. He'd retire to bed with a dozen Coca-Colas (which had replaced alcohol in his drinking habits), prop himself on pillows, and using a lapboard, he'd work for about five hours a day. A fatal heart attack prevented him from completing *The Last Tycoon*.

15. HUGH HEFNER (1926–   )

It seems appropriate that a man who made his fortune in sex should have done so in bed. For 20 years, Hef has controlled the *Playboy* empire from a massive bed in his Chicago mansion, where he has stayed awake for 60-hour stretches, fueled by amphetamines and Pepsi.

—R.W.S. & THE EDS.

8 MOVIE STARS WHO WORKED IN A GAS STATION OR GARAGE

1. DANA ANDREWS (1909–   )

While working as a gas-station attendant in Van Nuys, Calif.—a Los Angeles suburb—the aspiring actor made the rounds of the movie studios. His generous employers, Stanley Twomey and John Wardlaw, advanced him an extra $50 a week for singing lessons and living expenses until he won a $150 a week contract with Samuel Goldwyn in December, 1938.

2. SEBASTIAN CABOT (1918–1977)

Cabot, later known as a plump, courtly character actor, had to leave school at 14 to earn a living. Among his various jobs was that of garage mechanic while he was living in London.

3. CLINT EASTWOOD (1930–   )

To supplement his meager funds from the GI Bill—he was studying business administration at Los Angeles City College—Eastwood pumped gas at a station conveniently located near an unemployment office on Santa Monica Boulevard.

4. JAMES GARNER (1928–   )

During his youth, Garner held more than 50 different kinds of jobs in various towns across the country and in his hometown of Norman, Okla., including that of gas-station attendant. While pumping gas he made friends with a soda jerk named Paul Gregory. A few years later Gregory, who had become a producer, hired Garner to cue Lloyd Nolan in the Broadway production of *The Caine Mutiny Court-Martial.*

5. GENE KELLY (1912–   )

Before making it to Broadway in the chorus of Cole Porter's musical *Leave It to Me* in 1938, Kelly pumped gas in his hometown of Pittsburgh.

6. ALAN LADD (1913–1964)

The laconic tough guy best remembered for *This Gun for Hire* (1942) and *Shane* (1953) pumped gas and held a variety of jobs in Los Angeles before breaking into the movie business.

7. DEAN MARTIN (1917–   )

Quitting school in the 10th grade, young Dino Crocetti worked as a gas-station attendant in his native Steubenville, O.

8. VICTOR MATURE (1915–   )

Publicized as "The Hunk" in *One Million B.C.* (1940), Mature once worked as a car greaser and polisher in a Pasadena garage in order to pay his tuition at the Pasadena Playhouse. He lived in a tent fashioned out of a piano crate and a piece of canvas, which he set up in the backyard of playhouse director Gilmor Brown. Mature estimated later that his average daily budget was 46¢.

—M.E.P.

6 MOVIE STARS WHO WORKED IN A BARBERSHOP

1. HENRY ARMETTA (1888–1945)

At the age of 14, Armetta—an Italian stowaway—arrived in New York and first got work as a barber's helper. The venerable character actor often was typecast as an excitable Latin in scores of movies.

2. CHARLIE CHAPLIN (1889–1977)

By the time he was nine, Charlie was on his own. When not sleeping in Covent Garden market or in Hyde Park, he worked at several short-lived jobs, including that of lather boy in a barbershop. Years later one of his two roles in *The Great Dictator* (1940) was that of a barber.

3. PERRY COMO (1912–   )

This popular star of movie musicals made in the 1940s began working after school in a barbershop when he was 11. At 14, he was making installment payments on his own shop, and between 1929 and 1934 he operated a shop in Canonsburg, Pa., leaving it to sing first with Freddie Carlone's orchestra and then with Ted Weems. Five years later he returned to Canonsburg to reopen his shop but changed his mind when he was offered a job on radio.

4. GRETA GARBO (1905–   )

After her father's death in June, 1920, 14-year-old Greta Gustaffson worked as a *tvålflicka*—or "soaplather girl"—in a Stockholm barbershop owned by Arthur Ekengren. She tied the bib around the customer's neck, soaped his face after she mixed the lather, cleaned the razors, and warmed the towels. She often pirouetted on one leg while stropping a razor. Garbo recalled in the Swedish magazine *Lektyr* in 1931: "I was never as proud as of my first week's wages. . . ."

5. HARRY LANGDON (1884–1944)

The great baby-faced silent-film comedian—ranked with Chaplin, Keaton, and Harold Lloyd—worked as a barber before joining a medicine show in Omaha, Neb.

6. YVES MONTAND (1921–)

Ivo Livi, a 15-year-old Italian living in France with his family, worked as a ladies' hairdresser in his sister's beauty parlor in Marseilles. By the age of 23, he was Yves Montand—a popular music-hall singer and the *bon ami* of Édith Piaf.

—M.E.P.

17 MOVIE STARS WHO WORKED AS WAITRESSES

1. JACQUELINE BISSET (1944–)

When she was not making TV commercials, Jacqueline Bisset was a waitress in a London coffee bar in 1962.

2. JOAN BLONDELL (1909–1979)

While living with her parents at 84th Street and Lexington Avenue in Manhattan, the teenaged future comedienne tried in vain to get a job as a chorine. She ended up waiting tables instead.

3. JOAN CRAWFORD (1904–1977)

At the age of 11, Lucille LeSueur worked her way through St. Agnes Academy in Kansas City, Mo., by waiting tables. She again waited on her fellow students while attending Stephens College in Columbia, Mo. When she tried to pledge at a campus sorority, she was turned down because it did not take "girls who work."

4. BETTE DAVIS (1908–)

Because of the precarious financial status of her divorced mother— a fledgling photographer—Bette helped pay her tuition at Cushing Academy in Ashburnham, Mass., by waiting tables in the school cafeteria. Her classmates at the coeducational school did not, for the most part, ostracize her, which she had feared they would do. Miss Davis recalled this job as "my primer in pride."

5. OLIVIA DE HAVILLAND (1916–)

Because her dour stepfather, George Fontaine, opposed her starring in a Los Gatos, Calif., high school production of *Pride and Prejudice*, Olivia left home at 16 to work as a waitress in nearby Saratoga.

6. FAYE DUNAWAY (1941–)

After enrolling in Boston University's School of Fine and Applied Arts, Faye Dunaway was troubled with such feelings of inferiority and financial insecurity that she "waited on tables to stay abreast of the wealthy Pi Phi sorority kids I ran around with."

7. FRANCES FARMER (1914–1970)

The ill-fated blond star paid her expenses at the University of Washington by working as a singing waitress at Mount Rainier National Park, thus prefiguring her most famous movie performance—the dual role of Lotta, the cafe singer, and her daughter in *Come and Get It* (1936).

8. JOAN FONTAINE (1917–   )

Refusing to live in a house where her sister, Olivia de Havilland, was not welcome, Joan went to live at The Lundblads, a boardinghouse in Saratoga, Calif. She waited tables and also prepared vegetables in the afternoons and evenings.

9. LAUREN HUTTON (1944–   )

As an 18-year-old dropout from the University of Southern Florida, Hutton went to New York and ended up as a cocktail waitress. Later she recalled, "It was winter . . . I was starving . . . I took a job as a Playboy Bunny. The work was arduous and humiliating. Patrons assumed you were a whore."

10. GLENDA JACKSON (1936–   )

After graduating from London's Royal Academy of Dramatic Arts, Glenda Jackson toiled at several jobs, including that of a waitress, in the long stretches between acting jobs.

11. MADELINE KAHN (1942–   )

While attending Hofstra University on a scholarship in the early 1960s, the future Lili von Shtupp of *Blazing Saddles* (1974) was a singing waitress in a German dining hall in Bellmore, Long Island. Madeline recalled much later that anyone working there "really needed a sense of humor."

12. MAUREEN STAPLETON (1925–   )

During W.W. II, she worked as a waitress in the evenings while training for the stage at the Herbert Berghof Acting School in Manhattan.

13. MARY STEENBURGEN (1952–   )

After she left Hendrix College in Arkansas in 1972, she went to New York to study acting. But until Jack Nicholson cast her as his leading lady in *Goin' South* (1978), she spent more time waiting tables at the Magic Pan restaurant than at the Manhattan Theater Club.

14. LILY TOMLIN (1939–   )

Lily was a waitress in the mid-1960s at the busy Howard Johnson restaurant at Broadway and 49th Street in the heart of Manhattan's theater district. One day, to break the monotony, she announced over the restaurant's PA system: "Attention, diners: Your Howard Johnson's wait-

Lily Tomlin playing a waitress.

ress of the week, Miss Lily Tomlin, is about to make her appearance on the floor. Let's all give her a big hand!" She doubled her usual tips—but was fired by the manager, who did not have a sense of humor.

15. RAQUEL WELCH (1940–   )

After her divorce from tuna fisherman James Welch in 1963, she worked as a cocktail waitress in Dallas in order to support her two small children and to earn enough money for a nose job.

16. CINDY WILLIAMS (1947–   )

Following her graduation from Los Angeles City College, she was a waitress in Los Angeles until she was able to get bit parts in movies like *Gas-s-s-s* (1970) and *Drive He Said* (1971), directed by Jack Nicholson. She became a star on television as Shirley in the comedy series *Laverne and Shirley*.

17. JANE WYMAN (1914–   )

In the early 1930s she was fired from her job as a waitress at a Los Angeles coffee shop because she could not cut pie into six geometrically even pieces.

—M.E.P.

307

8 AILMENTS AND DISABILITIES THAT RESULTED IN THE FORMATION OF BIG BUSINESSES

1. STETSON HATS

New Jersey-born John B. Stetson learned hatmaking from his father, but just as John was setting up his own business, he was told he had consumption. He went West and joined a Pike's Peak expedition, hoping to build up his strength. When his comrades needed cloth for tents, Stetson told them of the felting process for making cloth without weaving. They laughed—until he changed a bit of fur into a hat which protected him from wind, rain, and sun, and a cowboy came along and bought it for $5. When Stetson's health returned, he went to Philadelphia and, in 1865, started producing the wide-brimmed, high-crowned felt hats which the world came to know as the Stetson. By 1906, when he died, Stetson's factory was turning out 2 million hats a year.

2. COUGH DROPS

During the mid-1800s, candymaker and restaurateur James Smith operated a restaurant in Poughkeepsie, N.Y. One day a patron noticed that Smith was being tormented by a heavy, hacking cough. The patron took a candylike lozenge from his pocket and told him it could soothe sore throats and relieve coughs. The diner later gave Smith the formula, and he whipped up a batch of the medicated candy. Seeing its commercial possibilities, Smith started packaging the drops and began an ad campaign in 1852. When James died, his sons William and Andrew inherited the business and, in 1866, it became the Smith Brothers Company. The famed Smith Brothers cough drops, now manufactured by F & F Laboratories, are still sold everywhere.

3. CARPET SWEEPER

Melville R. Bissell, a Grand Rapids, Mich., china dealer, was plagued by allergic headaches, a condition which was aggravated by the dusty packing straw he used in his shop. He overcame the problem by inventing a sweeper which scooped up the dust rather than scattering it. He patented his sweeper in 1876 and formed the Bissell Carpet Sweeper Company.

4. CASH REGISTER

Dayton, O., saloon owner James S. Ritty became so unnerved by his pilfering bartenders that his health began to fail, and his doctor advised him to take a relaxing ocean voyage. While aboard ship, Ritty noticed a device that counted the revolutions of the ship's propeller, and he deduced that the same principle could be applied to counting money. With the help of his brother, John, Ritty invented the cash register and patented the device in November, 1879. Five years later, Col. John Henry Patterson bought controlling interest in Ritty's operation and renamed it National Cash Register.

5. SHREDDED WHEAT

A victim of dyspepsia, lawyer and entrepreneur Henry D. Perky resolved to develop a food that was easy on the stomach. In accord with nutritional beliefs of the 1890s, he settled on the wheat berry as nature's most perfect food and devised a process for making shredded wheat. The earliest incarnation of the product was tested on some gastric patients, who thought that eating it was somewhat "like eating a whisk broom." After further refinements, Perky began taking out patents on his product and the machines used to make it in 1892, and his pillows of shredded wheat became a tasty fixture on the American breakfast table. In 1930 the National Biscuit Company (Nabisco) bought the company which produced shredded wheat.

6. RUBBER HEELS

Humphrey O'Sullivan, of Lowell, Mass., often got tired, cramped legs from standing on the concrete floor at the printing shop where he worked. A rubber mat eased the aches, but because it was inconvenient to carry the mat with him and because his fellow employees often walked off with it, he decided to nail patches of it to the heels of his shoes. That was in 1896. Once patented, that simple solution to a small problem made O'Sullivan a wealthy man. Today the company born of that brainchild is known as the O'Sullivan Corporation.

7. GROSSINGER'S VACATION RESORT

In 1914, a doctor advised Selig Grossinger to take a vacation from the fast pace of life on the Lower East Side of New York City. After three weeks in the mountains, Grossinger returned to the city rested, strengthened, and determined to buy a small farm in the Catskills for his family. The rock-strewn farm which the Grossingers purchased had no electricity or indoor plumbing and did not provide an income. So they took in boarders who sought good food, fresh air, and quiet surroundings. The Grossingers were such good hosts that, in spite of the farm's primitiveness, they soon had more guests than they could handle. Within five years, the family was able to buy a larger, more modern place nearby, which became the world-famous resort hotel, Grossinger's.

8. *READER'S DIGEST*

Spending three months in an Army hospital in France during W.W. I while recuperating from shrapnel wounds, Sgt. DeWitt Wallace of Minnesota had plenty of time to peruse magazines. He also practiced and perfected a technique of condensing articles which he thought were too long and tedious. He had long wondered what the prospects would be for a magazine containing selected articles and stories of general interest, condensed, but still retaining the substance. In 1922 he started publishing his original-format magazine, which eventually had a worldwide circulation of 100 million readers a month.

—T.B. & THE EDS.

11 ILLUSTRIOUS INCOME-TAX EVADERS

1. SPIRO AGNEW

On Oct. 10, 1973, the "law and order" vice-president resigned and pleaded *nolo contendere* (no contest) to a single charge of income-tax evasion following weeks of plea bargaining between the Maryland Republican's attorneys and the U.S. Justice Department. Although the usual punishment for such a crime was two to five months in jail, Judge Walter Hoffman fined Agnew $10,000 and placed him on three years' probation, because, the judge said, "the man has suffered enough."

2. ROBERT G. (BOBBY) BAKER

The onetime secretary to Senate Democrats was convicted in 1967 of income-tax evasion as well as theft, conspiracy, and fraud in connection with a scheme to funnel funds from California bank executives to Democratic Senate candidates. Authorities claimed Baker had reported less than $17,000 in taxable income for 1961 and 1962, when the actual figure for the two-year-period was more than $70,000.

3. CHUCK BERRY

Rock 'n' roll star Chuck Berry was indicted in May, 1979, for failing to pay nearly $110,000 in 1973 federal income taxes. He had falsified a series of contracts which indicated that he had received a scant $280 for each of 12 performances, when in fact he had been paid about $10,000 per concert. Berry was sentenced to four months in jail and ordered to perform 1,000 hours of community service in the form of benefit concerts.

4. EARL BUTZ

Former Secretary of Agriculture Earl Butz pleaded guilty in 1981 to "consciously underestimating" his 1978 income by more than $148,000. The fourth member of Richard Nixon's cabinet to be charged with a felony, Butz was fined $10,000, ordered to serve 30 days in jail, and placed on five years' probation. He was provided with comfortable shoes and a warm place to sleep at the Metropolitan Correctional Center in Chicago.

5. AL CAPONE

On Oct. 24, 1931, the Chicago gangster received the stiffest penalty—at that time—ever meted out to a tax evader: 11 years in jail, plus $80,000 in fines and court costs. Capone's request to post bail pending appeal was denied. He served eight years.

6. FRANK COSTELLO

Although Costello, reputed head of Murder, Inc., scrupulously kept no business records and operated on a strict cash-and-carry basis, federal agents patiently built a tax-evasion case against him. Testimony from 144 witnesses sent him to Lewisburg Penitentiary for 3½ years, beginning in 1958.

7. FORMER REP. CORNELIUS GALLAGHER (D-N.J.)

On June 15, 1973, six months after reversing his overall Not Guilty plea to Guilty on one of the seven counts lodged against him, Gallagher pleaded for over an hour for leniency. It did little good. The Bayonne Democrat drew a two-year sentence and a $10,000 fine for "willfully and knowingly" evading $75,000 in federal income taxes in 1966.

8. BERNARD GOLDFINE

In 1961, in U.S. District Court in Boston, the Russian-born textile magnate pleaded guilty to depriving the government of $450,961 in personal income taxes and another $340,784 in corporate taxes. Goldfine received a one-year prison sentence and a $110,000 fine.

9. JUDGE OTTO KERNER

The U.S. Circuit Court of Appeals judge was convicted in 1973 on 17 counts of income-tax evasion and other crimes growing out of a racetrack scandal in which he had played a central role while governor of Illinois. He drew a three-year sentence and a $50,000 fine.

10. SOPHIA LOREN

In May, 1982, actress Sophia Loren began serving a 30-day jail term in Italy for failing to report approximately $7,000 in income for 1970. She had been convicted of the offense in 1980 but had remained in self-imposed exile in Switzerland and France, out of reach of Italian authorities. She finally returned to her native country in spite of the jail sentence which awaited her because she missed "my mother, my country, and my roots." After serving 17 days in a jail near Naples, Loren was released.

11. SUN MYUNG MOON

Korean evangelist Sun Myung Moon, head of the Unification Church ("Moonies"), was convicted in May, 1982, for not reporting interest of more than $150,000 from his personal bank accounts. Moon contended that the money was not his but instead belonged to his Church. However, documents he produced to back up this claim proved fraudulent. Sentenced to 18 months in prison and fined $25,000, Moon is free on bond while appealing the conviction.

—W.A.D.

13 TAX PROTESTS AND PROTESTERS

1. LADY GODIVA

According to legend, this 11th-century noblewoman became a heroine to the people of Coventry, England, when—goaded by her husband, Leofric, Earl of Mercia—she rode naked on horseback through the marketplace. This convinced Leofric to abolish all taxes except those on horses.

2. BOSTON TEA PARTY

Angered by the fact that the British East India Company was seeking a monopoly on tea sales to the American Colonies, 150 Boston radicals known as the Sons of Liberty disguised themselves as Mohawk Indians, crept aboard three ships on Dec. 16, 1773, and dumped 342 tea chests into the sea. The loss to the East India Company was put at £18,000.

3. THE WHISKEY REBELLION

In 1794, some 3,000 farmers in western Pennsylvania organized to oppose the 1791 excise tax on liquor. President Washington sent in 13,000 militia to quell the disturbance and collect the tax. Of the 18 "whiskey boys" arrested, 16 were acquitted, and the two convicted of treason won presidential pardons a short time later.

4. HENRY DAVID THOREAU

Intending to leave the peace of Walden Pond just long enough to get his shoes fixed, Thoreau was arrested in 1845 for having failed to pay a poll tax. He refused to pay it because he believed the tax had been earmarked to fund the Mexican War, a war he denounced as designed to extend slavery. The essayist spent the night in jail and was released only after relatives paid the tax behind his back.

5. ABBY and JULIA SMITH

Born on a farm in Glastonbury, Conn., where they lived all their lives, the Smith sisters began their tax revolt in 1869 as an adjunct to the suffragette movement. Abby and Julia, aged 72 and 77, respectively, refused to pay taxes unless given the right to vote in town meetings. Authorities seized their land and cows, and the livestock became the center of international attention as the sisters twice bought them back and twice more had them seized. In 1877, Julia published *Abby Smith and Her Cows, with a Report of the Law Case Decided Contrary to Law*.

6. VIVIEN KELLEMS

In 1948, the feisty founder and president of a cable grip plant announced that she would no longer withhold income taxes from her employees unless the federal government put her on its payroll as a bona fide IRS agent. Rather than arrest her, authorities merely attached her bank account and "withdrew" the appropriate tax. Miss Kellems died in 1975.

Lady Godiva—the Howard Jarvis of the 11th century.

7. A. J. MUSTE

An active pacifist from W.W. I to the Vietnam War, Reverend A. J. Muste protested the cold war in 1951 by filing Thoreau's essay "On the Duty of Civil Disobedience" in place of his 1040 form. The year before his death, Muste joined Joan Baez in signing a tax protest ad in the *Washington Post*. (See entry 11.)

8. CORINNE GRIFFITH

The former silent-screen star (*The Last Man*, 1916; *The Garden of Eden*, 1928) and owner of the Washington Redskins football team launched a nationwide campaign in 1953 to abolish the personal income tax, the collection of which she called "legalized thievery." By the late 1960s, she had delivered nearly 500 speeches on the subject.

9. MAURICE McCRACKIN

A minister at Cincinnati's St. Barnabas Presbyterian and Episcopal Church, McCrackin refused to pay income taxes for several years rather than help fund the U.S. military. For failure to respond to an IRS summons, he drew a six-month jail sentence in December, 1958.

10. PAUL ROBESON

The celebrated black actor-singer who fell victim to the McCarthy inquisition fought for five years the federal government's attempt to tax the $25,000 Stalin Peace Prize he had won in 1953. Finally, in 1959, the IRS accepted his claim that the money should be tax-exempt, like Nobel and Pulitzer Prize winnings. Robeson died in 1976.

11. JOAN BAEZ

Protesting U.S. participation in the Vietnam War, the popular folk singer signed an ad which appeared in the *Washington Post* on Apr. 14, 1966, promising—together with 350 others—not to pay federal income taxes "voluntarily" as long as the war continued. She later sued the government for that portion of her taxes which went toward the war effort.

12. FRANKLIN McNULTY

After winning $128,410 in the 1973 Irish Sweepstakes, this retired bartender and carpenter refused to pay any income tax on his windfall and deposited the money abroad. In 1975, he received a five-year prison sentence for tax evasion, and he spent additional time in jail for civil contempt.

13. HARDENBURGH, N.Y.

Since 1976, nearly all of Hardenburgh's 236 citizens have become ministers of the Universal Life Church—a California-based church which grants mail-order ordinations—in order to claim the same tax benefits accorded other religious organizations in their town. Their case is still being litigated.

—W.A.D.

8 EXAMPLES OF GIFT EXCHANGES BETWEEN WORLD LEADERS

1. FREDERICK WILLIAM I OF PRUSSIA (1688–1740) FROM PETER THE GREAT OF RUSSIA (1675–1725)

Frederick William I was so absorbed in his army that he spent the equivalent of £16 million, or well over $30 million, to recruit and equip his favorite units. His prize battalions were two units of 600 men each made up of "giant" grenadiers. None of them—including those who played in the unit bands—were under 6 ft. tall, and many measured more than 7 ft. Frederick never subjected these battalions, which he called "my children in blue," to enemy fire, but he did drill them constantly. Even the battalion mascot, a huge bear, was expected to perform on command. Foreign rulers, acknowledging Frederick's obsession with his giant soldiers, sent the Prussian leader recruits as gifts. Peter the Great was the most generous donor. The czar sent Frederick 50 giant Russian recruits every year.

2. PRESIDENTS MILLARD FILLMORE (1800–1874) AND FRANKLIN PIERCE (1804–1869) OF THE U.S. TO EMPEROR KOMEI (1821–1867) AND SHŌGUN HITOTSUBASHI (1837–1902) OF JAPAN

After offering to begin trade with Japan in 1853, Commodore Matthew Perry returned the next year bearing gifts shipped from America to celebrate the anticipated positive Japanese response. The gifts included a complete telegraph set, clocks, American plant seeds, wines and liquors, several cases of Colt firearms, a variety of agricultural implements, and two sets of Audubon's beautiful plate books on birds and mammals of North America. But the main attraction was a miniature railway, consisting of a locomotive, tender, and passenger car, which steamed around on an 18-in.-gauge, 350-ft. circular track. In return, the shōgun (the emperor at that time was primarily a political figurehead) gave Pierce a lacquered box and writing case, a bronze censer, lengths of silk and pongee, and three spaniels of a breed only the emperor and shōgun formerly possessed.

3. PRESIDENT FRANKLIN D. ROOSEVELT OF THE U.S. (1882–1945) AND PRIME MINISTER WINSTON CHURCHILL OF THE UNITED KINGDOM (1874–1965) AND KING IBN SAUD OF SAUDI ARABIA (1880–1953)

In 1945, President Roosevelt delighted King Ibn Saud with a gift of a fully equipped C-45 airplane, complete with crew (the crew was on a one-year loan). Not to be outdone in courting favor with Ibn Saud, the British prime minister offered the king a Rolls-Royce. But upon returning to England, Churchill discovered that all Rolls-Royce plants had been converted to manufacturing aircraft engines for the war effort (by his own order). To save diplomatic face the British Ministry of Supply made an exhaustive search and finally found a prewar model in perfect condition sitting in a dealer's garage. It was metallic green with dark green fenders and matching leather upholstery and cabinetwork. Two custom features were added to the interior: a sterling silver bowl that could be filled from a copper water tank (to be used for Ibn Saud's ceremonial ablutions), and a wide royal throne in place of the rear seat. In return for Roosevelt's airplane and Churchill's automobile, the king gave each leader a collection of jewels, gold daggers, swords, and harem clothes.

4. PRESIDENT DWIGHT D. EISENHOWER OF THE U.S. (1890–1969) AND SHAH MOHAMMED REZA PAHLAVI OF IRAN (1919–1980)

During a six-hour stopover in Tehran on Dec. 14, 1959, President Eisenhower visited with the shah and addressed the two houses of the Iranian parliament. The people turned out in record numbers, with an estimated 750,000 lining the president's route to the airport. The standouts among the many gifts bestowed upon Eisenhower were a gold key to the city of Tehran and a silver peacock set with rubies and sapphires. The president gave the shah a transistor radio and a rare and ancient book on the history of Iran.

5. PREMIER NIKITA KHRUSHCHEV OF THE U.S.S.R. (1894–1971) TO THE FAMILY OF THE U.S. PRESIDENT JOHN F. KENNEDY

The White House has always received animal gifts, dogs in particular. But in June, 1961, the Kennedy family received an unusual 6-month-old puppy named Pushinka from the Soviet premier. Pushinka (the name means "fluffy" in Russian) was a mutt and not in herself unique. Her parentage, however, was—her mother, Strelka, was one of two dogs the Soviets had shot into orbit in Sputnik 5 on Aug. 19, 1960, and her father, Pushok, was used in a number of ground-based space experiments. Pushinka, who had her own passport, was examined thoroughly at Walter Reed Army Hospital, after which the U.S. government announced that the dog was not a carrier of any mysterious diseases, nor had it been implanted with transmitting spy devices. Pushinka later had a litter of four puppies fathered by Charlie, Caroline Kennedy's Welsh terrier. Accompanying Pushinka in 1961 was a gift sent especially for the president, a model of a 19th-century whaling vessel carved from walrus tusk and whalebone.

6. PRESIDENT RICHARD M. NIXON OF THE U.S. (1913–   ) AND SOVIET PREMIER LEONID BREZHNEV OF THE U.S.S.R. (1906–   )

President Nixon locked in on Premier Brezhnev's passion for fine cars as an answer to diplomatic gift-giving. Brezhnev already owned a Citroën-Maserati and a Renault 16, both gifts from French President Georges Pompidou, and a Rolls-Royce limousine when Nixon visited Moscow in May, 1972. As a parting gift, Nixon gave Brezhnev a new Cadillac, which had been donated by General Motors. Upon the occasion of Brezhnev's visit to the U.S. the following year in June, Nixon gave the Communist chief a dark blue, four-door Lincoln Continental, donated by Ford, with "Special Good Wishes—Greetings" engraved on the dashboard. Brezhnev also received a custom-made Pedersen-Mossberg hunting rifle, fitted with a stock featuring an inlaid gold American eagle, a Russian bear, and his initials. The Nixons were given a silver samovar and tea set. In June, 1974, on Nixon's return visit to Moscow, the president gave Brezhnev another car, this time a blue Chevrolet Monte Carlo from General Motors. In exchange, Mr. Nixon received a painting of Moscow by night, and Mrs. Nixon received a set of amber jewelry in gold settings.

7. ELIZABETH II OF THE UNITED KINGDOM (1926–   ) AND THE ARAB STATES

After what Queen Elizabeth and Prince Philip had initially considered a routine three-week tour of six Persian Gulf states in 1979, the British monarch returned home with extravagant gifts valued at well over $2 million. The prince was given the customary bejeweled swords on the tour, but it was the queen who was the object of gifts so lavish that even she was "slightly stunned." In Dubai, Sheik Rashid gave her a necklace of sapphires surrounded by 300 diamonds, plus matching earrings and a ring. The sheik also gave her a tray bearing two camels standing under two palm trees, all made of solid gold. In Bahrain, the queen received another solid gold palm tree—18-in. tall and hung with pearls—and a diamond and ruby brooch. From the emir of Kuwait she received a double string of pearls and a solid silver model of an Arab dhow (ship). More pearls and a lapis lazuli bowl encrusted with diamonds and mounted on two gold horses were among the gifts presented by the emir of Qatar. In Saudi Arabia, the gifts included a gold incense burner, a gold tray set with amethysts, a gold coffee jug shaped like a falcon (its talons of amethyst), and a pair of matching gold goblets. In return for such largesse, the queen presented each Arab leader with a sterling silver tray engraved with a picture of the royal yacht *Britannia* and "an appropriate message."

8. PRESIDENT MOBUTO SESE SEKO OF ZAIRE (1930–   ) TO PRESIDENT JIMMY CARTER OF THE U.S. (1924–   )

Much to the dismay of world wildlife preservationists, the president of Zaire presented President Carter with a rhinoceros horn and a carved ivory tusk on the occasion of a visit to the United States on Sept. 11, 1979. At the time, Carter and his national security adviser, Zbigniew Brzezinski, reportedly exchanged quips about the alleged aphrodisiac qualities of the rhino horn. The gift prompted Russell Train, head of the World Wildlife Fund, to send the president a telegram reminding him that, because of such folk beliefs (particularly in Asia), the rhino is in danger of extinction and urged Carter to call for a "worldwide campaign to stop the slaughter of rhinos."

—J.N.

THE 21 MOST EXPENSIVE ARTICLES EVER SOLD AT AUCTION

One of the world's leading auctioneers and autograph appraisers, Charles Hamilton lives in New York City, where he runs his own auction gallery. He is also the author of numerous books, including *Auction Mad-*

ness, American Autographs, Great Forgers and Famous Fakes, and *The Signature of America.*

1. PAINTING (INTERNATIONAL)

A painting by J. M. W. Turner, "Juliet and Her Nurse," was sold by Sotheby Parke Bernet in New York on May 29, 1980, for $6.4 million, top sum for any painting.

Juliet and Her Nurse by J.M.W. Turner sold for $6,400,000.

2. PAINTING (OLD MASTER)

A painting by Rubens, "Samson and Delilah," was knocked down at Christie's in London on July 11, 1980, for $5.4 million, biggest amount ever fetched for an old master.

3. PAINTING (AMERICAN)

A painting by Frederick E. Church, "The Icebergs," was knocked down at Sotheby Parke Bernet in New York in November, 1979, for $2.5 million, greatest amount for any American painting.

4. MANUSCRIPT

A 36-page manuscript by Leonardo da Vinci on cosmology sold at Christie's in London on Dec. 12, 1980, for $2.2 million, world's record for a manuscript.

5. BOOK

A copy of the Gutenberg Bible, first book ever printed from movable type, was sold by Christie's in New York on Apr. 7, 1978, for $2 million, highest price for a rare book.

6. CABINET

A Dubois corner cabinet was sold at Sotheby's Acker-Moyer sale in Monte Carlo in 1980 for $1.8 million, greatest sum for any piece of furniture.

7. CUP

A 15th-century Chinese "chicken cup" (for broth) sold at Sotheby's Hong Kong in 1980 for $1 million, record price for a piece of china.

8. STAMP

A unique British Guiana 1¢ stamp issued in 1856 sold at Sotheby Parke Bernet in New York in the spring of 1980 for $935,000, greatest sum ever fetched for a rare stamp.

9. COIN

A Brasher doubloon, a gold coin minted in New York by Ephraim Brasher and of which only seven are known, sold at Bowers and Ruddy in New York on Nov. 29, 1979, for $725,000, highest amount ever brought for a rare coin.

10. USED CAR

A 1936 Mercedes-Benz roadster sold via a telephone bid from Monaco at Christie's sale in Los Angeles on Feb. 25, 1979, for $421,040, top sum ever paid for a used car.

11. RUG

A Persian rug measuring 7 ft. 3 in. by 12 ft. 5 in., woven in Cairo about 1500, sold at Sotheby's in London on Mar. 29, 1978, for $229,900, highest amount ever for a carpet.

12. SNUFF BOX

A snuff box of gold and lapis lazuli signed by Juste-Oreille Meissonier, dated Paris, 1728, sold at Christie's in London on June 26, 1974, for $205,475, highest sum for a snuff box.

13. SWORD

A magnificent gold-hilted sword presented by the Continental Congress in 1779 to the Marquis de Lafayette sold at Sotheby Parke Bernet in New York on Nov. 20, 1976, for $145,000, world's record for a sword.

14. DOCUMENT

A document signed by Button Gwinnett, signer of the Declaration of Independence from Georgia, sold at Charles Hamilton Galleries in New York in October, 1979, for $100,000, world's record for an autograph.

15. PRINT

A print by Mary Cassatt, "Woman Bathing," was sold at Sotheby Parke Bernet in New York in February, 1980, for $72,000, a world's record for a print.

16. POSTER

A poster by Toulouse-Lautrec, "Moulin Rouge," sold at Phillips in New York in 1980 for $52,000, record price for a poster.

17. HAT

A hat worn by Napoleon in 1815 was sold by Maitres Liery in Rheims, France, on Apr. 23, 1970, for $29,471, top price ever paid for a hat.

18. WINE

A bottle of 1806 Château Lafite claret, one of two such bottles known, was sold at Heublein's 11th annual National Auction of Rare Wines on May 24, 1979, in Atlanta, Ga., for $28,000, highest price ever paid for a bottle of wine.

19. PHOTOGRAPH (PORTRAIT)

A photograph of Alexandre Dumas by Felix Nadar taken in 1857 was sold on Nov. 2, 1979, for $16,000, highest amount ever fetched for a single photographic image.

20. PHOTOGRAPH (20th-CENTURY)

A photograph by Ansel Adams, "Moonrise, Hernandez, New Mexico," was sold at Christie's in New York on Oct. 31, 1979, for $15,000, record price for a 20th-century photograph.

21. LETTER (BY A LIVING PERSON)

A handwritten letter by Ronald Reagan about Frank Sinatra sold at Charles Hamilton Galleries in January, 1981, for $12,500, highest price for a letter by a living person.

SOURCE: Charles Hamilton, *Auction Madness*. New York: Everest House, 1981.

15
LOVE STORIES

6 CURIOUS LOCATIONS FOR SEXUAL ACTIVITY

1. URBAN ATTRACTIONS

James Boswell, the biographer of Samuel Johnson and the quintessential libertine of 18th-century London, preferred St. James's Park for cooling his erotic passions with an endless string of prostitutes. He once copulated on the Westminster Bridge, thrilled by the flow of the Thames below.

2. MONASTIC PLEASURES

Grigori Rasputin—the debauched mystic monk who was a power behind the throne at the court of Nicholas II of Russia—was introduced to sexual orgies by the Khlysty sect in a cell of the Verkhoturye monastery in western Siberia in about 1892. Years later, a parade of women— from princesses to peasants—followed him there to indulge in untrammeled fornication.

3. PLAYING AROUND

Around the turn of the century, American-born Natalie Barney, the most famous lesbian in Paris, France, and the equally famous courtesan Liane de Pougy often made love in a theater box below stage level, while attending a play.

4. AIRBORNE MANEUVERS

Caroline "la Belle" Otero, mistress to royalty and millionaires, went up with Baron Lepic in a hot-air balloon in 1902. As the balloon rose 200 ft. over the Aude River in France, ". . . the baron and I made love," she later recalled. "It was an experience every woman should enjoy."

5. CLOSET ENCOUNTERS

During his first two years in the White House, President Warren G. Harding welcomed clandestine visits from his mistress, Nan Britton. On a visit there, Nan was taken by Harding to a safe and cozy place for their lovemaking—a 5 ft. by 5 ft. closet in an antechamber to the Cabinet Room.

6. ON LOCATION

While on a hunting trip in the 1930s, Hollywood idol Clark Gable had sex with actress Carole Lombard in a duck blind. He also bragged that he had made love to a woman in a canoe, a telephone booth, a swimming pool, and on a fire escape.

—R.J.R.

6 UFO ENCOUNTERS OF A SEXUAL KIND

1. THE PLOUGHMAN'S FANTASY (1957)

Antonio Villas Boas was ploughing a field near the town of São Francisco de Sales, Brazil, at 1:00 A.M. on Oct. 16 when a strange round object landed near his tractor. A group of small beings dragged Antonio into their craft. Once inside, they stripped him and coated him with a strange liquid. After they took a blood sample, they left him alone. Then a beautiful blue-eyed naked woman appeared and started to embrace Antonio intimately. Twice they made love in a normal humanoid manner. She never kissed Antonio—instead she grunted and bit him on the chin. He was released unharmed four hours after his abduction.

2. CHILD OF OUTER SPACE (1966)

Miss Marlene Travers defiantly told her interviewers, "Believe it or not, I was held captive in a flying saucer, raped and made pregnant by a man from outer space." As she was walking alone one night in the countryside near Melbourne, Australia, she saw a weird light in the sky. Suddenly it resolved itself into a large silvery disk and landed. A tall, handsome alien emerged from the craft. He transfixed her with his eyes and told her telepathically that she was to be the first human woman impregnated by a spaceman. She complied with his sexual demands, but whether the result of their union was a boy or a girl is unknown.

3. SATYRS FROM THE STARS (1966)

A Michigan woman named Jean Sheldon was relaxing in her parked car one summer evening when a large silvery object descended from the heavens and disturbed her peace. A kind of levitation beam drew her into the craft. Inside she met three naked male humanoids. Telepathically they transmitted this message: "My dear earthwoman . . . we wish to mate with you. It will be easier on your personality if you do this willingly." They stripped her, and on a bedlike machine all three males made love to her for at least an hour. She found the experience exciting and stimulating but was ashamed of the unusual delight she felt.

4. EXTRATERRESTRIAL EXHIBITIONISTS (1970?)

A farmer in France spotted a flying saucer as it landed in a nearby field. It was daytime and he clearly saw a naked female and a naked male

322

emerge from the craft. Unlike the majority of UFO occupants, who are usually observed by puzzled earthlings to be carrying out some elaborate "scientific" exploration of their landing area, these two occupants decided to indulge in a session of lovemaking. After satisfying their passions, the UFO occupants returned to their flying saucer. Then they rocketed into the sky, doubtless in search of new environments in which they might repeat their scene.

5. SEXPLORATION (1973)

A woman known only as Mrs. X was driving alone along a country road in Somerset, England, at 11:30 P.M. when the engine of her car stalled and she was suddenly confronted by a tall robot, whereupon she fainted. When she came to, she was strapped to a table inside a UFO, and three male occupants dressed like surgeons were examining her. One of them took a long look at the lower portion of her naked body before attaching a pin to her thigh, numbing her. Then he had sexual intercourse with her. He displayed no emotion during the performance.

6. ALIEN ORGY (1976)

Cowman Liberato Anibal Quintero of El Banco, Colombia, saw a beam of light, which was followed by the appearance of an egg-shaped luminous craft. After it had landed, several small beings emerged and captured Liberato, who fainted. On recovering, he found himself being massaged by three naked women inside the craft. He made love to one of the women, who was insatiable. His captors gave him a yellow-colored drink, which enabled him to accommodate the sexual demands of the other two women as well. After this orgy, he received a knockout injection in his back. When he regained consciousness, he was outside his home.

—N.W.

ROMANTIC PET NAMES OF 27 FAMOUS COUPLES

1. THOMAS CARLYLE, Scottish essayist and historian

Carlyle's wife, Jane, called her husband "Goody" or "Good-Good," and signed a letter to him "Your own Goody." He called her "Goody" too and "Wifekin."

2. CATHERINE THE GREAT, empress of Russia

Catherine, a woman of intense sexual appetites, had many pet names for her boorish, potbellied lover Grigori Potëmkin. Among them were "my marble beauty," "golden rooster," and "wolfbird."

3.–6. COLETTE, French writer

Colette gave pet names to her lovers, family, friends, and animals. Her detestable first husband, Henry Gauthier-Villars—known as Willy—she called "Kibi-la-Doucette," which means "the sweet one." (She also gave the name to one of her cats.) Her second husband, Henry de Jouvenel, became "Sidi the Pasha," or "the Sultan," for his love of luxury. At 47, close to divorcing Sidi, Colette may have had an affair with her stepson, 19-year-old Bertrand de Jouvenel, whom she called her "leopard." During her long, happy marriage to Maurice Goudeket, he was dubbed the "Devil" and the "great guy."

7. CHARLES DICKENS, British author

Dickens's letters to his wife, Kate, were full of endearments. He called her his "dearest Mouse" and his "dearest darling Pig."

8. ISADORA DUNCAN, U.S. dancer

Duncan's lover, theatrical designer Gordon Craig, called her "Topsy." Their passionate affair produced her first child.

9. JIM FISK, U.S. robber baron

Fisk had his major love affair with would-be actress Josephine Mansfield. He called her "dumplings," she called him "sardines" (because he loved sardines). When their relationship deteriorated, he began calling her "Lumpsum" after she asked him for a settlement.

10. CLARK GABLE and CAROLE LOMBARD, U.S. actor and actress

This husband-and-wife team gave each other the unlikely nicknames of "Pa" and "Ma."

11. WILLIAM GLADSTONE, British statesman

William and his bride Catherine Glynne were happily married for 59 years. He was "the oak" and she was "the ivy."

12. JOHANN WOLFGANG VON GOETHE, German writer

Goethe's wife, Christiane Vulpius, was an earthy girl who dubbed her husband's penis *Herr Schönfuss*, German for "Mr. Nice-foot."

13. HENRIK IBSEN, Norwegian playwright

Ibsen called his wife, Suzannah Thoresen, "my cat."

14. JAMES JOYCE, Irish novelist and poet

Joyce, one of English literature's most brilliant stars, was happily married to Nora Barnacle, who disdained his writing and called him "simpleminded Jim."

15. JOHN LENNON, British musician and songwriter

Lennon's pet names for his wife, Yoko Ono, were "Mother" and "Madam."

16. JACK LONDON, U.S. writer

London named his wife, Charmian Kittredge, "Mate-Woman."

17. KARL MARX, Russian political writer

Karl's wife, Jenny, dubbed her husband *Schwärzwildchen*—German for "little black wild one."

18. LORD HORATIO NELSON, British admiral

In a letter to his mistress, Lady Emma Hamilton, Nelson asked her to prepare "the dear thatched cottage" (his pet name for her genitalia) for his return.

19. ALFRED NOBEL, Swedish inventor and creator of the Nobel Prizes

Nobel had one love affair in his life, with Sofie Hess. It began when he was 43 and she was 18. He called her "charming child" and "The Troll." She called him *Brummbär*, German for "old gruff."

20. FRANKLIN D. ROOSEVELT, U.S. president

FDR called Eleanor "Babs," which meant "baby," and in the latter years of their marriage, the First Lady was "my missus."

21.–22. JEAN JACQUES ROUSSEAU, Swiss-born French philosopher and writer

Rousseau's first affair was with an older, experienced woman, Madame de Warens. He called her "mama," she called him "little cat." Rousseau's next liaison was with chambermaid Thérèse le Vasseur, with whom he lived for the rest of his life. He called her "Aunt" and "Boss."

23. GERTRUDE STEIN, U.S. writer

Stein called her lover, Alice B. Toklas, "pussy" and "baby." Toklas called Stein "Lovely."

24. MARK TWAIN, U.S. humorist and writer

Mark Twain worshiped and adored his wife, Livy Langdon. The equally adoring Livy regarded her husband as a wayward child, so she gave him the pet name "Youth."

25. CORNELIUS VANDERBILT, U.S. financier

Tennessee Claflin, sister of the famous feminist Victoria Woodhull, called Vanderbilt "old boy," and he called her "little sparrow."

26. H. G. WELLS, British writer

Wells's true love, writer Rebecca West, made up the pet names which the couple used constantly. Rebecca was "panther" and H. G. was "jaguar." He drew Rebecca "picshuas" of them as jungle cats and announced his decision to be faithful to her by writing in a letter, "Monogamous not Polygamous Jaguar now."

H. G. Wells's drawing of Panther and Jaguar, entitled "Vigil."

27. ÉMILE ZOLA, French writer and critic

Zola lived a double life—he had a wife and also a mistress, mother of his two children. The mistress, Jeanne Rozerot, called him her "Prince Charming."

—A.W.

9 MEN WHO LOVED THEIR WIFE'S SISTER

1. HEROD ANTIPAS (c. 25 B.C.–39 A.D.)

Herod Antipas, the ruler of Galilee, executed John the Baptist for questioning his right to marry his sister-in-law. Herodias, a beautiful and ambitious woman, also happened to be Herod's niece. Such a degree of consanguinity (whether to Herod or to his brother Philip, whom she left for Herod) was considered an abomination under local custom. "It is not lawful for you to have her," John the Baptist admonished Herod. Herodias retaliated through her daughter Salome who, according to legend, asked for John's head in reward for her erotic dancing. Herodias' scheming eventually led to her second husband's undoing, and they both died in exile.

2. SIR THOMAS MORE (1478–1535)

When the English scholar and lawyer decided to marry at the age of 27, he was offered a selection of three daughters from a country gentleman. More fell in love with one but decided to marry another, reasoning that it "would be both great grief and some shame also to the eldest to see her younger sister preferred before her." The choice of his head rather than his heart, Jane Colt More was bored and bewildered by her husband's academic preoccupations and died young. (Morally superior to the end, More was beheaded for refusing to sanction Henry VIII's marital and religious adventurism.)

3. HENRY VIII (1491–1547)

During his first marriage, to Catherine of Aragon, Henry enjoyed the favors of Mary Boleyn, daughter of a royal diplomat. Mary is said to have borne the king a child before she was superseded in the royal affections by her sister Anne. Profiting from Mary's experience, Anne Boleyn withheld her sexual favors until Henry offered marriage. In the process of divorcing Catherine of Aragon to marry Anne, the king attempted to get a papal dispensation dissolving his marriage to his first wife, and as a result he was excommunicated. Later, when Henry tired of Anne, he charged her with incest, among other things, and had her beheaded.

4. WOLFGANG AMADEUS MOZART (1756–1791)

In 1778 Mozart fell in love with Aloysia Weber, a young singer for whom he composed arias as amatory offerings. Apparently at her mother's prompting, Aloysia first encouraged the young composer, then brushed him off and married a Viennese actor. "I did not know, you see," she said later. "I thought he was such a *little* man." Perhaps to maintain contact with Aloysia—"even now, I feel she is not a matter of indifference to me," he wrote—Mozart took up lodgings with her scheming mother, who entangled him in a matrimonial web with her second daughter, Constanze.

5. JULIUS BEERBOHM (1810?–1891)

British actor-manager Herbert Beerbohm Tree and parodist Max

Beerbohm were rated as three-quarter brothers, born of their father's marriages to two sisters. A grain merchant from the Baltic port of Memel, Julius Beerbohm had four children (including Herbert, who added Tree to his name for dramatic effect) by his first wife, Constantia. After Constantia's death at 32, Julius proposed to her sister Eliza. Because British law prohibited marriage to a deceased wife's sister, they went to Switzerland for the ceremony. The second Beerbohm marriage produced another five children, the youngest of whom was Max.

6. CHARLES DICKENS (1812–1870)

Dickens loved not one but two of his sisters-in-law. When he married Catherine Hogarth in 1836, her younger sister Mary came to live with them and made her way "deeply and intimately" into the novelist's heart. After Mary's tragic death in 1837, Dickens wore her ring for the rest of his life and asked to be buried next to her. Mary's place in the household was soon filled by Georgina, the third Hogarth sister, who eventually replaced Catherine altogether. When Charles and Catherine Dickens separated after 22 years of marriage that produced 10 children, Georgina took her brother-in-law's side and remained in his household. This aroused wild rumors. In his will, Dickens left her a large bequest as well as his personal papers and belongings.

7. SIGMUND FREUD (1856–1939)

After Freud's marriage in 1886 to Martha Bernays, her sister Minna came to live with them and remained for 42 years. Martha was the submissive *Hausfrau* type, a devoted mother of six children, while the stronger-willed Minna was more intellectual. It was to Minna that Freud first confided his revolutionary new theories of human motivation and behavior. Martha Freud hated to travel, and Freud hated to travel alone, so Minna became his lifelong traveling companion. It is uncertain whether or not Freud and his sister-in-law were lovers. Freud's protégé, Carl Jung, held that they were, claiming that both Martha and Minna had separately confided to him that such was the case. Curiously, Minna's bedroom could only be reached by walking through the Freuds' bedroom.

8. GEORGE SANDERS (1906–1972)

"I always liked George," Jolie Gabor said in 1971 when Sanders married her daughter Magda, "but when a son-in-law comes back I really like it." Sanders, the sardonic British actor, had previously been married to Magda's sister Zsa Zsa. Or rather, as he put it, he was a paying guest in Zsa Zsa's Bel-Air mansion for five years (1949–54). "Zsa Zsa was like champagne, and I as her husband was hard put to it to keep up with her standard of effervescence," Sanders remarked. They remained good friends after divorcing. Sanders's marriage to Magda Gabor, a desperation move after the cancer death of his third wife, Benita, and before his own suicide, was annulled after two weeks.

9. STAVROS NIARCHOS (1909–   )

The marital history of Niarchos, the handsome Greek shipping tycoon, is as dramatic and tangled as a Greek tragedy. In 1947, he took as his third wife Eugenia Livanos, daughter of another powerful Greek shipper. They remained close after their Mexican divorce in 1965 and throughout Stavros's brief marriage to automobile heiress Charlotte Ford. The Mexican divorce was not considered valid under Greek law, so Niarchos and Eugenia resumed life together, without bothering to remarry, after Charlotte divorced him in 1967. Meanwhile, Eugenia's younger sister Tina had been married to Aristotle Onassis (1946–1961) and to the Marquess of Blandford (1961–1971). In 1971, after being cleared of guilt in the 1970 suicide death of Eugenia, Niarchos married her sister Tina. She died suddenly three years later of what was reported as an accidental overdose of sleeping pills.

—C.D.

13 FAMOUS SEXUALLY ACTIVE SENIOR CITIZENS

1. LOUIS XIV (1638–1715)

The profligate "Sun King" of France was morganatically married at the age of 45 to his children's former governess, Madame de Maintenon. A prudish and frigid woman, she complained of the king's extramarital dalliances and his unwelcome sexual advances to her until his death at nearly 77.

2. DUKE OF WELLINGTON (1769–1852)

The "Iron Duke" who defeated Napoleon at Waterloo had many affairs during a long love life. In his seventies, he carried on an ardent correspondence with a young evangelist and refused marriage proposals from two well-born ladies. Just before his death at 83, he was reported to be conducting a "highly unbecoming" love affair with the wife of a politician.

3. BRIGHAM YOUNG (1801–1877)

Upon divorcing the polygamous patriarch when he was 72, his 27th wife revealed that he became incensed when denied sex. And in his will, the Mormon leader acknowledged as legitimate any children born to his wives within nine months of his death. (In fact, his last child was born in 1870, when he was 69.)

4. VICTOR HUGO (1802–1885)

At the age of 70 the poet, novelist, and sexually indefatigable Hugo was carrying on an affair with a 27-year-old laundress. On the side, he seduced the young daughter of a famous novelist and may have dallied with actress Sarah Bernhardt—all while maintaining a 50-year intimate relationship with actress Juliette Drouet. Hugo's diary for 1885, when he was 83, records eight sexual acts, the last only six weeks before his death.

5. FRANZ LISZT (1811–1886)

On reaching his seventies, the great piano virtuoso complained of leg pains, shortness of breath, and orthodontic problems but did not seem to suffer flagging potency. He was rumored to be enjoying an affair with yet another of a long succession of admiring female music pupils. Liszt's last mistress was his "housekeeper," Lina Schmalhausen, who accompanied her septuagenarian master everywhere.

6. LEO TOLSTOI (1828–1910)

The celebrated Russian novelist and moralist was torn between his belief in asceticism and the "degrading madness" of sexual desire, which tormented him until the end of his long life. His wife, Sonya, noted in her diary for 1907 that her 79-year-old husband was "madly passionate last night." Only in his final year did Tolstoi enjoy freedom from lust.

7. HAVELOCK ELLIS (1859–1939)

British sex guru Ellis had his own personal problems, suffering from impotency until the age of 60. He was then cured thanks to the loving determination of Françoise Cyon, with whom he spent his last years. Besieged by adoring women in search of sexual succor, Ellis was at last able to offer something more than advice. Gloria Neville, a Canadian devotée who visited the 72-year-old Ellis in 1931, is said to have been his last lover before he lost his "body fire."

8. BERTRAND RUSSELL (1872–1970)

A veteran of three failed marriages and innumerable affairs, the philosopher and pacifist revived a long-standing affair with actress Colette O'Niel and enjoyed a three-year relationship with the wife of a Cambridge lecturer while in his seventies. At age 80 he married for the fourth time, explaining that he and Edith Finch "loved each other entirely." (In his newfound marital bliss, Russell noted, he almost forgot about the nuclear peril.)

9. W. SOMERSET MAUGHAM (1874–1965)

Maugham, the bisexual author who wrote *Of Human Bondage,* limited his sexual activity to men in later years. At age 72 he took on as secretary, companion, and bed partner 41-year-old Alan Searle. Searle described Maugham, with whom he underwent exotic rejuvenation therapy in Switzerland, as "the most marvelous lover I ever had," lusty at 75 and still randy at 84.

10. NATALIE BARNEY (1876–1972)

At 82 this American heiress, who lived in Paris, fell in love with "Gisele," the 58-year-old wife of a Romanian diplomat. Theirs was a "complete love affair" which lasted until Barney's death at 96. Barney's lover of nearly half a century, artist Romaine Brooks, tolerated the extracurricular affair for a decade, then broke with Barney.

11. PABLO PICASSO (1881–1973)

Before she left him in 1963, Françoise Gilot, Picasso's longtime mistress and the mother of his two youngest children, complained that the octogenarian artist was cheating on her with other women. After Gilot's departure, Picasso, who considered an amorous adventure a stimulus to his art, was soon consoling himself with Jacqueline Roque, whom he later married. "He's the only lover I've ever really wanted," Roque said.

12. LEOPOLD STOKOWSKI (1882–1977)

The flamboyant conductor was a notorious womanizer for over 50 years. In his late sixties he fathered two children by his young third wife, heiress Gloria Vanderbilt. After their divorce, the 80-year-old maestro lived the last 15 years of his life as an occasionally swinging bachelor.

Leopold Stokowski, a week before his 95th birthday.

13. CHARLIE CHAPLIN (1889–1977)

As a younger man, the great silent-film comedian became involved in several messy affairs with budding "Lolitas" (two of his first three wives were under 18). Married in 1943 to 18-year-old Oona O'Neill, daughter of playwright Eugene O'Neill, Chaplin matured into a doting *pater familias*, fathering his last two children when he was in his seventies.

—C.D.

DAN GREENBURG'S 7 BEST LINES FOR PICKING UP GIRLS

This three-time winner of the *Playboy* Humor Award got his start in advertising and has served as managing editor of *Eros* magazine. He is the author of *How to Be a Jewish Mother, How to Make Yourself Miserable*, and *Scoring*, "a socioautobiographical account of changing sexual mores." Greenburg's latest novel is *What Do Women Want?*

1. My aunt died and left me six million dollars with the stipulation that I find a wife by Friday. Would you like to have a drink?
2. Excuse me, do you happen to know where they're holding the Sexual Olympics this year? I'm a finalist in the 9-hour freestyle multi-orgasm event.
3. President and Mrs. Reagan would like the pleasure of your company at dinner, and they've asked me to escort you.
4. I'm Robert Redford and I'm wearing a disguise so I won't be recognized. May I buy you a drink?
5. Pardon me, but I think I might have once been married to you.
6. I have evidence that we were lovers in a previous life.
7. I have a .357 Smith & Wesson pointed at your pancreas. Would you like to come have coffee with me?

—Exclusive for *The Book of Lists 3*

18 WORST OPENING LINES

In 1981 psychologist Chris Kleinke, author of *First Impressions: The Psychology of Encountering Others*, conducted a study of opening lines used by men when meeting women. He polled 300 college students in California and Massachusetts, asking them to list opening lines used in general situations as well as at bars, restaurants, supermarkets, laundromats, and beaches. Kleinke then asked 1,000 college students, also from California and Massachusetts, to rate the 100 most frequently cited opening lines on a 7-point scale ranging from "excellent" to "terrible." According to Kleinke's study, the following openings should not be used if you want to impress a woman:

General Situations
1. Is that really your hair?
2. You remind me of a woman I used to date.
3. Your place or mine?

Bars
4. (Looking at a woman's jewelry) Wow, it looks like you just robbed Woolworth's.
5. Bet I can outdrink you.
6. I play the field, and I think I just hit a home run with you.

Restaurants
7. Do you think I deserve a break today?
8. I bet the cherry jubilee isn't as sweet as you are.
9. If this food doesn't kill us, the bill will.

Supermarkets
10. Do you really eat that junk?
11. You shouldn't buy that. It's full of cholesterol.
12. Is your bread fresh?

Laundromats
13. A man shouldn't have to wash his own clothes.
14. Those are some nice undies you have there.
15. I'll wash your clothes if you wash mine.

Beaches
16. Did you notice me throwing that football? Good arm, huh?
17. Let me see your strap marks.
18. Want to stroke with me?

18 BEST OPENING LINES

You should have better luck if you use these lines, according to Kleinke's survey:

General Situations
1. Hi.
2. I feel a little embarrassed about this, but I'd like to meet you.
3. That's a very pretty (sweater, dress, etc.) you have on.

Bars
4. Do you want to dance?
5. It took a lot of nerve to approach you, so can I at least ask what your name is?
6. What do you think of the band?

Restaurants
7. I haven't been here before. What's good on the menu?
8. Would you like to have a drink after dinner?
9. Can I buy you lunch?

Supermarkets
10. Can I help you to the car with those bags?
11. Excuse me. Which steak looks better to you?
12. Can you help me decide here? I'm a terrible shopper.

Laundromats
13. Want to go have a beer or cup of coffee while we're waiting?
14. Could you show me how to work this machine?
15. It's nice to see a person so neat with her clothes. I wish I were that way.

Beaches
16. Want to play Frisbee?
17. Can I bring you anything from the store?
18. The water is beautiful today, isn't it?

9 ANTISEX INVENTIONS

In 1760 Swiss physician S. A. Tissot created a sensation with the publication in French of *On Onanism, or a Physical Dissertation on the Ills Produced by Masturbation*. Using questionable case studies as examples, the book postulated that masturbation led to epilepsy, impotence, blindness, constipation, insanity, and more. Physicians and laypeople believed these fantastic claims. Inventors created a plethora of devices to prevent "self-abuse." One such invention was patented as late as 1932. The following list represents a mere sampling of such patents.

1. SLEEPING RING (Patent No. 14,739. Granted Apr. 22, 1856.)

During the 1850s, inventors energetically tried to create the ultimate penis ring, a device believed to prevent the irreparable physical and mental damage caused by wet dreams. Massachusetts inventor L. B. Sibley claimed his ring was an improvement over others commonly used at the time. Though the ring had several metal "spurs," which would "prick the penis only sufficiently hard to awaken the patient and warn him of danger as soon as the organ begins to distend," its novel construction avoided causing irritation while being applied, removed, or when a boy's penis was flaccid.

2. THE CUP (Patent No. 104,117. Granted June 14, 1870.)

"My invention," stated Daniel P. Cook in his "Self Protector" patent, "is a device for so covering up the sexual organs of a person addicted to the vice of masturbation . . . that he or she must refrain from the commission of the vicious and self-degrading act." Capable of being padlocked ("the key to which is to be carried by the person who has charge of the masturbator"), the invention was similar in construction to an athletic supporter, consisting of a series of bands of cloth, rubber, or leather, plus a cup for shielding the genitals. Cook recommended the use of a padded metal cup, and "the edges of the pouch fit close against the person so that it will be impossible for the wearer to touch the confined organ." The pouch contained a small hole "for the discharge of urine."

3. THE TRUSS (Patent No. 177,971. Granted May 30, 1876.)

To reduce "involuntary erections" and repress "inordinate amative desire, and too frequent emissions," Harvey A. Stephenson invented the simple but bizarre "Spermatic Truss." Attached to a waistbelt was a "pouch, made of cloth or other suitable material . . . and provided on the inner side with a loop" through which the penis was inserted downward. Penis in place, the lower end of the pouch was pulled tightly up the backside with a "fastening-strap" and attached to the waistbelt with a slipknot "so as to be readily loosened or moved laterally." A "pad" stretched between "the hips to prevent discomfort." Designed especially for use while sleeping, the truss allowed the scrotum and testicles to hang outside the pouch.

4. PENIS PLATE (Patent No. 587,994. Granted Aug. 10, 1897.)

Without explanation, Michael McCormick boasted that his "Surgical Appliance" would "control waking thoughts" in addition to preventing "involuntary nocturnal seminal emissions [and] self-abuse." His invention was a variant of the penis ring popularized during midcentury. Here, however, the ring was incorporated into an entire plate shaped to fit across a male child's abdomen and hung from a waistbelt. After the penis was pulled through the ring, its end was strapped to the plate's lower lip. Sharp screws were then adjusted "so as to lie in such proximity above . . . the organ, as may be found best." It is difficult to visualize a parent, screwdriver in hand, positioning these "pricking-points." In the case of an "irresponsible" self-abuser—one determined to slip off the device— the plate could be secured further either with a chain running up the child's backside and clipped onto the waistbelt, or with "sticking plaster." The patent guaranteed: "When from any cause expansion in this organ [penis] begins it will come into contact with the pricking-points, and the necessary pain or warning sensation will result."

5. SHEATH (Patent No. 826,377. Granted July 17, 1906.)

Raphael Sonn's hinged metal contraption was a sleeve that locked onto a child's penis. Once the sheath was in place, two pins were withdrawn, causing spring-loaded "inward-curving clamping members" made of celluloid or rubber to encircle further the boy's organ. The clamps in turn contained metal "teeth or prongs" for gripping the young flesh. The Atlanta, Ga., inventor claimed his device was novel, since it was adjustable for penile thickness; and one variation of the invention even permitted "lengthening of the appliance if found necessary." It was impossible to remove the "Sanitary Appliance" without "great physical pain and possible mutilation." And once removed, as Sonn pointed out smugly, "it cannot be replaced without the key, so that detection will be inevitable." The invention no doubt did more than "prevent and cure the habit of self-abuse in males."

6. HAND JIVE (Patent No. 973,330. Granted Oct. 18, 1910.)

The "Mitten" invented by Henry A. Wood was the simplest and most innocuous of all antisex devices. Even the patent politely avoided mention of sex, stating instead that the invention was "for use in the care of insane or incompetent persons." It consisted of an outer casing "having no thumb and constructed of some coarse stiff material such as heavy canvas or leather." This was sewed over an inner shell made of "some tough but light and flexible material." After the ventilated device was locked around the wrist, "the yielding inner mitten slips against the interior of the outer mitten and thus the hand is unable to grasp readily" either a permissible object or a body part.

7. LOCKING POCKETS (Patent No. 995,600. Granted June 20, 1911.)

Once a child was padlocked into J. E. Heyser's "Surgical Appliance," escape would require not merely "a vast amount of strength" but "unreasonably small hips" as well. The invention provided for a sheet metal plate fitted with "metal pockets . . . for the reception of the penis and testicles." The entire contrivance was "adjusted" to the body via a series of leather straps plus chains, which were covered with surgical tubing "to prevent chafing." With the child or insane patient's comfort in mind, Heyser perforated the pockets "for ventilation and . . . escape of urine" and gave a downward bend to the penile pocket "so as to permit the penis a natural position." Heyser claimed his device could be worn "with reasonable comfort and without danger of unduly wearing the clothes or garments of the patient." With entrepreneurial élan, he reserved the right to make "changes and alterations" if they fell "within the spirit and scope" of his invention and would "absolutely prevent any attempt on the part of the patient to masturbate."

8. LIVE WIRE (Patent No. 1,243,629. Granted Oct. 16, 1917.)

Edward Roddy, a British subject living in New York, employed the magic of electricity to curtail wet dreams "in persons suffering with certain forms of nervous and venereal diseases." His "Surgical Appliance," a small band with an open electrical circuit connected by wires to a waistbelt, was placed firmly into position around the penis. Additional wires, "of such length as to cause the patient no inconvenience upon retiring," fed from the belt to a case equipped with a battery and doorbell-like alarm. Assuming the patient didn't get entangled, the operation of the device was simple. Upon erection of the penis, the open circuit was closed, causing a surge of electricity to ring the alarm—placed beneath the bed—in order to "abort nocturnal emissions." Roddy claimed his invention was beneficial. He failed to indicate, though, what was to prevent the patient from removing the unit once the lights went out.

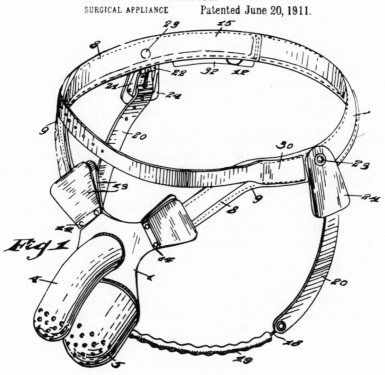

J. E. HEYSER.

SURGICAL APPLIANCE   Patented June 20, 1911.

J. E. Heyser claimed his device could be worn
"with reasonable comfort."

9. BODY SUIT (Patent No. 1,865,280. Granted June 28, 1932.)

Similar to a jumpsuit, Allan Risley's invention was to be worn underneath the nightclothes. Double ties and cords at the ankles, waist, and collar, plus a large industrial-size zipper running the length of the suit's torso prevented the wearer from making direct contact with the genitals. If the wearer was male, a guard of canvas or leather would be laced into the garment's crotch area, offering additional protection from a tyke's wandering hands. Risley patented a modified version, perhaps for use in hot climates, that looked like Bermuda shorts. It tied at the waist and leg openings and had a removable crotch guard. The inventor modestly called his creation a "Garment." "Simple, durable, and efficient," the invention prevented youngsters "from handling certain parts of the anatomy while asleep or partly asleep and thereby [curtailed] masturbation."

—Z.J.K.

13 PROSEX INVENTIONS

1. ANTICIRCUMCISION RING (Patent No. 2,538,136. Granted Jan. 16, 1951.

   For those who want the effect of circumcision without surgery, this device holds the foreskin in a retracted position. Fortunately, the ring is removable.

2. SCROTUM SLEEVE (Patent No. 2,576,024. Granted Nov. 20, 1951.)

   The scrotum is placed in a tubular sleeve, which holds the testicles downward. This is said to improve their well-being and functioning by stimulating the circulation of blood through the scrotum.

3. PROTECTIVE COATS (Patent No. 3,147,486. Granted Sept. 8, 1964.)

   Shrinking and discomfort of the penis in cold climates is prevented by this open-ended tube of plastic, sponge rubber, or the like.

4. ADHESIVE BRASSIERE (Patent No. 3,276,449. Granted Oct. 4, 1966.)

   This article is an elongated plastic strip with adhesive cups at both ends to contain the breasts. The center portion of the strip encircles the back of the neck. Transparent strips are favored so that it can be worn invisibly.

5. SEXUAL AID (Patent No. 3,401,687. Granted Sept. 17, 1968.)

   This is a tube of flexible material—plastic, leather, or rubber—which is placed over the penis for rigidity and support. It helps a man who has a flaccid penis during intromission. The tube is split longitudinally to allow for expansion if the penis becomes turgid.

6. BREAST DEVELOPING JACKET (Patent No. 3,500,832. Granted Mar. 17, 1970.)

   The jacket is connected via hoses to a source of warm water, which is circulated between the jacket's dual layers over the breasts. The circulation is said to enlarge the arteries and veins and cause storage of fat tissue in the heated areas.

7. PUBOCOCCYGEUS MUSCLE EXERCISER (Patent No. 3,502,328. Granted Mar. 24, 1970.)

   This muscle, which can contract voluntarily or involuntarily during coitus, can be exercised by women using this mechanism. The mechanism resembles a song flute with spaced protuberances along its length. After insertion of 1½ to 3 inches of the exerciser into the vagina, the muscle is voluntarily contracted, thus eventually improving muscle tone.

8. CONTRACEPTIVE ARTICLE (Patent No. 3,518,995. Granted July 7, 1970.)

   This article of clothing resembles a jockstrap and has a moisture-

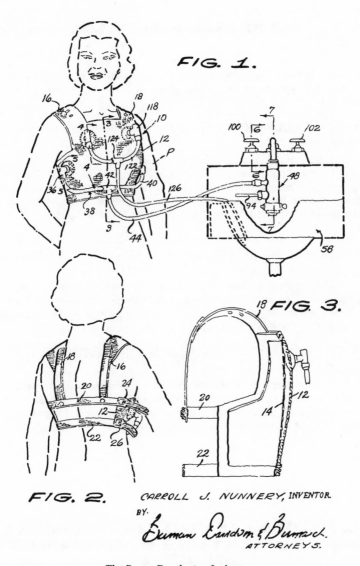

FIG. 1.

FIG. 3.

FIG. 2.

CARROLL J. NUNNERY, INVENTOR.

BY.

~~Berman Davidson & Burrack.~~
ATTORNEYS.

The Breast Developing Jacket.

resistant, heat-reflective panel to raise scrotum temperature 1.5 to 3°F and thus inhibit sperm production. The device is ineffective unless worn for some time prior to coitus, and infertility can last for three to eight weeks after using it.

9. HUMAN BIRTH-CONTROL APPLIANCE (Patent No. 3,536,066. Granted Oct. 27, 1970.)

Human conception is prevented by this appliance, which is worn like a panty. During intercourse the expandable crotch section is pushed into the vagina to provide a mechanical barrier to sperm.

10. CONTOURED PILLOW (Design Patent No. 220,823. Granted May 25, 1971.)

The pillow is provided with two conically shaped indentations for receiving breasts. The cushion affords more comfort to a large-breasted woman who prefers to lie on her stomach while she sleeps or during intercourse.

11. DUAL OCCUPANCY CRADLE (Patent No. 3,668,722. Granted June 13, 1972.)

Occasionally, sexual partners are mismatched in size, shape, or weight. This upholstered two-tiered cradle device props up the partner on top, who lies across a sling stretched between two support beams. The partner on the bottom has maximum freedom of movement; the partner on top, not having to worry about supporting his or her own weight, can stay relaxed.

12. METHOD AND DEVICE FOR ACHIEVING A PENILE ERECTION (Patent No. 3,853,122. Granted Dec. 10, 1974.)

This appliance is an elongated tube which is surgically implanted in the penis. The tube terminates in a bulb-shaped fluid container which is implanted in the scrotum. The victim of impotence achieves erection by squeezing the fluid container, which fills and elongates the tube.

13. SELF-CONTAINED GYNECOLOGIC STIMULATOR (Patent No. 3,996,930. Granted Dec. 14, 1976.)

One half of this V-shaped device fits into the vagina, while the other has an elongated trough for receiving the clitoris. The device can be worn beneath a pair of panties. The wearer can control the amount of stimulation by increasing or decreasing movement.

—J.R.L.

G. LEGMAN'S 13 MOST EROTIC BOOKS IN HISTORY (ARRANGED BY CHRONOLOGY, NOT QUALITY)

Possessor of one of the best private libraries of erotic folklore and literature, Legman has been bibliographer for the Kinsey Institute and writer-in-residence at the University of California. His books include *Love & Death: A Study in Censorship, The Horn Book: Studies in Erotic Folklore,* and *The Ballad: Unexpurgated Folksongs, American and British,* which is currently in progress. He is a resident of France.

1. *The Satyricon* by Petronius Arbiter
2. *The Perfumed Garden* by Sheikh Omar al-Nafzawi

3. *The Dialogues of Luisa Sigea* by Nicolas Chorier
4. *Fanny Hill, or the Memoirs of a Woman of Pleasure* by John Cleland
5. *The Porter of Chartreaux* by Gervaise de Latouche
6. *The Devil in the Flesh* by Andréa de Nerciat
7. *The Anti-Justine* by Restif de la Bretonne
8. *Tableaux Vivants* by Paul Perret
9. *My Secret Life* by H. Spencer Ashbee
10. *Josefine Mutzenbacher: A 16-Year-Old Prostitute* by Felix Salten
11. *Three Daughters of Their Mother* by Pierre Louÿs
12. *Delta of Venus/Little Birds* by Anaïs Nin
13. *Only a Boy* by Eugene Field

—Exclusive for *The Book of Lists 3*

16
SPORTS SECTION

THE 10 GREATEST SPORTS FIGURES IN AMERICAN HISTORY

The latest of many sports polls, this one was taken by David L. Porter, a professor of history at William Penn College in Iowa. In 1982, Porter polled America's leading sports historians on the 10 athletes or administrators they thought had "made the most outstanding accomplishments and had the most significant long-range impact on American sports history." Of the 40 historians polled, 31 (or 78%) replied. Herewith the results.

1. GEORGE HERMAN "BABE" RUTH (1895–1948) Baseball. 29 votes

Acclaimed by this poll "the greatest figure in American sports history." He started out as an excellent pitcher but became a legendary slugger on the New York Yankees, whom he led to seven pennants and four World Series triumphs. In his lifetime, he slammed 714 home runs (one every 8.5 times at bat), and in a single year, 1927, he hit 60 homers. His career batting average was .342, during which time he batted in 2,204 runs. A lusty and undisciplined folk hero, he earned a bigger salary than the president of the U.S. in 1930.

2. MILDRED "BABE" DIDRIKSON ZAHARIAS (1914–1956) Track, golf, basketball. 22 votes

Top female athlete of all time. She was a superwoman. In the 1932 Olympic trials, she won five events and broke three world records. In the 1932 Olympics in Los Angeles, she won gold medals and set world marks in the 80-meter hurdles and the javelin throw. Earlier, for Dallas, she had been a National AAU basketball All-American three times. Later, turning to golf, she won 22 amateur tournaments (14 in a row) and 34 professional tournaments (including three U.S. Open victories).

3. JACKIE ROBINSON (1919–1972) Baseball. 18 votes

He broke the color barrier in major league baseball, becoming the first black player in over 60 years. A four-sports athlete at UCLA, he began as a shortstop on the all-black Kansas City Monarchs. Defying the racists, Brooklyn Dodger owner Branch Rickey signed him on for a farm club, then in 1947 elevated him to the big leagues. With the Dodgers, Robinson built a .311 career batting average and helped the team to six pennant wins and one World Series victory. In 1962, he became the first black to be elected to the Baseball Hall of Fame.

Babe Ruth.

4. BILLIE JEAN MOFFITT KING (1943–   ) Tennis. 17 votes

Tough, flamboyant, court-smart, she won a Wimbledon doubles title at 17 and went on to win six Wimbledon singles titles (the most ever won by a woman) and four U.S. singles championships. A pioneer in establishing women's professional tennis, she earned over $100,000 in 1971. When male chauvinist Bobby Riggs taunted her, she took him on in Houston in 1973 and crushed him in straight sets. Always controversial, she remains an ardent feminist.

5. MUHAMMAD ALI (1942–   ) Prizefighting. 14 votes

A colorful showman, brilliant boxer, erstwhile poet, he won an Olympic gold medal in 1960 as a light-heavyweight. He took the world heavyweight championship from Sonny Liston in 1964 and successfully defended the title nine times. Converted to Black Muslim beliefs, Ali refused induction into the armed forces during the Vietnam era. He was stripped of his title and sentenced to prison, but the U.S. Supreme Court overturned his conviction. In 1974, he regained his heavyweight crown by beating the unbeaten George Foreman in Zaire, then defended his title successfully 10 times before losing it to Leon Spinks in 1978. However, Ali regained it later that same year. In his professional career, Ali has won 56 fights, lost five, and has earned over $45 million. He is America's most famous athlete worldwide.

6. JAMES FRANCIS "JIM" THORPE (1886–1953) Football, track, baseball. 13 votes

He was voted the greatest athlete of the half century by the Associated Press in 1950. A Sac and Fox Indian from Oklahoma, he led tiny Carlisle Indian School's football team to upset victories over Harvard, Army, and other big schools. At the Olympic games in Stockholm in 1912, he won gold medals in the decathlon and pentathlon and was named the world's greatest athlete by King Gustav V of Sweden. Thorpe helped popularize professional football in its early stages, playing for the Canton Bulldogs and similar teams from 1915 to 1926. Thorpe turned to big-league baseball between 1913 and 1919, playing for the New York Giants among other teams and compiling a .252 lifetime batting average.

7. WALTER CAMP (1859–1925) Football. 12 votes

His name was synonymous with early college football. He played halfback for Yale from 1876 to 1881, and he coached there from 1888 to 1892, turning out three undefeated teams that outscored their opponents 1,621 to 0. He was responsible for many modern-day football rules and practices, such as 11-man teams, four-man backfields, 10-yard first downs, and the forward pass. The All-American teams he selected annually from 1889 to 1924 were the most widely recognized.

8. JOE LOUIS (1914–1981) Boxer. 12 votes

"The Brown Bomber" beat the best of them. He defeated Primo Carnera, Max Baer, and finally knocked out James Braddock in 1937 to win the heavyweight championship. A year earlier Louis had suffered his first professional loss, to Germany's Max Schmeling in 12 rounds, but in a 1938 rematch he knocked out Schmeling in the first round. Louis fought 71 fights and won 68—54 by knockouts. He was the first black heavyweight champion since the superb but cocky and scandalous Jack Johnson. Unlike his black predecessor, the modest, quiet Louis was admired and loved by both whites and blacks.

9. JESSE OWENS (1913–1980) Track. 11 votes

For Ohio State University, at the Big Ten track championships in 1935 he broke three world records and tied another in 45 minutes—he shattered records in the 220-yard dash, 220-yard low hurdles, the broad jump, and tied the record in the 100-yard dash. At the 1936 Olympic

Games in Nazi Berlin, this black American won four gold medals, to the dismay of Adolf Hitler—setting world marks in the 200-meter dash, 400-meter relay, broad jump, and tying the record in the 100-meter dash.

10. HAROLD "RED" GRANGE (1903–   ) Football. 11 votes

"The Galloping Ghost," they called him. As a halfback for the University of Illinois, he went up against the University of Michigan, winner of 20 consecutive games, in 1924. He smashed Michigan single-handedly, running for five touchdowns and passing for a sixth. The following year, against the University of Pennsylvania, he ran for 363 yards and scored three touchdowns. In his college career, he covered 3,600 yards on the ground, scored 31 touchdowns, and became a three-time All-American. With the Chicago Bears in 1925, he turned pro football into a spectator sport. From 1932 to 1934, scoring 11 touchdowns, he led the Bears to three division titles and one National Football League championship.

—I.W., based on original annotations by David L. Porter

20 UNUSUAL BASEBALL RECORDS

1. Most consecutive games with extra base hit. PAUL WANER, outfielder for Pittsburgh, 14 from June 3 to 19, 1927.
2. Most triples in one game. BILL JOYCE, third baseman for New York Giants, 4 on May 18, 1897.
3. Hardest to double up. DON BUFORD, outfielder for Baltimore Orioles, $\frac{1}{138}$ ratio for his career.
4. Spoiled most no-hitters with only hit. CESAR TOVAR, outfielder for Minnesota, 5 during 1967–1975.
5. Best batting average at age 40. TY COBB, outfielder for Detroit, .357 in 1927.
6. Most steals of home. TY COBB, 35 during his career.
7. Most consecutive times struck out. BILL HANDS, pitcher for Chicago Cubs, 14 in 1968.
8. Most pitchers in combined no-hitter. OAKLAND, 4 on Sept. 28, 1975: Vida Blue, Glenn Abbott, Paul Lindblad, and Rollie Fingers.
9. Most wins for last-place team. STEVE CARLTON, pitcher for Philadelphia, 27 in 1972.
10. Oldest 20-game winner. WARREN SPAHN, pitcher for Milwaukee Braves, age 42 in 1963.
11. Last person to pitch two complete-game wins in one day. DUTCH LEVSEN, Cleveland, Aug. 28, 1926.
12. Best ERA (earned-run average) after age 40. CY YOUNG, 41-year-old pitcher for Boston Red Sox, 1.26 in 1908.
13. Best batting average for a 20-game winner. WALTER JOHNSON, pitcher for Washington, .433 in 1925 (with 20 wins).

14. Worst-hitting pitcher. RON HERBEL, San Francisco, .029 for career (6 hits in 206 at-bats).
15. Most consecutive errorless games. PAUL LINDBLAD, pitcher for Oakland (and Washington and Texas), 385 from 1966 to 1974.
16. Most lopsided win (since 1900). BOSTON RED SOX over ST. LOUIS BROWNS, 29–4 on June 8, 1950.
17. Most brothers in baseball. DELAHANTYS, 5 from 1888 to 1915 (Ed, Philadelphia Phillies outfielder; Frank, New York Highlanders outfielder; Jim, Brooklyn (Federal League) second baseman; Joe, St. Louis Cardinals outfielder; and Tom, Cleveland Spiders third baseman).
18. Most runs in one inning (since 1900). BOSTON RED SOX against Detroit, 17 on June 8, 1953.
19. Oldest ballpark still in use. COMISKEY PARK in Chicago since 1910.
20. Most .300 hitters in one season. ST. LOUIS CARDINALS, 8 in 1930: George Watkins, .373; Frankie Frisch, .346; Chick Hafey, .336; Jimmie Wilson, .318; Sparky Adams, .314; Jim Bottomley, .304; Charley Gelbert, .304; and Taylor Douthit, .303.

SOURCE: Joseph L. Reichler, *The Great All-Time Baseball Record Book.* New York: Macmillan Publishing Company, 1981.

10 PITCHERS WHO THREW NO-HITTERS FOR 9 INNINGS AND STILL LOST THE GAME

1. EARL MOORE, May 9, 1901

Pitching for the Cleveland Bronchos (now the Indians) against the Chicago White Sox, Moore allowed two unearned runs in the 4th, but his no-hitter remained intact until the bottom of the 10th, when Chicago erupted with two runs to win, 4–2.

2. HARRY McINTYRE, August 1, 1906

McIntyre of the Brooklyn Superbas (now the Los Angeles Dodgers) hurled 10 ⅔ no-hit innings against the visiting Pittsburgh Pirates. In the top of the 13th, the game still scoreless, Pittsburgh scored on two singles and a double to win the game. Brooklyn left nine men stranded on base and was allowed only five hits by Lefty Leifield, the Pittsburgh pitcher.

3. LEON AMES, April 15, 1909

An opening-day crowd of 30,000 at the Polo Grounds watched as Ames and the New York Giants lost to the Brooklyn Superbas after Ames had pitched 9 ⅓ no-hit innings. Still scoreless, Brooklyn rallied in the top of the 13th. With one out, Harry Lumley, the Brooklyn manager and right fielder, tripled off the center-field wall. Ames walked the next batter, then got tagged for two singles and a successful bunt down the third-base line which scored three runs. Though the Giants managed to put two men on in their half of the 13th, they couldn't bring them home.

4. THOMAS HUGHES, August 30, 1910

For nine innings Hughes pitched perfect baseball in the second game of a doubleheader between his New York Highlanders (later the Yankees) and the Cleveland Naps (later the Indians). With two out in the 11th inning, Cleveland exploded for five runs, giving Cleveland pitcher George Kahler a shutout.

5. JIM SCOTT, May 14, 1914

Scott of the Chicago White Sox lost his no-hitter against Washington in the last half of the 10th inning. Chick Gandil, the Washington first baseman, singled and came home on a double by leftfielder Howard Shanks. In losing, Chicago left two men on base in the top of the 10th.

6. JIM "HIPPO" VAUGHN, May 2, 1917

The Chicago Cubs' Vaughn lost his nine-inning no-hitter 1–0 to the Cincinnati Reds in the 10th inning. With one out, Larry Kopf, the Reds' shortstop, singled and went to third when the Cubs' centerfielder, Cy Williams, dropped a fly hit by Cincinnati's first baseman, Hal Chase. Kopf scored when Jim Thorpe singled on a slow bouncer to win the game. A big contributing factor to Vaughn's loss was that Fred Toney, the Cincinnati pitcher, threw a no-hitter in the same game. Actually, the game was as much a defensive battle as it was a pitchers' duel. In nine innings, the Cubs didn't permit a Reds runner to reach second base, though two men walked, and the Reds allowed only one Cubs runner to reach second, on a steal by Hal Chase.

7. LOUIS "BOBO" NEWSOM, September 18, 1934

Newsom's nine-inning no-hitter against the Boston Red Sox was marred by an unearned run in the second inning. The St. Louis Browns tied it up in the 6th but lost, 2–1, in the 10th when Newsom allowed two walks and a single, which combined to score the winning run.

8. HARVEY HADDIX, May 26, 1959

Haddix, of the Pittsburgh Pirates, threw 12 perfect innings against the Milwaukee Braves, who were leading the National League, and became the first pitcher in major-league history to carry a perfect performance beyond nine innings. Things fell apart for Haddix in the 13th inning when Felix Mantilla hit a grounder to third but was called safe at first on a throwing error. Eddie Mathews then sacrificed Mantilla to second. Hank Aaron came up and was walked, no doubt because he was the major leagues' leading batter. Joe Adcock, the next batter, connected with one of Haddix's pitches and put it over the fence but was declared out because in his excitement he passed Aaron on the base path between second and third. However, he was credited with a double and the game-winning RBI.

9. KEN JOHNSON, April 23, 1964

Johnson's no-hitter was the first of the 1964 season and came in a night game between Johnson's Houston Colt .45s (later the Astros) and the Cincinnati Reds. Ironically, it was Johnson who made the original mistake that led to his loss. In the 9th inning, the 30-year-old knuckle-baller fielded Pete Rose's bunt and threw wildly to first, sending Rose to second. Chico Ruiz, the next batter, grounded out, advancing Rose to third. Vada Pinson then grounded to second, but Nellie Fox muffed the ball, and Rose scored. Houston couldn't score in their half of the ninth.

10. JIM MALONEY, June 14, 1965

Maloney, of the Cincinnati Reds, lost his no-hitter in a night game at Crosley Field against the New York Mets. Throughout the first 10 innings, the Mets got on base only once—when Ed Kranepool walked in the 2nd. However, leading off the 11th, Johnny Lewis, with a .250 average, hit a 2–1 pitch against the center-field barrier for a game-winning ground-rule homer. During the game, Maloney had struck out 18 batters (including Lewis three times), tying a National League record. Maloney pitched another, more successful, no-hitter later that season, beating the Chicago Cubs, 1–0, in 10 innings.

—J.N.

THE 15 EASIEST BASEBALL PLAYERS TO STRIKE OUT (CAREER)

Player (main team, league, position)	Yrs.	AB	SO	Ratio
1. Dave Nicholson (Chicago, NL, OF)	7	1,419	573	2.48
2. Dave Kingman (San Francisco, NL, 1B)	10	3,839	1,139	3.37
3. Richie Allen (Philadelphia, NL, 1B & 3B)	15	6,332	1,656	3.82
4. Mike Schmidt (Philadelphia, NL, 3B)	9	4,261	1,077	3.96
5. Reggie Jackson (Oakland, AL, OF)	14	6,863	1,728	3.97
6. Bobby Bonds (San Francisco, NL, OF)	13	6,880	1,713	4.06
6. Donn Clendenon (Pittsburgh, NL, 1B)	12	4,648	1,140	4.06
8. Rick Monday (Chicago, NL, OF)	15	5,572	1,362	4.09
9. Willie Stargell (Pittsburgh, NL, OF)	19	7,794	1,903	4.10
10. Woodie Held (Cleveland, AL, SS & OF)	14	4,019	944	4.25
11. Frank Howard (Washington, AL, OF)	16	6,488	1,460	4.44
12. Deron Johnson (Philadelphia, NL, 1B)	15	5,902	1,307	4.51
13. Jimmy Wynn (Houston, NL, OF)	16	6,653	1,427	4.66

| 14. Mickey Mantle (New York, AL, OF) | 18 | 8,102 | 1,710 | 4.73 |
| 15. Harmon Killebrew (Minnesota, AL, 1B & 3B) | 22 | 8,147 | 1,699 | 4.80 |

SOURCE: Joseph L. Reichler, *The Great All-Time Baseball Record Book.* New York: Macmillan Publishing Company, 1981.

THE 8 HARDEST BASEBALL PLAYERS TO STRIKE OUT (CAREER)

Player *(main team, league, position)*	Yrs.	AB	SO	Ratio
1. Joe Sewell (Cleveland, AL, SS)	14	7,132	114	62.6
2. Lloyd Waner (Pittsburgh, NL, OF)	18	7,772	173	44.9
3. Nellie Fox (Chicago, AL, 2B)	19	9,232	216	42.7
4. Tommy Holmes (Boston, NL, OF)	11	4,992	122	40.9
5. Andy High (St. Louis, NL, 3B)	13	4,400	130	33.8
6. Frankie Frisch (St. Louis, NL, 2B)	19	9,112	272	33.5
7. Don Mueller (New York, NL, OF)	12	4,364	146	29.9
8. Sam Rice (Washington, AL, OF)	20	9,269	351	26.4

SOURCE: Joseph L. Reichler, *The Great All-Time Baseball Record Book.* New York: Macmillan Publishing Company, 1981.

13 GREAT PLAYERS WHO NEVER PLAYED IN A WORLD SERIES

Player *(main team, league, position)*	Yrs.	BA (hitters)	HR	ERA (pitchers)	W-L Pct.
1. Nap Lajoie* (Cleveland, AL, 2B)	21	.339	81		
2. Ted Lyons* (Chicago, AL, P)	21			3.67	.531
3. Luke Appling* (Chicago, AL, SS)	20	.310	45		
4. Mel Harder (Cleveland, AL, P)	20			3.80	.545
5. Gaylord Perry (San Francisco, NL, P)	20			2.99	.554
6. Ernie Banks* (Chicago, NL, SS & 1B)	19	.274	512		
7. Billy Williams (Chicago, NL, OF)	18	.290	426		

Ernie Banks.

8.	Jim Bunning (Det., AL, & Phil., NL, P)	17		3.27	.549
9.	Harry Heilmann* (Detroit, AL, OF)	17	.342	183	
10.	Ferguson Jenkins (Chicago, NL, P)	17		3.31	.567
11.	George Sisler* (St. Louis, AL, 1B)	15	.340	99	
12.	Rod Carew (Minnesota, AL, 2B)	15	.332	82	
13.	Ralph Kiner* (Pittsburgh, NL, OF)	10	.279	369	

*Designates member of Baseball Hall of Fame.

—A.S.

13 OF THE MOST UNUSUAL TOUCHDOWNS IN GRIDIRON HISTORY

1. YALE VARSITY v. YALE SCRUBS (1880s)

In an early practice game at Yale, the "maul in goal" rule, a carry-over from rugby, caused considerable consternation. The rule stated that the ballcarrier had to touch the ball to the ground behind the goal line for the touchdown to count and that opposing players could try to prevent this. Alex Coxe, a 290-lb. varsity guard, dragged the ball and several scrubs toward the goal line. On the next play, Coxe crossed the goal and fell on his back. One small opponent named Tillinghast clung to him and fought to keep him from rolling over and downing the ball. Since the rule further stated that only the man with the ball and whoever had his hands on him when he stepped over the goal line were allowed to fight it out, little Tillinghast struggled alone with Coxe for 15 minutes, while the other players stood around watching. Coxe grew winded and the feisty Tillinghast got the ball away from him before he could score.

2. HARVARD UNIVERSITY v. CARLISLE INDIAN SCHOOL (1903)

Since no rule specified that the ball had to be carried in a player's arms, Carlisle coach Glenn "Pop" Warner taught his Indians the "hidden ball" play, which they used against Harvard. On the kickoff, then quarterback Jimmy Johnson gathered in the ball on the 5-yd. line. The Indians went into a sort of huddle, except that they faced outward. Johnson, in the middle, slipped the ball under the jersey of lineman Charlie Dillon. The players moved downfield in a wedge formation, protecting Johnson, who pretended to have the ball. Meanwhile, Dillon, with a hump on his back, unnoticed by Harvard, broke into a run and headed into the end zone. Despite this ingenious play, Carlisle lost the game, 12–11.

3. ORANGE [N.J.] ATHLETIC CLUB v. FRANKLIN [PA.] ATHLETIC CLUB (1903)

After Franklin's two unsuccessful attempts to score from the Orange 5-yd. line in this tournament game of the second "World Series" of pro football, the ball was given to Doc Roller, a physician who wore kid gloves to protect his hands while playing. Herman Kerchoffe, Franklin's 260-lb. guard, picked up Roller and carried him over the line of scrimmage. With Roller still in Kerchoffe's arms, they crossed the goal line for a TD. Franklin won the game and the series.

4. UNIVERSITY OF CHICAGO v. CARLISLE INDIAN SCHOOL (1907)

Al Exendine, Carlisle's great right end, was covered by two backfield men from Amos Alonzo Stagg's Chicago team. On one play, Exendine went out of bounds and the backs therefore went after the other Indian end. Staying out of bounds, Exendine cut behind the Chicago bench and ran to the end zone, where Carlisle quarterback Pete Hauser hit him with a perfect 50-yd. spiral for a score.

5. LEHIGH v. LAFAYETTE (1918)

In the 1918 match between these ancient college rivals, Lehigh halfback Raymond "Snooks" Dowd took a handoff and scampered 15 yd. into the end zone—his own! Realizing his mistake, he circled back and ran the length of the field for a TD. His run covered 115 yd. in all.

6. NOTRE DAME v. NORTHWESTERN (1934)

Trailing, 7–6, in the final quarter, the Irish feigned a mix-up in signals so that Northwestern, sensing their confusion, would ease up on defense. Then halfback Andy Pilney took the ball and angled in 14 yd. for a TD. Notre Dame won, 20–7.

7. KANSAS STATE v. OKLAHOMA A&M (1935)

During this game, which was played in a torrential downpour, the referee spent most of his time under an umbrella near the sidelines. This situation did not go unnoticed by Kansas. As their quarterback dropped back with the ball, one of the halfbacks suddenly appeared from behind the referee and his umbrella, gathered in the ball, and sloshed downfield for the TD—a perfectly executed sleeper play.

8. WASHINGTON & LEE v. RICHMOND (1947)

Returning a kickoff from the 6-yd. line, Washington & Lee halfback Brian Bell broke free and raced to his own 40 with a blocker in front of him. As two Richmond tacklers caught up to him, a sidelines photographer shot off a flashbulb. The blinding light confused the Richmond players, who tackled the blocker. Bell ran in for the score, and W&L awarded a monogram to the photographer as the "star" of the game.

9. SAN JOSE STATE COLLEGE v. COLLEGE OF THE PACIFIC (1948)

Pacific's magician-quarterback Eddie LeBaron spun twice and handed off to a back, who was piled up at the line. The referee blew the play dead. However, unknown to him and nearly everyone else in the stadium, LeBaron still had the ball. As the players began unpiling at the line of scrimmage, Eddie faded back and threw a touchdown pass to Roy Kirsten. Now the officials had a dilemma. The "ball" had already been called dead at the line, even though it wasn't actually there. Should the touchdown be allowed, or could the referee nullify the 6 points? It was quickly decided that the score would not count, and the ball was returned to the place where the play had been blown dead. Pacific lost, 14–7—it was their only loss of the season.

10. NORTHWESTERN v. MICHIGAN (Sept. 11, 1971)

Michigan's Dana Coin attempted a 51-yd. field goal in the third quarter. Standing in front of the goalposts, Northwestern's Jack Dustin leaped up, hand extended over the crossbar, and batted the ball back into the end zone. Michigan receiver Bob Rather, who was running downfield on the play, fell on the ball for a Wolverine TD. Michigan won, 21–6.

11. FLORIDA v. MIAMI (Nov. 27, 1971)

A funny thing happened as Miami's John Hornibrook took the ball and began running toward Florida's goal line with a minute left to play: All of Florida's players fell to the ground, allowing him to score an 8-yd. TD. The reason: It was the last game of the season and they wanted their own quarterback, John Reaves, to get the ball one more time so he would have a chance to break Jim Plunkett's career passing record of 7,547 yd. After all, Florida led at the time, 45–8. After Hornibrook scored, Reaves did break Plunkett's record, on a 15-yd. pass to Carlos Alvarez.

12. MINNESOTA VIKINGS v. LOS ANGELES RAMS (Nov. 19, 1972)

As Minnesota's bulky, slow-footed fullback Bill Brown caught a pass, Ram linebacker Jim Purnell hit him from one side and defensive back Jim Nettles from the other. All they did was prop Brown up while they fell by the wayside. Brown resumed his run downfield, lumbering 76 yd. for a touchdown. The Rams lost, 45–41.

13. SAN DIEGO CHARGERS v. OAKLAND RAIDERS (Sept. 10, 1978)

With 10 seconds left to play, the ball on San Diego's 14-yd. line, and San Diego leading, 20–14, Oakland quarterback Kenny Stabler faded back to pass. Just as he was tackled, he fumbled the ball forward. Oakland running back Pete Banaszak pushed the ball farther along. So did Raider end Dave Casper, who recovered it in the end zone. The officials ruled it wasn't an intentional fumble (which is illegal) and allowed the score. Oakland won, 21–20. Of this football version of Tinkers-to-Evers-to-Chance, Stabler said afterward, "I fumbled it on purpose." Banaszak said, "Sure I batted it." Casper said, "I helped it along, then jumped on it." To guard against a recurrence, the NFL passed a rule stating that on any fourth-down fumble or fumble within the last two minutes of either half, the person who committed the fumble is the only offensive player who can recover the ball beyond the point of the fumble and run with it. If a teammate recovers the ball farther downfield, it comes back to the point of the fumble.

—M.H., S.H., & D.H.

THE 10 MOST COMBATIVE CHAMPIONS IN HEAVYWEIGHT BOXING

		Successful Defenses of Title
1. Joe Louis	25	(7 times in 1941)
2. Muhammad Ali	19	(5 times in 1966; 4 times in 1976)
3. Larry Holmes	12	
4. Tommy Burns	11	(6 times in 1908)
5. Jack Johnson	10	(4 times in 1909)
6. Ezzard Charles	8	(4 times in 1951)
7. James J. Jeffries	7	
8. Rocky Marciano	6	
9. Floyd Patterson	6	
10. Jack Dempsey	5	

—L.R.

ARTHUR ASHE'S 10 GREATEST MALE TENNIS STARS OF ALL TIME (IN NO PARTICULAR ORDER)

Ashe became the top-ranked tennis player in the world when he won the Wimbledon singles championship in 1975. Four years later his career ended abruptly after he suffered a major heart attack and underwent a quadruple bypass operation. Today, Ashe is captain of the U.S. Davis Cup team. He is also national campaign chairman for the American Heart Association.

1. Bjorn Borg
2. Rod Laver
3. Bill Tilden
4. Don Budge
5. Jack Kramer
6. Pancho Gonzales
7. John McEnroe
8. Fred Perry
9. Ken Rosewall
10. Frank Sedgman

—Exclusive for *The Book of Lists 3*

BJORN BORG'S 10 GREATEST MALE TENNIS STARS OF ALL TIME (IN NO PARTICULAR ORDER)

In 1974, at 18, Borg became the youngest man ever to win a major international tournament. Since then he has swept the Wimbledon singles championship six times (1975–1980) and has been named World Champion of Men's Tennis by the International Tennis Federation.

1. Rod Laver
2. Don Budge
3. Ken Rosewall
4. Jack Kramer
5. Bill Tilden
6. Roy Emerson
7. Jimmy Connors
8. Lew Hoad
9. Pancho Gonzales
10. John Newcombe

—Exclusive for *The Book of Lists 3*

ROD LAVER'S 9 GREATEST TENNIS PLAYERS OF ALL TIME (EXCLUDING MYSELF; IN NO PARTICULAR ORDER)

Throughout the 1960s, Laver's dazzling left-handed game won him four Wimbledon singles titles. Known as "the Rocket," the Australian became the only tennis player in history to win the Grand Slam (the U.S., British, Australian, and French championships) twice. He was also the first in the history of the sport to win over $100,000 in one year.

Ken Rosewall.

1. Bill Tilden
2. Don Budge
3. Jack Kramer
4. Bjorn Borg
5. Lew Hoad
6. Ken Rosewall
7. Pancho Gonzales
8. Fred Perry
9. John Newcombe

—Exclusive for *The Book of Lists 3*

GARY PLAYER'S 10 GREATEST MALE GOLFERS OF ALL TIME

Since taking up golf as a teenager in his native South Africa, Player has won millions of dollars in international tournaments. He is one of four golf champions ever to win all four top competitions in the world: the British Open, the Masters, the PGA Championship, and the U.S. Open.

1. Jack Nicklaus
2. Sam Snead
3. Ben Hogan
4. Arnold Palmer
5. Gene Sarazen
6. Walter Hagen
7. Bobby Jones
8. Bobby Locke
9. Byron Nelson
10. Lee Trevino

—Exclusive for *The Book of Lists 3*

ROGER STAUBACH'S 10 GREATEST LINEBACKERS (IN ALPHABETICAL ORDER)

A graduate of the U.S. Naval Academy (where he earned seven athletic letters), Staubach served four years in the Navy—including a tour in Vietnam—before signing on with the Dallas Cowboys. One of pro football's greatest quarterbacks, he led the Cowboys to four Super Bowls before his retirement in 1979, at age 37. Now a television sportscaster, Staubach was named in 1982 as the NFL's no. 1-rated all-time passer.

1. Chuck Bednarik, Philadelphia Eagles
2. Bill Bergey, Philadelphia Eagles
3. Dick Butkus, Chicago Bears
4. Chuck Howley, Dallas Cowboys
5. Sam Huff, Washington Redskins
6. Lee Roy Jordan, Dallas Cowboys
7. Jack Lambert, Pittsburgh Steelers
8. Ray Nitschke, Green Bay Packers
9. Tommy Nobis, Atlanta Falcons
10. Joe Schmidt, Detroit Lions

—Exclusive for *The Book of Lists 3*

JIM RYUN'S 10 GREATEST TRACK MILERS OF ALL TIME

Triumphing over various physical ailments, Ryun became the first high school student to run the mile in under 4 minutes. In 1966, at age 19, he set world records for the mile and for the 1,500-meter run and was voted the world's most outstanding athlete. In the 1970s he established Jim Ryun Distance Running Camps. Ryun credits his successes to his abiding religious faith.

1. Jim Ryun
2. Herb Elliott
3. Sebastian Coe
4. Steve Ovett
5. Kipchoge Keino
6. Peter Snell
7. Roger Bannister
8. Glenn Cunningham
9. John Walker
10. Michael Jazy

—Exclusive for *The Book of Lists 3*

ALFRED SHEINWOLD'S 5 GREATEST MOMENTS IN BRIDGE HISTORY

Bridge editor for the *Los Angeles Times,* Sheinwold is known to millions through his syndicated column "Sheinwold on Bridge." He is chairman of the board of governors of the American Contract Bridge League and has written *Five Weeks to Winning Bridge* and *Bridge Puzzles.*

1. EDMOND HOYLE PUBLISHES FIRST BOOK ON WHIST (1742)

Hoyle's *Short Treatise,* published in 1742, was the first full-length book on any card game. (Claudius wrote a treatise on dice and backgammon over 1,700 years earlier, before he became emperor of Rome.) Hoyle became a synonym for fair play, and the expression "according to Hoyle" is part of the language as a guarantee of honesty and of the rule of law.

2. HAROLD S. VANDERBILT "INVENTS" CONTRACT BRIDGE (1925)

Contract bridge, the latest in the family of games that began with whist, was an idea whose time had come in the 1920s, but Harold S. Vanderbilt invented rules and scoring which have survived, with a few minor changes, to the present day.

3. ELY CULBERTSON DEFEATS SIDNEY S. LENZ IN THE BRIDGE MATCH OF THE CENTURY (1931–1932)

Culbertson, a master of publicity as well as a great bridge player and theorist, put contract bridge on the front pages of newspapers in North America and Western Europe with his match against Sidney S. Lenz in the winter of 1931–1932.

4. U.S. WINS FIRST OFFICIAL WORLD CHAMPIONSHIP (1950)

The first "official" world championship took place in Bermuda in 1950, when the U.S. defeated Great Britain and a combined Sweden-Iceland team (in a three-cornered match).

5. ITALIAN "BLUE TEAM" DOMINATES WORLD CHAMPIONSHIPS (1957–1975)

In 1957 an Italian team began a series of world championship victories, ending in controversy and scandal in 1975 when an Italian pair were found to be playing "footsie" under the table in a world championship match, once again in Bermuda. Since that time Italy has won no world championships; the U.S. has won more than any other country, but Brazil, France, and Poland have also entered the winners' circle.

—Exclusive for *The Book of Lists 3*

"The bridge match of the century" took place in 1931–1932.
Seated left to right: Ely Culbertson, Sidney Lenz,
Josephine Culbertson, Oswald Jacoby.

6 FAMOUS PEOPLE WHO INVENTED GAMES

1. LEWIS CARROLL (1832–1898), British author and mathematician

A wizard at conventional games such as chess and billiards, the creator of *Alice in Wonderland* was a genius at inventing mazes, ciphers, riddles, magic tricks—even a paper pistol that popped when waved through the air. Wherever he traveled, especially to seaside resorts, Carroll always carried a black bag filled with delectable toys and games to enchant prospective female child-friends. His *Game of Logic*, published as a book in 1886, was an attempt to teach a dry, academic subject in a humorous, innovative way. Using "propositions," "syllogisms," and "fallacies," the game, though fairly complicated, was lively and filled with clever statements on everything from dragons and soldiers to pigs, caterpillars, and hard-boiled eggs. One of Carroll's syllogisms:

Some new Cakes are unwholesome;
No nice Cakes are unwholesome.
Therefore, some new Cakes are not-nice.

359

2. MARK TWAIN (1835–1910), U.S. author

"Mark Twain's Memory-Builder, a Game for Acquiring and Retaining All Sorts of Facts and Dates," was a particularly appropriate game for Twain, who was known for his absentmindedness. Played on a pegboard divided into 100 rectangles (representing the 100 years in a century), the history game tested players' abilities to remember dates of worldwide "accessions" (to thrones and presidencies), "battles," and "minor events" (such as important inventions). A player called out a date and event (such as 1815, Waterloo), then stuck a pin (each player had a set of colored pins) in the corresponding year and category ("battle"). Penalties were imposed when a player gave an incorrect date, and a point system determined the winner. Twain sold the game in 1891 and later revised it, hoping to organize nationwide clubs to compete for prizes. But the overhauled memory-builder proved too complex and was a commercial failure.

3. ROBERT LOUIS STEVENSON (1850–1894), Scottish novelist and essayist

The author of *Treasure Island* invented a German-style war game in the winter of 1881–1882 while residing in Davos, Switzerland, with his wife, Fanny, and 13-year-old stepson Lloyd. After clearing ample floor space in the lower story of their châlet, Stevenson, armed with *Operations of War* (a military strategy book), methodically set up a "theater of war" and carefully positioned opposing armies of lead soldiers. To shoot down the enemy, players used popguns—ingeniously loaded with "ems" from Lloyd's small printing press. Face-down cards provided the element of luck in the game, serving up valuable military secrets. The war game never had an official name, nor was it marketed, but Stevenson did write a long magazine article about it which was published in 1898. One reader, H. G. Wells, was so captivated by the game that he created his own—called *Little Wars*.

4. (HELEN) BEATRIX POTTER (1866–1943), British author and illustrator

A shy and repressed little girl, Beatrix Potter turned to animals for companionship. Secreted in her nursery was a menagerie of rabbits, mice, frogs, snails—even bats and a tame hedgehog. Years later many of them appeared in her children's books, which numbered over 30. Four of her most popular animal characters—Peter Rabbit, Squirrel Nutkin, Jemima Puddle-Duck, and Jeremy Fisher—became playing pieces on a board game, "Peter Rabbit's Race Game," marketed in 1920. To play: Choose a character, then roll a die and advance on a path of 122 squares (each player had a separate path) toward the winning goal, "The Meeting Place in the Wood." Just one of the obstacles waiting to impede Squirrel Nutkin: "Nutkin meets his friends and loses a turn while talking." But there were chances to jump ahead: Square 96 said, "Old Mr. Brown suddenly bites off Nutkin's tail and in terror he bounds off to 98."

5. H. G. WELLS (1866–1946), British novelist and historian

Wells's book/game *Little Wars* (1913) had simple rules but required an elaborate battleground. Players made houses, churches, castles, and sheds by gluing together wallpaper, cardboard, and corrugated packing paper; the structures (some over 1 ft. high) were handsomely

H. G. Wells playing his game "Little Wars," on an 18-ft. battlefield.

painted to show various details, such as windows and rainwater pipes. H.G. liked to play on an 18-ft. battlefield with 200 soldiers and 6 brass cannon (that could fire 1-in. wooden cylinders 9 yd.) per side. Playing the game was a serious event for Wells, a boisterous, red-faced commander always ready to rally his troops to anticipated victory. As one friend commented: "I have seen harmless guests entering for tea, greeted with the injunction, 'Sit down and keep your mouth shut' . . . it was a game which began at 10 and only ended at 7:30, in which Wells had illegitimately pressed noncombatants into his army—firemen, cooks, shopkeepers, and the like—and in which a magnificent shot from the other end of the floor destroyed a missionary fleeing on a dromedary—the last representation of a nation which had marched so gaily into battle so many hours before."

6. EDGAR CAYCE (1877–1945), U.S. clairvoyant and psychic healer

Known for his health "readings" (in self-induced trances he prescribed treatments for more than 14,000 patients) and psychic powers (among his correct predictions were the stock-market crash of 1929 and the beginnings and ends of both world wars), Cayce was a simple Kentucky farmboy who dropped out of school in the ninth grade. While working as head clerk in a bookstore in Bowling Green, O., in 1903, he invented a card game called "The Pit" or "Board of Trade." The 64 cards, dealt to two or more players, represented various commodities listed on the New York Stock Exchange, and the object of the game was "to corner the market." After the parlor game became popular at the local YMCA, Cayce sent it to a reputable game company in Massachusetts that bought it and successfully sold it throughout the U.S.

—C.O.M.

17
HEALTH AND HAPPINESS

7 ALMOST INDESTRUCTIBLE PEOPLE

1. GRIGORI RASPUTIN

The Russian mystic and orgiast held enormous political power at the court of the Romanovs from 1905 until his murder in 1916. That this decadent, vulgar peasant should hold such sway over the Empress Alexandra infuriated a group of five power-hungry aristocrats, who set out to destroy him. They arranged for Rasputin to take a midnight tea at the home of Prince Felix Yussupov. Some accounts say that Rasputin drank voluminous amounts of poisoned or opiated wine and remained unaffected, to Yussupov's great consternation. The frightened prince contrived an excuse to go upstairs, where the waiting gang furnished him with a gun, then followed him downstairs. According to Rasputin's daughter, Maria, the men assaulted her father and "used him sexually." Then Yussupov shot him. Again, according to Maria, they viciously beat Rasputin and castrated him, flinging the famed penis across the room. One of the conspirators—a doctor—pronounced the victim dead; but Yussupov, feeling uneasy, began to shake the body violently. The corpse's eyelids twitched—and opened. Suddenly, Rasputin jumped to his feet and gripped Yussupov by the shoulders. Terrorized, Prince Felix pulled himself free; Rasputin fell to the floor, and the other men dashed upstairs. In the midst of the brouhaha, they heard noises in the hallway: Rasputin had crawled up the stairs after them! Two more shots were fired into him, and again he was beaten with harrowing violence. The men (still doubting his death) bound Rasputin's wrists, and carrying him to a frozen river, they thrust his body through a hole in the ice. Rasputin was still alive. The icy water revived him, and he struggled against his bonds. When his body was found two days later, his scarred wrists and water-filled lungs gave this proof, as did his freed right hand, which was frozen in the sign of the cross.

2. SAMUEL DOMBEY

Dombey was a black gravedigger in post-Civil War New Orleans. Because he worked for such low rates, his fellow gravediggers decided to put an end to their competition. They called upon a certain Dr. Beauregard, reputed to have great magical powers, to use his $50 "supreme curse" involving an owl's head. The next morning, as Dombey began to dig a new grave, he heard a loud explosion. Someone, apparently injured, staggered from a nearby clump of bushes. There Dombey found a gun which, overloaded with buckshot, had blown up. Later, a much-bandaged Dr. Beauregard threatened to curse anyone who questioned him. The gravediggers took matters into their own hands. They placed a keg of explosive powder under the cot in the tool shed where Dombey took his daily nap and lit it while he slept. The explosion blasted Dombey out the doorway and plopped him 20 ft. away. The tool shed was completely destroyed, but Dombey was unhurt. The local police nicknamed him Indestructible Sam. But the best (or worst) was yet to come: Indestructible Sam was soon captured by masked men and taken in a boat to Lake Pontchartrain. Sam's hands and feet were tied, and he was dumped into the depths of the lake. These particular depths, however, turned out to be only 2 ft.; Sam wriggled free of his bonds and walked ashore. Next, Dombey's foes tried arson—and as Dombey ran from his burning home, he received a full load of buckshot in his chest. Firemen saved the house and rushed Sam to the hospital, where he lived up to his nickname. Sam had the last laugh. He continued to dig graves, and he died at 98, having outlived every one of his jealous competitors.

3. MICHAEL MALLOY

In 1933, a down-and-out drunken Irishman became the victim of an extraordinary series of murder attempts. Malloy was a bum who frequented the speakeasy of one Anthony Marino in the Bronx. Marino and four of his friends, themselves hard up, had recently pulled off an insurance scam, murdering Marino's girl friend and collecting on her policy; pitiful Michael Malloy seemed a good next bet. The gang took out three policies on him. Figuring Malloy would simply drink himself to death, Marino gave him unlimited credit at the bar. This scheme failed—Malloy's liver knew no bounds. The bartender, Joseph Murphy, was in on the plot and substituted antifreeze for Malloy's whiskey. Malloy asked for a refill and happily put away six shots before passing out on the floor; after a few hours, he perked up and requested another drink. For a week Malloy guzzled antifreeze nonstop. Straight turpentine worked no better, and neither did horse liniment laced with rat poison. A meal of rotten oysters marinated in wood alcohol brought Malloy back for seconds. In an ultimate moment of culinary inspiration, Murphy devised a sandwich for his victim: spoiled sardines mixed with carpet tacks. Malloy came back for more. The gang's next tactic was to dump the drunk into a bank of wet snow and pour water on him, on a night when the temperature had sunk to −14° F. No luck. So Marino hired a professional killer, who drove a taxi straight into Malloy at 45 mph, throwing him into the air—then ran over him again for good measure. After a disappearance of three weeks, Malloy walked into the bar, told the boys he'd been hospitalized because of a nasty car accident, and was "sure ready for a drink." Finally, the desperate murderers succeeded—they stuffed a rubber hose into Malloy's mouth and attached it to a gas jet until his face turned purple. The scheme was discovered, and four members of the five-man "Murder Trust" (as the tabloids dubbed Marino & Co.) died in the electric chair. One New York reporter speculated that if Mike Malloy had sat in the electric chair, he would have shorted out every circuit in Sing Sing.

4. DR. ARTHUR WARREN WAITE'S FATHER-IN-LAW AND MOTHER-IN-LAW

Dr. Waite was a New York dentist whose wife was the only daughter of a rich drug manufacturer in Grand Rapids, Mich. Waite decided to remove the only two obstacles in his path to riches: his parents-in-law. The doctor's efforts are neatly chronicled in Carl Sifakis's book *A Catalogue of Crime*: "Setting to work on his mother-in-law, Waite took her for a drive in a heavy rain with the windshield open. He put ground glass in her marmalade. He introduced into her food all sorts of bacteria and viruses—those that cause pneumonia, influenza, anthrax, and diphtheria. The lady did catch a cold, but that was all. In disgust, Waite shifted his attention to his father-in-law, trying the same disease producers—with absolutely no effect. He filled the old man's rubbers with water, dampened his sheets, opened a container of chlorine gas in his bedroom while he slept. Nothing. Then he tried giving the old man calomel, a purgative, to weaken him, and then a throat spray loaded with typhoid bacteria. People started commenting on how well the old man looked. Waite got off the disease kick and switched to arsenic. Amazingly, the poison failed. Finally, Waite polished off the old man by smothering him with a pillow. By now, however, other relatives were suspicious, and an autopsy on the father-in-law's body was ordered. Heavy traces of arsenic were found; although this was not the cause of death, the arsenic was traced to Waite and he finally confessed to his crime."

5. HERBERT "THE CAT" NOBLE

This Dallas racketeer earned his nickname after the first nine attempts on his life. He was shot at so often that he was also called "The Clay Pigeon." His third moniker was "The Sieve" because he had been riddled by so many bullets. The murder attempts were made by another Dallas gangster, the crude, illiterate "Benny the Cowboy" Binion. A retired police captain revealed the details of their rivalry to Ed Reid and Ovid Demaris, authors of *The Green Felt Jungle*, an exposé of Las Vegas crime. Binion was taking a 25% cut of Noble's crap games and wanted to up it to 40%. Noble refused, and the fireworks began. In a dramatic car chase, Binion's thugs splattered Noble's car with bullets, and one slug lodged in Noble's spine. Binion moved to Las Vegas, but the feud continued long-distance—Benny wanted to save face by nailing Noble with hired killers. Hollis "Lois" Green, a depraved murderer, succeeded in wounding Noble on his third attempt. The following year, in 1949, explosives were found attached to Noble's car, and he was soon shot again. Real tragedy struck when Noble's beloved wife, Mildred, was literally blown to bits by an explosion of nitrogelatin planted in his car. This loss unhinged Noble's mind—his prematurely gray hair (he was 41) turned snow-white, he lost 50 lb., and he began to drink heavily. Another shooting put him in the hospital, where he was fired upon from across the street. Noble's attempts at retaliation included equipping a plane with bombs to drop on Binion's home, but Noble was shot again before he could carry out his plan. Next, Noble miraculously survived the bombing of his business and a nitroglycerin explosion in one of his planes. Binion finally killed Herbert the same gruesome way he'd killed Mildred—with nitrogelatin hidden near Noble's mailbox. On Aug. 7, 1951, the top part of Noble's body was blown clear over a tree—there was nothing left of the bottom. The retired police captain who revealed all this commented, "I think Noble had more downright cold-blooded nerve than anyone I've ever known. He was ice water in a tight place."

6. DAVID HARGIS

The 23-year-old Marine drill instructor was murdered in San Diego on July 21, 1977—but it wasn't easy. His wife, 36-year-old Carol, took out an insurance policy on her husband to the tune of $20,000. Her accomplice was 26-year-old Natha Mary Depew. First, the ladies went to the woods to find a rattlesnake; instead they found a tarantula, which they made into a pie. David didn't really like the taste of tarantula pie, so he ate only a few pieces. The women then tried to (1) electrocute him in the shower, (2) poison him with lye, (3) run him over with a car, and (4) make him hallucinate while driving by putting amphetamines in his beer. Their plan to inject a bubble into his veins with a hypodermic needle—thereby causing a heart attack—failed when the needle broke. They considered putting bullets into the carburetor of David's truck, but Depew objected because she wanted to keep the truck after his death. Frustrated, they resorted to a more old-fashioned method—they beat him over the head with a 6½-lb. metal weight while he slept. This worked. The murderesses were apprehended while trying to dump the body into a river. Depew told the jury, "If it had not been for Carol I would never have touched him. . . . He looked so beautiful lying there sleeping."

Carol Hargis (L) tried several times to kill her husband.
Her efforts included baking him a tarantula pie.

365

7. BERNADETTE SCOTT

Between 1979 and 1981, Peter Scott, a British computer programmer, made seven attempts to kill his 23-year-old wife after taking out a $530,000 insurance policy on her. First he put mercury into a strawberry flan, but he put in so much mercury that it slithered out. Next, Peter served Bernadette a poisoned mackerel, but she survived her meal. Once in Yugoslavia and again in England, Peter tried to get her to sit on the edge of a cliff, but she refused. When Bernadette was in bed with chicken pox, her husband set the house on fire, but the blaze was discovered in time. His next arson attempt met with the same result. Bernadette had her first suspicion of foul play when Peter convinced her to stand in the middle of the street while he drove their car toward her, saying he wanted to "test the suspension." He accelerated, but he swerved away moments before impact. "I was going to run her over but I didn't have the courage," he later confessed to the police. Pleading guilty to several charges, he was jailed for life. The Scotts had been married for two years.

—A.W.

12 UNUSUAL ACCIDENTS

Our choice of the 15 most unusual accidents compiled by *Family Safety Magazine.*

1. In Smethwick, England, a machine got drunk. The machine, designed to give instant computer readouts of blood alcohol levels, started to give readings high enough to suggest drivers had more alcohol than blood in their bodies. Smethwick police officers found that the machine had become befuddled by alcohol fumes and sent it to central headquarters to dry out.

2.–3. A 1977 traffic jam occurred on a freeway connecting road near Los Angeles. The jam was caused by cars slowing down and skidding around in a pool of 250 gallons of chocolate syrup. The syrup had spilled from 50 drums that toppled off a truck carrying them for an ice cream company. In 1978, a similarly sticky situation occurred in Marietta, Ga. A truck overturned, spilled $10,000 worth of honey, and freed 28 million bees. It took 14 beekeepers to control the insects.

4. In Washington, D.C., Wage and Price Stability Council Director Barry Bosworth, trying to hold down prices and inflation, opposed a proposal to require lawn mower manufacturers to install devices to turn off mowers automatically when an operator releases the controls. Bosworth said the safety benefits didn't justify the increased cost. A few days later Bosworth cut a finger while trying to clear some grass from his still-running mower—exactly the kind of injury the safety device would have prevented.

5. Jake McKinney of Bakersfield, N.C., decided to step out of his camper one night for some fresh air. However, he forgot that the camper was traveling down the highway at 55 mph, with his son at the wheel. McKinney stepped right out into nothing and fell to the pavement but managed to get up and scramble out of the way of oncoming traffic. He suffered only minor cuts.

6. In Oswestry, England, expert pool player Stuart Russell leaned over the table at the Eagles Inn and took aim. He coughed, sending his two false front teeth flying into the corner pocket. When he attempted to retrieve them, his right arm got stuck in the pocket. Two police officers, six fire fighters, and some 50 customers tried to help. Finally, the tabletop was lifted, Russell's arm was released, and his teeth were recovered. He stuck them back in his mouth and continued the game, which he won.

7. After a 1980 overtime victory against the Detroit Lions, Chicago Bears defensive end Dan Hampton raced across the field to join his teammates in celebration. He got right in the middle of the pummeling, pounding, and patting. Hampton suffered a broken nose when someone smashed his face mask into it.

8. Robert P. Doherty—a Salem, Va., attorney—was sitting in his office waiting for a client who was charged with drunk driving. Doherty was thinking about the case when he heard a crash, and a car plowed right through his front door and stopped in the middle of the room. The driver of the car was none other than Doherty's client.

9. Young Brent Hartford went sleepwalking on the second floor of his family's new cabin and fell through a hole cut for a stovepipe. He landed in a tub of water which had been left heating on the stove below, thus scalding himself and sending a cascade of hot water across the floor. His father, Rex Hartford, came running—barefooted. While he howled and hopped on blistered feet, another son, Rex, Jr., rushed from his bedroom, fell down a flight of stairs, and broke his leg in three places. Peg Hartford went for help in the family pickup but got stuck in a snowbank. Eventually all three Hartford men made it to a Lander, Wy., hospital.

10. In Westwood, N.J., 500 motorcyclists demonstrated to head off legislation requiring that they wear helmets. Two of the bikers collided and were sent to the hospital—with head injuries.

11. In San Fernando, Calif., a 3-in. communications cable sagged so low over Mission Boulevard that it was snagged by the exhaust stack of a truck. The truck stretched the lead-covered, ½-mi.-long cable for 30 ft. The tension turned the cable into a slingshot and it sprang back, ripping through five blocks of telephone wires and whipping 30 cars, three traffic signals, two billboards, and a neon sign.

12. In a game in 1977 against Georgia, Wiley Peck, a center for the Mississippi State University basketball team, slam-dunked the ball for two points. It rocketed through the net, hit the floor, bounced back up, and struck him on the head. The blow knocked him unconscious for several minutes.

—T.D. & A.W.

18 HEALTH EXPERTS AND HOW THEY DIED

1. EDWARD BACH (1886–1936) Age at death: 50

A respected bacteriologist and homeopath, Bach was convinced that the underlying causes of illness always reflected abnormal mental or emotional states. He found remedies for these negative attitudes in 38 different wild flowers. When in the presence of any one of these healing plants, he experienced peace of mind. Mustard, for example, seemed to dispel gloom, and heather worked against feelings of loneliness. A month after his 50th birthday, Bach became so weak that he was confined to bed. Apparently he was unafraid of his impending death, for he believed that an important part of his work could be accomplished only after he had shed his physical body. He died quietly in his sleep.

2. ARNOLD EHRET (1866–1922) Age at death: 56

As a young man Ehret was beset by illnesses, including Bright's disease, a heart disorder, and bronchial weakness. He gradually regained his health by alternating between a fruit-based diet and periodic fasting, a regimen which he claimed rid the body of mucus—a substance he attributed to disease. Thus was born Ehret's Mucusless Diet Healing System. His career as a health lecturer came to an abrupt end after he delivered a successful speech in Los Angeles on Oct. 8, 1922. The man who had hiked thousands of miles to demonstrate his renewed strength and vigor slipped while stepping into the street and fell backward, hitting his head on the curb. He suffered a basal fracture of the skull and died within minutes, never having regained consciousness.

3. SYLVESTER GRAHAM (1794–1851) Age at death: 57

A clergyman and temperance leader, Graham believed that good health could be achieved through a strict regime which included cold showers, daily exercise, and a vegetarian diet. In 1847 he spoke to an audience in Boston and triggered a near riot by butchers and bakers who were angered by his advocacy of vegetarianism and homemade bread. He was deeply shaken by the attack, and his health began to decline. Treatment with stimulants, mineral water, and tepid baths proved to be of no lasting help, and he died broken in body and spirit. He is remembered today chiefly for his creation of the Graham cracker, though the present-day commercial product—containing bleached flour, sugar, and preservatives—would have horrified him.

4. EUGENE SANDOW (1867–1925) Age at death: 58

Through the application of scientific methods of muscle development, Sandow transformed himself from a weak youth into the "world's strongest man," as show-business promoter Florenz Ziegfeld billed him at the 1893 World's Columbian Exposition in Chicago. In 1911, Sandow was appointed professor of physical culture to King George V. However, Sandow's primary concern was to convince the average man that anyone could achieve strength and vigor by exercising for as little as 20 minutes a day. The strong man pushed himself beyond even his immense capacities when, without any assistance, he lifted a car out of a ditch after an accident. He suffered a severe strain and died soon afterward from a burst blood vessel in the brain.

Eugene Sandow.

5. PHILIP HANDLER (1917–1982) Age at death: 64

Handler, a former head of the National Academy of Sciences, was an internationally recognized authority on the connection between nutrition and disease. Principal among his discoveries was the link between vitamin-B deficiency and pellagra, a disease common among people who eat a corn-based diet. Handler died of cancer complicated by pneumonia.

6. ÉMILE COUÉ (1857–1926) Age at death: 69

Trained as a pharmacist, Coué became interested in hypnotism and developed a health treatment based on autosuggestion. He told his patients that their health would improve dramatically if, morning and evening, they would repeat faithfully: "Every day and in every way, I am becoming better and better." Prior to W.W. I, an estimated 40,000 patients flocked to his clinic each year, and Coué claimed a 97% success rate. Coué kept up a demanding schedule. After one of his lecture tours he returned to his home in Nancy, France, and complained of exhaustion. He died there of heart failure.

7. ADELLE DAVIS (1904–1974) Age at death: 70

"You are what you eat," claimed Davis, the well-known American nutritionist who advocated a natural diet rich in fresh fruits and vegetables along with large doses of vitamins. When she was diagnosed as having bone cancer at age 69, her first reaction was disbelief. "I thought this was for people who drink soft drinks, who eat white bread, who eat refined sugar, and so on," she said. Eventually she came to accept her illness as a delayed reaction to the "junk food" eating habits she had acquired in college and which had lasted until the 1950s. Her hope was that those who had faith in her work would not be disheartened by her fatal illness.

8. MAX BIRCHER-BENNER (1867–1939) Age at death: 71

One of the first exponents of proper nutrition, Bircher-Benner advocated the ingestion of raw fruits and vegetables—"living" food. He also believed that a patient's mind played an important role in the cause of illness and that psychological as well as physical treatment was necessary to cure disease. A premature baby, Bircher-Benner had been born with a weak heart which doctors said would prevent him from ever living a normal life. Through vigorous physical exercise and careful diet he had attained remarkable health as an adult, but the coronary weakness was not entirely overcome. On Jan. 24, 1939, he died from a ruptured heart vessel.

9. ÉLIE METCHNIKOFF (1845–1916) Age at death: 71

Through extensive longevity research, the Nobel Prize-winning bacteriologist concluded that the human body was meant to last 100 to 150 years. He became known particularly for his "Sour Milk Cure," in which he advocated the consumption of yogurt to cleanse the large intestine. In addition, he discovered a bacterium (found only in the intestines of dogs) which he believed could further retard the aging process—and he proceeded to inoculate himself with the microbe. Shortly before his death from heart disease, Metchnikoff detailed in his diary the reasons for his untimely demise: "intense and precocious activities, fretful character, nervous temperament, and tardy start on a sensible regime."

10. J. I. RODALE (1899–1971) Age at death: 72

The head of a multimillion-dollar publishing business, Rodale promulgated his belief in "organic food" (food free from chemicals and artificial additives) supplemented by natural vitamins through his popular magazines *Organic Gardening* and *Prevention*. He was at the height of his fame when he appeared on *The Dick Cavett Show* on June 9, 1971. After describing the dangers of milk, wheat, and sugar, Rodale proceeded to say, "I'm so healthy that I expect to live on and on." Shortly after the conclusion of the interview, Rodale slumped in his chair, victim of a fatal heart attack.

11. SEBASTIAN KNEIPP (1821–1897) Age at death: 76

As a young seminary student, Kneipp cured himself of an attack of nervous prostration through hydrotherapy. When he became a priest he continued his cold-water cures. Eventually he abandoned his priestly duties altogether to give advice to as many as 500 patients a day. The empress of Austria and Pope Leo XIII, were among those who consulted him. Kneipp believed that the application of cold water—plus exercise, fresh air, sunshine, and walking barefoot over grass and through snow—could cure virtually any mental or physical disorder. An inflammation of his lungs, which had been weak since childhood, resulted in his death.

12. FRANZ MESMER (1734–1815) Age at death: 80

Mesmer believed that a person became ill when his "animal magnetism" was out of balance. To correct this condition, the Viennese doctor made use of magnets and held séancelike therapeutic sessions for his patients. Hounded out of Vienna on charges of practicing magic, Mesmer moved to Paris, where a royal commission (whose members included Benjamin Franklin and Antoine Lavoisier) concluded that Mesmer's "cures" were due solely to his patients' imaginations. Mesmer was convinced that he would die in his 81st year, as a Gypsy woman had foretold. Her prediction came true two months before his 81st birthday, when he succumbed to an extremely painful bladder condition that had troubled him for years.

13. D. C. JARVIS (1881–1966) Age at death: 85

This country doctor became an overnight sensation in 1958 with the publication of *Folk Medicine: A Vermont Doctor's Guide to Good Health*. Part of his appeal derived from the simplicity of his remedies. For example, he suggested that one could stay healthy through a daily dose of two teaspoons each of honey and apple cider vinegar in a glass of water. Jarvis had many supporters, in spite of a Harvard professor's comment that "This claptrap is strictly for those gullible birds stung by the honey bee." He died in a nursing home in Vermont after suffering a cerebral hemorrhage.

14. F. MATTHIAS ALEXANDER (1869–1955) Age at death: 86

As a young actor Alexander solved the problem of losing his voice during performances by paying careful attention to how he held his head

371

and used his throat muscles. From this experience he developed the Alexander technique, a system which teaches how to use the body to achieve optimum functioning. His students included George Bernard Shaw, Aldous Huxley, and John Dewey. In 1947 Alexander injured himself in a fall and then suffered a stroke which paralyzed his left side. He recovered quickly and was soon teaching again, amazing his students with his suppleness and agility. He remained active for eight more years until, after a day at the races, he caught a chill and died.

15. BERNARR MACFADDEN (1868–1955) Age at death: 87

Billing himself as a kinestherapist, Macfadden ran a chain of health food restaurants and sanitariums which pushed his program of exercise, fresh air, personal hygiene, and wholesome diet. He also published the popular but controversial magazine *Physical Culture*, which featured photos of men and women posing nearly naked—considered obscene by some in the early 20th century. Throughout his long life Macfadden was almost always in the news for one reason or another—his marriages, his attacks on the medical establishment, or his founding of a new religion, the Cosmotarian Fellowship. Macfadden celebrated his 83rd birthday by parachuting 2,500 ft. into the Hudson River. The master showman finally succumbed to a jaundice attack which he had tried unsuccessfully to combat through fasting.

16. SAMUEL HAHNEMANN (1755–1843) Age at death: 88

A German physician at crosscurrents with the medical beliefs of his day, Hahnemann developed the system of homeopathy. Its basic tenet is that a drug which produces symptoms of illness in a healthy person will cure a sick person who exhibits those symptoms, when that drug is administered in minute doses. Hahnemann died from an inflammation of the bronchial tubes, which had plagued him for 20 years. Although he had come to terms with death ("My earthly shell is worn out," he stated), his wife was less accepting of the inevitable. She kept his embalmed corpse with her for nine days before giving it up for burial.

17. MARY BAKER EDDY (1821–1910) Age at death: 89

Eddy founded the Christian Science religion after experiencing what she believed to be Christ's method of healing. At the time, she was suffering the effects of a serious fall on the ice. She taught that healing is accomplished not by drugs or medicines but through the affirmation of spiritual truth. Although Eddy enjoyed a remarkably active old age, when her health began to fail she was convinced that it was due to Malicious Animal Magnetism engendered by her enemies. The official verdict was that she died from "natural causes" after a brief bout of pneumonia. The undertaker who examined the corpse stated: "I do not remember having found the body of a person of such advanced age in so good a physical condition."

18. J. H. KELLOGG (1852–1943) Age at death: 91

A Seventh-Day Adventist and lifelong vegetarian, Dr. Kellogg ran a sanitarium in Battle Creek, Mich., where he made his patients' diets more palatable by devising new vegetarian products. His brother Will marketed some of these products, including the now famous Kellogg's cornflakes. (Another breakfast-food magnate, C. W. Post, was one of Kellogg's patients.) J. H. Kellogg died from pneumonia shortly after waging a successful court battle to keep the Adventists from assuming control of his sanitarium.

—F.B.

5-YEAR RELATIVE SURVIVAL RATES FOR 10 TYPES OF CANCER

In 1980, the National Cancer Institute published the five-year survival rate for both black and white cancer patients diagnosed between 1970 and 1973. This rate is defined as the probability of escaping death from cancer for five years following its diagnosis. The listing for whites and blacks gives survival rates, where appropriate, for males and females combined.

	Percent White	Percent Black
1. Endometrium (uterine lining)	81	44
2. Breast (females only)	68	51
3. Cervix	64	61
4. Prostate	63	55
5. Bladder	61	35
6. Colon	49	37
7. Rectum	45	30
8. Stomach	13	13
9. Lung	10	7
10. Pancreas	1	2

SOURCE: *Cancer Patient Survival Experience.* U.S. Department of Health and Human Services, June, 1980.

12 FAMOUS PEOPLE WHO HAD NIEHANS THERAPY

Dr. Paul Niehans (1882–1971) was already a famous Swiss surgeon in 1927, the year he began testing regenerative therapy on human beings. In the belief that tissue from a young organ could revitalize a diseased organ, he grafted parathyroid tissue from a calf onto the parathyroid of a young male dwarf who, Niehans reported, grew 14 in. taller after the treatment. In 1931, Niehans substituted cell injections for tissue grafts. He prepared solutions from the ground-up organs of a fetal lamb taken by Cesarean section from the womb of a black sheep. The mixture was then injected into the buttocks of the patient—if he had liver problems he received liver cells, if he had thyroid problems he got thyroid cells. Niehans claimed success against a wide range of diseases, including the ravages of old age, anemia, excessive perspiration, arteriosclerosis, ulcers, and even mongolism.

Today, other physicians who have entered the field are being well paid by clients who submit to an estimated 300,000 individual injections yearly. Most patients declare that the therapy relieves their major complaints and makes them more youthful and energetic. Many scientists assert that cell therapy is quackery and that any "cure" is in the mind. In spite of the debate, a lot of famous people have had cell therapy. Here is a list of just a few.

1. KONRAD ADENAUER (1876–1967)

The former West German chancellor received cell therapy injections about once a year beginning in 1958, though it was not made public. He was 91 at the time of his death.

2. GEORGES BRAQUE (1882–1963)

Braque, the 75-year-old father of abstract art, reportedly visited the Niehans clinic in 1957. He lived another six years and, in 1961, was the first living artist to have his works displayed in the Louvre.

3. WINSTON CHURCHILL (1874–1965)

Though Churchill received three or perhaps four cell treatments between 1953 and 1955, it was not at the hands of Dr. Niehans. Patrick McGrady, author of *The Youth Doctors*, says some believe it was because Niehans's patients were not allowed to smoke or drink after the treatments and that Churchill was unwilling to give up those pleasures. But it may also have been that Niehans, nephew of Kaiser Wilhelm II of Germany, refused to treat the British leader who was responsible for bombing German cities in W.W. II. Churchill died at the age of 90.

4. MARLENE DIETRICH (1901–   )

The famous German-born actress sought out cell therapy three times during the 1960s and 1970s in order to overcome the stresses and strains of her work.

5.–6. LILLIAN GISH (1896–   ) and DOROTHY GISH (1898–1968)

On Jan. 15, 1966, *Vogue* magazine quoted actress Lillian Gish as saying that she thought the Niehans injections, which she and her sister had received in the early 1960s, were "little short of miraculous." Still, Dorothy died at 70. But Lillian, who has had at least two treatment series, celebrated her 86th birthday in October, 1982.

7. GAYELORD HAUSER (1895–   )

Author and nutritionist Gayelord Hauser discovered cell therapy when he was 84. He was so impressed with the treatment that he held a reception for Dr. Claus Martin, a cell therapist who runs a clinic in Germany, in order to spread the word among Americans. (The therapy is illegal in the U.S.) Hauser, who was 87 in May, 1982, advises patients at Martin's clinic about special diets and weight-loss menus.

8.–9. W. SOMERSET MAUGHAM (1874–1965) and ALAN SEARLE (1904?–   )

When the author was 64 and his secretary was about 34, they underwent Niehans's cell therapy together—Maugham because he was slowing down, Searle because he had psoriasis. Both men considered the therapy successful, with the added bonus of renewed sexual vigor. Maugham had the treatments again when he was 84 and 88. He died at 91. (Maugham's brother, who did not have cell therapy, also died at 91.)

10. POPE PIUS XII (1876–1958)

Niehans probably received more publicity for treating this Roman Catholic pontiff than for any other single patient. Niehans was called to the Vatican to treat Pius XII in 1954 for exhaustion, hiccups (caused by a hiatus hernia), and vomiting. The pope lived another four years after the treatment, dying when he was 82.

11. GLORIA SWANSON (1899–   )

American film star Gloria Swanson claims to have had cell injections once as part of her research on an article. She was not impressed with the therapy—it gave her a headache. Swanson was 83 in March, 1982. She insists that the secret of staying young is eating wholesome, natural foods.

12. HENRY A. WALLACE (1888–1965)

Late in life, Wallace—who was an editor, an author, and the vice-president of the U.S. from 1941 to 1945—developed amyotrophic lateral sclerosis (also known as Lou Gehrig's disease). There is no known cure for this affliction, which destroys the central nervous system, yet in the months before his death at the age of 77, Wallace tried several experimental treatments, including cell therapy.

—V.S.

14 BODY PARTS NAMED AFTER PEOPLE OF DIFFERENT NATIONALITIES

1. BUNDLE OF HIS (German)

A group of modified muscle fibers of the heart which serve to conduct electrical impulses from the atrium through the ventricles. Named after physician Wilhelm His, Jr. (1863–1934).

2. CIRCLE OF WILLIS (English)

Arteries of the brain which connect the principal vessels supplying blood to the cerebrum. Named after Thomas Willis, physician (1621–1675).

3. DOUGLAS'S CUL-DE-SAC (Scottish)

Peritoneal fold between the uterus and the rectum. Named after anatomist James Douglas (1675–1742).

4. GERDY'S FIBERS (French)

A ligament collection found in the fingers. Named after surgeon Pierre N. Gerdy (1797–1856).

5. GEROTA CAPSULE (Romanian)

The perineal fascia. Named after anatomist Dumitru Gerota (1867–1939).

6. HASNER'S FOLD (Czech)

A fold of mucous membrane at the opening of the nasolacrimal duct. Named after ophthalmologist Joseph R. Hasner (1819–1892).

7. HOUSTON'S MUSCLE (Irish)

Portion of the muscular structure of the penis. Named after surgeon John Houston (1802–1845).

8. McBURNEY'S POINT (American)

A point of severe tenderness in cases of acute appendicitis—between the umbilicus and the top of the hip bone. Named after surgeon Charles McBurney (1845–1913).

9. MOLL'S GLAND (Dutch)

Modified sweat glands near the eyes. Named after oculist Jacob A. Moll (1821–1914).

10. PEYER'S PATCHES (Swiss)

Nodules of lymphatic tissue found in the ileum of the small intestine. Named after anatomist Johann K. Peyer (1653–1712).

11. PRUSSAK'S SPACE (Russian)

A tiny space in the middle ear. Named after otologist Alexander Prussak (1839–1897).

12. PURKINJE CELLS (Bohemian)

Large nerve cells situated in the cerebellum. Named after physiologist Johannes E. Purkinje (1787–1869).

13. VON EBNER'S GLAND (Austrian)

Glands of the tongue which secrete a watery fluid. Named after histologist A. G. von Ebner (1842–1925).

14. WORMIAN BONES (Danish)

Small, irregular bones of the cranium. Named after anatomist Ole Worm (1588–1654).

—K.A.M.

8 PEOPLE WHO CARRIED BULLETS IN THEIR BODIES

1. ANDREW JACKSON

In 1806, the future president of the U.S. fought a duel with Charles Dickinson, who had made disparaging remarks about Mrs. Jackson. Dickinson got off the first shot and his ounce ball struck Jackson in the left breast. Jackson staggered but remained on his feet and with deliberate aim wounded Dickinson fatally. Jackson carried Dickinson's lead ball the rest of his life, since it was lodged too close to his heart to be removed.

2. CHARLES B. NELSON

In 1897 Nelson, a Cadillac, Mich., resident, was shot in the chest as he was sitting with a girl in a Chicago park. He was at first pronounced dead by his doctors, but he lived and thrived for many years thereafter, carrying a bullet in his heart. Later he fell from the top of a high wagon and landed on his head, and his physicians feared the sudden shock might cause the bullet to move and kill him, but once again he survived. A turn-of-the-century newspaper account reported he had returned to Chicago in an attempt to discover who had shot him and why. There is no indication that he succeeded in his quest, but as the glowing report happily informed readers, "Nelson suffered no inconvenience" from the bullet in his body.

377

3. FREDERICK GILMER BONFILS

In 1900, the fiery co-owner of the *Denver Post* was shot twice by an irate lawyer. One bullet entered Bonfils's chest, grazing his heart, and the other struck his shoulder, plowing upward to lodge near his throat. The position of the second bullet made removal inadvisable, and as a result Bonfils had to give up smoking, which he greatly enjoyed. Thereafter visitors were often treated to a bizarre sight in the city room of the *Post*. As Bonfils sat at his desk, an employee would puff on a cigarette and blow smoke in his face. This way he could at least enjoy the odor of tobacco.

4. LILY DEBUSSY

In 1904, Lily, the wife of Claude Debussy, saw her four-year marriage disintegrating as the womanizing composer took up with a married woman who had deserted her husband. Lily sent Debussy a suicide note and then shot herself twice, once in the breast and once in the groin. When Debussy returned home he found his wife badly wounded, but he left her to recover by herself. Lily carried the bullet in her breast, as well as the love she still felt for Debussy, the rest of her life.

5. THEODORE ROOSEVELT

Teddy, second U.S. president to carry a bullet permanently, was shot by John F. Schrank in October, 1912, while campaigning in Milwaukee, Wis., during his unsuccessful Bull Moose campaign for the presidency. Schrank, a New York bartender who had stalked Roosevelt for months, said he had been commanded to kill him by the ghost of William McKinley. The .38 bullet, fired at point-blank range, struck Roosevelt's chest and would have penetrated his heart had it not been deflected by his metal eyeglass case and the folded multipage speech tucked in his inside coat pocket. Roosevelt placed a handkerchief over his bleeding wound and insisted on going to the auditorium where he was to deliver his speech. Afterward, he was taken to a hospital, where it was determined that the bullet threatened no vital organ, and the doctors decided to leave it alone. Roosevelt made a complete recovery and lived another seven years, not troubled in the least by the bullet.

6. RICHARD DWYER

U.S. diplomat Dwyer, second in command at the U.S. embassy in Guyana in 1977, was with U.S. Rep. Leo J. Ryan of California when the congressman and four other Americans were shot to death by members of cult leader Jim Jones's Peoples Temple. Dwyer himself still carries a bullet at the base of his spine.

7. CLEVELAND DAVIS

In 1978, this ex-con was arrested after his car crashed several blocks from where two police officers had been killed in a Brooklyn shootout with an unknown assailant. Davis was bleeding from a bullet wound in his leg, but he denied having anything to do with the murders. The district attorney wanted the bullet removed from Davis's leg to see if it came from the gun of either murder victim. However, Davis refused to permit such an operation, and an appeals court upheld his refusal, since such surgery would be "a major intrusion" upon him.

8. ILIJA SESUM

In 1981, Sesum, a 90-year-old Yugoslav living in a village north of Belgrade, coughed up a rifle bullet that he had carried since 1916. He had been wounded in a battle on the Italian-Austrian frontier during W.W. I.

—C.S.

13 CHRONIC HEADACHE SUFFERERS

1. CAROLUS LINNAEUS (1707–1778), Swedish botanist

Linnaeus had frequent migraines for 20 years, in midlife. They were sometimes triggered by cold weather or strong winds and often by alcohol, even in small amounts. Sour wine was particularly dangerous for Linnaeus, and a glass of sloe gin produced devastating effects. The worst triggers of all were anger, disappointment, or excitement. Once, a student brought the botanist a jar containing a plant laden with precious insects from Surinam. Linnaeus's gardener, not aware of the importance of the insects, cleaned the plant and washed them away. The insects died, and Linnaeus had one of the worst headaches of his life. Linnaeus believed that the sedentary life of scholars made them susceptible to migraines and attributed his own improvement in later life to drinking fresh spring water and exercising in the morning.

2. THOMAS JEFFERSON (1743–1826), 3rd president of the U.S.

"They came on every day at sunrise and never left till sunset," said Jefferson of his headaches, which sometimes lasted six weeks. Associated with inner conflict and repressed anger, they occurred through most of his life at seven- or eight-year intervals but ceased after he left the presidency. Unlike most migraine victims, Jefferson forced himself to work despite the pain.

3. ULYSSES S. GRANT (1822–1885), 18th president of the U.S.

Grant got migraines every three or four weeks. His wife, Julia, recalled in her memoirs those days when he would return from his office saying, "Oh, do not ask me to speak. I have a dreadful headache." Then she would go through the ritual of ministering to him: a dark room, a hot mustard footbath, one of her "little pills"—until he finally slept. In an hour or two he would wake refreshed, ready for a cigar. When Julia expected to be commended for curing him "nicely and quickly, he was ungracious enough to laugh and say: 'You did not cure me. Why, I got well myself, did I not?'" For two days before the climax of the Civil War, as Grant rode toward Appomattox, he suffered from a vicious migraine, which no amount of mustard plasters would relieve. The instant he read General Lee's note of surrender, his headache completely disappeared.

4. ALFRED NOBEL (1833–1896), Swedish inventor and manufacturer and founder of the Nobel Prizes

Nobel's work caused him immense stress, often resulting in headaches so terrible that he had to write with his head wrapped in wet towels. When the pain was too great, he put aside his serious work and wrote experimental literary essays and parodies for relief. Sometimes, in periods of extreme suffering, he would disappear for weeks on end. His distressed friends and assistants would eventually find that he had returned to his laboratory wearing dark glasses and wet towels, recovering from what he called his "visits from the spirits of Niflheim."

5. ALEXANDER GRAHAM BELL (1847–1922), U.S. inventor

Bell had headaches all his life, sometimes lasting as long as a week when he was "worn out with work and anxiety." As a boy, he had attacks of what his mother called "musical fever." Listening to music affected him so deeply he couldn't sleep, leaving him with a headache in the morning. In later life, overwork and stress gave him insomnia, and the resultant morning suffering. His mother suggested cures: Keep off pickles, try a little beer, and put cold water on your eyes. Aleck chose "plenty of Porter or Portwine every day, as a kind of medicinal course." Even when Bell slept soundly, a morning awakening before 9:00 A.M. gave him a headache; if he had an early morning appointment, he preferred to stay up all night.

6. GUY DE MAUPASSANT (1850–1893), French writer

De Maupassant lived for years with a galaxy of agonizing symptoms caused by syphilis; migraine was one of them. Few doctors recognized this venereal disease in the 1800s, and Guy sought relief—to no avail—in spas, morphine, sunbathing, and endless "cures." The agony of the headaches or the effects of painkilling drugs halted his work for long periods. He wrote to a friend, "My body is strong but my head is worse than ever. There are days when I long to stick a bullet in it." And later, "My headaches are so agonizing that I clasp my head between my hands and it feels like a death's head." Syphilis, so easily cured today, killed the brilliant author at the age of 43.

7. GEORGE BERNARD SHAW (1856–1950), Irish playwright

Shaw became a vegetarian for two reasons: to emulate the poet Shelley and to cure himself of the monthly headaches that left him surprised to be alive after each bout. His various regimes helped but never fully cured him. Active as his life was, Shaw felt he needed more exercise to work off the protein he consumed. In 1918 he wrote, "Probably the secret of the sedentary life—the no-exercise life—is meat, tea, and alcohol whenever you feel low. . . . I prefer to be really alive; but the penalty is that I want an hour and a half of navvying every day to work off all my steam; and society is organized to suit the boozy people. . . . The consequence is that the steam accumulates; gets stale and poisonous; and finally explodes about once a month in a devastating headache. No avoidance of uric acid foods helps me in the least." However, at the age of 70, Shaw switched from the staples of his diet—beans, lentils, and macaroni—to fresh fruits and vegetables and succeeded in making his last 24 years more comfortable.

8. SIGMUND FREUD (1856–1939), Austrian founder of psychoanalysis

Freud suffered from migraine attacks all his life, usually accompanied by sinusitis. He took only mild painkillers, such as aspirin, for the headaches, though for the nasal problems he often applied cocaine. Freud's friend and physician for a decade, Wilhelm Fliess, suffered from exactly the same ailments, and the two men exchanged many letters on the subjects of their noses and heads. One cause of Freud's headaches was the *Föhn*—a warm, dry wind which blows down the slopes of the Alps and dramatically changes the atmospheric pressure and temperature. During the 1890s, Freud related migraines largely to sexual deprivation. This was the same period when he and his wife were trying to avoid adding to their brood of six children, and Freud was writing with interest on the subject of "anxiety neurosis" caused by "coitus interruptus." Eventually, Freud's headaches decreased in number as he freed himself of many of his neuroses through careful self-analysis—but he never ceased to suffer on the days of the *Föhn*.

9. WOODROW WILSON (1856–1924), 28th president of the U.S.

"I am too intense," wrote Woodrow Wilson. The nervous, hardworking Wilson began having his "ominous headaches"—which were accompanied by severe indigestion—as a child. His sickliness prevented his parents from sending him to school, and he didn't learn to read until he was 11. Throughout his life, despite his wife's tender ministrations and neck massages, his special diets, fasting, and a variety of medicines, Wilson never found a cure. In 1932, Sigmund Freud coauthored a psychological biography of Wilson. The book, not published until 1967, chronicles 14 periods of physical breakdown during the course of Wilson's life, during which his headaches, nervousness, and indigestion completely dominated his life. Freud concluded that "the conflict between his femininity and his exalted Super-Ego which demanded that he should be all masculinity" caused Wilson's health crises.

10. UPTON SINCLAIR (1878–1968), U.S. writer and reformer

The author of *The Jungle* spent 40 years of his life seeking the cause of his migraine torment. He tried to cure himself with a beef diet, a macrobiotic diet, and fasting, all to no avail. It was not until he was in his late 70s that he found a diet that worked. It consisted basically of brown rice, fresh fruit, and celery. He ate no wheat or meat.

11. PRINCESS MARGARET (1930–   )

Princess Margaret has suffered migraines for most of her life and is a patron of the British Migraine Trust. James Brough, author of *Margaret: The Tragic Princess,* advances the theory that she is a victim of hereditary porphyria, an incurable illness with a myriad of painful symptoms, among them migraine. Brough believes that the insanity of Margaret's ancestor King George III was caused by severe porphyria. Doctors prescribed a diet of frequent high-carbohydrate snacks, which combats low blood sugar, as a treatment for Margaret's headaches. Margaret was criticized by fashionable London society for "letting herself go" when she gained weight on this regime.

Kareem Abdul-Jabbar described one of his excruciating migraine
headaches by saying, "It felt like the Alien was inside my head,
trying to get out my eyes."

12. JOAN DIDION (1934–   ), U.S. writer

In 1968, Didion wrote an essay called "In Bed," an eloquent account of her life as a victim of hereditary migraine. She had her first
migraine at the age of eight, during a school fire drill. Her attacks come
three to five times a month, and without migraine-preventive drugs, she

wrote, "I would be able to function perhaps one day in four." Didion's husband, writer John Gregory Dunne, also has migraines, "which is unfortunate for him but fortunate for me: perhaps nothing so tends to prolong an attack as the accusing eye of someone who has never had a headache. 'Why not take a couple of aspirin,' the unafflicted will say from the doorway, or 'I'd have a headache, too, spending a beautiful day like this inside with all the shades drawn.' All of us who have migraine suffer not only from the attacks themselves but from this common conviction that we are perversely refusing to cure ourselves by taking a couple of aspirin. . . . That no one dies of migraine seems, to someone deep into an attack, an ambiguous blessing."

13. KAREEM ABDUL-JABBAR (1947–   ), U.S. basketball player

In 1980, during a Lakers 16-game winning streak, it was announced over the Los Angeles Forum's public-address system that Kareem Abdul-Jabbar would not be able to play that day due to a migraine headache. Without their star center, the team was barely maintaining a lead over Houston when Abdul-Jabbar appeared and strode onto the court. The Lakers won. Afterward, Kareem told the press, "I haven't had a migraine bad enough to make me miss a game in two years. . . . The pain was so bad this morning, I was crying. I couldn't move. I had to lie in a dark room in total silence. You know what it felt like? It felt like the Alien was inside my head, trying to get out my eyes." Abdul-Jabbar's headaches tend to be seasonal, coming between February and June, and sometimes they send him to the hospital. Also, they have a history of descending during periods of extreme stress—in 1973, when one of his friends was murdered; in 1977, when he was surrounded by political turmoil; and in 1980, while he was proceeding with a painful divorce.

—A.W.

6 FAMOUS FAINTERS

1. CHARLES DARWIN (1809–1882)

Darwin, the great naturalist who postulated the survival of the fittest in his *Origin of Species,* was a chronic invalid for the last 40 years of his life and was prone to fainting spells. Numerous psychological theories have been given to explain Darwin's poor health. Recent findings reveal, however, that he probably suffered from Chagas's disease contracted while he was traveling in South America in 1835. He was bitten by a bug (*Triatoma infestans*) that carries trypanosome, which remains in the blood many years after infection. The disease was not discovered until 1909.

2. FRANZ LISZT (1811–1886)

The greatest bravura pianist of all time, Liszt began a concert by tossing his long blond hair and throwing his green gloves to the floor. Women worshiped him, fought over him, and collapsed in orgasmic swoons (lisztomania, it was called) while he played. The pianist, who since childhood was subject to mild cataleptic seizures, himself fainted at least once in public, at the climax of a concert in Paris.

3. CHARLES DICKENS (1812–1870)

In addition to his skill as a writer, Dickens was a consummate actor whose dramatic public readings from his novels were highly celebrated. During his reading tours of Britain—and his 1867 tour of the U.S.—he occasionally worked himself up to such a pitch of excitement while performing that he collapsed in a faint. Some considered these episodes a form of demonic possession; others attributed them to the declining state of the novelist's health.

4. J. P. MORGAN (1837–1913)

After recovering from a severe case of inflammatory rheumatism at age 15, Pierpont Morgan became subject to strange fainting fits, probably of nervous origin. Later in life, particularly when he faced monetary setbacks on Wall Street, the financier suffered similar nervous collapses.

5. SIGMUND FREUD (1856–1939)

The founder of psychoanalysis fainted on several highly significant (that is, Freudian) occasions. Most of the incidents involved male colleagues, prompting a self-diagnosis of repressed homosexual feelings. In 1909 and again in 1912, Freud fainted during arguments with Carl Jung, his heir apparent. After these disputes about the child's (Jung's) wish for the death of the father (Freud), the two men ended their friendship. Jung later remarked: "Just like a woman. Confront her with a disagreeable truth, she faints."ˋ

6. MARIE CURIE (1867–1934)

As a student in Paris, Marie Curie was so poor and so absorbed in her scientific studies that she nearly starved to death. Many of her meals consisted of nothing more than buttered bread and tea. After falling in a faint several times, the future Nobel Prize winner (for her work on radioactivity) was forced to concede that the human body cannot live on air alone.

—C.D.

14 PERSONS WHO SUFFERED FROM SEVERE DEPRESSION

1. LOUISA MAY ALCOTT (1832–1888)

As a child, Louisa May Alcott was prone to periods of hyperactivity followed by long days of depression and listlessness. It was to be a recurrent pattern for her—one moment working toward a bright future, and the next moment contemplating suicide. She served for a time as a nurse during the Civil War, until she became ill with typhoid pneumonia and was treated with massive doses of calomel, a side effect of which was acute mercury poisoning. She lost her hair, and her mouth was full of sores. She had richly Gothic nightmares and hallucinations in which a cruel Spaniard in black velvet would leap Zorro-like through her bedroom window at night and urge her, "Lie still, my dear." Although she recovered to some degree from her wartime illness and the horrendous cure, she remained a tormented and depressed soul even as she penned such heartwarming novels as *Little Women* (1868).

2. EDWIN "BUZZ" ALDRIN (1930–   )

As pilot of Apollo 11's lunar module—"Eagle"—Aldrin was the second man to set foot on the moon. Getting back to earth, however, turned out to be a much easier task than getting his feet back on the ground psychologically. After his historic space flight, Aldrin slowly began to sink into a state of severe depression, a condition that was difficult to rationalize in the light of his *Life* magazine image as an astronaut. "We looked to be happy, open-faced, well-adjusted people," he said, "with no skeletons in the closet." Through a combination of psychiatric therapy, psychological exercises, and antidepressant drugs, he gradually emerged from his dark mental state. Aldrin candidly reveals the details of his illness and recovery in his book *Return to Earth* (1973).

3. CLARA BARTON (1821–1912)

Extremely timid as a child, Barton, the founder of the American Red Cross, confessed in her diary that she experienced periodic low moods, most taking place during hiatuses in her busy life. One of these occurred in April, 1864. Fresh from the battlefields of the South, where she had patched together many a wounded soldier left for dead, Miss Barton tried to rest up in Washington but found herself sinking into depression. Despite her attempts to keep busy—cleaning up her rooms, shopping for groceries, fussing with her dark hair, or strolling through the nation's capital on the arm of John Brown's brother Frederick—nothing boosted her spirits. On April 18, she wrote of "the old temptation to go from all the world," and predicted, erroneously as it turned out, that suicide would one day be her fate.

4. CHARLES BAUDELAIRE (1821–1867)

This great French poet received virtually no critical recognition in his lifetime and no financial success. He contracted syphilis in his youth, and its debilitating effects were compounded by worry over money, a tortured relationship with his mother and stepfather, an obscenity trial which he lost, and a long, unhappy love affair. At 24, Baudelaire made a halfhearted suicide attempt, leaving a note which read, "I *kill* myself without unhappiness. . . . I am killing myself because I cannot live anymore, because I find that the tedium of going to sleep and the tedium of waking up are intolerable. I am killing myself because I am useless to others and *dangerous to myself.*" Perhaps only work kept Baudelaire alive for 22 more years. Among his greatest achievements were the first French translations of the writings of Edgar Allan Poe—a kindred spirit in genius and suffering. Baudelaire died at 46 in his mother's arms, a smile on his face.

5. ROBERT BURTON (1577–1640)

Plagued throughout his life with chronic depression, this English scholar began writing *The Anatomy of Melancholy* as a form of therapy. He produced five editions of *Melancholy* during his lifetime, examining in detail every facet of his affliction. As an Oxford librarian, an Anglican churchman, and a lifelong bachelor, Burton led a reclusive and colorless life, which no doubt contributed to his dour state of mind. His contention that "all the world is melancholy or mad" was a bold assumption from a man who limited himself to a solitary existence.

6. FLETCHER CHRISTIAN (1764–1793)

The handsome British naval officer had frequent lapses into brief "black moods" even before he cast Captain Bligh adrift from the *Bounty* in 1789. Just hours prior to the famous mutiny, Christian was so depressed that he determined to jump ship using a makeshift raft, but his fellow crewmen talked him out of it. Unlike the other mutineers, he could not enjoy his newly won freedom from the oppressive rule of William Bligh. Instead, the sight of his former captain adrift in a puny boat—facing what seemed to be certain death—sank Christian's spirits to a new low. These frequent bouts of depression followed him to his Pitcairn Island refuge. There, as the mutineers fell to squabbling among themselves, Christian often went off alone, for days at a time, to brood.

7. WINSTON CHURCHILL (1874–1965)

Throughout his life, Britain's greatest 20th-century prime minister confronted what he called his "Black Dog" of gloom and despair. Churchill confided to Lord Charles Moran, his physician, that as a young back-bencher in the House of Commons he had spent a hellish two or three years lost in the doldrums. Although talking things over with his wife helped a bit, he often was so depressed that he refused to stand near the edge of a train platform or a ship deck for fear that in an acute moment of despair he might jump.

8. FËDOR DOSTOEVSKI (1821–1881)

An epileptic, the Russian author was a bundle of raw nerves, phobias, and ills, both real and imagined. Usually he was in a sullen mood. The specter of imminent death haunted him constantly. He was so terrified of being buried alive that, when sleeping away from home, he often left a bedside note asking his host not to bury him immediately should he appear to be dead the next morning. Every ache and pain convinced him that the end was near. His worst spells came at night, and try as he might to shake them with logic and reason, they persisted, as he put it, "like some inescapable fate, terrible, hideous, and implacable." Reflecting on this depressed period in his life, Dostoevski grew convinced that he had for a time gone insane. His son and namesake also wrestled with bouts of depression.

9. STEPHEN FOSTER (1826–1864)

Shy and introspective as a child, Foster resisted his parents' efforts to channel him into a steady profession and instead became a songwriter. Although he achieved great fame in his lifetime with such hits as "Oh, Susanna" and "Old Folks at Home," both wealth and happiness eluded him. Often depressed and irritable, Foster quarreled repeatedly with his wife, and the couple found it more convenient to live apart from time to time. The composer drifted to New York, where he drank heavily, scratched out a batch of lackluster tunes on any scrap of paper handy at the time, and lived a hand-to-mouth existence, often reduced to a diet of apples and turnips. Yet even while in these depths, he managed to rekindle his creative flame long enough to compose "Old Black Joe" and "Beautiful Dreamer," the latter published posthumously.

10. SIGMUND FREUD (1856–1939)

For Freud, it was a busman's holiday to analyze his own wild mood swings. "I am now experiencing myself all the things that as a third party I have witnessed going on in my patients. . . . [There are] days when I slink about depressed," Freud commented during an acute downslide which occurred while he was putting together his classic treatise *The Interpretation of Dreams.* Freud could work neither in the depths of depression nor on the peaks of euphoria. Rather, he undertook his most profound studies amid what he called "the moderate misery necessary for intensive work."

11. NATHANIEL HAWTHORNE (1804–1864)

Perhaps the author's gloomy spells sprang from his lonely childhood. His mother, widowed when Nathaniel was four, lived with her son in near-total seclusion. Hawthorne would slump into depression over life's most trivial discomforts. A windy day was often enough to upset him. Brief separations from his wife and children always depressed him. And once he went into a tailspin because his wife served peas and baked Indian pudding for breakfast two days in a row. He felt life had boxed him in and said so in a letter to his old college chum Henry Wadsworth Longfellow: "I have secluded myself from society; and yet I never meant any such thing. I have made a captive of myself and put me into a dungeon, and now I cannot find the key to let myself out."

12. SAMUEL JOHNSON (1709–1784)

Johnson's state of mind began crumbling during his penurious student days at Oxford, where he suffered the wisecracks of the wealthier students. But it was after he left Oxford, at age 20, that he plunged into an unrelieved depression which lasted two years. He tried to reason his way up from utter despair and found some solace by putting his crippled mind to work on mathematical problems, but for the most part he remained idle, a financial and emotional burden to his poor parents. He reportedly contemplated suicide at one point. At 22 he had passed the worst, and in another three years he was functioning normally.

13. ABRAHAM LINCOLN (1809–1865)

The man famous as a knee-slapping, frontier raconteur, whose biggest asset on the stump was his endless supply of down-home jokes, anecdotes, and witty retorts, suffered at times from what then was called "melancholia." Even before he entered the White House to confront problems which would have unsettled the most stable of minds, Lincoln frequently was depressed. "I looked up at him," said Joshua Speed, the first man to befriend Lincoln when the rawboned 25-year-old lawyer ar-

Said Edgar Allan Poe, "I am wretched, and know not why."

rived in Springfield, Ill., "and I thought then, as I think now, that I never saw so gloomy and melancholy a face in my life." The presidency offered Lincoln little relief. The uncertain course of the Civil War, public charges that his wife was a Confederate spy, the sudden death of his 11-year-old son Willie while living in the White House—all drove Lincoln to despair.

14. EDGAR ALLAN POE (1809–1849)

Poe looked to alcohol and occasionally opium as refuges from his frequent periods of black depression. In his last days, barely out of his thirties, he tramped the streets, oblivious to all around him, mumbling darkly to himself. Undoubtedly, a greater measure of popular acclaim would have soothed his troubled spirit somewhat. But even during his relatively successful period, when he was contributing editor of the *Southern Literary Messenger*, he remained unhappy. "I am suffering under a depression of spirits such as I have never felt before," Poe wrote to a friend during this time. "I have struggled in vain against the influence of this melancholy. . . . I am still miserable in spite of the great improvement in my circumstances. . . . I am wretched, and know not why."

—W.A.D. & M.J.T.

RATING 36 HOME-GROWN VEGETABLES

You can grow vegetables for fun, food, or both. Nowadays, produce costs are sky-high except during seasonal surpluses. Hence, more home gardeners are demanding maximum value from the vegetables they grow. Three dozen of the top home-garden experts in the U.S. were asked by the National Garden Bureau to rate vegetables according to garden value. They considered total yield per sq. ft., average value per lb. harvested, and seed-to-harvest time. Here are the ratings. (Ten is the maximum; no vegetable rated the maximum, since no single vegetable performs well under all soil and climate conditions.)

Rank	Vegetable	Value Rating
1.	Tomatoes, grown on vertical supports to save space	9.0
2.	Green bunching onions	8.2
3.	Leaf lettuce	7.4
3.	Turnips, grown for greens and root crop	7.4
5.	Summer squash: zucchini, scallop, and yellow types	7.2
6.	Edible podded peas	6.9
6.	Onion sets for storage after harvest	6.9
8.	Beans, pole or runner types, green or wax pod	6.8
9.	Beets, grown for greens and root crop	6.6
10.	Beans, bush green or wax pod	6.5
10.	Carrots	6.5
10.	Cucumbers, grown on vertical supports	6.5

13.	Peppers, sweet green or yellow	6.4
14.	Broccoli	6.3
14.	Kohlrabi	6.3
14.	Swiss chard	6.3
17.	Mustard greens	6.2
17.	Spinach	6.2
19.	Beans, pole lima	6.1
19.	Radishes	6.1
21.	Cabbage	6.0
22.	Leek	5.9
23.	Collards	5.8
24.	Okra	5.7
25.	Kale	5.6
26.	Cauliflower	5.3
26.	Eggplant	5.3
28.	Peas, green or "English"	5.2
29.	Brussels sprouts	4.3
29.	Celery	4.3
29.	Peas, southern (black-eyed, crowder, purple hull)	4.3
32.	Corn, sweet	4.1
33.	Squash, winter, vining types	3.8
33.	Melons	3.8
33.	Watermelons	3.8
36.	Pumpkins	1.9

SOURCE: National Garden Bureau, Inc., 1186 Los Altos Ave., Los Altos, Calif. 94022.

NATHAN PRITIKIN'S 7 HARDEST-TO-RESIST FOODS FOR DIETERS

An advocate of a low-fat, high-carbohydrate diet along with plenty of exercise, Nathan Pritikin exudes good health. He's brought his program for healthful living to millions through his books, which include *The Pritikin Program for Diet & Exercise* and *The Pritikin Permanent Weight Loss Manual*, as well as the numerous Pritikin Longevity Centers. According to Nathan Pritikin, participants at the longevity center in Santa Monica, Calif., find the following foods hardest to resist.

1. Häagen-Dazs chocolate chip ice cream
2. Kentucky fried chicken
3. Tamari roasted cashew nuts
4. Pecan pie
5. New York cheese cake
6. Fettucini Alfredo
7. Brie cheese

—Exclusive for *The Book of Lists 3*

10 TOP ICE CREAM FLAVORS

Flavor	1981	1976	
1. Vanilla	35.1%	(1)	42.1%
2. Chocolate	12.4%	(2)	12.0%
3. Neapolitan	7.4%	(5)	6.9%
4. Chocolate chip	5.9%	(8)	2.1%
5. Strawberry	5.6%	(6)	2.6%
6. Vanilla fudge	4.2%		
7. Butter pecan	2.7%		
8. Cherry	2.5%	(10)	1.5%
9. Butter almond	1.6%		
10. French vanilla	1.4%		
Others	21.2%		

Note: Flavors for 1976 were for both ice cream and ice milk. Other top 10 flavors in 1976 were: (3) nut, 9.4%; (4) variegated, 8.1%; (7) candy and crunch, 2.6%; (9) peach, 1.7%; and others, 11.0%.

SOURCE: *Latest Scoop* (1981 edition), International Association of Ice Cream Manufacturers. *Dairy & Ice Cream Field,* April, 1977.

4 GROUPS OF DRUGS AND FOODS THAT CAN KILL YOU WHEN COMBINED

1. If you take these anticoagulant drugs: (1) Coumadin, (2) Dicumarol, (3) Liquamar, (4) Panwarfin, (5) Sintrom, (6) Miradon

In combination with vitamin-K-containing foods such as (1) asparagus, (2) bacon, (3) beef liver, (4) broccoli, (5) cabbage, (6) kale, (7) lettuce, (8) spinach, (9) turnip greens, (10) watercress

This could result: Vitamin K may reverse the effectiveness of the medication. It is not so much what you eat as maintaining a consistent vitamin intake. Once you are stabilized you should maintain the pattern or else you could end up with a clot. Periodic blood tests will tell the story.

2. If you take these drugs: (1) Aldoril, (2) Anhydron, (3) Aquatag, (4) Aquatensen, (5) Butizide, (6) Digoxin, (7) Diupres, (8) Diuril, (9) Diutensin, (10) Enduron, (11) Exna, (12) Hydrochlorothiazide, (13) Hydropres, (14) Hydrodiuril, (15) Hygroton, (16) Lanoxin, (17) Lasix

In combination with licorice

This could result: More than three quarters of an ounce of licorice eaten regularly can really mess up body chemistry and can lead to fluid buildup and high blood pressure. Licorice can reduce the effectiveness of your medication and if you are also taking a diuretic, licorice can deplete your body potassium. This can be lethal if you are also on a digitalis heart medicine.

3. If you take these MAO-inhibitors: (1) Eutron, (2) Eutonyl, (3) Furoxone, (4) Marplan, (5) Matulane, (6) Nardil, (7) Parnate

In combination with tyramine-containing foods such as (1) avocados, (2) bananas, (3) bologna, (4) Brie cheese, (5) Camembert cheese, (6) canned figs, (7) caviar, (8) cheddar cheese, (9) chicken liver, (10) Emmenthaler cheese, (11) fava beans, (12) Gruyére cheese, (13) meat tenderizer, (14) pepperoni, (15) pickled herring, (16) salami, (17) sour cream, (18) soy sauce, (19) summer sausage

This could result: The combination of tyramine-containing foods and MAO-inhibitors that are used to treat high blood pressure, psychological depression, infections, and cancer could cause blood pressure to go so high that you could have a stroke. Early warning signs of this reaction include: terrible headaches, chest pain, sweating, palpitations, rapid pulse, changes in vision, and coma.

4. If you take the antabuse Disulfiram, or these antidepressants: (1) Aventyl, (2) Elavil, (3) Marplan, (4) Nardil, (5) Norpramin, (6) Parnate, (7) Pertofrane, (8) Sinequan, (9) Tofranil, (10) Vivactil, or these barbiturates: (1) Butabarbitol, (2) Donnatal, (3) Nembutal, (4) Pentobarbital, (5) Phenobarbital, (6) Seconal, or these sedatives, tranquilizers, and sleeping pills: (1) Ativan, (2) Clonopin, (3) Dalmane, (4) Doriden, (5) Equanil, (6) Haldol, (7) Librium, (8) Miltown, (9) Serax, (10) Tanxene, (11) Valium, (12) Quaalude

In combination with alcohol (including beer, wine, liquor, cold remedies, cough medicine)

This could result: Effects range from high blood pressure, excessive sedation, and lack of coordination to death. Taken in combination with even a small amount of alcohol could make driving or operating machinery extremely dangerous.

Source: Joe Graedon, *The People's Pharmacy-2.* New York: Avon Books, 1980.

18
ENCORES

In *The Book of Lists 1* and *2* there appeared certain lists that proved to be immensely popular with our readers. Many of our readers wrote us inquiring if we could go on with the same subjects again, only adding new material. After researching these subjects further, we were able to tell our inquiring readers that we had found considerably more new material on their favorite topics. We are presenting these lists now—the headings, you will see, may be familiar, but the entries under these headings are all brand new.

THE 5 MOST HATED AND FEARED PERSONS IN HISTORY

Annually, since 1970, Mme. Tussaud's Waxwork Museum in London polls 3,500 of the international visitors to their exhibition by handing them questionnaires which ask them which persons, of all time, they hated the most. Simultaneously, the Mme. Tussaud's Waxwork Museum in Amsterdam conducts the same kind of poll of its visitors. These are the results of those two polls taken in 1981.

London Poll

1. Adolf Hitler
2. Ronald Reagan
3. Yorkshire Ripper
4. Margaret Thatcher
5. Leonid Brezhnev

Amsterdam Poll

1. Ronald Reagan
2. Leonid Brezhnev
3. Dracula
4. Muammar al-Qaddafi
5. Adolf Hitler

17 MORE GREAT SLIPS OF THE TONGUE IN AMERICAN POLITICS

1. "[Nuclear war is] something that may not be desirable."
   (Edwin Meese III, White House counselor, 1982)

2. "We may be finding that in some blacks when it [the chokehold] is applied the veins or arteries do not open up as fast as they do on normal people."
(Los Angeles Police Chief Daryl Gates, 1982)

3. "How are you, Mr. Mayor? I'm glad to meet you. How are things in your city?"
(Ronald Reagan, failing to recognize Samuel Pierce, his secretary of housing and urban development, at a White House reception for U.S. mayors, 1981)

4. ". . . a great man who should have been president and would have been one of the greatest presidents in history—Hubert Horatio Hornblower . . . er . . . Humphrey."
(Jimmy Carter, 1980 Democratic convention)

5. "It's wonderful to see all these beautiful white faces . . . I mean black and white faces."
(Nancy Reagan, 1980 presidential campaign)

6. "To you, and the people you represent, the great people of the government of Israel."
(Gerald Ford toasting Egyptian President Anwar Sadat at a Washington, D.C., dinner, 1975)

7. "Don't confuse me with the facts. I've got a closed mind."
(Rep. Earl Landgrebe, R-Ind., upon being told of the "smoking gun" Watergate tape, 1974)

8. "This is a great day for France."
(Richard Nixon, in Paris for the funeral of French President Georges Pompidou, 1974)

9. "The president is aware of what is going on in Southeast Asia. That is not to say anything is going on in Southeast Asia."
(Nixon press secretary Ron Ziegler, during an embargo on news about South Vietnam when asked if U.S. troops were about to invade Laos, 1971)

10. "We will once again have an administration that is inept in putting up with problems."
(Mario Procaccino, trying to convince voters to elect him mayor of New York, 1969)

11. "I don't think anyone in his right mind would say he wanted a bloodbath."
(Paul Beck, press secretary of California Governor Ronald Reagan, commenting on Reagan's statement, "If it takes a bloodbath" to silence campus radicals, "let's get it over with. No more appeasement." 1970)

12. "A fellow like myself would never be mayor of this great city without a Democratic party."
(Chicago Mayor Richard Daley, 1967)

13. "Killing, rioting, and looting are contrary to the best traditions of this country."
(Lyndon B. Johnson, 1965)

14. "You vote the straight Democratic ticket, including Senator Kuchel."

(California Gov. Edmund Brown, 1962 [Sen. Tom Kuchel was a Republican])

15. "I am running for governor of the United States."
(Richard Nixon, running for governor of California, 1962)

16. "You could say the senator [John Tower of Texas] is doing a lousy job, but I don't use that kind of words."
(Richard Daley, 1962)

17. "A man running for a public office to make such a statement without consulting the statue [sic] of Illinois and the laws of Illinois, gentlemen, it's ridiculous."
(Richard Daley, attacking his opponent for Cook County clerk, 1954)

—E.F.

11 NAMES OF THINGS YOU DIDN'T KNOW HAD NAMES

1. COLUMELLA NASI

The bottom part of the nose between the nostrils.

Columella Nasi

2. DRAGÉES

Small beadlike pieces of candy, usually silver-colored, used for decorating cookies, cakes, and sundaes.

3. FERRULE

The metal band on a pencil that holds the eraser in place.

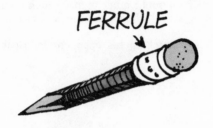

4.–7. JARNS, NITTLES, GRAWLIX, and QUIMP

Various squiggles used to denote cussing in comic books.

JARNS

NITTLES

GRAWLIX

QUIMP

8. KEEPER

The loop on a belt that keeps the end in place after it has passed through the buckle.

9. ROWEL

The revolving star on the back of a cowboy's spurs.

10. SADDLE

The rounded part on the top of a matchbook.

11. SNORKEL BOX

A mailbox with a protruding receiver to allow people to deposit mail without leaving their cars.

—D.W.

20 VERY ODD JOBS

1. ARMPIT SNIFFER

Sniffs armpits to test deodorant effectiveness.

2. BALL PICKER

Picks up unclaimed baseballs, golf balls, and the like to keep recreation areas clean.

3. BONER

Inserts stays (bones or steels) into prepared pockets of women's foundation garments, such as corsets or brassieres.

4. BOTTOM BLEACHER

Applies bleaching liquid to bottom of leather outsoles of lasted shoes, using brush or cloth, to lighten color of outsoles.

5. CABBAGE SALTER

Fills wooden tubs, barrels, or containers with cabbage and covers with salt and other preservatives to keep contents from spoiling.

6. CAN CATCHER

Stands at end of conveyor belt and catches falling cans in hands in order to keep cans from colliding and denting each other.

7. DINKEY OPERATOR

Controls dinkey engine powered by electric, gasoline, steam, compressed air, or diesel engine to transport and shunt cars at an industrial establishment or mine.

8. DOG- AND CAT-FOOD COOK

Controls battery of steam-jacketed kettles that cook ingredients for preparation of dog and cat foods.

9. EASTER BUNNY

Impersonates Easter Bunny to promote sales activity in retail stores, at conventions or exhibits, and to amuse children at hospitals, amusement parks, and private parties.

10. EXTERMINATION SUPERVISOR

Supervises and coordinates activities of exterminators engaged in destroying vermin with insecticides, rodenticides, or fumigants.

11. FISH HOUSEKEEPER

Cleans, dresses, wraps, labels, and stores fish for guests at resort establishments.

12. PRUNE WASHER

Tends machine that washes prunes preparatory to canning, packaging, or making specialty foods.

13. PUFF IRONER

Slides material back and forth over heated, metal, ball-shaped form to smooth and press portions of garments that cannot be satisfactorily pressed with flat presser or hand iron.

14. QUEEN PRODUCER

Raises queen bees.

15. REEFER ENGINEER

Operates refrigeration or air-conditioning equipment aboard ships.

16. ROOTER OPERATOR

Tends machine that roots (stitches) prescribed quantity of hair onto doll heads.

17. SLIME-PLANT OPERATOR

Tends agitation tanks that mix copper ore slime and acid solution preparatory to precipitation of copper.

18. SQUEAK, RATTLE, AND LEAK REPAIRER

Drives automobiles of service customers to determine origin of noises and leaks, and repairs or adjusts components to eliminate cause of complaint.

19. SUCKER-MACHINE OPERATOR

Tends machine that automatically forms lollypops of specified shape on ends of wooden sticks.

20. THRILL PERFORMER

Entertains audiences at fairs, carnivals, and circuses by performing daredevil feats, such as diving from high diving board into tank of water, parachuting from airplane, or being shot from cannon onto net.

—E.N. & THE EDS.

15 WINNERS OF THE
GOLDEN FLEECE AWARD

Every month Sen. William Proxmire of Wisconsin presents a Golden Fleece Award in honor of the biggest, most ridiculous, or most ironic example of government spending or waste.

1. AIR FORCE

In September, 1979, budget officers at Clark Air Force Base in the Philippines discovered that they had $715,000 left over from their annual allotment. Not wanting to return the money to the government, the officers alerted the base that the money had to be spent overnight. In an era when the Pentagon is constantly bemoaning its need for more money for national defense, Clark Air Force Base came up with the following expenditures: $20,000 for new televisions and fans (the latter were back-ups for the new air conditioners which had also been bought), $9,000 to resurface four tennis courts, $45,000 for supplies to clean up the base swimming pools and for pool furniture, and $115,000 to purchase new furniture for the John Hay Air Base recreational cottage. The Security Police accepted $30,000 to buy new refrigerators, televisions, stereos, jungle fatigues, boots, and berets, while the Maintenance Department picked up $35,400 for boots, tools, and microwave ovens.

2. COAST GUARD

In early 1976, the Coast Guard got the idea of saving space by converting 35,000 officer and enlisted personnel records from paper files to microfiche. Later in the year it was decided to convert 24,000 files of reservists' personnel records as well. After three years, someone decided to check the progress of the project, whereupon it was discovered that only 7% of the files had been transferred despite the fact that $525,000 had already been spent. (The original budget estimate had been $261,000.) Fortunately, the Coast Guard had enough good sense to cancel the project. The 4,200 files that had already been transferred to microfiche were changed back to paper files—at an undetermined cost.

3. DEPARTMENT OF COMMERCE

Although the department had 112 public-relations experts whose salaries totaled $4.8 million, the associate deputy secretary of the Dept. of Commerce requested $9,800 to hire an outside public-relations firm to evaluate the work of the department's office of public affairs. The outside firm concluded that the Dept. of Commerce should spend more money on public relations.

4. GOVERNMENT NATIONAL MORTGAGE ASSOCIATION

To commemorate the issuance of $100 billion in mortgage-backed securities, the GNMA spent $6,918 to buy 1,200 imitation-leather binders, which it sent to savings and loan associations across the country.

5. DEPARTMENT OF DEFENSE

The DOD received the award for annually understating by $1.5 million the cost of maintaining the homes of high-ranking generals and admirals. Some $500,000 was spent to manicure the lawns of generals and admirals on 22 bases, while $65,000 was used to repair gazebos adjacent to 13 generals' quarters at Bolling Air Force Base in Washington, D.C. Although DOD Instruction 4260.21 states that officers are personally responsible for routine maintenance, minor repairs, and housekeeping, it is usually the taxpayers who get stuck with the bill. For example, at Fort Belvoir, Va., "emergency" orders were issued for repairs at the residence of one senior officer when his garage lights wouldn't go out and when the doorbells didn't work.

6. FEDERAL HIGHWAY ADMINISTRATION

The FHA spent $241,764 to create a computerized system to give travel directions to drivers who can't or won't read maps and who can't or won't ask for directions at the nearest gas station. To operate the system, the user must negotiate a list of 16 instructions. It also does not help with the most confusing part of a trip—the small local roads closest to your destination. It is unlikely that a person who is not able to use a map or follow the directions given by a human being would do any better with a computerized system.

7. PRESIDENTIAL INAUGURAL COMMITTEE

When Ronald Reagan became President, he staged the most expensive inauguration ceremony in U.S. history, all the while proclaiming that no public funds were being used. Unfortunately, this was not true. The most flagrant example was the inaugural committee's use of 1,120 marines, soldiers, sailors, and other service personnel as chauffeurs and escorts for VIPs, including members of Reagan's kitchen cabinet. The military chauffeurs logged an amazing 250,000 mi. Total costs for this aspect of the inauguration alone were $1.8 million. The records of the Senate Appropriations Committee show that an additional $2.5 million of inaugural expenses were billed to the taxpayers. Additional money was lost to the Treasury because the $10 million which was contributed to the inaugural committee was tax-deductible.

8. NATIONAL AERONAUTICS AND SPACE ADMINISTRATION

Overlooked in the publicity blitz surrounding the launchings of the space shuttle was the unpleasant fact that delays in the shuttle also caused a $1 million-a-day delay in the launch date of the Tracking Data Relay and Satellite System (TDRSS), a space-based equivalent of the current ground-based space tracking network. Realizing that it would be impossible to convince Congress to pay for the development of such an expensive satellite, NASA decided to lease the system, thus adding $689 million in interest payments. Ninety days after a contract was negotiated, a serious satellite weight problem developed, which meant that the original launch vehicle, an Atlas Centaur, could not be used. So a three-year delay was created until the space shuttle was ready to do the job. Meanwhile, other problems developed as well, including one involving radio frequency interference, which cost $75 million plus interest to fix. Originally, development costs for the TDRSS were estimated at $841.8 million, but they eventually rose to well over $2 billion.

9. DEPARTMENT OF COMMERCE

In 1980 federal bureaucrats actually awarded $28,600 to the city and county of Honolulu to study how to spend another $250,000 for a good surfing beach. The $250,000 was paid to Honolulu by the Hawaiian Electric Company, which ruined a surfing beach on Oahu by expanding a power plant without making an environmental-impact study. Hawaii, of course, is filled with expert surfers, many of them already on the government payroll, who would be happy to participate in a study to improve surfing spots. Honolulu officials, however, simply could not resist the chance for a federal handout, and so an outside consultant was hired to do the job.

10. UNITED STATES ARMY

The Army's Natick Research and Development Laboratories in Massachusetts spent $6,000 to prepare a 17-page document that tells the federal government how to buy Worcestershire sauce. Paragraph 4.5.1.1 of Federal Specification EE-W-600F for Worcestershire sauce explains how to check the label to see if it is stuck on correctly: *"Water-resistant examination for label adhesive (no alternative procedures permitted).* The label adhesive shall be examined for water resistance as follows: Submerge glass container, with label affixed, into room temperature water for four hours. Remove from water and remove excess water by blotting with paper towel. Press finger firmly against the label (in areas where the adhesive has been applied) and move finger (still pressed against the label) towards the bottom of the bottle. Displacement of the label indicates failure to meet this requirement."

11. TREASURY DEPARTMENT MANAGERS OF THE SOCIAL SECURITY TRUST FUNDS

While private money managers earned 13% interest on their investments in 1980, the Treasury managers earned only 8.3% interest, causing a loss of $2 billion for the Social Security funds. The worst part is that this was done on purpose. The major problem is the existence of a conflict of interest on the part of the Treasury Dept. Every secretary of the treasury since 1935 has chosen to put the interests of the Treasury Dept. ahead of the interests of the Social Security trust funds. Instead of investing for maximum returns, they invested the funds in low-interest issues in order to minimize the interest on the national debt.

12. ECONOMIC DEVELOPMENT ADMINISTRATION OF THE DEPARTMENT OF COMMERCE

In 1979 the Carter administration approved a grant of $500,000 to build a 10-story-high limestone replica of the Great Pyramid of Egypt in Bedford, Ind. Two years later, the Reagan administration, not to be outdone, allocated an additional $125,000 to complete the project as well as $200,000 to build an 800-ft. limestone replica of the Great Wall of China. Perhaps someday Bedford, Ind., will become a major tourist attraction, but one wonders why taxpayers are forced to put up the money for this gamble.

13. FEDERAL HIGHWAY ADMINISTRATION

When Congress first approved the Federal Highway System in 1958, the estimated cost was $37.6 billion. Since then the project has set a record for cost overruns: $100.3 billion or 267%. And the system isn't finished yet. This cost growth is bigger than the combined 1982 budgets for the Depts. of Agriculture, Education, Energy, Housing and Urban Development, Interior, Justice, State, and Transportation. The worst example of spending in the highway program has been "Westway" in New York City. The final cost of this 4-mi. highway will reach $1 billion a mile, making it the most expensive road, inch for inch, ever built anywhere in the world. The FHA accounts for 30% of all federal cost overruns.

14. DEPARTMENT OF DEFENSE

In 1974 Deputy Secretary of Defense William Clements, Jr., told the chairman of the House Defense Appropriations Subcommittee that the Navy was using a bull in Wisconsin to test for possible biological effects of the Extremely Low Frequency (ELF) system, a submarine communications device. When Clements learned that no such bull existed, he became extremely upset and ordered the Navy to get a bull to the Wisconsin Test Facility at Clam Lake within a week. So an 18-month-old bull named Sylvester was purchased and installed in a 10-ft.-by-10-ft. enclosure at Clam Lake. The Navy knew the ELF bovine test was a phony, but no one wanted to challenge Secretary Clements. Finally, six years and $13,000 later, the Navy put an end to the charade by cruelly shooting Sylvester to death.

15. SYNTHETIC FUELS CORPORATION

The Synthetic Fuels Corporation, a useless government organization which deserves to be abolished as quickly as possible, paid $44,226 for a study which recommended increasing executive salaries to as high as $190,000 or about 173%. As part of the corporation's spending splurge, they spent $522,919 to decorate their offices, including $83,260 for velvet carpet.

—D.W.

10 BEST-CENSORED STORIES
OF THE 1980s

Project Censored is a nationwide research project begun at Sonoma State University in California in 1976. Significant news stories that have been ignored by the mass media are located, evaluated, and submitted to a panel of prominent judges, who rank them annually. The Sonoma State researchers stress that the suppression of these stories is not so much the result of a "conspiracy" as the media's lack of perception, their drive for profits, their common interest with big business, and a general desire not to rock the boat.

1. THE REAL CAUSE OF OUR ECONOMIC CRISIS

Tight money, federal budget deficits, foreign imports, and decreased productivity have been blamed for the current economic problems being faced by the U.S. However, the real cause of the deterioration of our economy is the disappearance of a truly competitive economy. Monopoly, militarism, and multinationalization have destroyed the free-enterprise system and created inflation, stagnation, and unemployment.

2. EVERY TWO SECONDS A HUNGRY CHILD DIES

While world leaders fight over arbitrary boundaries and get lost in geopolitical games, 50 million people quietly starve to death each year. Some 40,000 children die each day, and 17 million of the children who will be born this year will die before their fifth birthday.

3. DISTORTED COVERAGE OF THE WAR IN EL SALVADOR

Although the civil war in El Salvador received ample coverage by the U.S. media, the situation was consistently misrepresented. While the press presented the image of a "moderate" junta fighting left- and right-wing extremists, the fact was that the "left" was actually a mixture of peasants, students, teachers, priests, nuns, and middle-class businessmen who made up 80% of the population. Although the press perpetuated the myth that the bulk of El Salvador's 10,000 assassinations a year were the work of Marxist guerrillas or reactionary right-wing forces, the records of the Legal Aid Office of the Catholic Archdiocese of San Salvador show that 80% of the assassinations were actually committed by government military units.

4. BIG BROTHER IS LISTENING TO YOU

The biggest security agency in the U.S. is not the CIA or the FBI, but the NSA: the National Security Agency. The NSA, with an annual budget of over $2 billion, records every telephone call and wireless or cable message to and from the U.S. Despite the fact that this activity is completely illegal and unconstitutional, the NSA has gone unchallenged by the press or by Congress.

5. CORNERING THE SOLAR MARKET

In recent years, oil companies have quietly developed a monopoly on solar energy. For over a decade, the oil industry criticized solar technology as expensive and impractical. But when support for solar energy grew rapidly throughout the population, the oil companies switched tactics and started buying into the solar industry. Their strategy seems to be to control development so that alternative energy sources don't threaten their investments in fossil fuels and nuclear power. The federal government has actively aided this monopolization by awarding over 90% of solar research and development grants to the largest corporations, such as Shell, Atlantic-Richfield, Northrop, Amoco, Exxon, and Mobil. Solarex, an independent company, was denied financial assistance from the Dept.

of Energy. However, after Amoco bought 20% of Solarex's stock, Solarex received a $7 million grant.

6. THE BENDECTIN COVER-UP

Richardson-Merrill, Inc., the company that gave us thalidomide, is still marketing Bendectin, an antinausea drug for pregnant women which is responsible for over 3,000 birth deformities a year. Bendectin also produces annual profits of $15 million, since it is used by 25% of the pregnant women in the U.S.

7. THE GLOBAL SUPERMARKET

Much has been written about the increase in worldwide food production that has been brought about by modern technology. What hasn't been written about is the fact that this has caused more starvation and malnutrition rather than less. Along with the modern technology has come a conversion from subsistence farming by small farmers to the growing of cash-export crops by transnational agribusiness firms. All over the world, peasant farmers have been driven from their lands and forced to find seasonal work or move to cities.

8. NUCLEAR CENSORSHIP

Among the nuclear-related stories which have been bypassed by the media are the following:
1. Despite the claims by the nuclear power industry that "No one died at Three Mile Island," a study by Dr. Ernest J. Sternglass, professor of radiation physics at the University of Pittsburgh, showed that the accident at TMI led to a minimum of 430 infant deaths.
2. The U.S. detonates an atomic bomb once every 3½ weeks at underground test sites in Nevada. Unfortunately, radiation from these tests has been seeping into the groundwater as well as into the atmosphere.
3. A symposium held by Physicians for Social Responsibility concluded that 30 days after a 20-min. nuclear war 90% of all Americans and Soviets would be dead.
4. From 1946 to 1970 radioactive trash was jettisoned in 50 ocean dumps up and down the East and West coasts of the U.S., including prime fishing areas. No major effort has been made to study the possible health hazards of this dumping.
5. Since the 1950s, over 500,000 gallons of radioactive liquid waste have leaked from storage tanks at Hanford, Wash.
6. Scotland was almost obliterated on Nov. 2, 1981, when a fully armed Poseidon missile was accidentally dropped 17 feet from a crane during a transfer operation between a U.S. submarine and its mother ship.
7. In the fall of 1980, 49 lb. of enriched uranium was discovered missing from the naval reactor fuel facility at Erwin, Tenn.
8. An estimated 1,200 nuclear weapons are stored in California alone, half of them in or near major urban areas.

9. TRAINING TERRORISTS IN FLORIDA

While the Reagan administration publicly opposes international terrorism, Cuban and Nicaraguan exiles are being trained in terrorism at

Anticommunist terrorist training camp in Florida.

Camp Libertad and other camps in southern Florida. These camps are in direct violation of the U.S. Neutrality Act as well as other federal laws which prohibit private citizens from organizing to overthrow or undermine foreign governments.

10. POISONED WATER

Each year 78 billion lb. of poisonous chemicals are dumped into 51,000 sites across the U.S. Regulation of these dumps is inadequate, and many of these hazardous wastes enter our groundwater supply.

—D.W.

9 FAMOUS HEMORRHOID SUFFERERS

1. ALFRED THE GREAT (849–899)

As a very young man, King Alfred of Wessex expressed the wish that God would send him a disease that would suppress lust but would not deprive him of the ability to rule. Soon he became afflicted with hemorrhoids, and once, after a painful day out hunting on horseback, Alfred stopped at St. Neot's shrine in Cornwall to pray for relief.

2. NIKOLAI GOGOL (1809–1852)

In 1831, the young Russian author wrote to his mother, "Suffering from hemorrhoids, I had the foolish idea that it was some other and more dangerous ailment. Later I learned that there was not one man in St. Petersburg free from this nuisance." Lifelong overeating worsened his condition.

3. DAVID LIVINGSTONE (1813–1873)

The African explorer and medical missionary suffered innumerable bouts with hemorrhoids. In 1864, he refused surgery to remove them because he feared he would be disabled and thus prevented from returning to Africa. Livingstone is the only well-known person known to have died from hemorrhoids.

4. KARL MARX (1818–1883)

While writing *Das Kapital,* Marx was plagued by hemorrhoids. He wrote to his friend Friedrich Engels, "To finish I must at least be able to *sit down.*" He added, "I hope the bourgeoisie will remember my carbuncles."

5. EARL WARREN (1891–1974)

Sitting on the bench of the U.S. Supreme Court from 1953 to 1969 may have been uncomfortable for Chief Justice Warren, but he did not allow his hemorrhoids to deter him from participating in many landmark court decisions.

6. GERALD FORD (1913–)

The 38th president of the U.S. has always been athletic. Before earning his law degree at Yale University, he was a football and boxing coach there. But in later years, as hemorrhoids restricted his activities, Ford began finding less strenuous sports—such as golf—more to his liking.

7. JIMMY CARTER (1924–)

In 1974 Carter underwent surgery for hemorrhoids. But the 39th president of the U.S. was so incapacitated by hemorrhoidal pain that on one occasion he was forced to cancel his day's work at the White House. One sympathizer from Egypt sent the following message: "May Allah cure you. This illness should have been inflicted on an unjust ruler rather than you, O Carter."

8. ELIZABETH TAYLOR (1932–)

A movie star since she was a teenager, Taylor has had an equally impressive career of medical difficulties—an emergency tracheotomy, skin cancer, dislodgement of a chicken bone in her throat, back traction, and two operations to remove persistent hemorrhoids.

9. GEORGE BRETT (1953–   )

After the first game of the 1980 World Series, the Kansas City Royals announced that their star hitter was incapacitated by hemorrhoids. Brett had corrective surgery, and 30 hours later he left the hospital in time to play in the third game of the Series. He commented to reporters, "My problem's behind me now."

—R.J.F.

PRIMARY SOURCE: Stephen Berger, *Of Natural Causes: The Disease and Death of Just About Everybody.* New York: Vantage Books, 1982.

13 STRANGE DEATHS

1. REVENGE OF THE PLANT KINGDOM

On Feb. 4, 1982, 27-year-old David M. Grundman fired two shotgun blasts at a giant saguaro cactus in the desert outside Phoenix, Ariz. Unfortunately for Grundman, his shots caused a 23-ft. section of the cactus to fall on him, and he was crushed to death.

2. KILLED BY A ROBOT

Kenji Urada, 37, was a worker at the Akashi plant of Kawasaki Heavy Industries in western Japan. On July 4, 1981, he entered a restricted zone to repair a machine on a processing line for automobile gears. Although reports of the incident are confusing, Urada apparently became so engrossed in his work that he failed to notice the approach of a transport robot which delivered parts to the machine. The robot came up on Urada from behind and crushed him to death against the machine.

3. THE PERFECT LAWYER

Clement L. Vallandigham was a highly controversial Ohio politician who engendered much hostility by supporting the South during the Civil War. Convicted of treason, he was banished to the Confederacy. Back in Ohio after the war, Vallandigham became an extremely successful lawyer, who rarely lost a case. In 1871 he took on the defense of Thomas McGehan, a local troublemaker who was accused of shooting Tom Myers to death during a barroom brawl. Vallandigham contended that Myers had actually shot himself, attempting to draw his pistol from his pocket while trying to rise from a kneeling position.

On the evening of June 16, Vallandigham was conferring in his hotel room with fellow defense lawyers when he decided to show them how he would demonstrate his theory to the jury the next day. Earlier in the day, he had placed two pistols on the bureau, one empty and one loaded. Grabbing the loaded one by mistake, Vallandigham put it in his trouser pocket. Then he slowly pulled the pistol back out and cocked it.

"There, that's the way Myers held it," he said, and pulled the trigger. A shot rang out and Vallandigham explained, "My God, I've shot myself!" He died 12 hours later.

Vallandigham's client, Thomas McGehan, was subsequently acquitted and released from custody.

4. THE ELECTRIC GUITARIST

Keith Relf, who had gained fame as the lead singer of The Yardbirds, a 1960s blues-rock group, was found dead at his home in London on May 14, 1976. The cause of death was an electric shock received while playing his guitar. Relf was 33 years old.

Keith Relf of The Yardbirds.

5. TOO MUCH OF A GOOD THING

It is almost impossible to die of an overdose of water, but Tina Christopherson managed to do it. The 29-year-old Florida woman, who had an IQ of 189, became obsessed with the idea that she suffered from stomach cancer, a disease which had killed her mother. In an attempt to cleanse her body, Christopherson went on periodic water fasts, during which she ate no food but drank up to four gallons of water a day. By Feb. 17, 1977, she had consumed so much water that her kidneys were overwhelmed and the excess fluid drained into her lungs. She died of internal drowning, otherwise known as "water intoxication."

6. THE BURDEN OF MATRIMONY

William Shortis, a rent collector in Liverpool, England, and his wife, Emily Ann, had not been seen for several days. Worried friends and a policeman entered the house on Aug. 13, 1903, and were horrified to discover William, dazed and dying, at the foot of the staircase pinned to the floor underneath the body of his 224-lb. wife. A coroner's jury concluded that the elderly couple had been walking up the stairs when Emily Ann fell backward, carrying her husband with her. Mrs. Shortis died immediately from a concussion, but William remained in his unfortunate position for three days, too seriously injured to be able to extricate himself.

7. THE DEADLY DANCE

In August, 1981, 11-year-old Simon Longhurst of Wigan, England, attended a Sunday afternoon junior disco session where, along with other youngsters, he performed the "head shake," a New Wave dance in which the head is shaken violently as the music gets faster and faster. The following day, young Simon began suffering headaches and soon a blood clot developed. Three weeks later he died of acute swelling of the brain. The coroner ruled it "death by misadventure."

8. A WISH FULFILLED

American revolutionary patriot James Otis often mentioned to friends and relatives that as long as one had to die, he hoped that his death would come from a bolt of lightning. On May 23, 1783, the 58-year-old Otis was leaning against a doorpost in a house in Andover, Mass., when a lightning bolt struck the chimney, ripped through the frame house, and hit the doorpost. Otis was killed instantly.

9. A FATAL TEMPER

On Apr. 15, 1982, 26-year-old Michael Scaglione was playing golf with friends at the City Park West Municipal Golf Course in New Orleans. After making a bad shot on the 13th hole, Scaglione became angry with himself and threw his club against a golf cart. When the club broke, the clubhead rebounded and stabbed Scaglione in the throat, severing his jugular vein. Scaglione staggered back and pulled the metal piece from his neck. Had he not done that, he might have lived, since the clubhead could have reduced the rapid flow of blood.

10. THE WORST NIGHTMARE OF ALL

In 1924, British newspapers reported the bizarre case of a man who apparently committed suicide while asleep. Thornton Jones, a lawyer, woke up to discover that he had slit his throat. Motioning to his wife for a paper and pencil, Jones wrote, "I dreamt that I had done it. I awoke to find it true." He died 80 minutes later.

11. A DAREDEVIL'S FINAL FALL

Bobby Leach was a colorful character who first became famous in 1911 when he went over Niagara Falls in a barrel. He continued to perform dangerous exploits, including parachuting over the falls from an airplane. In April, 1926, Leach was walking down a street in Christchurch, New Zealand, when he slipped on a piece of orange peel and broke his leg so badly that it had to be amputated. Complications developed and he died.

12. KILLED BY JAZZ

Seventy-nine-year-old cornetist and music professor Nicola Coviello had had an illustrious career, having performed before Queen Victoria, Edward VII, and other dignitaries. Realizing that his life was nearing its end, Coviello decided to travel from London to Saskatchewan to pay a final visit to his son. On the way, he stopped in New York City to bid farewell to his nephews, Peter, Dominic, and Daniel Coviello. On June 13, 1926, the young men took their famous uncle to Coney Island to give him a taste of America. The elder Coviello enjoyed himself but seemed irritated by the blare of jazz bands. Finally he could take it no longer. "That isn't music," he complained and he fell to the boardwalk. He was pronounced dead a few minutes later. Cause of death was "a strain on the heart."

13. WHAT A WASTE TO GO

The 70-year-old mayor of Betterton, Md., Monica Myers, considered it part of her duties to check the sewage tanks at the municipal facility. On the night of Mar. 19, 1980, she went to the Betterton treatment plant to test for chlorine and sediment. Unfortunately, she slipped on a catwalk, fell into a tank of human waste, and drowned.

—D.W.

REMAINS TO BE SEEN—
14 PRESERVED PARTS

1. ST. BONAVENTURE'S HEAD

This great Catholic theologian and philosopher is one person who definitely did not rest in peace. Almost three hundred years after his death in 1274, his remains were caught in the middle of a French religious war that pitted the Roman Catholic Church against the Protestant Huguenots. In 1562, St. Bonaventure's tomb at Lyons was plundered. While his body was publicly burned, the head—said to be perfectly preserved—was saved and hidden by one of the faithful. It disappeared, however, during the French Revolution and has not been seen since.

2. PAUL BROCA'S BRAIN

In one of the less-frequented corners of the Musée de l'Homme (Museum of Man) in Paris are numerous bottles containing human brains. Some belonged to intellectuals, others to criminals. But perhaps the most distinguished of the specimens is that of Paul Broca, a 19th-century physician and anthropologist who was the father of modern brain surgery.

3. GEORGE FREDERICK COOKE'S SKULL

Even though Irish-born actor George Frederick Cooke has been dead for over 170 years, he still gets steady work in bit parts. That is, a bit of his parts still gets steady work. Cooke's skull is owned by the Thomas Jefferson University Medical School library in Philadelphia, which lends it out to theatrical groups as a prop.

4. BARON PIERRE DE COUBERTIN'S HEART

Lausanne, Switzerland, and Olympia, Greece, are the two most revered sites of the modern Olympic movement. Baron Pierre de Coubertin, the founder of that movement, left a part of himself in each place. His will requested that his body be buried at Lausanne, the site of the International Olympic Committee headquarters. But first his heart was to be removed and placed in a marble column at Olympia, where the ancient games were held.

5. ALBERT EINSTEIN'S BRAIN

What might have been the greatest brain of the 20th century was not buried with the body that housed it. Albert Einstein asked that after his death his brain be removed for study. And when the great physicist died in 1955, this was done. The brain—which was neither larger nor heavier than the norm—was photographed, sectioned, and sent around the country to be studied by specialists. Some of the largest specimens are in Wichita, Kans.

6. GALILEO'S FINGER

The great astronomer died in 1642, but his body wasn't interred in its final resting place until 1737. During that final transfer to the Church of Santa Croce in Florence, an aristocratic admirer cut off three of Galileo's fingers as keepsakes. Two now belong to an Italian doctor, but the third—a middle finger—sits in Florence's Museum of the History of Science pointing skyward.

7. JOSEPH HAYDN'S HEAD

The Austrian composer died in 1809. Soon after his burial, a prison warden who was an amateur phrenologist—a person who tries to corre-

411

Galileo's middle finger.

late head bumps with character traits—hired grave robbers to steal the head. The warden examined the skull, then gave it to an acquaintance, and a remarkable 145-year-long odyssey began. The theft of the skull was discovered in 1820, when the family of Haydn's patron had the body disinterred. Eventually they got a skull back, but it wasn't Haydn's. The real item was passed from one owner to another, some of them individuals, others organizations. Finally, it found a home in a glass case at Vienna's Society of Friends of Music. In 1932, the descendants of Haydn's patrons once again tried to get it back. But W.W. II and then the cold war intervened—the body was in Austria's Soviet quarter, but the skull in the international zone. It wasn't until 1954 that body and skull were finally reunited.

8. CHARLES LOWELL'S PELVIC BONES

Lowell, of Lubec, Maine, fractured his pelvis in a fall from a horse in 1821. The pelvis was treated by Dr. Micajah Hawkes. Lowell walked on it too soon, and it didn't heal well. Lowell blamed the physician and sued. After three highly publicized trials, the judge threw the case out of court. Lowell, however, apparently couldn't forget it. His will directed that after his death, which occurred in 1858, a postmortem examination be made. It showed that Lowell had been wrong. The celebrated pelvic bones were preserved in a Boston anatomical museum while the rest of the body was buried in Maine.

9. MAJ. JOHN W. POWELL'S BRAIN

Geologist John W. Powell donated his brain to the Smithsonian Institution, of which he was an official, in order to settle a bet with an associate over whose brain was larger. Although Powell's gray matter is still in the museum's collection, that of his associate is nowhere to be found, which makes Powell the winner by default.

10. JOSÉ RIZAL'S VERTEBRA

José Rizal, the national hero of the Philippines, was accused of sedition and executed by the Spanish in 1896 and buried without a coffin. He was exhumed in August, 1898, after the Americans took Manila. Most of Rizal's remains are interred beneath the Rizal Monument in Luneta—all except one of his cervical vertebrae; the vertebra is enshrined like a holy relic in Fort Santiago.

11. DAN SICKLES'S LEG

Sickles was a colorful New York congressman who organized and led a brigade of volunteers at the outbreak of the Civil War. He was involved in some of the bloodiest fighting at Gettysburg, losing his own right leg in the battle. That trauma, however, apparently didn't diminish Sickles's personal flair. He had the leg preserved and sent to Washington, where it was exhibited in a little wooden coffin at the Medical Museum of the Library of Congress. Sickles frequently visited it himself.

12. LAZZARO SPALLANZANI'S BLADDER

When Italian biologist Spallanzani died in 1799, his diseased bladder was excised for study by his colleagues. Afterward, it was placed on public display in a museum in Pavia, Italy, where it remains today, a monument to the inquisitive mind.

13.–14. GEORGE WASHINGTON'S HAIR AND TOOTH

In June, 1793, George Washington gave a locket containing a clipping of his hair to his aide-de-camp, Col. John Trumbull. When Trumbull died, he willed the lock of hair to a first cousin of the president's, Dr. James A. Washington, who passed it along to his family as a sort of "hairloom." George Washington's dentist, John Greenwood, managed to acquire another collectible which the president shed from his person—the last of his natural teeth. Washington mailed the tooth to Greenwood to use as a model in making a new set of dentures. The dentist kept the tooth as a souvenir, and it remained in the Greenwood family for generations.

—E.F. & M.J.T.

PRESERVING OUR HERITAGE—
10 STUFFED OR EMBALMED HUMANS
AND 1 GORILLA

1.–2. SUZANNE AND JACQUES NECKER

Spirits of wine preserve the bodies of the French couple in a black marble basin inside a mausoleum at Coppet, Switzerland, her head on his shoulder, his large red cape floating above them. Fearing a lonely eternity, Mme. Necker, author and salon hostess, worked out details of their lasting togetherness during their 30-year marriage. After her death in 1794, Necker—France's director of finance—built the mausoleum, filled it with alcohol, and placed his wife's body in it. A decade later he joined her in the tomb. The coffin of their daughter, Mme. de Staël, was placed at their feet in 1817, and the tomb was sealed.

3. COLONEL MORLAND

Noted for his lush, drooping moustache, this officer in Napoleon's army was killed in action during the Battle of Austerlitz in 1805. Surgeons buried his viscera in Brunn but shipped his body back to Paris sealed in a barrel of rum. The barrel stood in the Paris School of Medicine awaiting construction of a monument (never built) and was still there in 1814 when Napoleon lost the empire. Shortly afterward, the barrel broke and Morland fell out; his moustache, some said, had grown to waist length.

4. ANONYMOUS COAL MINER

A Fort Smith, Ark., newspaper carried a poignant story of discovery in 1869. Miners found the perfectly preserved body of a young man who had disappeared in the airless coal pits 40 years before. When they brought his body to the surface, a gray-haired old woman slipped through the crowd and threw herself upon the youthful corpse, pouring out a stream of endearments. The dead miner was to have become her husband on the day following his disappearance. The contrast in features— he so young, she worn and wrinkled—eloquently told how time had changed the living but stopped for the dead.

5. ST. BERNADETTE

In 1858, at the age of 14, Bernadette Soubirous saw several visions of the Virgin Mary at a spring in Lourdes, France. Bernadette later joined the Sisters of Notre-Dame of Nevers, and today the site of the apparitions is one of the most famous Catholic shrines. After her death at age 35, Bernadette's body was buried and exhumed three separate times in the next 45 years in attempts to verify the incorruptibility of her corpse (according to Catholic tradition, a sign of sainthood). Although there has been some decomposition, owing in part to numerous examinations, Bernadette's remains are remarkably intact. Today her body is on display in the chapel of the Convent of St. Gildard at Nevers.

6. "STONE WILLIE"

The modern technology of embalming was far from perfected in 1895 when an unidentified male inmate died in a Reading, Pa., jail. Mortician Theodore C. Auman, Sr., seizing the opportunity to improve upon preservation techniques, promptly embalmed the body with an over-strong dose of chemicals similar to those used today. To learn how long "Willie" would last in his mummified state, the mortuary kept the cadaver in storage. At last report in 1982, "Stone Willie," though dehydrated and darker, had otherwise changed little and "still gets an occasional change of pajamas and a periodic soap-and-water bath."

7. "SYLVESTER"

In the hot alkaline sand and dry air of Arizona's Gila Bend Desert in 1895, two cowboys found a naked, perfectly preserved mummy with a bullet wound in its stomach. The hair, moustache, nails, and blue eyes of the tall, mummified man remained intact. "Sylvester," the unclaimed mummy, traveled the country with freak shows for the next 30 years. During the 1930s, he rested under sofa cushions in the living room of a doctor who liked to surprise his guests. At last report, Sylvester was startling customers in a Seattle curiosity shop.

8. ENRICO CARUSO

During the six years that followed his death in 1921, the great Italian tenor surely qualified for the "best-dressed corpse" list. Each year solicitous friends ordered a new outfit for Caruso's body, which lay on public display in a crystal casket. In 1927, his widow decided enough was enough and had a white granite slab placed over the casket. It now remains sealed and undisturbed with Caruso in old clothes at Del Planto Cemetery near Naples, Italy.

9. CHARLES "SPEEDY" ATKINS

Always nattily dressed in a blue suit and necktie, "Speedy" has served as a Paducah, Ky., mortician's "silent partner" for over half a century. The black handyman, born about 1878, acquired his nickname because of his quick efficiency in performing odd jobs for mortician A. L. Hamock. When Atkins drowned in 1928, Hamock embalmed him with a super formaldehyde solution that virtually petrified the corpse. For years the stonelike body stood in a corner of the mortuary as testimonial to Hamock's skills. Still well preserved if a bit grotesque, the cadaver continued to draw sightseers to the mortuary—now operated by Hamock's widow—in 1982.

10. SAMUEL PERRY DINSMOOR

Nightmarish demons, devils, and serpents leer from 113 tons of sculptured concrete statuary fashioned by this Civil War veteran during his last 19 years. Dinsmoor's 1932 will stipulated that his body be on perpetual display in his triangular mausoleum. Operated by his Lucas, Kans., neighbors and funded by an admission fee, the Garden of Eden contains Dinsmoor's remains, which lie behind a sealed glass window.

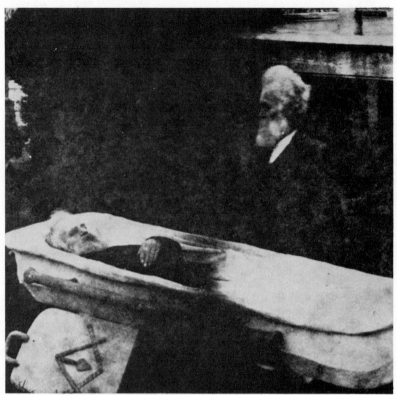

This postcard was made by Mr. S. P. Dinsmoor in the early 1900s,
depicting him looking down at himself in his coffin. Today,
Dinsmoor's remains are a tourist attraction in Lucas, Kansas.

11. BUSHMAN

More than 3 million people viewed the huge, chest-thumping go-
rilla in Chicago's Lincoln Park Zoo over a period of 20 years. While alive
Bushman often became moody when zoogoers ignored him. In death, his
stuffed and mounted carcass continues to awe visitors at Chicago's Field
Museum of Natural History, where he glares from a sealed glass case
filled with insecticidal gases.

—J.E.

19
TILL DEATH DO US PART

14 PEOPLE WHO DIED
WHILE PERFORMING

1. MOLIÈRE

The great French actor and playwright collapsed onstage during the third performance of his play *Le Malade Imaginaire* (*The Imaginary Invalid*) on Feb. 17, 1673. He was taken to his home on rue de Richelieu, where he died of a hemorrhage resulting from a burst blood vessel.

2. JAMES BOSWELL

Renowned clown James Clement Boswell suffered a stroke while performing his "broken-ladder trick" in 1859. Stricken in the midst of the stunt, he fell from the ladder and died a short time later.

3. CHUNG LING-SOO

Chung Ling-soo (a.k.a. William E. Robinson), the American-born magician famous in England for his round-the-clock impersonation of Chinese magician Ching Ling-foo was shot to death on Mar. 23, 1918, while performing the "Defying the Bullets" trick at the Wood Green Empire in Middlesex, England. The act normally featured Robinson appearing to "catch" miraculously in a plate two bullets fired at him from separate guns. That night, however, a mechanical failure in one of the fixed guns caused a bullet actually to discharge and hit him. Shot in one of his lungs, Robinson yelled, "My God! Something's happened! Lower the curtain!" He died the following morning at Wood Green Cottage Hospital.

4. CLARENCE SMITH

Pianist Smith was at the keyboard at a Chicago jazz club on Mar. 14, 1929, when he was shot to death by an unknown gunman.

5. LILLIAN LEITZEL

Originally a member of the "Leitzel Sisters," Lillian wowed the spectators at three-ring circuses by doing more than 200 aerial plunges in one continuous effort. She also could accomplish as many as 40 complete revolutions using only one hand. The famed aerialist died during a 1931 performance in Copenhagen after she fell from a high wire when its swivel mechanism broke.

6. LEONARD WARREN

Warren collapsed on the stage of New York's Metropolitan Opera House at 9:55 P.M. on Mar. 4, 1960, while playing the lead role of Don Carlo in Giuseppe Verdi's *La Forza del Destino* (*The Force of Destiny*). During the second act, Warren dropped a prop and fell forward onto his face. Thirty-five minutes later, the audience was informed of the baritone's death.

7.–8. DIETER SCHEPP AND RICHARD FAUGHAN

Schepp and Faughan—nephew and son-in-law, respectively, of Karl Wallenda, patriarch of The Great Wallendas acrobatic troupe—were killed in a 38-ft. fall when their "human pyramid" act collapsed in Detroit, Mich., on Jan. 30, 1962. Karl saved his niece, Christiana, and himself by clinging to the balance wire with his legs. An adopted son, Mario, was paralyzed from the waist down in the accident.

9. LILLIAN HARDIN

Louis Armstrong's second wife died of a heart attack while performing a memorial tribute to her husband at the Civic Center Plaza in Chicago, Ill., on Aug. 27, 1971. A jazz pianist who had played with Armstrong and in numerous bands, the 73-year-old widow collapsed while performing "The St. Louis Blues."

10. RICHARD GUZMAN

During a 1972 performance at the Wheeling Island Stadium in West Virginia, Richard Guzman accidentally touched a live electrical wire while climbing a pole to join his father-in-law, Karl Wallenda, atop a balance cable. The shock caused Guzman to lose his grip and plunge to his death.

11. LES HARVEY

Singer Les Harvey was killed onstage at Swansea University, Wales, in 1972 during a performance with his band, Stone the Crows. Death was caused by shock from electrocution, which occurred when Harvey touched his microphone.

12. CARL BARNETT

Carl Barnett, musical director at Will Rogers High School in Tulsa, Okla., suffered a heart attack in 1974 while conducting the school's 75-piece orchestra at its annual spring concert. The 59-year-old Barnett collapsed as the band played Bach's *Komm Suesser Todd* (*Come Sweet Death*) before an audience of 300 people. He was pronounced dead on arrival at St. John's Hospital.

13. SID JAMES

Comedy actor Sid James did not rise from his chair on cue 15 minutes into the opening-night performance of *The Mating Season* at Sunderland, England's Empire Theatre on Apr. 26, 1976. The curtain was dropped as James toppled onto the stage floor. His wife, Valerie, accompanied him to the nearby Royal Infirmary, where he died within minutes. The audience of 400 was sent home, and the play was canceled.

14. KARL WALLENDA

High-wire acrobat Karl Wallenda plunged 100-ft. to his death while promoting the Pan American Circus in San Juan, Puerto Rico, on Mar. 22, 1978. Negotiating his way across a 750-ft. cable bridging two hotels, Wallenda began to lose his balance and attempted to squat as his associates yelled, "Sit, Poppy, sit!" A gust of wind blew him off the wire, sending him crashing down onto a taxicab on the street below. He was pronounced dead at a nearby hospital.

—D.B.

20 FAMOUS PEOPLE KILLED IN AUTO ACCIDENTS

1. Marc Bolan, British rock star, died on Sept. 19, 1977, at age 29, in London, England.
2. Albert Camus, French author, died on Jan. 4, 1960, at age 46, in Villeneuve-la-Guyard, France.
3. Harry Chapin, U.S. folk-rock composer and singer, died on July 16, 1981, at age 38, in Long Island, N.Y.
4. James Dean, U.S. actor, died on Sept. 30, 1955, at age 24, in Cholame, Calif.
5. Brandon De Wilde, U.S. actor, died on July 6, 1972, at age 30, in Lakewood, Colo.
6. Charles Richard Drew, U.S. physician who developed "blood banks," died on Apr. 1, 1950, at age 45, near Burlington, N.C.
7. Randall Jarrell, U.S. poet, died on Oct. 14, 1965, at age 51, near Chapel Hill, N.C.
8. Jack A. Johnson, U.S. heavyweight boxing champion, died on June 10, 1946, at age 68, near Raleigh, N.C.
9. Hal Kemp, U.S. bandleader, died on Dec. 21, 1940, at age 36, near Madera, Calif.
10. Prince Aly Khan, Italian/Persian international playboy and Pakistani ambassador to the United Nations, died on May 13, 1960, at age 48, in Suresnes, France.
11. Ernie Kovacs, U.S. comedian, died on Jan. 13, 1962, at age 42, in West Los Angeles, Calif.
12. Jayne Mansfield, U.S. actress, died on June 29, 1967, at age 34, near New Orleans, La.
13. Margaret Mitchell, U.S. author, died on Aug. 16, 1949, at age 49, in Atlanta, Ga.
14. Tom Mix, U.S. film actor, died on Oct. 12, 1940, at age 60, near Florence, Ariz.
15. George S. Patton, Jr., U.S. army general, died on Dec. 21, 1945, at age 60, in Heidelberg, Germany.

16. Jackson Pollock, U.S. painter, died on Aug. 11, 1956, at age 44, in Long Island, N.Y.
17. Peter Revson, U.S. race car driver, died on Mar. 22, 1974, at age 35, in Johannesburg, South Africa.
18. John D. Rockefeller III, U.S. philanthropist, died on July 10, 1978, at age 72, in Pocantico Hills, N.Y.
19. Bessie Smith, U.S. singer, died on Sept. 26, 1937, at age 42, in Clarksdale, Miss.
20. Nathanael West, U.S. author, died on Dec. 22, 1940, at age 37, near El Centro, Calif.

—H.G.

11 GUNFIGHTERS WHO DID NOT DIE IN GUNFIGHTS

1. (ROBERT) CLAY ALLISON (1840–1887)

Allison is credited with killing between 12 and 18 men in gunfights during his adult life. When he was 47 years old, his life ended in a freak wagon accident near Washita, Tex.

2. JOHN SLAUGHTER (1841–1922)

Slaughter was involved in at least eight gun battles as a cattleman and sheriff between 1876 and 1901. The Cochise County, Ariz., lawman who gave varmints "24 hours ter git!" died at his apartment in Douglas, Ariz., of complications from high blood pressure at age 81.

3. VIRGIL W. EARP (1843–1906)

Virgil, Wyatt Earp's older brother, survived four gunfights between 1876 and 1881, including the one at the OK Corral, where he was wounded. He died at age 63 of pneumonia at his home in Goldfield, Nev.

4. FRANK JAMES (1843–1915)

Frank and his kid brother Jesse were the co-inventors of train robberies and daylight bank robberies. Jesse died at the hands of a member of their outlaw band, but Frank lived through two dozen skirmishes. When he was 73 years old, he died of heart disease on his Kearney, Mo., farm.

5. THOMAS COLEMAN YOUNGER (1844–1916)

Younger ended his criminal career with the James Gang by serving 25 years in a Minnesota prison. He later made the rounds on a lecture circuit before succumbing to heart trouble at age 72 in his Lees Summit, Mo., home.

6. WILLIAM M. (BILLY) BREAKENRIDGE (1846–1931)

The Tombstone, Ariz., deputy wasn't fast with a gun, but he lived through five showdowns, including one in which the infamous Johnny Ringo died. Breakenridge died after an appendectomy at age 85 in Tucson, Ariz.

7. WYATT EARP (1848–1929)

Earp may have survived his five face-offs between 1878 and 1884 because he wore a steel vest. The Tombstone, Ariz., lawman who had led the faction that included two of his brothers (Virgil and Morgan) and Doc Holliday against the Clanton gang at the OK Corral was bedridden off and on in his last years. In his weakened condition, the 81-year-old Earp suffered a relapse after going out to send a telegram to a friend. It is believed that the exertion killed him. He died in Los Angeles.

Wyatt Earp in 1925.

8. JOHN HENRY (DOC) HOLLIDAY (1851–1887)

Holliday was responsible for shooting Tom McLowry in the gun battle known as the "gunfight at the OK Corral" in 1881. That was one of eight showdowns for the dentist turned gambler, who died of tuberculosis at 36 in Glenwood Springs, Colo.

9. WILLIAM BARCLAY (BAT) MASTERSON (1853–1921)

As a lawman in Dodge City, Kans., and a gambler in Tombstone, Ariz., Masterson killed three men in shoot-outs. He had been sports editor on the *Morning Telegraph* in New York City for about 14 years when a heart attack killed him at his desk. He was 67.

Bat Masterson.

10. FRANK (BUCKSKIN) LESLIE (1858?–1948?)

Leslie shot Billy Claiborne in a classic Main Street-style gun battle in Tombstone, Ariz., in 1882. Leslie faded into obscurity but reportedly entered a San Diego, Calif., hospital in 1948 under a false name. The ailing, decrepit man, probably in his 90s, died of unknown causes shortly thereafter.

11. JEFF DAVID MILTON (1861–1947)

He "never killed a man that didn't need killing," Milton once said. During his 50-year career the Texas lawman notched up eight gunfights, but he died in bed at the ripe old age of 85 in Tucson, Ariz., after years of suffering from hardening of the arteries.

—T.C.

GONE WITH THE WIND, SORT OF: ASHES OF 19 FAMOUS PEOPLE—AND 1 DOG

1. MAUSOLUS, Ruler of Caria (?–c. 353 B.C.)

In what must have been a highly ritualized performance, his widow—and sister—Artemisia mixed his ashes in water and drank him. Having swallowed her beloved, she then erected a splendid memorial tomb for him at Halicarnassus in Asia Minor. This structure became one of the Seven Wonders of the World and gave us the word "mausoleum."

2. HENRY LAURENS, U.S. diplomat (1724–1792)

Reputedly the first white person cremated in America, Laurens had a horror of being buried alive. He charged his son to wrap his body in a 12-yd.-long tow-cloth winding sheet and let it burn until consumed. This was accomplished at Mepkin, the family estate near Charleston, S.C., where his ashes were buried.

3. JOAQUIN MILLER, U.S. poet (1839–1913)

Miller spent years constructing a massive granite cremation oven for himself on "The Hights," his estate at Oakland, Calif. However, when he died, civil authorities required that the actual cremation occur in Oakland facilities. Friends later deposited Miller's ashes on the faggots he had prepared and "recremated" him on the homemade pyre, then scattered the ash mixture over his estate.

4. HENRY JAMES, U.S.-born author (1843–1916)

After he was cremated in London, the novelist's ashes were smuggled past war-tightened customs inspection into America by his sister Alice. His ashes were buried in the James family plot at Cambridge, Mass.

5. GEORGE BERNARD SHAW, British playwright (1856–1950)

The ashes of Shaw's wife, who preceded him in death, were kept in a crematory for seven years. When Shaw himself died, his ashes were added to hers according to his instruction, and his doctor scattered the mixture over the garden of Shaw's home at Ayot St. Lawrence, England.

6. MOHANDAS K. GANDHI, Indian political leader (1869–1948)

Amid solemn ceremony, the body of the assassinated Hindu leader was burned atop a large sandalwood pyre on the banks of the Jumna River. Most of his ashes were then scattered at the confluence of India's most sacred rivers—the Ganges, Jumna, and Saraswati. However, small portions of Gandhi's ashes were given to some of his friends. Those given to Yogi Paramahansa Yogananda are enshrined in the Gandhi World Peace Memorial, a sarcophagus at the Self-Realization Fellowship Lake Shrine in Pacific Palisades, Calif.

7. JOE HILL, Swedish-born U.S. labor organizer and songwriter (1879–1915)

If you "dreamed [you] saw Joe Hill last night," maybe it wasn't just a dream; though hardly corporeal, he is, in fact, just about everywhere. Convicted of murder, the labor activist died in front of a Utah firing squad. From Chicago's Graceland Cemetery went dozens of envelopes to "Wobbly" (Industrial Workers of the World) locals in every state in the union except Utah and to every continent except Antarctica. Each envelope contained a pinch of Hill's ashes and a note. On May 1, 1916, the envelopes were opened at their destinations, and the ashes of Joe Hill were scattered and entered the world ecosystem.

8. CHARLES COBURN, U.S. actor (1877–1961)

"I am not in sympathy with burial," said Coburn, and friends carried out instructions to scatter his ashes in five separate locations: in Gramercy Park, New York City, at the base of Edwin Booth's statue and at the foot of a tree planted in memory of his first wife; on the stage of Union College's outdoor Mohawk Drama Theater in Schenectady, N.Y.; on his parents' and sister's graves in Savannah, Ga.; and along the Mohawk Trail (N.Y. State Highway 2) in the Berkshires.

9. DAMON RUNYON, U.S. author (1880–1946)

A portrayer of Broadway night people in his stories, Runyon desired to have his ashes scattered over Manhattan, "the place that I truly loved." Accordingly, the writer's longtime friend, Capt. Eddie Rickenbacker, piloted Runyon's son and the ash container over Manhattan, and the author's remains drifted down over the city "that was good to me."

10. JOSEPH W. STILWELL, U.S. general (1883–1946)

As he wished, there was no public funeral. Three of his W.W. II personal pilots carried his ashes aboard the Army transport plane he had used throughout the war. After twice circling his home in Carmel, Calif., the plane headed out over the Pacific and dropped Stilwell's "cremains" into the sea.

11. SINCLAIR LEWIS, U.S. author (1885–1951)

Lewis's ashes were brought from Italy, where he died, to the cemetery in Sauk Centre, Minn.—the hometown he had fiercely satirized in *Main Street*. When his brother, who wanted to keep the urn, carelessly poured the contents into the grave, a sudden gust of wind scattered a quantity of Sinclair Lewis over Minnesota.

12. HIDEKI TOJO, Japanese prime minister (1885–1948)

Hanged as a war criminal after W.W. II, Tojo and six others executed the same day were cremated. Gen. Douglas MacArthur refused to allow the families to claim possession of the remains, but Japanese workers salvaged some of the ashes and hid them until the end of the Allied occupation. A granite tomb containing these remains was unveiled at Hazu in 1960 with the inscription "Tomb of Seven Martyrs."

13. ALEXANDER WOOLLCOTT, U.S. journalist (1887–1943)

A friend, presumably, picked up witty Aleck's last tab in the kind of story that Woollcott himself liked to collect. His ashes were destined for burial at Hamilton College—his alma mater—in Clinton, N.Y., but were delivered by mistake to Colgate University in Hamilton, N.Y. Forwarded to Clinton, they arrived with 67¢ postage due.

14. ROBERT BENCHLEY, U.S. humorist (1889–1945)

Benchley's last joke, though hardly planned, was nevertheless characteristic. Somewhere between the crematory and his intended grave in Nantucket, Mass., the contents of his burial urn disappeared. When his widow discovered that she had driven miles for the solemn occasion with an empty container, she was quiet for a moment, then smiled and said: "I can hear him laughing now."

15. THOMAS "FATS" WALLER, U.S. musician (1904–1943)

The jazz pianist and composer died of pneumonia on a train en route to New York City from Los Angeles. An unidentified W.W. I aviator known as the "Black Ace" flew the urn containing Waller's ashes over Manhattan Island and, according to his wishes, scattered them directly on Harlem, his boyhood home.

16. WILLIAM SAROYAN, U.S. author (1908–1981)

Prolific author of short stories, novels, plays, and essays, Saroyan won a Pulitzer Prize for his 1939 play *The Time of Your Life*. Born the son of Armenian immigrants in Fresno, Calif., Saroyan felt an allegiance to both his homeland and his heritage. Half of his ashes are interred in Fresno, and half are in the Armenian capital of Yerevan, in the U.S.S.R.

17. WOODY GUTHRIE, U.S. folk singer, composer (1912–1967)

The canister containing his ashes "looked like an institution-size can of beans," according to biographer Joe Klein. Guthrie's family took the container to his favorite spot in Coney Island, intending to scatter his ashes on the sea, but no one could open the metal can. They punctured holes in the top with a beer-can opener, but the contents wouldn't pour— so son Arlo finally hurled the container seaward off the jetty. It floated awhile, then sank. Knowing that Woody would approve, the family had hot dogs afterward.

18. MARIA CALLAS, U.S. opera singer (1923–1977)

Following her cremation, the diva's ashes rested in a special urn at Père Lachaise Cemetery in Paris while awaiting settlement of a lengthy family dispute over their custody. The urn was stolen late in 1977 but was recovered a short time later. Finally in 1979, a Greek Navy vessel transported the urn 37 mi. southeast of Athens, and friends fulfilled the singer's own request by scattering her ashes over a choppy Aegean Sea.

19. JIM JONES, U.S. cult leader (1931–1978)

Jones had taken many of his followers deep into the Guyanan jungle, where they carved out the village of Jonestown. Almost one month after he convinced his disciples that they were as sick of life as he was, the organizer of the mass suicide-murder of 913 people was cremated in New Jersey. The state's attorney general charged the next day that there had been no proper authorization for the action. While the legalistic flap raged, Jones's ashes added to the Atlantic Ocean's pollution.

20. PASCHA, U.S. police dog (1973–1981)

During his four-year career with the Santa Monica Police Department, Pascha saw more than his share of the sordid pink underbelly of society, helping to capture no less than 30 armed suspects and aiding in over 200 felony arrests. A man high on PCP once knifed him so badly he almost lost a paw. On another occasion he saved the life of his handler, Sgt. Barney Melekian, by warning him a split second before a shotgun blast shattered their car window. Pascha died of heart failure soon after his retirement. His ashes are buried under a Christmas tree in the Melekian backyard.

—J.E.

7 PEOPLE WHO WERE BURIED ALIVE— AND LIVED

1. MAX HOFFMAN (buried 1865, U.S.)

When five-year-old Max "died" of cholera, he was buried in the cemetery of the small Wisconsin town near his family's farm. The next night, his mother had a nightmare—she saw Max turned over in his coffin, struggling to escape, with his hands clasped beneath his right cheek. She begged her husband to disinter their child, but he refused. The next night, Mrs. Hoffman had the same dream. Her demands were so urgent that her husband complied—at one o'clock in the morning, he and a neighbor began digging. Max's body lay just as it had in his mother's dream but showed no signs of life. The body was brought to the doctor who had pronounced the boy dead. Reluctantly, he attempted to revive him, and after an hour the lad's eyelid twitched. Hot bags of salt were placed under his armpits, and he was given brandy. Within a week he had fully recovered. Max Hoffman lived to be nearly 90 and treasured until his death the little metal handles of his boyhood coffin.

2. SISTER DELPHINE DE ST. PAUL (buried 1876, U.S.)

Minnie Keusch was born in Detroit, Mich., in 1859. At 17 she contracted typhoid fever, was certified dead, and was sealed in her coffin. Minnie's bereaved sister begged for a final look, which she was granted. The sister bent down and kissed the "dead" girl—and Minnie opened her eyes. On that day Minnie decided to become a nun. She died in 1958, just three months short of her 100th birthday. She had served for 75 years as Sister Delphine de St. Paul, in the order of the Little Sisters of the Poor.

3. MARJORIE ELPHINSTONE (buried 17th century, Scotland)

Marjorie and her husband, wealthy landowner Walter Innes, lived on a small estate called Ardtannies on the banks of the River Don. Marjorie "died" in the first decade of the 17th century and was buried wearing her jewelry. The night after the funeral the gravedigger exhumed Marjorie and began pulling her rings from her fingers. Waking from her coma, she groaned, which sent the thief running. Marjorie gathered up her jewelry and retraced the path of the funeral cortege to Ardtannies. Inside, relatives were tending her grief-stricken husband. Hearing a sound at the door, Walter said that had he not seen his wife dead and buried, he would have sworn it was her knock. Marjorie died for good in 1622, outliving her husband by six years. Her tombstone can be seen today in the churchyard at Inverurie in rural Aberdeenshire.

4. MARGARET HALCROW (buried in the 1670s, Scotland)

Margaret Halcrow was an Arcadian woman who "died" soon after her marriage in 1674 to Rev. Henry Erskine, the minister of Chirnside in the Scottish Lothians. Knowing that Margaret was being buried with valuable jewelry, the sexton covered her grave lightly with dirt. When he dug her up later, he tried to cut off her ring finger. Margaret screamed, leaped out of the coffin, and raced to her home, shroud billowing behind her. Knocking at the entrance, she said, "Open the door, for I'm fair clemmed wi' the cauld."

5. ANONYMOUS WOMAN (buried 1980, U.S.)

On Nov. 20, 1980, a 26-year-old woman met a man she knew slightly at Jumbo's Bar in Hollywood, Calif. The man, 38-year-old James Earl Gibbs, offered to take her home, saying he had to drop by his apartment first. There, Gibbs punched her, tore off her clothes, and raped her. Then he took her to a wooded area on the grounds of Hollywood's Immaculate Heart College. Gibbs maniacally began to stab her—20 times in all—severing her jugular vein, carotid artery, and larynx. "I kept screaming until I began gurgling with blood," she later testified. After the stabbing, Gibbs buried her in a shallow grave and covered her with dirt and

427

leaves. These she pressed into her wounds to keep from bleeding to death. After clawing and crawling her way out of the grave, she was discovered by a security guard and rushed to surgery. She was so horribly wounded that Dr. Eugene Flaum said he thought he was "probably operating on a corpse." Her testimony in May, 1982, resulted in Gibbs receiving a maximum sentence of 27 years. About five years before, Gibbs had stabbed and killed his wife and discarded her body in a wooded area. He had served only three years in prison for that crime.

6. VICTORINE LEFOURCADE (buried 1810, France)

Victorine was young, beautiful, and born to a rich and noble family. She loved a poor young journalist, Julius Bossuet, but her parents would not let them marry. Instead, they "forced her to reject her lover and marry a certain Monsieur Renelle, a banker and politician without any heart, who treated her cruelly." After a few years of misery, Victorine "fell sick of grief and sorrow, and died." Her wish was to be buried simply in the village where she was born. When Bossuet heard of her death, his despair drove him to seek a remembrance of his love—a lock of her beautiful hair. He traveled from Paris to the village churchyard and at midnight dug out Victorine's coffin and unscrewed the lid. As he was about to cut off a lock of hair, she opened her eyes. Reunited, the lovers stayed hidden until Victorine had regained her health, and then went to the U.S. After 20 years, they returned to France, feeling sure that no one would recognize her. However, she *was* recognized—and when Renelle heard about it, he had her arrested and laid claim to her. The court refused to honor his claim, and Victorine and Bossuet were finally free to love in their native France.

7. ANONYMOUS MAN (buried 1831, England)

Four days after his burial, this victim of typhoid fever was exhumed and brought to a group of medical students for dissection. He was placed on a marble slab, where a professor cut into his chest. The "corpse" suddenly let out a cry and grabbed the professor's arm. This Englishman lived for many years afterward and published a rare, lengthy account of his conscious recollection of his death and burial. As his physical strength waned from the typhoid fever, he never lost his mental awareness, but he lost all ability to speak or communicate in any way. He heard his doctor say, "All is over!," felt his face being covered with a cloth, and heard his family crying. He lay in state, completely alert, as his friends and relatives mourned for three days. Then he was given to the undertakers, who "treated me with revolting brutality." The following description reads like a story by Edgar Allan Poe: "I heard the crashing of the wood as they drove in the nails in fastening the lid . . . crammed into that narrow box . . . I experienced a sensation as if my head and limbs were being torn asunder . . . I would never have believed that a heart could suffer so much without breaking." He heard a friend reading his sermon at the graveside and heard the dirt crashing over his coffin. He hoped to die quickly but remained alert for four days and throughout the exhumation. In the dissecting room he recognized two friends from medical school. And finally, with the cut of the knife, "I succeeded in crying out, the bonds of death were separated, and I returned to life."

—A.W.

3 AMERICANS BURIED IN THE KREMLIN

1. WILLIAM DUDLEY HAYWOOD (1869–1928)

A native of Salt Lake City, labor leader "Big Bill" Haywood presided over the founding of the Industrial Workers of the World (IWW) in Chicago in 1905. While IWW secretary, he was convicted of sedition for his denunciation of W.W. I as a capitalist attack on workers worldwide. Sentenced to 20 years in prison, he jumped bail in 1921 and fled to the Soviet Union. There he was greeted enthusiastically by the Soviet masses and awarded a medal recognizing him as a revolutionary hero. He spent the remainder of his life in Moscow.

2. JOHN REED (1887–1920)

A journalist and author of *Ten Days That Shook the World,* Reed was an outspoken supporter of radical causes. A native of Portland, Ore., he observed and wrote about the 1917 Russian Revolution and became a close friend of Lenin. After Reed returned to the U.S., he helped found the Communist Labor Party and was indicted for sedition, then sought asylum in the U.S.S.R. At age 33, he was stricken with typhus and died in a Moscow hospital. After a funeral procession through the streets of the Soviet capital, Reed was buried in the Kremlin. In 1981 he was the hero of the Hollywood film *Reds.*

3. CHARLES EMIL RUTHENBERG (1882–1927)

One of the first general secretaries of the U.S. Communist party, Ruthenberg was a Cleveland salesman and office manager who helped the Communists split off from the Socialists in the U.S. in 1919. He ultimately became the party's top leader in the U.S. and died in Chicago of peritonitis while free on bail pending trial in Michigan (he was appealing a conviction on criminal syndicalism). His ashes were sent to Moscow for interment in the Kremlin wall.

—R.T.

10 WILLS THAT WERE IGNORED

1. VERGIL, Roman poet; died 19 B.C.

Anticipating his own death, the perfectionist author of the *Aeneid* worried about his 12-book epic poem, which was in rough draft form. He left instructions that the manuscript should be burned, since it had not been polished to his absolute satisfaction. However, Caesar Augustus nullified Vergil's will, and the poem was published after minimal polishing by others.

2. CAROLUS LINNAEUS, Swedish botanist; died 1778

Some years before his death, Linnaeus left specific instructions as to how he should be planted: "Lay me in a coffin unshaven, unwashed, unclothed, wrapped only in a sheet. Nail down the coffin forthwith, that none may see my wretchedness. . . . Entertain nobody at my funeral, and accept no condolences." In spite of the Swedish botanist's request that no funeral feast be held, his wife ignored the order, inviting everyone in the region to a luncheon.

3. CHARLES LEE, U.S. Revolutionary War general; died 1782

"I desire most earnestly that I may not be buried in any church, or churchyard," Lee stated in his will, explaining that "I have kept so much bad company when living, that I do not choose to continue it when dead." Historian Benson J. Lossing commented, "He neither feared nor loved God or man." Lee openly opposed his superior, General Washington, and eventually was dismissed from service. Nevertheless, when Lee died in Philadelphia, he was buried with military honors in the cemetery of Christ Church.

4. VISCOUNT AMBERLEY, British freethinker; died 1875

Lord Amberley stipulated in his will that friends should rear his son—the future philosopher, mathematician, and peace activist Bertrand Russell—as an agnostic. But to most upper-class Britons, Christianity is tantamount to patriotism. Hence a British court set aside Amberley's provision, and the boy was brought up by his liberal Puritan grandmother. Ironically, by age 18 and despite Lady Russell's influence, Russell had arrived at agnosticism on his own.

5. FRANZ LISZT, Hungarian pianist, composer; died 1886

Liszt, who had taken minor orders as a Roman Catholic *abbé* in 1865, requested in his will that he be buried in his Franciscan cassock and that a requiem mass be celebrated at his funeral. Instead, his death was treated as a bothersome distraction, since the Wagner musical festival was then in progress at Bayreuth. A quickly summoned Lutheran minister pronounced the benediction.

6. FRANK WORK, American businessman; died ?

Frank Work despised the British aristocracy after the breakup of his daughter's marriage to James Burke-Roche, an English nobleman. He tried to dispose of his $15 million fortune so as to prevent his grandchildren from visiting their father and marrying Europeans. Because his descendants rejected his chauvinistic will, however, his great-great-granddaughter—Diana, Princess of Wales—will probably become the next Queen of England.

7. FLORENCE NIGHTINGALE, British nurse and hospital administrator; died 1910

In her will she donated her body to medical science, requesting that the final interment of her remains be "in the nearest convenient burial ground." And she also specified that "not more than two persons without trappings" should escort her body to the grave. Public opinion overruled her wishes on all three counts: She was not dissected; six sergeants from the Guards regiments carried her coffin; and she was interred in the Hampshire cemetery where her parents lay.

8. FRANKLIN DELANO ROOSEVELT, U.S. president; died 1945

On the morning of Roosevelt's funeral, his penciled burial instructions were discovered in his White House bedroom safe. By then, the ceremonial machinery of a presidential funeral had advanced far beyond his wishes, which stipulated a simple casket of "dark wood" (the actual casket was a 600-lb. bronze deluxe model); that his body "be not embalmed or hermetically sealed" (both were done); and overnight placement of the casket in "the big room" at his Hyde Park, N.Y., estate (burial was immediately after arrival of the funeral train at Hyde Park).

9. W. C. FIELDS, U.S. film comedian; died 1946

Fields wanted his body cremated with no religious ceremony whatever. His estranged Roman Catholic wife, however, vetoed these wishes, which were stated in his will. Both she and his mistress, Carlotta Monti, had separate religious ceremonies conducted before his body was interred in a Los Angeles mausoleum. In addition, nothing came of his provision that a "W. C. Fields College for orphan white boys and girls" be established.

10. VIVIEN LEIGH, British actress; died 1967

Her will bequeathed her eyes, after death, to an eye bank. However, she had suffered for years from flare-ups of tuberculosis and finally died of this disease, which precluded the use of her corneas as transplants. Following a requiem mass in London, her body was cremated.

—J.E.

GEORGE PLIMPTON'S 10 PERSONS IN HISTORY WHOSE LIVES HE WOULD LIKE TO HAVE LIVED IN 10 PAST INCARNATIONS

He has lived his books: played with the New York Philharmonic, quarterbacked for the Detroit Lions, entered the boxing arena with Archie Moore, and stepped onto the tennis court with Pancho Gonzales. On top of all that, Plimpton has impressive literary credentials as the cofounder of *Paris Review*, an associate editor for *Harper's*, and a special contributor to *Sports Illustrated*. His books include *Paper Lion, Shadow-Box,* and *Open Net.*

1. Richard Haliburton
2. Amelia Earhart

431

3. Captain of the *Mary Celeste*
4. Ambrose Bierce
5. Judge Crater
6. James Hoffa
7.–10. and four of the leaders of the lost tribes of Israel

Note: The *Mary Celeste* was discovered floating in the Atlantic in November, 1872, with no one aboard. Captain Benjamin Briggs, his wife, baby daughter, and seven-man crew had vanished; their fate has never been discovered. Judge Joseph Crater (1889–?), a New York Supreme Court justice, disappeared on Aug. 6, 1930. It was speculated that he was involved in political corruption through Tammany Hall and possibly murdered or that he decided to leave his old life and begin anew somewhere else. He has never been found.

—Exclusive for *The Book of Lists 3*

20
ENDPAPERS

MANHATTAN'S 5 LARGEST
TICKER-TAPE PARADES

The U.S. traditionally honors its heroes by showering them with shredded paper as they proceed past the skyscrapers of Manhattan. The tonnage listed below represents the weight of the refuse—mainly ticker-tape, Teletype, and tissue paper—found in the streets after some of the largest parades. The fact that less paper has been swept up in recent years is attributed to sealed skyscraper windows, a shorter route that runs through what is called the "Canyon of Heroes," and the replacement of the ticker-tape machine by the computer.

1. John Glenn (1962)	3,474 tons
2. Gen. Douglas MacArthur (1951)	3,249 tons

In 1962, astronaut John Glenn was showered by the largest ticker-tape parade in New York history.

3. Charles Lindbergh (1927)   1,750 tons
4. Returned Iranian hostages (1981)   1,260 tons
5. N.Y. Mets baseball victory (1969)   1,254 tons*

*These were thrown during a spontaneous celebration following the Mets' World Series victory on Oct. 16, 1969. A formal victory parade four days later produced 578 tons.

SOURCE: The City of New York Department of Sanitation.

10 DISAPPEARANCES OF LARGE OBJECTS

1. ATLANTIS (disappeared around 1200 B.C.)

The riddle of the lost continent of Atlantis has mystified historians and geographers for centuries. Plato, the original source for the tale of Atlantis, described it as a lush paradise with mountain ranges and every kind of fruit and animal. The capital city was laid out in perfect concentric circles of alternating land and water, interconnected by bridges and tunnels. In the center circle stood a temple of ivory, silver, and gold. Presumably an Aegean island, it may have been destroyed by a volcanic explosion 3,200 years ago. However, not only is the existence of Atlantis disputed, but its location as well. Recently, a giant wall was discovered underwater near North Bimini in the Bahamas, and speculation arose that it was a remnant of the lost land of Atlantis.

2. FRIESLAND (disappeared in the late 17th century)

A large populated island south of Greenland, Friesland occupied a place on world maps for at least a century—from the 1550s to the 1660s. According to Nordic legends, the people of Friesland were skilled craftsmen who traded with Greenland and with European visitors. But by the late 17th century, Friesland had disappeared from most maps for some unknown reason. One possibility is that the land mass sank. Another possibility is that it had been mistaken for a nearby island which did sink. The place, called Buss, was referred to as the "Sunken Land of Buss" on a Dutch chart dated 1745.

3. AURORA ISLANDS (disappeared c. 1820)

These three snowcapped subantarctic islands located halfway between the East and West Falklands (Islas Malvinas) and their South Georgia dependency were first sighted by a Spanish ship in 1762. The same ship reported seeing them several times after that, and in 1794 the islands were surveyed by the Spanish captain of the *Atrevida*, who charted their longitude and latitude, putting them on the map. But 26 years later, Antarctic explorer Capt. James Weddell searched in vain for the Auroras, and an American sealer could find no trace of them in 1822. Subsequent searches for the Auroras have been equally unsuccessful.

4. TUANAKI ISLANDS (disappeared between 1842 and 1844)

Inhabited by a group of peaceful Polynesians, these three small South Pacific islands were near the Isle of Mangaia in the Cook Archipelago. A sailor who spent six days there in 1842 described the natives as a friendly, seafaring people who loved to sing and dance. Two years later, the Tuanaki Islands had completely disappeared. A group of British missionaries en route to the islands, combed the area but couldn't find any trace of them or their inhabitants. Since the islanders were expert sailors, whatever happened to the Tuanakis must have occurred quickly with no warning, giving them no chance to escape by sea.

5. AMERICAN COLONY OF ELLENA (disappeared in 1866)

This obscure lost American colony in Borneo lasted less than a year before being swallowed up by the Malayan jungle. Also known as Ambong and Maroodu, the colony was established as a land boondoggle by two American schemers. One of the rascals, Charles Lee Moses, managed to be appointed U.S. consul to Borneo in 1864. The Yankee next convinced the sultan of Brunei to lease most of North Borneo to the colony, and thus Moses and his partner, Joseph Torrey, became rajas over a vast territory. At its peak, Ellena's population consisted of 11 Americans and 60 Chinese. Eventually Moses and Torrey quarreled over money, and the colony of Ellena (which was never recognized by the U.S.) expired through neglect and lack of funding in 1866. The jungle soon reclaimed the area, and a Navy lieutenant who went looking for the colony years later failed to find it.

6. *IRON MOUNTAIN* RIVERBOAT (disappeared June, 1872)

The last time anyone saw the *Iron Mountain*, it was rounding a bend in the Mississippi River. Carrying 55 passengers and crew members, the 180-ft. riverboat had left Vicksburg, Miss.—laden with a cargo of molasses and towing barges of cotton—to head north. Two hours later another riverboat, the *Iroquois Chief*, nearly collided with a string of runaway cotton barges from the *Iron Mountain*. The *Iroquois Chief*'s captain noticed the ropes that had connected the barges to the *Iron Mountain* had been cut deliberately. Other ships joined the search for the lost riverboat, but neither survivors nor debris could be found.

7. COLUMBIAN LIBERTY BELL (disappeared July, 1893)

The baffling disappearance of the Columbian Liberty Bell has remained a mystery for nearly a century. Cast for the 1893 World's Columbian Exposition in Chicago, the 7-ft.-tall bell was rung for the first time on the Fourth of July, 1893. More than 200,000 people contributed to its making, donating watches, silver spoons, wedding rings, gold and silver thimbles, and over 250,000 pennies. Historic metal pieces—including a copper kettle that had belonged to Thomas Jefferson and a surveyor's chain used by George Washington—also became part of the bell. Its sponsors, the Daughters of the American Revolution, had planned to use the bell after the exposition to promote world peace, but when the exposition closed, the huge 13,000-lb. bell was nowhere to be found.

8. YUMA MISSION (disappeared in 1970)

No one is quite sure exactly where the Mission of the Four Evangelists rests. Believed to be within a 40-mi. radius of Yuma, Ariz., the lost Spanish mission hides under desert sands for years, then magically reappears. Possibly located in Arizona, the mission more likely is on the Mexican side of the border, along a lake called the Laguna Prieta, though no one has seen the brackish lake either in recent years. The mission's disappearing act is attributed to a natural phenomenon called "walking dunes"—knolls of sand that form around solid objects and constantly change shapes. Since some walking dunes reach heights of 300 ft., they may be covering up the lost mission. A student aviator who spotted a belfry sticking up from the sand dunes in 1970 is the last person to report seeing the mission.

9. ITALIAN LAKE (disappeared July, 1980)

A calm, peaceful body of water, the small lake had nestled next to Comelice Supiriore in the Italian Dolomites for hundreds of years. Then one warm summer day, the water inexplicably vanished, leaving nothing but mud and a few fish where the lake had been. At 5:00 P.M. people had been fishing and children were splashing about in the lake. Five minutes later, there was a roar of rushing water and a great spiral of water rose out of the center of the lake. With a giant gurgling noise, the lake disappeared. Hydraulic engineers and geologists have been unable to explain the lake's vanishing act.

10. S.S. *POET* (disappeared Oct. 24, 1980)

Bound for Egypt with a cargo of corn, the U.S. freighter S.S. *Poet* and its crew of 34 vanished the day it left Philadelphia. The last communication with the *Poet* was a ship-to-shore telephone conversation that day between the third mate and his wife. When the freighter failed to radio its position after a week, the owner unsuccessfully tried to contact it. Finally, he notified the Coast Guard, which launched a 10-day search covering over 300,000 sq. mi. But not a trace of the ship or its crew was ever found. A congressional investigation revealed that two other vessels owned by the same company had sunk from overloading. It was also revealed that two days after the ship's departure, there were stormy 40-ft. seas. Why no distress signal was sent remains a mystery.

—L.K.S.

6 GREAT SAUSAGE EVENTS

1. COMIC SAUSAGE

Epicharmus, a Greek dramatist who lived during the golden age of Sophocles and Aeschylus, wrote a comedy titled *Orya* (*The Sausage*) around 500 B.C. Because the play exists today only as a fragment, we will never know exactly what the Greeks thought was funny about sausage.

The African sausage tree blooms at night,
emitting a mouselike odor.

2. HEATHEN SAUSAGE

The ancient Romans were so fond of pork sausage spiced with pine
nuts and pepper that the dish became a staple of the annual Lupercalian
and Floralian festivals. Since these pagan celebrations usually degener-
ated into orgiastic rites, the early Christians looked upon them with dis-

approval. When Constantine the Great, a Christian, became emperor in 324 A.D., he outlawed the production and consumption of the sinful sausage. But the Romans refused to cooperate and developed a flourishing black market in sausage. They continued to eat the bootlegged delicacies throughout the reigns of several Christian emperors until the ban was finally lifted.

3. FATAL SAUSAGE

At a simple peasant meal in Wildbad, Germany, in 1793, 13 people shared a single sausage. Within hours they became seriously ill, and six of them died. Their disease became known as botulism—a word coined from the Latin for sausage, *botulus*. The powerfully toxic bacteria *Clostridium botulinum* inside the sausage could have been easily killed by boiling it for two minutes. Once in the body, botulism toxins attack the nervous system, causing paralysis of all muscles, which brings on death by suffocation.

4. HUMAN SAUSAGE

Adolph Luetgert, a Chicago sausagemaker, was so fond of entertaining his mistresses that he had a bed installed in his factory. Louisa Luetgert was aware of her husband's infidelities, and in 1897 their marriage took a dramatic turn for the worse. Louisa subsequently disappeared, and when the police arrived to search Luetgert's factory, they found human teeth and bones—as well as two gold rings engraved "L.L."—at the bottom of a sausage vat. During his well-publicized trial, Luetgert maintained his innocence, but he was convicted of murder and spent the rest of his life in prison.

5. MUCKRAKING SAUSAGE

Upton Sinclair's novel *The Jungle*, an exposé of conditions in the Chicago stockyards and meat industry, contained shocking descriptions: "There was never the least attention paid to what was cut up for sausage . . . there would be meat stored in great piles . . . thousands of rats would race about on it . . . these rats were nuisances, and the packers would put poisoned bread out for them; they would die, and then rats, bread, and meat would go into the hoppers together." Americans were deeply alarmed by the filth described, and in the same year the book was published, Congress passed the Pure Food and Drug Act of 1906.

6. INSOLENT SAUSAGE

In October, 1981, Joseph Guillou, an engineer on the Moroccan tanker *Al Ghassani*, was arrested, fined £50, and sentenced to two years in jail for insulting Morocco's King Hassan. Guillou's offense was hanging a sausage on the hook normally reserved for a portrait of the monarch. A sausage, said Guillou, was "more useful than a picture of the king."

—K.P.

MOST OFTEN REQUESTED LIST:
10 LINCOLN-KENNEDY COINCIDENCES

The authors of *The Book of Lists, The People's Almanac,* and "Significa"—a weekly column in *Parade* Magazine—have received scores of letters from readers who would like to see a list comparing the eerie coincidences between the lives of two great U.S. presidents, Abraham Lincoln and John F. Kennedy. To the many readers who have contributed entries to this list, the authors say thank you.

1. SONS AND BROTHERS

Two of Lincoln's sons were named Edward and Robert. Edward died at age three, Robert lived on. Two of Kennedy's brothers were named Robert and Edward. Robert was assassinated, Edward lived on.

2. TAKING OFFICE

Lincoln was elected president in 1860. Kennedy was elected president in 1960.

3. SECRETARIES

Lincoln's secretary was named Kennedy. Kennedy's secretary was named Lincoln.

4. WIVES

Mary Lincoln and Jackie Kennedy both had children who died while their husbands were in the White House.

5. THE ASSASSINATIONS

Both presidents were with their wives, and both were shot in the back of the head. And they were both shot on a Friday.

6. THE ASSASSINS

Lincoln's assassin, John Wilkes Booth, and Kennedy's alleged assassin, Lee Harvey Oswald, were both Southerners who were in their 20s.

7. SCENE OF THE CRIME

Booth shot Lincoln while he was sitting in a theater, then hid in a warehouse. Kennedy was shot from a warehouse; Oswald was found hiding in a theater.

8. NEVER BROUGHT TO JUSTICE

Booth and Oswald were both killed before they could be tried in court.

9. THE SUCCESSION

Abraham Lincoln was succeeded by Andrew Johnson, who was

born in 1808. John Kennedy was succeeded by Lyndon Johnson, who was born in 1908. Both Johnsons had served in the U.S. Senate.

10. NUMEROLOGY

The names Lincoln and Kennedy each contain seven letters, Andrew Johnson and Lyndon Johnson each have 13 letters, and John Wilkes Booth and Lee Harvey Oswald each total 15 letters.

—THE EDS.

10 GOOD THINGS THAT HAPPENED ON FRIDAY THE 13TH

Superstition tells us that Friday the 13th is a day of bad luck. It's true that some of history's worst disasters have happened on that day, and people everywhere tend to get jumpy and use extra caution on Friday the 13th. Winston Churchill refused to travel on the "unlucky" Friday—a practice many others would agree with, whether it be flying across the Pacific Ocean or walking to the corner store. Nevertheless, the old superstition doesn't hold up that well, for we have discovered quite a few *good* things that have happened on the fateful day and date. Here are some notable examples.

1. NORTHWEST ORDINANCE PASSED (July 13, 1787)

Among the most important laws the U.S. Congress ever adopted, the Northwest Ordinance offered the territories assurance of participation in the national government. The Northwest Territory was later divided into the states of Ohio, Indiana, Illinois, Michigan, Wisconsin, and eastern Minnesota.

2. ENGLAND INAUGURATES ITS FIRST ELECTRIC STREET-LIGHTING SYSTEM (Dec. 13, 1878)

Electric cables laid beneath the streets of London carried the charge from a dynamo housed in a shed to 20 Jablochkoff candles which lighted up that city's Holborn Viaduct. Summed up the *London News* the following Monday, "The quality of the light, as well as its quantity, appears to be establishing it firmly in public favor. . . ."

3. ALFRED DREYFUS IS REINSTATED IN THE FRENCH ARMY (July 13, 1906)

Twelve years after Dreyfus was wrongly convicted of treason and banished to Devil's Island, the sad affair finally came to a just conclusion.

On this day the French Senate and Chamber of Deputies approved a government bill restoring the Jewish officer to the army and promoting him to the rank of major.

4. ASCAP ORGANIZED TO PROTECT COMPOSERS AND LYRICISTS (Feb. 13, 1914)

The American Society of Composers, Authors, and Publishers was formed in New York City for the purpose of collecting royalties when copyrighted music is performed in public for profit. Music publisher George Maxwell was elected president of the new organization, whose first members included composers Irving Berlin, Victor Herbert, and John Philip Sousa.

5. U.S. SECRETARY OF STATE FRANK B. KELLOGG FORMALLY PROPOSES BANNING WAR AS AN INSTRUMENT OF NATIONAL POLICY (Apr. 13, 1928)

Inspired by French Foreign Minister Aristide Briand's proposal that the U.S. and France forge a bilateral treaty to renounce war forever, Kellogg expanded Briand's concept to include the other major powers. Thus on Aug. 27, 1928, 15 nations signed the unprecedented Pact of Paris. While nearly all of the signatories abrogated its spirit upon the outbreak of W.W. II, the idealistic effort earned Kellogg the Nobel Peace Prize in 1929.

6. FIRST WOMAN GRANTED AIRPLANE INSTRUCTOR'S LICENSE (Oct. 13, 1939)

After completing 200 hours of flight, Evelyn Pinckert Kilgore received the first instructor's license ever issued to an aviatrix under the Civil Aeronautics Authority. Kilgore put her license to work during W.W. II when she trained pilots at her flight school in Pomona, Calif.

7. GREEK PATRIOTS RETAKE ATHENS (Oct. 13, 1944)

"The great hour of freedom has come." So began the broadcast which announced to the world that the 3½-year Nazi occupation of history's oldest "democratic" city had ended. But as the Greek flag was unfurled above the Acropolis that day, the turmoil of the past few years was far from over, and civil war soon erupted in the country.

8. ANNOUNCEMENT OF RETURN OF THE *KITTY HAWK* (Feb. 13, 1948)

On this date the Science Museum in London announced that the *Kitty Hawk*, the Wright brothers' airplane, would be returned to the U.S. for permanent display at the Smithsonian Institution. The biplane was sent to England in 1928 after an indignant Orville Wright (Wilbur had died in 1912) refused to give it to the Smithsonian because it had labeled another plane, the Langley Aerodrome, as "the first airplane capable of sustained free flight with a man." When Orville died in 1948, his will specified that the *Kitty Hawk* be given to the Science Museum. The famous flying machine was formally installed in the place of "highest honor" in the Smithsonian's Arts and Industries building on Dec. 17, 1948.

9. PRESIDENT LYNDON JOHNSON CRACKS DOWN ON SEX DISCRIMINATION IN GOVERNMENT (Oct. 13, 1967)

In signing an executive order to this effect, President Johnson ensured that the existing machinery designed to abolish discrimination on the basis of race, creed, color, and national origin henceforward would just as zealously rid the government of sex bias.

10. NASA SELECTS FIRST WOMEN ASTRONAUTS (Jan. 13, 1978)

Fifteen years after a female Soviet cosmonaut orbited the earth 48 times, the National Aeronautics and Space Administration chose six women to join the astronaut corps as mission specialists to perform medical, scientific, and engineering tasks on space shuttle flights starting in the mid-1980s. All but one of the previous 73 astronauts had been white males.

—W.A.D.

12 AMAZING ATTIC EVENTS

1. THE RESIDENCE OF MADAME DE POMPADOUR (1745–1750)

Madame Jeanne-Antoinette d'Étoiles was known throughout Paris as one of the most beautiful and cultured women of her day. In 1745, she met King Louis XV of France. The two immediately fell in love, and Madame d'Étoiles obtained a legal separation from her husband. She was then given the title of the Marquise de Pompadour and installed in the attic apartment of Versailles as the king's mistress. Her apartment became known as the meeting place for some of the most celebrated people of France, and her guests were assisted in the steep 100-stair ascent by an elementary lift dubbed the "flying chair." But her private life with the king was less than ideal. After two blissful years together, Pompadour lost her physical passion for the king. She feared losing him and believed that a diet of vanilla, truffles, and celery would stimulate her desire for sexual activity. It only worsened her already weak physical condition. After five years in the attic, the king moved her to a flat on the ground floor of the palace. It was clear he had now taken new mistresses. Pompadour, however, retained her powerful position as the king's political and artistic adviser until her death in 1764.

2. THE SUICIDE OF THOMAS CHATTERTON (1770)

As a boy, Thomas Chatterton was a prodigious poet and scholar, and early Romantic who at age 10 wrote on a par with his adult contemporaries. His family was poor, his mother a widowed seamstress, and privacy was difficult to come by in their small Bristol home. So young Thomas set up a writing room in the attic, which he jealously guarded as his secret domain. In the attic room, among his books and papers, stood Ellinor, a life-size doll made of woven rushes, which his mother used for dress fittings. Thomas loved Ellinor and always took care to powder her face and fix her hair. However, when he moved to London to pursue his literary career, he left his beloved Ellinor behind. He rented a garret reminiscent of his attic study at home, and there, after suffering repeated personal and professional disappointments, including failure to sell a series of forgeries he claimed had been written by a 15th century monk, Chatterton took arsenic and died at age 17.

3. THE LITERARY GARRET OF EDMOND DE GONCOURT (1885–1896)

Edmond and his brother Jules were French novelists. Both are best remembered for the detailed journals they kept on literary people of the late 19th century. Jules died in 1870, and in 1885, Edmond turned the two attic rooms of the house into a salon. Each Sunday afternoon, he would entertain such notables as Guy de Maupassant and Émile Zola. The following are some excerpts from Edmond's journal on these afternoons.

Feb. 1, 1885 On the French poet Robert de Montesquieu-Fezenac: "Somebody described his first love affair with a female ventriloquist who, while [he] was straining to achieve his climax, would imitate the drunken voice of a pimp."

May 24, 1885 Edmond comments on Zola's reaction to the recent death of Victor Hugo: "He walked around the room as if relieved by his death and as if convinced he was going to inherit the literary papacy."

Apr. 19, 1896 A description of the removal of Paul Verlaine's death mask: "The conversation turned to Verlaine's alcoholism and the softening effect it had had on his flesh . . . [Stéphane] Mallarmé had said he would never forget the wet, soggy sound made by the removal of the death mask from his face, an operation in which his beard and mouth had come away too."

4. MARCONI INVENTS THE WIRELESS TELEGRAPH (1894–1896)

Guglielmo Marconi was 20 years old when he began experimenting in earnest with radio waves. Because his father took a dim view of such "childish" pursuits as physics and even went so far as to destroy his son's electronic equipment, young Marconi had to set up a secret laboratory in the attic of their villa in Bologna. There, among his mother's trays of silkworms, Marconi determined that radio waves could carry a message in Morse code across the room. In time, he proved that the effectiveness of his invention was not bound by the four attic walls, but that it could transmit messages over great distances.

5. THE ATTIC LOVER (1916–1922)

Late one evening in 1922, neighbors heard gunshots at the Los Angeles home of Fred and Dolly Oesterreich. When police arrived, they found Dolly locked in the closet and Fred dead on the floor. Dolly claimed robbers had locked her up and then shot her husband, but police could find no signs of forcible entry or theft. Dolly was charged with murder the following year, but due to insufficient evidence, charges were

Dolly Oesterreich.

dropped. While she was in jail, she entrusted her lawyer with a secret: Her "half brother" Otto Sanhuber was living in her attic. After Dolly's release, her lawyer insisted that Otto leave the Oesterreich home. Probably no one would ever have found out Otto's true identity if Dolly and her lawyer had remained on friendly terms. But after they had a quarrel, the lawyer went to the district attorney. It was now 1930, eight years since the murder. Since there is no statute of limitations on murder, police issued a warrant for Otto's arrest. When they picked him up, he confessed to the crime but said it was an accident. He also admitted to having been Dolly's lover and said he had lived in her attic for several years—first in Milwaukee, then in Los Angeles. The jury sympathized with Otto, who was 20 years younger than Dolly, and convicted him of manslaughter instead of first-degree murder. But since there is a three-year statute of limitations on manslaughter, the state was forced to let him go. Dolly was tried separately. The jury was hopelessly deadlocked, 10 to 2 for conviction. A mistrial was declared, and Dolly also went free.

6. THE CONSTRUCTION AND DEMONSTRATION OF THE FIRST TELEVISION (1922–1926)

In 1922, British scientist John Logie Baird rented an attic room at 8 Queen's Arcade in Sussex to continue research on his primitive television sets. He used a tea chest as the base for his motor, a biscuit tin to house the projection lamp, and he held the whole contraption together with darning needles, scraps of wood, string, and sealing wax. In 1924, he took his "working" apparatus to London. There he rented two attic rooms at 22 Frith Street in Soho. He struggled for another two years before he gave the first demonstration of true television on Jan. 26, 1926, for an audience of 50 scientists. The British Broadcasting Corporation inaugurated Baird's system in 1929 and used it until 1935, when a more sophisticated system was adopted.

7. ADOLF HITLER'S ATTEMPTED SUICIDE (1923)

After the failure of his Beer Hall Putsch in Munich, Germany, Hitler hid in an attic bedroom at Uffing, the country estate of his follower Putzi Hanfstaengl. Hitler tried to commit suicide by shooting himself when the police came to arrest him. A police agent managed to disarm him before he could pull the trigger.

8. ESPIONAGE AT PEARL HARBOR, HAWAII (1939–1941)

Ruth Kühn was only 17 years old when she became the mistress of Nazi leader Joseph Goebbels. But like all of his mistresses, Ruth was soon discarded. When the affair ended in 1939, Goebbels decided to send Ruth out of Germany. He arranged for her and her parents, Bernard and Friedel, to move to Hawaii and act as espionage agents for the Japanese. Ruth set up a beauty parlor in Honolulu, which became her chief source of information, since it was frequented by American military men's wives. The next step was to figure out a way of transmitting this information to the Japanese. The Kühns devised a simple code system and sent signals from the attic window of their small house overlooking Pearl Harbor. On Dec. 7, 1941, toward the end of the Japanese surprise attack, their signals were noticed by two American naval officers. The U.S. Navy Shore Patrol arrested the family, and all were imprisoned for espionage.

9. ANNE FRANK WRITES HER DIARY (1942–1944)

Forced into hiding when the Nazis overran the Netherlands, Anne Frank, her parents and sister, and four other Jews shared a musty Amsterdam attic above a warehouse and office building. They hid there for two years, obtaining food and other necessities from Gentiles on the floor below. Anne, a precocious girl in her early teens, kept a diary in which she chronicled not only the details of their imprisonment but also her personal feelings about life, love, the future, and her budding sexual awareness. Finally, in August, 1944, the Gestapo, acting on a tip by Dutch informers, raided the hiding place. All the Franks died in concentration camps (Anne of typhus), except Otto Frank, the father. He returned to the attic after the war and found his daughter's diary, which was published under the title *The Diary of a Young Girl*.

10. THE DISCOVERY OF FRANZ SCHUBERT'S LOST PIANO SCORE (1969)

The score for a fantasy for piano by Franz Schubert was discovered in an attic in Knittlefield, Austria, in 1969. The piece is believed to have been written by the Viennese composer in 1817.

11. THE DISCOVERY OF FRÉDÉRIC CHOPIN'S LOST WALTZES (1978)

Several waltzes dedicated to Clementine de la Panouse were discovered by Vicomte Paul de la Panouse in the attic of the family château near Paris in 1978. The waltzes were stored in a heavy trunk belonging to the French aristocratic family. The waltzes were hidden—along with many other documents—in various locations prior to the German invasion of France during W.W. II.

12. THE SAN JOSE PEEPING TOM (1980)

A man and his girlfriend were in the bedroom of their condominium in San Jose, Calif. when they heard a noise in the attic. Thinking it was a mouse, the man crawled into the attic and confronted not a rodent, but a neighbor who was peering into the couple's bedroom through a hole in the ceiling. Douglas Anthony Carr, 33, was arrested, and it was later revealed that he had tunneled through the entire row of condominium attics and drilled tiny peepholes into the bedroom ceilings of each unit. Carr pleaded no contest to a charge of misdemeanor trespassing, was sentenced to 75 days in jail, and was ordered to undergo psychological counseling. He was also obliged to pay for repair of the peepholes.

—L.O. & M.J.T.

VIDAL SASSOON'S 10 HISTORICAL CHARACTERS HE WOULD LIKE TO HAVE MADE UP OR STYLED

London-born Sassoon began cutting hair at 14 and rapidly developed his art. He came to prominence in the 1960s when he cut the hair of fashion designer Mary Quant. Since then he has become the hair stylist of countless celebrities. He is founder and chairman of the board of Vidal Sassoon, Inc., which operates boutiques and beauty salons throughout the U.S. and Europe.

1. Delilah
2. Nikita Khrushchev
3. Albert Einstein
4. Eleanor Roosevelt
5. Tallulah Bankhead
6. George Washington

7. Mona Lisa
8. Buffalo Bill
9. Orphan Annie
10. Rasputin

—Exclusive for *The Book of Lists 3*

30 THINGS AND THEIR SPEEDS

	Speed (mph)
1. The tip of a ⅓-in.-long hour hand on a wristwatch.	0.00000275
2. The growth rate of some bamboos (3 ft./day).	0.0000237
3. The average ground speed of the three-toed sloth (*Bradypus tridactylus*).	0.068–0.098
4. The speed of a giant tortoise.	0.17
5. The average current of the Mississippi River.	3
6. A brisk walking pace for a human.	3.75
7. The average wind speed in Washington, D.C., during 1980.	9.3
8. The average speed of Roger Bannister during his 4-min. mile.	15
9. The average speed of the current world record holder in the 1-mi. run, set by Steven M. J. Ovett on July 1, 1980 (time: 3:48.8).	15.73
10. The fastest passenger elevator (in the "Sunshine 60" building, Ikebukuro, Tokyo).	22.72
11. Eric Heiden's speed in the 500-meter speed-skating event at 1980 Winter Olympics (time: 38.03 sec.).	29.41
12. A fast warthog.	30
13. A cheetah in a hurry.	60
14. The "Beast" roller coaster, King's Island, near Cincinnati, O.	64.77
15. A cricket ball bowled by Jeff Thompson of Australia (vs. the West Indies), December, 1975.	99.7

16. Speed of ball in world's fastest recorded pitch, by Nolan Ryan on Aug. 20, 1974. — 100.9

17. The fastest bird in level flight, the white-throated spine-tailed swift (*Hirundapus caudacutus*). — 106.25

18. The fastest-ever steam train, no. 4468 "Mallard" of the London & North Eastern Railway. — 126

19. The approximate speed attained in the head-first free-fall position of sky diving. It is reassuring to know that if you fall out of an aircraft, you would probably never fall faster than this (unless you were really high up). — 185

20. The speed of a nerve impulse along a nerve in your body (approximately 400 ft./sec.). — 205

21. The speed of sound at sea level at 20° C. — 758

22. The speed of the fastest aircraft, the Lockheed SR-71A. — 2,193

23. The speed of a bullet from a standard U.S. army M16 rifle (3,250 ft./sec.). — 2,250

24. The highest man-made rotary speed of any earthbound object (a swirling, tapered 6-in. carbon-fiber rod in a vacuum). — 4,500

25. The speed reached by the space shuttle Columbia on its first flight approximately 9 min. after takeoff. — 16,700

26. Escape velocity from the earth. — 25,200

27. An Atlas SLV-3C launcher, with a modified Centaur D second stage, and a Thiokol Te-364-4 third stage, which left the earth's atmosphere on Mar. 2, 1972. (The first space vehicle to attain the speed necessary to break out of the solar system.) — 32,114

28. The average orbital speed of the earth around the sun. — 66,641

29. The orbital speed of an electron in a uranium atom. — 5,406,077

30. The speed of light (that's 186,181 mi./sec.). — 670,251,600

—D.O.

9 PERSONAL EVERYDAY LISTS FROM OUR READERS:

6 BEST LINES FROM DRUNKS AT AUTO ACCIDENTS

From: Michael C. O'Reilly, member of a rescue squad in Scotch Plains, N.J.

1. "I'm not drunk and I didn't see that house."
2. "We were only trying to take a shortcut by jumping the brook."
3. After hitting two cement posts, a bridge abutment, a dirt mound, and a sizable oak tree: "Can't I just back out?"
4. "What tree?"
5. "Oops!"
6. "It was his fault." (The driver hit a telephone pole; no other cars were involved.)

6 UNUSUAL COCKTAILS

From: Ann Roubal, a bartender in Wauwatosa, Wis.

1. Courvoisier and Coke
2. Peppermint schnapps and Coke
3. Gin and root beer
4. Amaretto and Tab
5. Scotch and Kahlúa
6. Chivas and Grape Tang

11 UNPLEASANT FEELINGS (rated on a scale from 0–100)

From: Steve Dawson, a college student in Kinston, N.C.

1. Having your watchband pull the hair out of your arm. (35.0)
2. A piece of popcorn shell between your back teeth. (35.7)

3. Sand in your swimsuit. (38.0)
4. Morning breath. (55.0)
5. Your dog's morning breath. (65.0)
6. A cold toilet seat. (70.0)
7. A wet toilet seat. (75.0)
8. Knowing that a patrolman's flashing blue light is for you. (80.0)
9. Being drafted. (95.0)
10. Death. (100.0)
11. Marriage. (102.0)

7 DUMBEST SAYINGS IN THE ENGLISH LANGUAGE

From: Sue Campbell, a 13-year-old in Peekskill, N.Y.

1. "It's as cold as hell."
2. "Sleep tight."
3. "Head over heels in love." (Most people are like that even when they're not in love!)
4. "Working like a dog." (All my dog does is eat!)
5. "Drunk as a skunk." (Who's even seen a drunk skunk?)
6. "Out of your mind."
7. "Paying through the nose."

30 STATEMENTS THAT CHILDREN HEAR FROM ADULTS

From: Donna and Deana Meyer (mother and daughter) in Chula Vista, Calif.

1. "No!" (the answer most often heard)
2. "Don't give me those excuses!"
3. "Let me put it another way . . ."
4. "I don't have time now, maybe later."
5. "Do you think I'm made out of money?"
6. "Just wait 'til you have kids of your own!"
7. "What in the world do you think you're doing?"
8. "Don't eat a snack; dinner's almost ready!"
9. "Be nice to your little brother [sister] or *else*!"
10. "Clean your room!"
11. "When I was your age . . ."
12. "Are you lying to me?"

13. "Eat your dinner; there are children starving all over the world!"
14. "Can't you understand what I'm trying to tell you?"
15. "Can't you ever do [get] *anything* right?"
16. "Who do you think you are, anyway?"
17. "Why don't you grow up?"
18. "This is going to hurt me more than it will hurt you!"
19. "When are you *ever* going to learn?"
20. "Do it *now!*"
21. "Can't you kids get along with each other?"
22. "Why can't you be like _____?"
23. "Go to your room!"
24. "Do your homework!"
25. "Don't use that tone of voice with me!"
26. "Shut up and listen to me!"
27. "You're not old enough to understand that yet!"
28. "Here, let me show you how to do it right!"
29. "I'm doing this for your own good!"
30. "Turn that radio down [off]!"

6 QUESTIONS STUDENTS ASK TO STUMP RELIGION TEACHERS

From: Cristina deVivero, religion teacher in Ft. Lauderdale, Fla.

1. "If God created the world, who created God?"
2. "If Jesus is God, why did he talk and pray to himself?"
3. "If Christians are supposed to 'turn the other cheek,' why did they slaughter so many people during the Crusades?"
4. "If popes were as bad as what *The Book of Lists* says, why is the pope considered infallible today?"
5. "If there is a God, why is there so much evil in the world?"
6. "Why is religion class graded?"

8 ANNOYING THINGS CATS DO

From: Josephine O'Halloran, Howell, N.J.

1. Sleep on your face.
2. Pee in the bathtub.
3. Sit on the dinner plates.
4. Lay across newspapers, books, or magazines you're trying to read.
5. Shed on all your black, brown, and navy clothes.

451

6. Stare at your face until you wake up—usually at 5:30 A.M.
7. Try to steal roast beef, ham, and turkey roll out of your hero sandwich.
8. Whack a plastic ball against the bathroom tiles at 2:00 A.M.

10 THINGS PEOPLE STAND IN LINE FOR IN POLAND (IN ORDER)

From: A woman reader in Warsaw

1. Meat
2. Cigarettes
3. Washing powder
4. Soap
5. Toilet paper
6. Eggs
7. Alcohol
8. Shampoo
9. Mayonnaise
10. Everything else

Average time in line is 2 hours, although in the case of meat it can be 12 hours or more.

Waiting in line in Poland.

17 THINGS THAT COULD NEVER BE

From: Patty Mulrooney and her students, Shaun Brady (grade 1), Merin Gwinn (grade 2), Eric Voigt, Elaine Herr, and Alison Frantz (grade 3), at McVey Elementary School, Newark, Del.

1. Fall up.
2. Turn into a cartoon.
3. Have a foot on your nose.
4. Charlie Brown would give his dog away.
5. A frog can never wear glasses.
6. An ant cannot speak Japanese.
7. Two women can't marry nine men at the same time.
8. The Eiffel Tower cannot be in Tokyo.
9. The world could never be a yo-yo.
10. No one could ever eat a 10-ft.-tall elephant in one bite.
11. There could never be a real marshmallow as big as the world.
12. Pat Boone playing football.
13. A ghost with two front teeth.
14. The Easter Bunny going on strike.
15. My goldfish on a skateboard.
16. Me coming back as a peanut shell.
17. Cherry pie being left over.

THE AUTHORS' 7 THOUGHTS FOR YOU, THE READER

1. Thank you for having read this far. We hope you will let us hear from you, if you are so moved.
2. Please tell us what you enjoyed most, and least, about this book, and why.
3. If you come across any errors or omissions—or have any suggestions or requests for the next edition—let us know.
4. Send us any clippings or items that you feel we might enjoy or that would help us prepare *The Book of Lists 4*. Please include the sources for any facts or lists you send in, and accompany these with a self-addressed stamped envelope if you want a response.
5. If you send in a *completed* list and we find it acceptable for publication, we will compensate you and give you credit.
6. If you just feel like sounding off about something, please get it off your chest to us. We read every letter that reaches us.
7. Here is how to get in touch with us. Write to:

> *The Book of Lists 3*
> P.O. Box 49699
> Los Angeles, Calif. 90049

—A.W., D.W., & I.W.

A

Aaron, Hank, 347
Abbandando, Frank "the Dasher,"
  45
Abbott, Glenn, 345
Abelard, Peter, 280
Abstemious, 175
Abstentious, 175
Accardo, Tony "Joe Batters," 45
Accidents
  unusual, 366
  of U.S. nuclear weapons, 94–96
Acheson, Dean, 33
Acker, Jean, 277
Acronyms, 174–75
Acton, John Emerich Edward, 169
Adams, Ansel, 36–37, 320
Adams, John Quincy, 32
Adams, Samuel Hopkins, 236
Adams, Sparky, 346
Adams, W. Claude, 251
Adams, Will, 283
Adcock, Joe, 347
Addams, Charles, 178
Adenauer, Konrad, 374
Adoption of famous people, 289
Adoula, Cyril, 44
Aeschlimann, J. F., 237
"A.F.," 54
Agdulos, Ernesto, 93
Agnew, Spiro, 310
Agriculture, programs proposed in,
  35–36
Agriculture Department, U.S., 165
Ailments, big businesses resulting
  from, 308–9
Ainsworth, Macie Marie "Sunny,"
  279
Ainsworth, Robert, 241
Air Canada, 93
Air Force, U.S., 94, 399

Air France, 94
Airliners, near-crashes of, 92–94
Airlines ranked by number of pas-
  senger complaints, 156–57
Aiuppa, Joseph "Ha Ha," 45
Akkad, king of Sargon, 289
Alabama, 38, 39
Alaska, 39
Albee, Edward, 289
Albert, Carl, 29
Albert, British prince consort, 271
"Alcatraz, Battle of," 83–84
Alcatraz, escape attempts from,
  80–85
Alcohol consumption, geographic
  distribution of, 39–40
Alcoholic beverages, unusual, 449
Alcott, Amos Bronson, 139
Alcott, Louisa May, 232, 385
Alda, Alan, 219
Alden, Ginger, 274
Alderman, Israel "Icepick Willie,"
  45
Aldrin, Edwin "Buzz," 385
Alexander, F. Matthias, 371–72
Alexander III, czar of Russia, 176
Alexander the Great, 194
Alexandra, British queen consort,
  15
Alfred the Great, king of Wessex,
  405–6
Allen, Gracie, 7
Allen, Irwin, 205
Allen, James, 256
Allen, Richie, 348
Allison, (Robert) Clay, 420
Allyson, June, 189
Alvarez, Carlos, 352
Amazon River, 268
Amberg, Louis "Pretty," 45
Amberly, Viscount, 430
American Airlines, 92–93

Burton, Sir Richard, 241–42
Burton, Robert, 386
Businesses, big
  ailments and disabilities result-
    ing in formation of, 308–9
  popular songs commissioned by,
    182–83
Bussey, Woodrow W., 72
BUSTOP, 174
Butkus, Dick, 357
Butler, Frank E., 275
Butte, Mont., 116
Butz, Earl, 310
Byrd, Robert, 289
Byron, George Gordon, Lord, 241

C

Cabinda, Angola, 119
Cabot, Sebastian, 303
Cabot family, 70
Caesar, Gaius Julius, 59
Caesar, Sid, 218
Caesar Augustus, 429
Caesious, 175
Cagney, James, 214
Caillaux, Henriette, 77–78
Cairo, Egypt, 149
California, 39, 158
Callas, Maria, 426
Calloway, Cab, 21
Callwood, June, 230–31
Calmette, Gaston, 77–78
Calomaris, Anthony, 23
Cambodian coup, 44
Cambridge, England, nuclear
  weapons accident in, 94
Camembert, France, 118
Cameron, Lucille, 284
Camp, Walter, 344
Campbell, Rodney, 231
Campbell, Sue, 450
Campbell, William Wallace, 259
Campione, Italy, 119
Camus, Albert, 419
Canada, 151
  cruelty to animals in, 145

Cancer, survival rates for, 373
Cantalupo, Italy, 118
Capone, "Scarface Al," 46, 310
Capra, Frank, 200
Capranica, Robert R., 251
Carew, Rod, 286, 350
Carlton, Steve, 345
Carlyle, Jane, 241, 323
Carlyle, Thomas, 241, 323
Carmen y Ruiz, Maria del, 73
Carnegie, Andrew, 289–90
Carnegie, Margaret Hodge,
  289–90
Carnera, Primo, 344
Carnes, Clarence, 83–84
Carney, Art, 219, 221
Carr, Douglas Anthony, 446
Carr, John Dickson, 238
Carroll, Lewis, 359
Carroll, Madeleine, 210
Carter, Benny, 185, 187
Carter, Jimmy, 21, 162, 165, 317,
  401, 406
Carter, Rosalynn, 1
Cartoonists, favorite cartoons of,
  178–81
Caruso, Enrico, 415
Casals, Pablo, 280–81
Cash, Johnny, 18
Casper, Dave, 353
Cassatt, Mary, 319
Cassius Longinus, Gaius, 59–60
Caston, Bob, 274
Catachresis, 171
Catherine of Aragon, 327
Catherine the Great, empress of
  Russia, 323–24
Cats
  annoying acts of, 451–52
  most popular names for, 130
Cayce, Edgar, 316
Cayenne, French Guiana, 118
Celebrities
  as admirers of Hitler, 3–5
  adopted, 289
  ashes of, 423–26
  bed as workplace for, 299–302
  born on date of another's death,
    14–15

as chronic headache sufferers, 379–83

with dogs as sleeping companions, 128–30

as draft dodgers and resisters, 102–4

as fainters, 383–84

as fathers-in-law and sons-in-law pairs, 10–11

as former barbershop employees, 304–5

as former gas station or garage employees, 303–4

as former intelligence agents, 100–102

as former teachers, 210–12

as former waitresses, 305–7

games invented by, 359–61

as hemorrhoid sufferers, 405–7

as income-tax evaders, 310–11

killed in auto accidents, 419–20

known by middle names, 1–2

marriage proposals of, 271–74

married before age of sixteen, 274–76

married for less than one month, 277

with mother fixations, 289–93

as Niehans therapy patients, 373–75

part-American Indian, 18–20

preserved body parts of, 410–13

as runaways, 294–97

U.S. citizenship renounced by, 40–41

as victims of severe depression, 385–89

Cell regeneration therapy, 373–75

Censorship
of news stories, 402–5
of notable books, 226–29

Center for National Security Studies (CNSS), 268

Central Intelligence Agency (CIA), 268, 403
secret armies of, 42–44

Cervix, cancer of, 373

Cessna, 93–94

Cézanne, Paul, 194

Chain, Ernst, 266

Chamberlin, George Agnew, 236

Chamberlin, Neville, 1

Champagne, France, 118

Champion boxers, most combative, 353

Chandka Forest, India, 92

Chandler, Raymond, 6

Chapin, Harry, 419

Chapin, Dr. James P., 134–35

Chaplin, Charlie, 11, 304, 332

Chaplin, Oona O'Neill, 332

Chapuis, Alfred, 254

Charles Pfizer and Company, 265

Charles, Ezzard, 353

Charles, Ray, 183, 186

Chase, Hal, 347

Chastain, A. B., 58

Chateaubriand, François René de, 8

Chatterton, Sarah Young, 287

Chatterton, Thomas, 287, 442–43

Cheddar, England, 118

Chekov, Anton, 239

Cher, 18

Chesselet, Alyn, 71–72

Chesterton, G. K., 236

Chevalier, Maurice, 197

Cheyenne, Wyo., 159

Chianti mountains, Italy, 118

Chicago, Ill., 115, 149, 222, 223

Chicago Bears, 367

Chicago Seven, 78

Children
books for, 247
delivered after father's death, 287–88
raising of, 293

Chinese brigade in Burma, 42

Chopin, Fréderic, 446

Chorier, Nicholas, 341

Chou En-lai, 7

Chrétien, Henri, 207

Christian, Fletcher, 284, 386

Christie, Agatha, 236

Christopherson, Tina, 409

Chromite, 109

Chung Ling-soo (William E. Robinson), 417

DuBois, W.E.B., 40
Duels, unusual, 97–99
Dulles, John Foster, 6, 34
Dunaway, Faye, 305–6
Duncan, Isadora, 324
Dunleavy, Yvonne, 231
Dunne, John Gregory, 382
Dunsany, Lord, 238
Durango, Colo., 116
Durant, Ariel. *See* Kaufman, Ida
Durant, Will, 281
Duryea, Etta Terry, 284
Dustin, Jack, 352
Duvall, Robert, 202–3
Dwyer, Richard, 378
Dylan, Bob, 297

E

Earhart, Amelia, 431
Earp, Virgil W., 420, 421
Earp, Wyatt, 420, 421
Earth Resources Experimental
    Package (EREP), 268
Earth's core, 263
Easter Island, 149
Eastwood, Clint, 251, 303
Eckler, A. Ross, 224–25
Economic Development Admin-
    istration, 40
Ecuador, 269
Edam, Netherlands, 118
Eddy, Mary Baker, 246, 281, 372
Ederle, Gertrude, 216
Edison, Thomas Alva, 8, 260
Edward VII, king of Great Britain,
    410
Edward VIII, king of Great Britain,
    5, 129
Edwards, Bonita Francine,
    278–79
EGADS, 174
Egville, Henri d', 97
Egypt, cruelty to animals in, 144
Ehret, Arnold, 368
Einstein, Albert, 169, 264, 411,
    446

Eisenhower, Dwight D., 6, 18, 21,
    316
Eisenhower, Mamie, 302
Eldridge, Roy, 185
Eldridge, Walter, 68
Eleanor of Aquitaine, 274
Electromagnetic spectrum, com-
    plete, 263
Eliot, T. S., 40, 282
Elizabeth I, queen of England,
    195, 212
Elizabeth II, queen of Great Brit-
    ain, 317
Ellena, American colony of, 435
Ellington, Duke, 21, 187
Elliott, Herb, 357
Ellis, Havelock, 169, 330
Elman, Mischa, 187
Elphinstone, Marjorie, 427
El Salvador, 403
Elwood, Roger, 273
Emerson, Ralph Waldo, 168, 169
Emerson, Roy, 354
Emmy Awards, performers win-
    ning greatest number of,
    220–22
Empire State Building, 91, 114
Endometrium, cancer of, 373
Energy, proposed programs for,
    34–35
Enesco, Georges, 188
Entertainers
    deaths of, 417–19
    Las Vegas one-time-only-appear-
        ances of, 188–89
Environmental Protection Agency
    (EPA), 165–66
Epenthesis, 170
Epicharmus, 436
Erickson, Eric, 41
Ernst, June, 278
Erotic books, 340–41
Erskine, John, 236
ERTS satellite, 268, 269
Escape attempts from Alcatraz,
    80–85
Estonia, 120
Eugene, Oreg., 116
Evans, Larry, 157–58

465

N

Nadar, Felix, 320
Nafzawi, Omar al-sheikh, 340
Names
for figures of speech, 170–71
not commonly known, 395–96
Names, middle, celebrities known
by, 1–2
Names, place
food or drink as, 118
longest, 116–17
Namgyal, Palden Thondup, king
of Sikkim, 285
Napoleon I, emperor of France,
70–71, 198, 207
Nashville, Tenn., 160
Natick Research and Development
Laboratories, 401
National Advisory Committee on
Oceans and Atmospheres, 219
National Aeronautics and Space
Administration (NASA), 269,
400
National Congressional Club
(NCC), 30
National Conservative Political Ac-
tion Committee (NCPAC), 30
National Front for the Liberation
of Angola (FNLA), 44
National Garden Bureau, 389
National Security Agency (NSA),
403
National Union for the Total Inde-
pendence of Angola (UNITA),
44
Nauru, 152–53
Nazism, non-Nazi admirers of,
3–5
Necker, Jacques, 414
Necker, Suzanne, 414
Nelson, Byron, 356
Nelson, Charles B., 377
Nelson, Lord Horatio, 325
Nelson, Lester "Baby Face," 49
Nelson, Rick, 11
Nerciat, Andréa de, 341
Nettles, Jim, 353
Nevada, 38, 39, 158
Neville, Gloria, 330

New Brunswick, Canada, 117
Newcombe, John, 354, 356
Newell, Alton S., 70
New England, 36
dark day in, 113
Newfoundland, 122
New Hampshire, 38, 39
Newhart, Bob, 2
New Jersey, 38, 158
New Jersey Division of Gaming
Enforcement, 165
Newman, Edwin, 171–72
New Mexico, 36, 38
Newsom, Louis "Bobo," 347
News stories, censorship of,
402–5
Newton, Isaac, 240–41
New York, N.Y., 107–8, 115, 149,
222, 223
New York State, 38
New Zealand, 116
Nguyen Cao Ky, 5
NHOMTPIABOPARMBETZHEL-
BETRABSOMONIMONI-
MONKONOTDTEKHSTRO-
MONT, 174
Niarchos, Eugenia Livanos,
328–29
Niarchos, Stavros, 328–29
Nicaragua, 270
Nichols, Red, 7
Nicholson, Dave, 348
Nicklaus, Jack, 356
Nicknames
of famous couples, 323–26
of underworld figures, 45–49
Niehans, Dr. Paul, 373–75
Niehans therapy, celebrity pa-
tients in, 373–75
Nietzsche, Friedrich, 16, 169, 246
Nightingale, Florence, 430–31
Nimbus 6 satellite, 269, 270
Nin, Anaïs, 341
Niobium, 111
Nippon Airways, 93
Nitschke, Ray, 357
Niven, David, 2
Nixon, Pat, 253
Nixon, Richard M., 25, 29–30, 230,
253, 310, 316–17, 394, 395

478

O

P

Pope, Alexander, 167
Pope, Allen, 42
Popular Movement for the Liberation of Angola (MPLA), 44
Porter, Cole, 7
Porter, David L., 32
Portraits hated by subject, 190–93
Post, C. W., 10, 373
Potemkin, Grigori, 323
Potter, Beatrix, 359
Pougy, Liane de, 321
Powell, John W., 413
Powell, Mary, 277
Power, Debbie Montgomery Minardos, 288
Power, Tyrone, 288
Pregnancies, at time of husband's death, 287–88
Preservation
  of bodies, 414–16
  of body parts, 410–13
Presidential Inaugural Committee, 400
Presley, Elvis, 23, 274, 292
Presley, Gladys, 292
Previn, André, 188
Price, Eleanor, 235–36
Prineville, Ore., 116
Pritchard, Dr. Peter C. H., 254
Pritikin, Nathan, 390
Procaccino, Mario, 394
Profumo, John, 216
Project Censored, 402–3
Prokofiev, Sergei, 188
Prosex inventions, 338–40
Prosopopoeia, 171
Prostate cancer, 373
Proust, Jeanne Weil, 292
Proust, Marcel, 239, 243, 292, 302
Proxmire, William, 399
Prussak, Alexander, 377
Prussia, 122
Prytz, Ulla, 248
Puppy mills, 146–47
Pure Food and Drug Act (1906), 438
Purkinje, Johannes E., 377
Purnell, Jim, 353
Putnam, George, 236

Q

Qaddafi, Muammar al-, 393
Quaker Oats Company, 164
Quant, Mary, 446
Quarks, 264
Queen, Ellery, 238
Quelis, Comte Jacques de Lévis de, 97
Quiller-Couch, Arthur, 245
Quinlan, Karen Ann, 289
Quinn, Anthony, 11.
Quintero, Liberato Anibal, 323
Quisling, Vidkun, 106
Quotations
  erroneous, 167–68
  great, 168–69
  misattributed to movie stars, 214–15
  of U.S. politicians, 393–95

R

Racicot, Marc, 228
Radio stations, most listened to, 222–23
Raimondi, Giuseppina, 277
Rainfall
  most in one minute, 114
  point, 114
Rains, Claude, 2, 6
Rajachandra, Shrimad, 140
Raleigh, Sir Walter, 87
Rao, R. G., 250
Rapid City, S.Dak., 116
Rappe, Virginia, 76
Rasputin, Grigori, 321, 362, 447
Rather, Bob, 352
Rather, Dan, 231
Rauschenberg, Robert, 20
Rawson, Clayton, 238
Ray, James Earl, 62
Ray, Johnnie, 20
Reagan, Nancy Davis, 273, 394
Reagan, Ronald, 30, 31, 53, 78, 164–65, 189, 196, 226, 273, 320, 393, 394, 400, 404
Realtors Political Action Committee (RPAC), 31

S

Wright, W. H. (S. S. Van Dine), 236
Wright, Wilbur, 441
WRKS-FM, 222
Wullschleger, Julie, 72
Wyatt, Edith, 236
Wyman, Jane, 307
Wynn, Jimmy, 348
WYNY-FM, 222
Wyoming, 39

Y

Yachats, Ore., 115
Yardbirds, 408
Yellow plague, 264
Yevtushenko, Yevgeny, 216
Yonge, Charlotte Mary, 235–36
York, Alvin C., 103–4
Yorkshire Ripper, 393
Yorktown, Battle of, 252
Yosemite National Park, Calif., 36
Young, Brigham, 329

Young, Caesar, 75
Young, Cy, 345
Young, Henry, 81
Young, Lester, 185
Young, Robert M., 203
Younger, Thomas Coleman, 420
Ysaye, Eugène, 188
Yuma Mission, Ariz., 435–36
Yussupov, Felix, Russian prince, 362

Z

Zaharïas, Mildred "Babe" Didrikson, 342
Zangwill, Israel, 238
Zanuck, Richard D., 204–5
Zapata, Emiliano, 60
Zeiglin, Ella, 97
Ziegfeld, Florenz, 368
Ziegler, Ron, 163, 394
Zioncheck, Marion, 27–28
Zola, Émile, 77, 326, 443

Franz Liszt.

PHOTO CREDITS

ABOUT THE AUTHORS

AMY WALLACE is coauthor of *The Book of Lists, The Book of Predictions, The Intimate Sex Lives of Famous People, The Two* (a biography of the original Siamese twins), and *The Psychic Healing Book*. She and her husband, Josef, live in Berkeley, California.

DAVID WALLECHINSKY created and coauthored *The People's Almanac*. He also coauthored *The People's Almanac #2* and *#3, The Book of Lists, The Book of Predictions, The Intimate Sex Lives of Famous People, Chico's Organic Gardening and Natural Living, Laughing Gas*, and *What Really Happened to the Class of '65*. He is currently writing *The Encyclopedia of the Olympics*. He lives with his wife, Flora, in Santa Monica, California.

IRVING WALLACE, named one of the five most widely read authors in the world, has written twenty-seven books, which have sold an estimated 156 million copies worldwide. Besides coauthoring books with Amy and David, he has written such best-selling novels as *The Chapman Report, The Prize, The Man, The Seven Minutes, The Word, The Pigeon Project,* and *The Almighty*. He and his novelist wife, Sylvia, live in Los Angeles, California.